PSYCHOLOGY OF ADJUSTMENT

personal growth
in a
changing world

Second Edition

Eastwood Atwater

PRENTICE-HALL, INC., Englewood Cliffs, New Jersey 07632

Library of Congress Cataloging in Publication Data

ATWATER, EASTWOOD, [date]
   Psychology of adjustment.

   Bibliography: p 383
   Includes indexes.
   1. Adjustment (Psychology) 2. Adulthood.
3. Interpersonal relations. 4. Self-actualization
(Psychology)   I. Title.
BF335.A88 1983   158   82-16588
ISBN 0-13-734855-X

Interior design and text supervision: Serena Hoffman
Cover photo: Fred Burrell
Cover design: Anne T. Bonanno
Manufacturing buyer: Ron Chapman

PRINTED IN THE UNITED STATES OF AMERICA

10 9 8 7 6 5

ISBN 0-13-734855-X

PRENTICE-HALL INTERNATIONAL, INC., *London*
PRENTICE-HALL OF AUSTRALIA PTY. LIMITED, *Sydney*
EDITORA PRENTICE-HALL DO BRASIL, LTDA, *Rio de Janeiro*
PRENTICE-HALL OF CANADA, LTD., *Toronto*
PRENTICE-HALL OF INDIA PRIVATE LIMITED, *New Delhi*
PRENTICE-HALL OF JAPAN, INC., *Tokyo*
PRENTICE-HALL OF SOUTHEAST ASIA PTE. LTD., *Singapore*
WHITEHALL BOOKS LIMITED, *Wellington, New Zealand*

To Kay, Susan, and Gail

Contents

2   Motivation

3   Stress

4   **Emotions**   **79**

5   **Self-concept**   **107**

8 Love and Marriage   189

9 Work and Leisure   218

10 Freedom and Decision Making   248

11 Self-directed Change   274

12   Psychotherapy   300

13 Growth and Adult Life Stages   330

14 Death and Bereavement   359

Preface

Preparing the revised edition of this book has given me an opportunity to incorporate many of the changes suggested by students and faculty, as well as the findings of recent studies. A major addition is the chapter on death and bereavement. The new chapter on decision making, which includes some of the material from an earlier chapter on personal freedom, now has a more practical orientation to aid students. Much of the chapter on sexuality has been rewritten, with a new section on sex roles. I have also rewritten the chapters on work and leisure and adult life stages to include recent findings in these areas. The reader will find new material and revised sections in all chapters, especially those on adjustment and growth, self-concept, and love and marriage.

As in the earlier edition, the chapters are organized around three related themes of adjustment and growth: *personal behavior* (Chapters 1–5), *interpersonal relationships* (Chapters 6–9), and *change* (Chapters 10–14).

Throughout the book the reader is encouraged to apply the material to his or her own personal experience. To this end, I have included many examples and illustrations, as well as relevant boxed material. At the end of each chapter there are questions for self-reflection, recommended readings, and exercises for personal growth. The latter may be especially helpful in applying the ideas and findings in the book to personal experience.

I am grateful for the suggestions received from faculty colleagues, especially Emory Holland, Carol Rae Hoffman, and Elmer Ritzman. I'm also indebted to those who reviewed the earlier edition of this book and made suggestions for the present revision, including: Robert A. Brown, University of Maryland-College Park; Ronald G. Evans, Washburn University of Topeka; Walter Lundstrum, Northwestern Wisconsin Technical Institute; Roger P. Seaman, Yuba College; and Patricia A. Cote, Community College of Rhode Island.

I am especially thankful for the invaluable help from my wife Kay, the special assistance of Mary Jane Burns, and the patience and cooperation of all my family throughout the preparation of this book.

Finally, it is my hope that all who read this book will find it a helpful and rewarding experience.

EASTWOOD ATWATER

Psychology of Adjustment

Adjustment and Growth

Actress Laraine Newman hated school and made such poor grades that she couldn't get into college. But once she became interested in acting and comedy, her life changed dramatically. "Basically I'm lazy," she says, "but I'm not lazy if something interests me. And what interests me is being a comic actress. Then I have endless energy, great strength to pursue goals."*

Laraine Newman is fortunate in having discovered a special interest that she enjoys and excels in. Not everyone does. Many people spend a good part of their lives in frustration, disappointment, and boredom. Worse still, they begin to doubt their own abilities and chances of ever succeeding at anything. Yet, in our own way, each of us has the potential for boundless energy and impressive achievement. What is most needed is to discover our own special interests and abilities and to appreciate our own uniqueness.

In this chapter, after presenting an overview of adjustment and growth, we will turn to a consideration of personal growth. We will also discuss the idea of growth as self-actualization, including the importance of discovering our potential and how we go about actualizing it. Finally, we will look at the all-important matter of personal motivation.

ADJUSTMENT

Most days I ride a bike to the college where I teach. It's a pleasant trip through a familiar neighborhood that includes the homes of many people I know. I'm often preoccupied with what I plan to do in class that day. But sometimes as I pass a house my thoughts turn to the people who live there.

I think of a young lawyer's wife, Kathy, who regrets quitting college to get married. Now that their kids have begun school, Kathy wants to complete her degree part time. But her husband feels a wife's place is at home, especially when the children are young. Meanwhile, Kathy feels torn between furthering her education and being loyal to her family.

Around the corner live a couple having trouble getting over the death of their son, who was killed in an automobile accident. Even though the father appears to have gotten over his son's death, friends say he is "holding it all in." They say his wife isn't coping at all. She stayed home from work three months after the accident and still avoids talking with her neighbors about it. She cries easily and sleeps a lot. Now, six months after her son's death, she continues to think about him but asks, "Is something wrong with me?"

A couple of doors away lives Julie, an attractive sophomore at a nearby university who feels confused about her career plans. She has changed her college major from special education to psychology. But since she doesn't plan to attend graduate school, she wonders what she can do with an undergraduate degree in psychology. She has heard that the job outlook is much brighter in the fields of business and computer programming, but she feels badly about changing her mind so much and "wasting" her parents' money.

By now, I've reached the campus and head toward Founder's Hall, where I teach. After securing my bike and greeting some students, I walk toward my classroom, still pondering the various plights of my neighbors.

The Concept of Adjustment

All of these problems have several things in common. One is concern with *ourselves.* Up to a point, self-interest is a normal and necessary part of life. Another common element is the need to get along with *others.* At work or at home, life's biggest problems often turn out to be "people" problems. At the same time, some of life's greatest satisfactions come from relationships with friends and lovers. A third common element is *change.* In recent years change has become so rapid and all-encompassing that it may be no exaggeration to say that life itself *is* change. Yet, as Alvin Toffler (1971) has said, what we need is neither blind acceptance nor blind resistance to change, but rather an array of creative strategies for using it selectively.

Much of our effort is aimed at every-day survival. (Teri Leigh Stratford)

All three of these elements—ourselves, others, and change—are interwoven in the concept of adjustment. Simply put, *adjustment consists of the changes in ourselves and our circumstances necessary to achieve a satisfactory relationship with others and with our surroundings.*[1] Just think of all the energy we spend trying to satisfy our needs, meeting other people's demands, and fulfilling our responsibilities. When given the familiar greeting "How are you?" people often respond with phrases such as "I'm coping," "I'm hanging in there," "I'm keeping my head above water," or "I'm going to make it." When asked what they mean by such phrases, people readily admit that "life is a struggle." In other words, much of our effort is aimed at everyday survival. The *process* of adjustment continues to usurp much of our energy; the *labels* we use to describe it change with the times.

Our understanding of adjustment has also changed. Until recently, the emphasis was on *changing ourselves to fit into our surroundings,* and it implied a great deal of social conformity. The well-adjusted person—always more of an ideal than a reality—was highly stable and more inhibited with his or her desires and feelings than people are now. Today we sometimes feel it necessary to *change our surroundings* as a way of satisfying our needs. Consequently, people are busy improving their skills in assertiveness and stress management. They are also more willing to change jobs or careers or find a more satisfying marriage partner than ever before. In short, there is more awareness that healthy adjustment is

[1]Benjamin B. Wolman, defines adjustment as: "1. A harmonious relationship with the environment involving the ability to satisfy most of one's needs and meet most of the demands, both physical and social, that are put upon one. 2. The variations and changes in behavior that are necessary to satisfy needs and meet demands so that one can establish a harmonious relationship with the environment." (*The Dictionary of Behavior Science,* pp. 9–10. Copywright © 1973 by Van Nostrand Company. Reprinted with permission of Van Nostrand Reinhold Company.)

a two-way process involving an active role for the individual. In some instances it may mean joining organizations for social change and working for it directly through demonstrations.

In the case of Kathy, who wants to complete college part time while her children are in school, a healthy adjustment will require resourcefulness on her part, as well as the ability to give and take in her relationship with her husband. Kathy needs to explain why she feels so strongly about completing her degree and be willing to listen to her husband's reasons for feeling the way he does. He needs to listen to her side, too. Perhaps they could agree that Kathy try attending school for a semester and see how it goes.

Another woman found her husband's objections pertained mostly to the considerable amount of time she spent commuting to a distant college, so she began taking courses at a nearby community college. After it became clear that her sense of personal fulfillment gave her more satisfaction as a wife and mother, her husband enthusiastically supported her transfer to the college of her choice. In both instances, successful adjustment involves individual initiative, willingness to communicate, and concern for the mutual satisfaction of needs.

The Emphasis on Growth

The emphasis on growth and personal fulfillment has greatly enriched our understanding of adjustment. The movement toward self-fulfillment has served as a corrective to the excessive element of self-denial implicit in the traditional notion of adjustment, thereby modifying the giving/getting compact between ourselves and the environment.

"Growth" psychology had its origins in such seminal thinkers as Carl Rogers and Abraham Maslow, who adopted the *organismic model of personality*. According to this view, the human organism behaves as a unified whole of mind and body, driven by the sovereign motive of self-actualization. While the individual is not regarded as immune to external demands, the emphasis clearly has shifted from mastery of the environment to unleashing the organism's potential for growth and psychological health. Yet many of the terms used to describe psychological health—such as competence and mastery—still emphasize the person's ability to function in the environment. Maslow warned, "We must not fall into the trap of defining the good organism in terms of what he is 'good for,' as if he were an instrument rather than something in himself" (Maslow, 1978, p. 16). Instead, the goal of living should be seen in terms of the inherent human potential that partially transcends the environment. The work of Maslow and Rogers has played a major role in the rise of humanistic psychology and the human potential movement. The popularity of personal growth at the national level eventually led to the 1970s being dubbed as the "me" decade.

At the same time, the search for personal fulfillment has come under increasing attack. While this emphasis may be a healthy corrective for the uptight, oversocialized person, it easily leads to unbridled selfishness among those who are not yet adequately socialized. Lacking the sense of responsibility and concern for others so central to Maslow's view of the mature, self-actualizing person, an immature, self-centered person becomes even more subjective and hedonistic. Furthermore, for many people the search for personal fulfillment has come to supersede adjustment to the larger world.

In their book *The Inner American* (1981), Joseph Veroff, Elizabeth Douvan, and Richard Kulka report that Americans have moved from a socially integrated approach to well-being to a more personal or individuated one. The concern for personal satisfaction has become the primary orientation for most people. But rather than indicting the shift toward personal fulfillment as "selfishness," these authors see this as an adaptive response (or adjustment) to the increasing complexity, impersonality, and uncertainty of social institutions. Having lost faith in the worth of institutions like the government, people retreat to the realm of personal fulfillment. As a result, young and old alike now see their personal futures mostly in positive terms, while at the same time they have a pessimistic outlook about their country and the rest of the world (Bachman & Johnston, 1979).

Daniel Yankelovich (1981) points to another contradiction in the search for self-fulfillment. On the one hand, it presupposes continued economic prosperity and affluence; yet we've been experiencing one of the most prolonged periods of economic and social uncertainty in our history. Consequently, people are now searching for self-fulfillment in a "world turned upside down." Young people who have grown up with increased expectations about the quality of life and who now face a world of diminishing resources and heightened competition are especially susceptible to frustration, disappointment, and cynicism. Yankelovich disagrees with those who feel we are witnessing a return to the old values. Instead, he feels we are moving toward a new, more inclusive orientation that encompasses concern for both commitment and community. There is an increasing realization that self-fulfillment can be achieved only in a web of shared meanings that transcend the isolated individual. Even in this new era, we must still deal with the individual *and* his or her environment, with growth *and* adjustment.

Adjustment and Growth

Actually, adjustment and growth refer to complementary life processes. Both involve satisfying our needs as well as the demands of our surroundings. But the emphasis is different in each. In adjustment, it is the relationship with our surroundings that is foremost. In growth, the emphasis falls on the individual. Similarly, there is stability and change in both processes. But stability is more valued in adjustment, while change is the key to growth. Each process also brings its own kinds of satisfaction. For example, moving ahead in a career despite certain misgivings may bring a sense of recognition, achievement, and security. Yet setting out on a new career that promises greater personal fulfillment may give one a new lease on life that outweighs the risks involved. Some people may seek a more challenging job within the same vocation, thus combining the satisfactions of adjustment and growth.

The process of living involves both growth and adjustment. For example, Julie, the college student mentioned earlier, may experience significant growth in resolving the uncertainty over her career. After talking with different people and entertaining new ideas about possible careers, Julie may come to a more satisfying decision about her college major. Throughout the process of making a decision, however, she must continue to meet classes, do the assignments, and keep up some social life. In short, she must be able to cope with (adjust to) everyday demands while going through a growth crisis in regard to her career.

In a similar way, the couple grieving over the death of their son may eventually discover that their grief has become an occasion for growth. Parents who have lost a child often say they are no longer the same. They no longer take so many things for granted. They are more appreciative of life and of their other children. Yet throughout the slow, painful period of bereavement, each of them must continue to meet their everyday responsibilities. The husband must go back to work. The wife must eventually return to work to keep her job. They must keep up the house, pay the bills, and take care of their other children. In short, life goes on. People who adjust to their grief too quickly may fail to benefit from it. But those who use it as an excuse to withdraw from life may fail to adjust or grow. The interplay of adjustment and growth leads away from this kind of stalemate.

As you can see, there is no sharp separation between adjustment and growth. We must adjust in order to survive. Yet it is the experience of growth that lends enthusiasm and direction to our lives. Because the experiences of adjustment and growth are so completely intermeshed, one is often indistinguishable from the other. It is mostly in looking back that we realize how much we have grown. Accordingly, throughout this book, we will be dealing with both adjustment and growth, though the emphasis falls on growth.

WHAT WAS YOUR MOST DIFFICULT ADJUSTMENT?

If you were to name the most difficult adjustment you've had to make, what would it be? Was it overcoming a physical handicap or illness? Did it involve coming to terms with disappointment or failure in school? Or was it the breakup of a close relationship?

Some people say their most difficult experience was overcoming a drug or drinking problem, partly because it posed a test of willpower, and partly because it required a change of lifestyle. Others say that their most difficult time was going through a divorce or getting over the death of a parent, spouse, or child. The loss of someone who has meant so much to us is like losing a part of ourselves, evoking deep emotions that are not easily resolved.

Interestingly, what people say was their most difficult adjustment varies widely from one person to another. Can you explain why your experience was the most difficult for you? What did you learn about yourself from it?

PERSONAL GROWTH

Essentially, personal growth refers to change or development in a desirable direction. We usually say someone has "grown as a person" when he or she becomes more understanding, competent, responsible, and considerate of others. In this sense, we have some general expectations of what constitutes growth that are desirable for everyone. At the same time, personal growth is a complex and varied process.

Variations in Growth

There are as many different views of the growth process as there are major psychological viewpoints. For purposes of presentation, however, we have chosen to incorporate these various views into the most relevant chapters throughout the book. For example, since Maslow emphasizes the motivational aspects of growth, his view will be included in the chapter on motivation as well as in this one. On the other hand, Carl Rogers's emphasis on changes in the self fits more naturally into the chapter on the self-concept. Although Erik Erikson's concept of life-long growth is appropriate to any phase of growth, it will be dealt with in the section on the achievement of self-identity at adolescence as well as in the chapter on adult life stages.

Another reason our ideas of growth vary is because of the differences among individuals themselves. What constitutes change in a desirable direction often differs from one person to another, depending on their needs, values, and past development. For example, we may feel that a highly aggressive person has grown by learning how to respond to others in a more sensitive, cooperative way. Or we may feel that an excessively shy person grows by speaking up and acting more assertively. Our ideas of growth may also vary in different stages of life or according to our concept of appropriate sex roles. In all these instances, we are dealing with growth. But the content and direction of growth varies somewhat according to individual development.

Conditions for Growth

Some conditions tend to facilitate growth more than others—especially physical and environmental changes, significant life events, and all kinds of changes in the inner, personal realm of life.

The stage for growth is often set by physical changes. This can be seen most dramatically during adolescence, when the rapid increases in weight, height, and sexual characteristics bring new ways of seeing oneself and relating to others. Although the physical changes associated with middle and old age occur more gradually, they are no less influential in changing our outlook and personality. Illness and accident may trigger a regression or remarkable inner growth, depending on how well we accept these changes.

A change in environment, such as a move to another neighborhood or city, attending a new school, or working in a new company, often leads to growth. Such moves provide the stimulus and opportunity for desirable change. Isn't this one reason we seek out new surroundings in the first place?

Significant life events such as graduation, marriage, the birth of a child, or retirement also become occasions for growth. So do unpleasant events or family crises like the loss of a job, divorce, or the death of our parents. In each instance, such events set the stage for growth by confronting us with new roles and responsibilities.

Often the stimulus for growth comes from within, from the personal realm of feelings and self-perceptions. A sense of dissatisfaction with ourselves, building up for months or years, may finally spur us toward growth. A vague sense of stagnation or stimulation may be the force that urges us on. Gail Sheehy (1977) has correctly observed that all too often we displace these inner feelings onto external events, as if we're embarrassed by an inner need to grow. For example, if asked why they've left a job after only a few years, many people look for some external justification, like their boss or the company. Yet, these may have been only part of the reason for the change. People more in tune with their inner world might readily admit, "Frankly, I was getting bored and felt the need for a change."

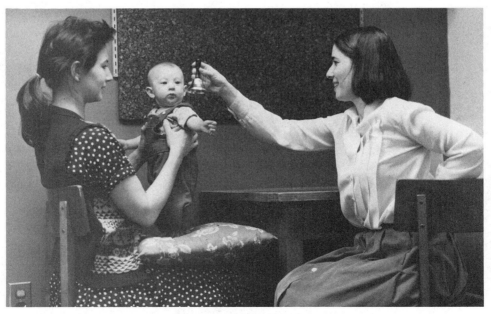

Significant life events such as the birth of a child become occasions for personal growth. (Ken Karp)

A Phenomenology of Growth

Recognizing the importance of such inner changes in the growth process, Sidney Jourard (1975) has given us a *phenomenology of growth:* an account of how we subjectively experience growth.

According to Jourard, our subjective experience of growth tends to follow a three-phase cycle. Typically, an experience of growth begins with (1) acknowledging some change within ourselves or our surroundings, which evokes (2) a sense of dissonance or dissatisfaction within, which in turn leads us to (3) reorganize our experience in some way, such as adopting a new attitude toward ourselves or others.

Like all growth, our inner experience of growth tends to be uneven, with spurts and plateaus. We may be willing to try out something new one minute and feel a need for consolidating our gains the next. Since we experience our inner world more as a continuous flow of ideas, feelings, and meanings, we are more apt to realize that we've grown in retrospect than when we are in the midst of a particular growth cycle.

ACKNOWLEDGING CHANGE. Growth usually begins with the acknowledgment of change. Actually, changes are occurring all the time, but we're not always aware of them. A constant awareness of change would be too disturbing. Instead, we strive to construct an image of ourselves and our world that pictures reality as more stable and under our control than it really is. As a result, we become more acutely aware of changes at some moments than at others. Sometimes we become aware of change rather suddenly through the experience of surprise, such as receiving an unexpected compliment or criticism. Times of uncertainty and decision making also remind us that more changes will be forthcoming, such as when we are wrestling with the choice of a college major or a career. Experiences of disappointment and failure, such as being fired from a job without warning, force us to acknowledge change. The common denominator in all these experiences is the acknowledgment that things are different from what they were— or what you believed or expected they would be.

A SENSE OF DISSONANCE OR DISSATISFACTION. Whether or not the awareness of change leads to growth depends on how it affects you. Sometimes you may react to change defensively, with little awareness of your real feelings, such as the man who dismisses his failure to get a promotion by saying, "I really didn't want it anyway." Because this man is denying his feelings about the change, he minimizes the possibility for growth. In contrast, when you feel dissatisfaction from such experiences, you may be aroused or motivated to further change. This is why the growth cycle is so often tripped by an experience of disappointment or failure. For example, a student may learn how to study more effectively only after going through the agony of failing a test or a course and getting remedial help. Of course, you may also grow under happier conditions, when your feelings of discomfort come from dissatisfaction or unmet growth needs rather than from basic deficiencies. An example would be a woman who returns to school after many years of raising a family because she feels the need for a challenge, rather than because she feels she has been inadequate as a mother.

This phase of growth is inevitably accompanied by a certain degree of anxiety and discomfort. When your motive for growth proceeds out of a sense of challenge or mastery, such as when you take up a new sport, you may simply feel stimulated or mildly apprehensive about the outcome. But when your motive springs from a profound dissatisfaction with yourself, your feelings tend to be more turbulent and agonizing. Either way, the old saying, "How can something that feels so bad be so good?" reminds us that these unsettling feelings are more often than not a necessary part of achieving some desired goal.

REORGANIZING YOUR EXPERIENCE.   In conventional terms this is often expressed as acquiring new ideas and then altering your beliefs, attitudes, values, or self-concept. In some instances, such as the discovery that most people feel anxious about tests, additional knowledge or insight may alter your understanding of yourself or others. Or you may become more aware of your own largely unconscious processes, such as the realization that your chronic sense of anxiety during tests masks an undue fear of criticism and failure. Or you may adopt a new attitude toward another person, becoming more willing to listen to someone's criticism because you know that person wants to help rather than hurt you. Growth may also take the form of new self-perceptions, such as the increased self-acceptance and confidence that often comes with an achievement like getting a degree or getting over a difficult problem like divorce. The main point is that each inner adjustment or change you make affects the whole of your experience, so that growth consists in the continuous reorganization of your experience.

We're more likely to have positive, gratifying feelings at this point than in the earlier stages. We're also more apt to understand how we've grown. Kierkegaard, an existentialist philospher, once put it, "Life must be understood backwards, but it must be lived forwards." Haven't you looked back at a very trying time in your life that eventually led to growth and said to yourself, "Now I realize what I was going through"?

Jourard's phenomenology of growth implies that growth ordinarily proceeds out of our inner response to change, which may eventually result in more lasting changes in our personality and behavior. But sometimes we may change our behavior directly—for example, when we give up the habit of smoking—as we discuss in the chapter on self-directed change. In these instances external changes may give rise to a new attitude or feelings of self-confidence. The important thing to recognize is that overall growth involves both inner and outer changes, with inner changes sometimes leading to behavioral changes and vice versa.

Either way, we must have a willingness to grow. And yet, whether we grow is not entirely up to us. For in another sense we are predisposed to growth. At least this is the view of psychologists who interpret growth in terms of self-actualization.

HABITS AND PERSONAL GROWTH

If someone were to ask, "Which shoe did you put on first this morning?" could you answer with certainty? Most of us couldn't because we usually dress from habit—actions that have become automatic through repetition.

The famous psychologist William James realized that habits can work for us or against us. He observed that our bad habits are among our greatest obstacles to personal growth. The worst habit, he said, was overlooking or ignoring our other bad habits.

James also championed free will—the power to change habits. In fact, it was his own belief in free will that helped him to overcome a serious bout of depression. Yet he maintained that it is not enough merely to want to or to intend to change our behavior. We must seize the first opportunity to put that intent into action! Otherwise, our resolve simply evaporates, making it that much more difficult to act on future resolutions. Each lapse is like letting a ball of string drop; a single slip undoes much more than many turns can wind.

Do you have any bad habits you would like to change? Would you agree that the longer you wait to act on your good intention, the harder it gets? What are some desirable habits you would like to cultivate? What's keeping you from starting?

William James, *Talks to Teachers on Psychology and to Students on Some of Life's Ideals* (New York: Henry Holt and Company, 1899), pp. 33–36. Unaltered republication, New York: Dover, 1962.

GROWTH AS SELF-ACTUALIZATION

According to humanistic psychologists like Maslow and Rogers, the human organism exhibits a tendency to actualize its own potential. (The term *it* has been used here because such a tendency is assumed to operate at the biological level.) In speaking of this actualizing tendency, Rogers says:

> *By this I mean the directional trend which is evident in all organic and human life—the urge to expand, extend, develop, mature—the tendency to express and activate all the capacities of the organism, or the self. This tendency may become deeply buried under layer after layer of encrusted psychological defenses; it may be hidden behind elaborate façades which deny its existence; it is my belief, however, based on my experience, that it exists in every individual, and awaits only the proper conditions to be released and expressed* (1961, p. 351).

Rogers reserves the term "self-actualizing tendency" for the individual's push to realize his or her own sense of fulfillment, which operates in addition to the unconscious thrust of the actualizing tendency. However, Maslow uses the term "self-actualizing tendency" more generally, sometimes referring to the organism's biological tendency and sometimes to the individual's self-conscious desire and effort to grow.

Fulfilling Our Potential

The notion of such an actualizing tendency suggests that each of us has many more possibilities for growth than we have realized. We tend to set premature limits on what we can do and become. William James recognized this at the turn of the century, hypothesizing that the average person functioned at only 10 percent of capacity. More recently, Herbert Otto (1980) has gone a bit further and estimated that we use only about 4 percent of our potential. Perhaps the precise figure would vary depending on which aspects of ourselves we're considering. For example, you might be using a greater part of your potential for playing the guitar than, say, learning to think logically in your philosophy course. Then too, the figures would probably change at different stages of your life.

People sometimes feel freer to explore their potential more fully in their later years. (Ken Karp/Sirovich Senior Center)

Some individuals explore their potential more vigorously in their twenties, while others grow more at later periods of their lives. However, psychologists who rely on the self-actualizing model of growth would agree on one point: Each of us has many more abilities and resources for growth than we are now using. Would you agree?

Some Tantalizing Questions

As promising as all this sounds, the notion of fulfilling our potential also raises some tantalizing questions. For one thing—how can you know your potential capacity for something until you have realized it? Of course, there's no simple answer to this question. Maslow (1968) pointed out that, while all of us share some capabilities that are generally known, such as the capacity to love and be loved, each of us also has distinctive potentials, such as a talent for music, that must be discovered individually. Perhaps this is the reason why psychologists using the self-actualizing model provide us with so little specific content for describing our potential—because it varies so much from person to person. Yet, we're not without clues. For what a person likes and does well provides valuable information about that person's inherent potential. You may also get an idea of your capabilities by objective means, such as an IQ or aptitude test. Or you may catch a glimpse of your potential from something you've accomplished, like a car you've rebuilt or a swimming class you've taught. Perhaps the best indication of all is your own sense of satisfaction in developing some skill or talent.

WHAT'S IT LIKE TO ACTUALIZE YOUR POTENTIAL?

"If I say something about the human potential hypothesis and 10 percent hypothesis, people often say, 'Gee, here comes someone who is putting us under even more pressure, when I am already doing the very best I can.' My answer to that is, 'Do you remember a day in your life when things were going tremendously well, when you were creatively, fantastically productive and you were happy, your heart was singing inside you and things were just going beautifully?' All of us have had days like that. That is how it feels when you are actualizing more of your potential. It is basically a joyous experience. Yet, what leads up to that point may be turmoil because it involves change. Growth involves change, but the realization of the growth, the step forward, is basically joyous for most of us. It is a tremendous feeling of satisfaction and joy."

Herbert A. Otto, "New Light on Human Potential," in Abe Arkoff, ed., *Psychology and Personal Growth,* 2nd ed. (Boston: Allyn and Bacon, 1980), p. 340. Revised and reprinted by permission from *Families of the Future* by College of Home Economics. © 1972 by Iowa State University Press, Ames, Iowa 50010.

An equally troublesome question is—how do you go about actualizing your potential? Again, there is no simple answer. Maslow (1968) makes it clear that actualization is only partly a result of discovering what is in us already. Reliance on such a passive process suggests the erroneous notion that our potential is fully determined biologically—which it isn't. Our potential is also greatly affected by our environment and learning. Accordingly, Maslow stresses that growth is an active process of trial and error in which we partly choose and create ourselves. Such conscious efforts are also more appropriately directed at *specific* areas of growth, such as playing a better game of tennis or communicating more effectively with our marriage partner, than toward self-actualization in general. Self-actualization itself is more of a by-product than the aim of our conscious efforts. While it may help to believe in the general idea of self-actualization, it is more important to spend our efforts in achieving specific goals.

Ideally, we feel freer to engage in this process when we're in favorable surroundings, when we can relax our defenses and take risks. But as we explain more fully in the next chapter, this is not always the case. In actual practice, the conditions that facilitate growth are varied indeed. Many times we get the incentive to grow only after painful experiences of disappointment and failure, such as losing a job or getting divorced. Sometimes we may need an outside push because of the risk involved in growth.

Growth and Risk

Growth understandably involves taking calculated psychological risks. Growth involves stepping into unfamiliar and potentially dangerous situations, thereby leaving us more vulnerable to hurt and disappointment. Each step forward may result in a step backward. Therefore, the decision to grow often has to be made in spite of these dangers and requires courage and the willingness to take risks. Interestingly enough, a surprising number of highly successful men have had incidents of stealing or delinquent behavior in their past, perhaps because they were risk takers even in their youth (Bardwick, 1974). The willingness to take risks is a key to personal growth.

In less obvious ways, of course, we run a risk whenever we avoid growing. Each time we pass up an opportunity to develop a new skill or put security before a challenge, we run the risk of becoming stagnant or bored. When we habitually suppress or deny the underlying actualizing tendency of the human organism itself, we risk becoming ill, sometimes in obvious ways, sometimes in subtle ways, sometimes immediately and sometimes later. In fact, many of the characteristic disorders of our time such as the "stunted person," the "amoral person," or the "apathetic person" result from the failure to grow (Maslow, 1968). Either way, then, we run a risk. But the self-reinforcing qualities of the growth process imply that more often than not the satisfaction of growing outweighs the risks involved.

SELF-ACTUALIZING PEOPLE

Maslow believed that some people have reached a healthier, more optimal level of functioning than the average person has. He called these self-actualizing people, and claimed that the study of them may teach us much about our own potential for growth.

The two main criteria for including such people were that they must be relatively free from neurosis or major problems and they must have made the best possible use of their talents and strengths. Maslow included both historical figures like Abraham Lincoln and Jane Addams and recent figures like Albert Einstein and Eleanor Roosevelt.

When compared to the average person, self-actualizing people tend to exhibit the following characteristics or traits: more adequate perception of reality; greater acceptance of themselves and others; greater spontaneity and naturalness; more focused on problems outside themselves; need for privacy and solitude; high degree of autonomy or independence; greater freshness of appreciation of the basic things in everyday life; more frequent peak or mystic experiences (though not necessarily in a religious way); increased feeling of kinship with other people; satisfying, intimate relationships with a few friends or loved ones; democratic personality; highly developed sense of right and wrong; healthy, unhostile sense of humor; highly creative (though not necessarily in the arts); and a resistance to conformity (Maslow, 1970).

Yet it is clear from Maslow's writings that self-actualizing people are not perfect. Even though they have transcended the problems of becoming, or growth, they remain vulnerable to the problems of being, or the existential concerns that plague all people, such as frustration, anxiety, or guilt. But their problems tend to be real ones that come from coping with a troubled world, rather than neurotic distortions of it (Maslow, 1968). At times, however, self-actualizing people can be boring, irritating, or depressed, as all humans can be. For they are not special beings as much as they are "the ordinary person with nothing taken away." That is, self-actualizing people are like the rest of us, but without the inhibited capacities so characteristic of the average person (Maslow in Lowry, 1973).

Maslow's writings on self-actualizing people have been criticized on several grounds. First, they tend to be clinical impressions more than empirically documented studies, prompting Maslow himself to propose such studies before his death. Second, they tend to be more descriptive than explanatory, in that they tell us what it is like to be actualized but not how to get that way. As a result, Maslow's last book (1971) contains more specific suggestions for increasing our self-actualization:

> Experience life fully, be alive and absorbed with what you are doing at the moment.
> Learn to trust your own judgment and feelings in making life choices, such as marriage and career.
> Be honest with yourself and take responsibility for what you do.
> Whenever possible choose growth, rather than safety or security.
> Recognize your defenses and illusions, and then work to give them up.
> Even though peak experiences are transient, keep the inspiration of these moments of self-actualization alive in your everyday thoughts and actions.
> Remember that self-actualization is a continual process; it is never fully achieved.
> Commit yourself to concerns and causes outside yourself, since self-actualization comes more as a by-product of developing your full capacities than the ego-centric pursuit of growth itself.

SELF-ACTUALIZATION AMONG HANDICAPPED PEOPLE

Some of the most dramatic examples of self-actualization can be seen among people afflicted with various handicaps, whether from birth, accident, or illness. Many of them are leading full lives by learning how to actualize a greater degree of their potential than is the case with most of us. Blind people have learned how to play musical instruments, swim, ski, and sky-dive. Amputees in wheelchairs have excelled in business and athletics. Artists have learned to paint by holding the brush in their mouths. One woman born without arms learned to use her feet so well that she drives a car, shops, cooks, and serves meals to her family, all without a trace of self-pity.

A particularly inspiring example of self-actualization was seen in a Philadelphia courtroom when a quadriplegic woman fought to gain custody of her infant daughter. The woman was born with an inherited birth defect called arthrogryposis multiplex, a condition that affects the muscles, skin, and soft tissues of the body. As a result, she gets around by thrusting her body along the floor. Despite her useless limbs, however, this woman has refused to settle for anything short of a full life. She received a high school diploma by passing an equivalency test and hopes to attend college. She is writing her autobiography, typing much of it with her tongue. She also plays the organ with her tongue. In the courtroom she demonstrated her ability to care for her child by changing the infant's diapers with her tongue and lips. The judge ruled that through her "tremendous love and interest" she has offset her disabilities and is capable of caring for her own children.

Reported by Ellen Karasik in *The Philadelphia Inquirer*, January 21, 1979, p. 6B.

IT'S UP TO YOU

By now it should be clear that growth is an active and personal process. Others may make suggestions or challenge you. Psychology may provide you with helpful information. But ultimately growth is self-directed. It's really up to you.

We may realize only a fraction of our potential because of the limitations of time and circumstance. But, often, we fail to actualize ourselves because of the choices we make—or don't make.

Making Choices

This is such an important topic that the better part of Chapter 10 has been devoted to decision making. At this point we will simply point out an aspect of choosing that is especially relevant to personal growth—namely choice as commitment.

So often growth occurs because of a personal decision. Occasionally, when a student does considerably better on a test compared to an earlier one, I will comment on the improvement and ask what made the difference. Typical responses are, "I studied harder" or "I just made up my mind to do better." While most students would *like* to do better, only those who have reached a *decision* to do something about it expend greater effort at study, which in turn increases the likelihood of improving their performance. Tangible evidence of improvement, such as a higher grade, then serves to strengthen their positive self-image and sense of competence. I've also been struck with how often people who overcome a problem with drinking or drug abuse do so only after making a conscious choice to that effect. Many times the events that precede their decision include rejection by loved ones or a sense of personal failure or disgust. But at some point that individual has to make a personal decision to give up drinking or drugs.

Many opportunities for personal growth are associated with major life choices, such as the choice of attending college or graduate school or the choice of a career or marriage partner. Daniel Levinson (1978) has pointed out the paradox that we are expected to make such critical choices *before* we have the necessary experience or judgment to choose wisely! Yet, if such choices are delayed until we feel ready, the delay may produce even greater costs. This paradox is especially true in regard to the choice of a career or marriage partner. Much of the anxiety among young people comes with the feeling that their choices are irrevocable. When they choose not to attend graduate school or have children, they have the feeling they will have to live with that choice forever. Yet this is generally a false fear, since change is not only possible, but some modification of earlier choices is inevitable (Sheehy, 1977). Consequently, one of the distinctive requirements of youth and early adulthood is that we make sufficient choices to give us roots and direction while putting off firmer commitments until our options are clearer.

Clarifying Values

Many times we have trouble choosing because of a conflict in our values—what is desirable and of worth to us. We share many of our values with others, but some are highly personal. What one person finds worthwhile may not be at all satisfying to another. Then too, we do not always choose values compatible with our needs. We may take a job mostly for the money, rather than the personal satisfaction involved. Furthermore, in a rapidly changing world, an emerging set of values may conflict with our existing ones. An example would be the increasing value put on personal happiness, which often conflicts with the traditional value of a long-term commitment to marriage. Since the question of values is often the hardest part of making decisions, it helps to be clear about our values, so that we know what we want, and the kind of person we're trying to become. In practice, however, it often works the other way around, so that we examine our values only when we have to make a difficult choice. The important thing is that we realize the significant part played by values. For a choice is good or bad mostly in terms of whether it expresses our personal values.

Personal Responsibility

Personal freedom can be frightening because of the responsibility that goes with it. We become acutely aware of this fact while making difficult life choices such as choosing a mate or a career. At these times we realize that we stand alone. It's an awesome feeling from which we often feel like escaping either by not deciding at all, or by deciding not to change. That's why personal growth requires what theologian Paul Tillich has called "the courage to be," that is, the courage to affirm ourselves and our possibilities in spite of the risks involved. Psychologists such as Carl Rogers, Fritz Perls, and Rollo May also agree that we grow only by affirming the sense of responsibility implicit in our personal freedom. Rogers (1961) has observed that while there is little or no sense of responsibility for one's problems early in psychotherapy, as an individual gains insight there is more acceptance of "self-responsibility" for one's life and problems. The same is true throughout life. As long as we blame others or circumstances for our shortcomings, even when these have contributed to our problems, we fail to grow. Growth comes through assuming responsibility for our own lives.

There's a humorous saying that "I was halfway through life before I discovered it was a do-it-yourself affair." Like all proverbial sayings, it's only half-true. But the sooner we discover this truth, the more freedom and growth we will experience.

SUMMARY

We began the chapter with the view that adjustment and growth are complementary processes. We must continually adjust in order to survive. Yet it is the experience of growth that gives us a sense of enthusiasm and direction.

Although personal growth refers to change in a desirable direction, there are many views of growth because of the variations in individual development as well as major psychological viewpoints. However, our subjective experience of growth tends to follow a three-phase cycle: an initial acknowledgment of change, which evokes a sense of dissatisfaction within ourselves, which in turn leads us to reorganize our experience in some way, such as adopting a new attitude toward ourselves or others.

Those who interpret growth as a process of self-actualization point out that there's an actualizing tendency at work in all of us and that we have a much greater potential for growth than we're aware of. Yet growth is not simply the result of passively discovering our inborn potential, but is an active process of choosing and creating ourselves in relation to specific goals.

Implicit in the concept of self-actualization is the notion that personal growth is an individual and self-determined process. It's primarily up to us. Although we ordinarily actualize only a fraction of our potential because of the limitations of time and circumstances, we can maximize our growth through the choices we make, the values we hold, and the sense of personal responsibility for our lives.

QUESTIONS FOR SELF-REFLECTION

1. What is the most difficult adjustment you have had to make in life?
2. Do you find it easier to acknowledge periods of marked personal growth more in retrospect than at the time?
3. Would you agree that we "live in a forward direction" but "understand in a backward direction"?
4. Do you agree that we use only 4 to 10 percent of our capabilities? What figure would you give for yourself?
5. How much guidance can you reasonably expect from courses and books in psychology?
6. In what ways would you like to grow as a person in the next five years? What are you doing to bring this about?
7. Why does it often take painful experiences such as personal failure to motivate us to change?
8. Do you sometimes take calculated psychological risks that may enhance your growth?
9. What kinds of changes are needed in society to help more people realize their potentialities?
10. Do you feel personally responsible for your life? Or do you frequently complain and blame others?

EXERCISES

1. Your most difficult adjustment

Think back to some condition, event, or situation that required a major adjustment on your part. It could be a physical handicap, a difficult course in school, a traumatic event, or a trying experience like divorce.

Explain why it was such a difficult adjustment for you. How well did you cope with the situation? How passive or resourceful were you throughout this period? What did you learn about yourself from this experience? Would you consider yourself a survivor?

2. An experience of personal growth

Select some way in which you feel you have grown significantly in the past several years, such as the ability to express yourself more assertively. Then examine your experience in relation to the three phases of Jourard's growth cycle. Remember that, as in all stages of growth, the growth phases overlap considerably. They are rarely as clear-cut in experience as they appear on paper.

a. What events made you aware of the need for growth? Did such events involve a sense of disappointment or failure? Or did the need for growth arise more out of a sense of challenge and mastery? Did the awareness of change come as a surprise or shock, or was it more or less expected?

b. Can you identify some of your inner reactions as you look back at this stage of growth? Did you waste time in feelings of anger, resentment, discouragement, or self-pity? Did the reaction of others challenge or inspire you to change? How much personal initiative did you take?

c. In what ways have you grown as a result of your experience? Has it resulted in change of attitude, self-perception, specific skills or strategies used? Have you received feedback from others? Was it favorable or unfavorable? Has your experience of growth been mostly satisfying?

3. Assessing your growth potential

Experts have estimated that the average person operates at only about 4 to 10 percent of capacity. To see how this applies to you, select half a dozen categories and estimate how well you have developed your inborn potential. Possible categories include physical conditioning, natural abilities, the senses, memory, reasoning and judgment, personality, social skills, special aptitudes, and so forth. Estimate the percentage of your potential that you have developed in each area.

How do your figures compare with those given by the experts? Would you agree that much of your potential is undeveloped? How much of your potential do you believe will ever be actualized? What are your plans for developing more of your potential?

4. Discovering your growth potential

Even though discovering your potential is an attitude and an approach to all of life, sometimes you may get helpful clues from particular activities. In addition to the following suggested activities, you may want to add others.

Take a course or workshop in improving your study skills.

Select some personal limitation and work on it.

Take an aptitude test or vocational-type inventory in the college counseling center.

Participate in a growth-type group improving your personal skills (preferably sponsored by your college).

Take lessons or a course improving a sport of your choice, such as tennis.

Read a self-help book, preferably written by a professional such as a psychologist.

When it seems appropriate, volunteer to give an oral report or talk in class.

5. Risk-taking and growth

Growth involves the willingness to take calculated psychological risks, such as asking a friend out, soliciting someone's opinion of your work, or expressing your feelings. What are some appropriate psychological risks that might lead to growth on your part? Since these will vary from one person to another, make a list that especially applies to you. Select a suggestion you feel comfortable with and act on it for several days, then write up your experience.

6. Self-actualization among handicapped people

Some of the most dramatic examples of self-actualization can be seen among people who have overcome a handicap present from birth or caused by an illness or accident.

One woman born with only stubs in place of her arms has become the mother of two children, takes care of the children herself, is getting a master's degree in psychology, and is writing her life story and typing it with her toes. To get an idea of how difficult this is, try typing your name with your toes.

Watch for news clippings or stories about such persons and bring them to class. You might have each member of the class bring in such an article and then share them.

What can we learn from such people? To what extent have they developed their potential? Why are they so much more motivated than the average person?

RECOMMENDED READINGS

Johnson, D.W. *Reaching Out: Interpersonal Effectiveness and Self-Actualization,* 2nd ed. Englewood Cliffs, N.J.: Prentice-Hall, 1981 (paperback). Contains practical aids for discovering areas of needed improvement and exercises for developing interpersonal skills.

Lazarus, A. and F. Allen. *I Can If I Want To.* New York: William Morrow, 1975 (Warner paperback, 1977). A guide to personal growth and self-actualization.

Otto, H.A. *A Guide to Developing Your Potential.* North Hollywood, Calif.: Wilshire, 1974 (paperback). A guide to self-actualization by one of the leaders in the field.

Rogers, C. *A Way of Being.* Boston: Houghton Mifflin, 1981 (paperback). One of the pioneers of growth psychology explains how to develop your personal power in humane ways.

Shostrom, E. *Freedom To Be.* New York: A Bantam Book, 1974 (paperback). A practical guide to achieving your full human potential as a human being.

Motivation

2

Like a detective searching for a motive, we are constantly trying to find out why people behave the way they do. If a student drops out of school for no clear reason, we often say that he or she is "not motivated to study." On the other hand, if students obviously enjoy school despite the pressures of work or family responsibilities, we may say they're "highly motivated." In both instances, we're attempting to explain behavior through motivation. But what do we mean by "motivation"?

We'll begin by explaining the concept of motivation. Then we'll examine the major physiological motives, such as hunger, as well as some of the more important psychological motives, such as the striving for achievement. We'll also point out how our motives change with the satisfaction of our needs, so that we often act out of what Maslow has called "growth motives." A better understanding of the latter is especially important for fulfilling our human potential, as discussed in Chapter 1.

THE CONCEPT OF MOTIVATION

Essentially, *motivation* (from the Latin word for "movement") refers to the inner state that moves or causes us to behave the way we do. In a sense, the entire field of psychology has to do with explaining behavior in terms of its underlying causes. But what has traditionally been called motivation refers specifically to the study of *inner* causes. That is, the "why" of behavior is explained in terms of the sequence of inner forces involved. Motivation refers to the inner conditions that energize and direct us toward purposive, goal-seeking behavior. A particular motive such as hunger refers to the more specific goal-directed activity of obtaining food.

Sometimes our motives are rather obvious, such as the hungry teenager who asks, "How long before dinner?" At other times, our motives are not so apparent, as when a person unexpectedly resigns from a successful position. In many instances, our motives are mixed and unclear even to ourselves.

Motives Are Inferred

Basically we infer motives from our observations of behavior. For example, suppose you are taking a hike or bicycle trip. You may start out vigorously and continue at that pace for several hours. Then you notice that you and some of your companions are moving at a slower speed, drinking from your canteens and dipping into your knapsacks more often. Rest stops occur more frequently. Well into the afternoon more of you start asking, "When do we stop to eat?" You'll probably interpret all these things to mean that you and your friends are hungry. But how do you know? Nobody can see "hunger." Rather, hunger is something you've inferred to account for the difference between earlier and present behavior. Or to put it in a fancier way, hunger explains the difference between the input conditions of exercise combined with hours of food deprivation and the resulting external conditions of less vigorous behavior, more frequent snacks, and talk about eating. Rather than attempting to trace all the causal connections between the input and output events, we posit an intervening or motivational variable to explain such behavior (Zimbardo, 1980).

Motivational variables such as hunger, thirst, sex, or curiosity also help to explain the variations in human behavior. When two people are performing poorly in tennis, why does one person give up while the other tries all the harder? Why does one person take the initiative to learn to play while another has to be prodded into it? Why do some people readily assume responsibility for their performance while others are ready to blame something or someone else for it? Or, for that matter, why does our own behavior vary from one occasion to the next? We say the difference lies in our motivation. But motivation is essentially a *construct,* or an idea that psychologists and others use to explain the variations in behavior that are not obviously attributable to the situation itself.

1 Push-and-Pull Motives

The way motives affect us has been explained largely through homeostatic principles. *Homeostasis* (from the Greek words for "steady state") is the process by which our bodies maintain a sufficiently steady state to ensure our survival. Many of our vital body processes—such as temperature, amount of oxygen available to our cells, or the amount of sugar in our blood—can vary only within certain limits. When anything disrupts this delicate balance, homeostatic mechanisms automatically go into action to rectify the imbalance. For example, when you become chilled, the blood vessels on the surface of your skin automatically constrict to retain warmth, and you develop goose pimples and shivering as a means of raising your body temperature.

When the imbalance of inner forces exceeds the usual range of these homeostatic mechanisms, we tend to speak of motivated behavior. Initially, we become aware of this imbalance as a state of tension or a *need*. Some needs, such as thirst, are so urgent they are often referred to as *drives*, because we feel driven to satisfy them. The tension of our unmet needs or drives in turn serves to arouse or energize us to seek the appropriate gratification, which we refer to as a *motive* or collectively as motivation. Of course, external cues help make us more aware of our needs and thus act on them, such as the smell or sight of food. But according to the *drive-reduction model* of motivation, it is mainly the unresolved tension of our unmet needs that motivates us. In addition, the feeling of satisfaction that follows the reduction of tension serves to reinforce our motives, so that we're likely to repeat the sequence of behavior in the future.

At times we act in ways that do not readily fit the familiar drive-reduction theory of motivation, as described above. How about mountain climbing, car racing, or seeking out a more challenging job even though it presents more risks? Studies on behavior associated with curiosity, stimulation, and mastery suggest that we often act in ways that deliberately *increase* tension. As a result, psychologists such as Abraham Maslow (1970) speak of a growth or actualization model of motivation, which takes into account our tendencies to grow and change as well as to restore equilibrium. We shall deal with this idea more fully later in the chapter.

Psychologists are also questioning whether our motivation always comes from within, as traditionally viewed in the drive theory. They see behavior as also shaped by *incentives:* objects or conditions in the environment that attract or repel us. College degrees and promising jobs serve as positive incentives that attract us toward these objects. Loneliness and failure are negative incentives that repel us enough to act to avoid them. Incentives direct our behavior toward a goal, like the cue of the smell of a pizza directs us toward food. But unlike cues, incentives also help arouse or energize us to seek these goals. When an incentive is interpreted as a reinforcer, as in behaviorist theory, it is usually referred to as a reinforcing stimulus rather than a motive.

The lack of consensus in the use of these terms derives largely from conflicting theories of motivation in the field of psychology. Traditionally, psychologists have emphasized the inner forces or how we are pushed from within in explaining motivation. But not all psychologists agree with this view. Behaviorist psychologists such as B. F. Skinner emphasize the role of environmental reinforcers and the pull that these external forces exert on our behavior. Most psychologists tend to include both inner and outer types of causal forces in their explanations of behavior. They would probably agree that in actuality "the question is how much of motivation is push and how much is pull" (Bolles, 1967). In the final analysis, our overall motivation comes from an interaction between inner and outer influences, whether we call these drives, incentives, reinforcers, or motives. In this chapter, we focus on the inner forces, or the push aspects of motivation, with consideration of the environmental influences, or pull aspects of motivation, reserved for Chapter 11.

Classification of Motives

One familiar classification of motives distinguishes between primary and secondary drives or motives. *Primary drives* are considered to be innate, while *secondary drives* are acquired largely through learning. Hunger would be a primary motive, and achievement a secondary one. But many motives, like curiosity and sex, don't fall exclusively under either heading.

Another arrangement follows Maslow's (1970) distinction between survival motives and growth motives. Hunger and sleep are examples of survival motives,

Our motivation is affected by both inner and outer influences. (Ken Karp)

while the search for meaning and equality are examples of growth motives. One shortcoming of this scheme is that it doesn't distinguish between the physical priority of a motive and the urgency, time, and energy we spend on satisfying it. For example, we may give little thought to sleep though it is crucial to our survival, but we spend a lot of time learning things like psychology and religion that mean much to us but are not life-and-death matters.

It should be clear at this point that any classification of motives is relative at best. What follows is more of a continuum of motives, with motives that are predominantly physiological toward one end and those that have more to do with our psychological well-being toward the other end. While all these motives are affected by our environment to some degree, psychological motives are especially affected by learning.

PHYSIOLOGICAL MOTIVES

Hunger and Thirst

Hunger is one of the most widely investigated motivational states. Early investigators explained that the sensations of hunger were caused by the contractions of an empty stomach. Later discoveries have shown that a lowered glucose or sugar level in the blood is also part of the hunger motive. More recent studies have indicated that the hypothalamus (located at the base of the brain) plays a central role in our eating habits. A "feeding center" and a "satiety center" in the hypothalamus act in opposite ways to regulate when and how much we eat. Factors such as an empty or full stomach, blood sugar level, and brain temperature stimulate these control centers to make us feel hungry or full.

Although most wild animals maintain a constant weight level throughout their lives despite changing supplies of food, human weight tends to fluctuate because our eating behavior is strongly influenced by learning and emotions. Psychodynamic theories of behavior, such as Freud's, claim that people sometimes overeat because they are starved for affection. For these people, food and drink have become symbolic substitutes for love. More recent studies suggest that obese people tend to be oversensitive to external cues, like the availability of food, but undersensitive to internal cues, like the sensations of hunger or satiety (Schachter, 1971). Eating habits are also influenced by the sameness or variety of food available to us. Perhaps you have noticed how you tend to eat more than usual during Thanksgiving dinner. One explanation is the greater variety of food stimulating your palate. Since eating is largely a social habit, you may also notice that you eat more and linger longer over a meal when you are socializing with others.

While we can survive for weeks without food, we can live only a few days without water. Furthermore, while the pain of hunger tends to lessen as we get more and more hungry, the sensation of thirst becomes more intense with in-

FASTING

Fasting (abstaining from food) is a time-honored tradition that may serve a variety of purposes, including weight loss, resting the intestines, revitalizing the body, and enhancing alternate states of consciousness such as dreaming and meditation. It is no accident that the first meal of the day is called "breakfast," suggesting that each of us has abstained from food for a respectable period during the night. Prolonged fasting has also been used as a means of political protest, as among the imprisoned Irish activists in recent years.

People who fast may feel hungry for the first few days but usually have no hunger sensations by the end of the first week. When deprived of food, the body begins to feed on itself by burning up the stored fat. As the fat stores are exhausted, the body draws more heavily on the protein deposits. Since the biggest deposits of protein are in the muscles, the muscles gradually waste away, including the heart muscles. Starvation also disrupts the electrical rhythm of the heart, so that death sometimes occurs very suddenly long before the available calories are burned up. Since the body's natural immune system is also weakened by malnutrition, one of the most common causes of death from prolonged fasting is infection. People rarely survive prolonged fasting beyond the third month.

creasing hours of deprivation. Even when we've found water, we may experience an insatiable thirst for hours afterwards.

There appear to be metering mechanisms in the mouth, throat, and stomach associated with the hypothalamus that help regulate our water intake. There is also an interrelated system of physiological processes that helps to maintain a fluid balance in our system as a whole, so that even when we fail to consume adequate fluids our bodies will recover water from our kidneys. For example, you may notice that your urine usually has a darker color in the morning than later in the day. This results from a heavier concentration of urine to satisfy your thirst during sleep.

Thirst is also affected by external influences and learning. As with eating, so we sometimes drink from habit rather than physiological need. There also appears to be an association between our eating and drinking behavior, so that once either is begun, the other tends to follow.

Avoidance of Pain and Extreme Stimuli

The sense of pain differs from other physiological motives in several ways. We do not feel pain as a result of being deprived. Nor is it cyclical in occurrence or gratification. When we do feel pain, it arouses us to avoid or escape something that is injurious or threatening to us. Pain is a warning essential to survival. Although the sense of pain usually results from tissue damage, it can be elicited directly by stimulation of the appropriate brain centers.

The sense of pain can be blunted by lack of exposure to normal stimuli. For example, puppies raised without normal pain-arousing stimuli tend not to respond appropriately when pricked with a pin or when their tails are stepped on (Scott, 1968). In those instances where the experience of pain is sought as a means of excitement or pleasure, such as sadistic and masochistic behavior, the sense of pain has become pathological, usually through some form of conditioning.

Actually, any intense or extreme stimulus, whether light, sound, heat, cold, or inflammation or damage to our tissues, can be painful. Fortunately, our built-in homeostatic mechanisms automatically act to redress the balance in many of these instances. For example, if our bodies overheat, our blood vessels dilate, our sweat glands perspire, and we adapt to the change. And, vice versa, when cold, we shiver, thereby generating more body heat to offset the drop.

Sleep and Dreaming

Someone has estimated that by the time you are 60 years old you will have slept the equivalent of 20 years! You will have spent over one-third of your life relatively unconscious of your surroundings, 15 years in dreamless sleep, and 5 years in vivid dreams (Jouvet, 1967). "What a waste of time!" you may say. But if you look at some of the symptoms of people who are seriously deprived of sleep, you may think otherwise. For example, Peter Tripp, a New York disc jockey, staged a 200-hour "wakathon" for the benefit of the March of Dimes. During this time, psychological tests and observations by physicians showed that he suffered from marked lapses of attention, a variety of visual and auditory disorders, disorientation of time and place, hallucinations, and paranoid symptoms (Luce, 1965). However, other studies have shown that even after 10 days without sleep, people usually exhibit few psychological effects of sleep deprivation (Goleman, 1982).

After years of investigating sleep habits, Wilse Webb (1976) has concluded that sleep is a biological rhythm that may be altered within certain limits. That is, away from time cues lab subjects tend to wake and sleep in a 25½-hour day. Each night volunteers go to sleep later and each morning they get up a little later. But within our time-conscious society, each of us learns to modify this biological rhythm in order to function within a 24-hour day.

How much sleep do you need? It tends to vary from person to person. But each of has has a natural sleep length. The best way to tell if you are getting enough sleep is that you wake up spontaneously, feel well rested, and don't have to struggle through periods of sleepiness during the day. If you are not sure try this regimen. One night during the first week go to bed at 5 A M and get up at 7 A M Observe yourself all day to recognize the symptoms of not getting enough sleep. One night during the next week, go to bed at 3 A M and get up at 7 A M, and see how you feel. Then let yourself sleep two hours longer one night each successive week, until you wake up spontaneously and don't feel tired during the day. That is your natural sleep length (Goleman, 1982).

The need to dream is just as basic as the need to sleep. Young adults dream a total of about two hours each night; older adults dream somewhat less. Each person's sleeping pattern alternates between various levels or stages of sleep, with the deepest stage of sleep occurring within the first hour or so after falling asleep. During the later hours of sleep, sleep alternates between REM (rapid eye movement) sleep and various stages of non-REM sleep. Dreams tend to occur more frequently and in greater detail and vividness in REM sleep. Since the periods of REM sleep and dreaming grow progressively longer toward the end of our sleep, we often wake up in the morning toward the end of a dream. Upon awakening, most of us do not remember our dreams. We are more likely to recall our dreams when we are awakened in the middle of a dream (Dement, 1974).

Most of us are familiar with Freud's notion that dreams express wish-fulfillment of repressed impulses. But Jung emphasized that dreams are also revelations of our unconscious self, hinting of untapped potential or warning us of personal weaknesses. Rosalind Cartwright (1978) found that dreams may also help with problem solving. She presented students in a sleep laboratory with problem stories dealing with common concerns of young adults, like separation from home, before bedtime. Then she allowed some subjects to dream, while others were awakened during REM sleep or not allowed to sleep at all. She found that those who were allowed to dream proposed more creative solutions to the stories. Cartwright suggests that dreams may serve a positive purpose, helping us to repair self-esteem and competence in our lives.

Sex

The sexual motive exhibits many unique characteristics. In some ways, sex functions in accordance with the drive-reduction model of motivation, in that sexual desire increases psychological tension and can be relieved through orgasm. But unlike hunger and thirst, sexual arousal is actively sought as enjoyable in itself. Sex also defies simple classification as to whether it is a physiological or psychological motive. Nobody dies from a lack of sex, since individual survival doesn't depend on it, although survival of the species does. Nor is there any sound evidence that abstinence from sexual activity is detrimental to a person's health. Rather, the urgency of sexual desire is often influenced more by psychological and social factors than by hormones, so that it is doubtful sex should be considered a drive like hunger and thirst. In short, the sexual motive is a unique blend of inborn and learned influences.

Psychological and social motives play a larger role in regulating sexual behavior in humans than in animals. Thus, in addition to being a means of reproduction, sexual intercourse often becomes an expression of love. In fact, the phrase "making love" has become synonymous with sexual intercourse for many people. Sexual intercourse is also sought as a pleasurable activity in itself, especially among those with liberated lifestyles. But people also engage in sex for a variety of other motives, including the need for approval or conquest, calming the nerves, or escape from depression. Teenagers may seek sexual intercourse out of curiosity or peer pressure. The forbidden quality of sex outside marriage heightens its attractiveness for many people. Some married couples admit that they enjoyed sex more when they were living together before marriage. Married partners may seek extramarital affairs out of a desire for adventure or to relieve the boredom of marital sex.

Probably the greatest change in our attitude toward sex is the realization that sexual feelings are present in everyone. Sex is not just for young, attractive people anymore. Sexual desire is present in older people, unattractive people, and handicapped people (see the boxed material on sex and the handicapped).

Sexual feelings normally persist in people as they grow older. Much of the decrease in sexual responsiveness that occurs with age is due more to psychological than physical causes. For example, the frequency of intercourse among married couples generally declines with age and length of marriage, from an average of several times a week among partners in their twenties to about once a week among those in their fifties (Hunt & Hunt, 1975). Yet there is great

Sex isn't just for young people anymore. (Teri Leigh Stratford)

variation from one person or couple to another. The more sexually active individuals have been in their twenties and thirties, the more likely they will remain relatively active in their later years. Individuals who change their marital status tend to become more sexually active with a new partner, but many married couples remain sexually active with the same partner. A study of sexual desire among couples who had been married fifty years or more showed that almost four out of ten spouses still experienced moderate or strong sexual desires (Roberts & Roberts, 1975).

SEX AND THE HANDICAPPED

The movie *Coming Home* helped to change the public's attitude toward sex and the handicapped. In the movie a handicapped Vietnam war veteran fell in love with a character played by Jane Fonda, and the couple eventually became active sexually. The movie showed that being in a wheelchair doesn't necessarily end a person's interest in sex or the ability to enjoy it. Many men are capable of a partial or complete erection, depending on their injury.

What is important is how handicapped people feel about themselves and their sexuality, as well as how their partners feel about sex and the handicapped. Men who are paralyzed from the waist down may be plagued by questions such as "Will I be able to perform satisfactorily?" or "Can I still satisfy my partner?" Women may initially find it awkward too. Yet able-bodied people can learn much about sex from the handicapped, for the physically impaired soon discover that the main sex organ is the brain. They learn to make greater use of their imagination and fantasies and to take advantage of the full range of erogenous zones in the body.

PSYCHOLOGICAL MOTIVES

Psychological motives refer to motives that are primarily learned and have more to do with psychological functioning and sense of well-being than with physical survival. Some of these motives, like sex, are derived from physiological needs, but are not consistently connected to them. Other motives, such as achievement, are more exclusively influenced by learning. There is no one authoritative list of psychological motives because learning experiences and key motives vary so widely among individuals. There are some motives, however, that are common to all of us.

Security

Children early in life express a preference for security. They feel more secure with their own parents, their own rooms, and their familiar routines. They feel more comfortable knowing the rules and what is expected of them. Like Linus, each child needs a security blanket, something that he or she can cling to in the face of an uncertain world.

As we grow up, our security motive assumes different forms. For example, we prefer satisfying our physiological needs in familiar ways, such as eating our favorite foods or sleeping in our own rooms. Once we've learned to satisfy our needs in specific ways we acquire a preference or appetite for these familiar things. We build a kind of groove for ourselves.

Another form of security is reflected in our desire to understand and predict the world around us. We want to know what kind of person we're working for and whether our job has a future or not. Much of this has to do with keeping anxiety at a minimum. To do this, we acquire all sorts of security operations, like making excuses or putting ourselves down to protect ourselves in the face of criticism and failure.

Our strong inclination toward consistency is another form of the security motive. Festinger's theory of *cognitive dissonance* (1957) holds that individuals cannot tolerate inconsistency and will work to reduce or avoid it whenever possible. Whenever we have two ideas or beliefs that are cognitively or psychologically (but not necessarily logically) incompatible, we unconsciously strive to get rid of the tension caused by that incompatibility. The same principle applies to the tension between our beliefs and behavior, our beliefs and another's behavior, or our behavior and another's behavior.

For example, suppose I smoke a pack of cigarettes a day, but become worried about the risk of getting cancer. I could resolve this tension by giving up smoking. But there are also more effortless ways to reduce the tension. I could belittle the danger of smoking, pointing out that they haven't yet proven that smoking actually causes cancer. Or, I could emphasize positive reasons for smoking, such as the refreshing taste or how much it calms my nerves. The main point is that we have such a distaste for inconsistency and the anxiety it arouses that we resort to all kinds of self-justifying mechanisms to avoid such tension when possible.

Stimulation and Exploration

By now you probably think that we are little more than security-minded creatures who shrink from all change. But this is only part of the story. There is also mounting evidence from experiments with deprived and enriched environments that suggests we also have basic motives toward stimulation and exploration.

For example, in one study college students were given up to $25 a day (good pay in the 1960s) to do nothing but lie on a comfortable bed in a small cubicle, being allowed to get up only for the bathroom and meals. The stimulation from their surroundings was drastically reduced by such means as goggles on their eyes and cotton wrapping on their arms. Sounds like a good deal? They thought so too, and at first spent most of their time in sleep. However, the students gave up the experiment after only two or three days. While some of them experienced extreme effects, such as disturbances in their thinking and hallucinations, all of them felt extremely bored and restless (Heron, 1961).

Similar studies with variations in procedure have had similar results. Individuals become bored, restless, and emotionally upset, which suggests that we have a basic need for stimulation. Although the reasons for this are not completely understood, some psychologists suggest that our cerebral cortex needs a minimum stimulation from our senses to function normally.

The desire for stimulation and challenge helps to explain why people do such things as climbing snow-topped mountains or rowing across the ocean. A good example is the adventuresome flight of the *Double Eagle V* balloon over the Pacific Ocean by three businessmen. Throughout the flight their lives were threatened by thunderstorms, a buildup of ice, and finally a crash landing in the California mountains during which one man was knocked unconscious. Asked why they did it, one man admitted that it was mostly for the adventure and the challenge. Soon afterwards the crew announced plans to balloon around the world (*Time*, November 23, 1981).

Individuals differ in the desire for novel experiences. People who score high on measurements of the sensation-seeking motive are likely to experiment with drugs, engage in a variety of sexual practices, and seek excitement in risky sports. Those who score low in the sensation-seeking motive may prefer more peaceful and familiar patterns of behavior. Studies suggest that a person's sensation-seeking tendencies may be determined partly by biological factors, with sensation seekers having a higher optimal level of arousal than nonsensation seekers. Also, after the college years, the sensation-seeking motive tends to get weaker (Zuckerman, 1979).

Affiliation

The desire to be approved and to belong arises from several related needs such as attachment, dependency, affiliation, and love or acceptance. While it's difficult to separate the learned from the unlearned aspects of these needs, we do feel and act differently when such needs are unmet.

Let us think for a minute about attachment and dependency needs. The fact that human children have a relatively long period of helplessness makes these needs essential for their survival. When children are deprived of parental affection in the first few years of life, studies have shown that they suffer serious effects in their emotional and intellectual development (Bowlby, 1973). Interestingly enough, such deprivation has its greatest effect when an intense attachment has been formed in the first six months of life and is then disrupted. For this reason agencies often suggest that prospective foster parents make arrangements for adoption as soon as possible after the birth of a child.

The fact that first-born children tend to show stronger affiliative tendencies throughout their lives is usually attributed to the generous amount of undivided parental attention they received in their formative years. Yet studies have not always confirmed this finding, suggesting that many other influences affect our affiliative tendencies in addition to birth order. One such influence is the experience of anxiety and fear. For example, in one study, half of a group of female university students were led to expect a series of painful shocks by an ominous-looking scientist, while the other half expected only mild shocks. All the women were then given an opportunity to spend a 10-minute waiting period either alone or with another woman before receiving the shock. The results showed that a higher percentage of the women expecting the painful shocks chose to affiliate than did those expecting the mild shocks. Furthermore, the more intense the fear, the greater the intensity of the affiliative motive (Schachter, 1959).

A later study showed that the type of person one affiliates with is also important. Fearful subjects chose to affiliate more often with other people who were in a similar emotional state (Zimbardo & Formica, 1963). Such studies suggest what each of us has already discovered from personal experience, namely, that the more fearful we become, the more we want the company of others as a means of allaying our anxiety.

When our affiliative needs are seriously deprived, the result is loneliness. Although the incidence of loneliness varies from about 10 percent among workers in Los Angeles (Seeman, 1971) to about 80 percent among those seeking psychiatric help (Graham, 1969), it is a common experience among college-aged people. In a study of 401 students in four universities, over 80 percent of them had experienced loneliness that was "quite upsetting," "very upsetting," or even more severe (Sermat, 1972). While the experience of loneliness among these students led to psychiatric disturbances or suicide attempts in 13 percent of the cases, the fear of loneliness probably drives many more students into casual dating, friendships, all kinds of groups, and even marriage, sometimes compulsively so. Yet many of these relationships remain at the "social-pleasant" level, with little acceptance of the people as they are. For example, one study of female university students disclosed that those with the highest loneliness scores showed the greatest discrepancy between how they saw themselves and how others saw them (Moore, 1972). (See the boxed material on loneliness in Chapter 6.)

The irony of loneliness while surrounded by others indicates that we need more than just social contacts or participation in groups. We also need to share ourselves more deeply and experience mutual acceptance in more personal, intimate relationships. We need to be loved and accepted as we really are and to do the same for others, as in true friendships and satisfying marriages. We shall explore this more in later chapters on interpersonal relationships and love and marriage. But here it should be pointed out that as our society changes and becomes more and more impersonal, we tend to place an even higher value on true friendship and love. When we have found sufficient love and acceptance and feel that we belong, then we can be alone without being lonely, as Thoreau did in the Walden woods. Yet the shortness and uncertainty of life itself bears with it a certain amount of inevitable loneliness that all humans experience, suggesting that our affiliative needs have existential as well as psychological dimensions.

Achievement

Have you ever noticed how some people succeed more consistently in whatever they do? They seem to have a stronger achievement motive, or the desire to perform well according to some internal standard of excellence.

Since the achievement motive is largely learned, it should not surprise us that it is strongly affected by parental behavior. Studies have shown that parents of high-achieving students tend to give a generous amount of nonspecific help, such as suggestions and positive reinforcement, but little specific help on how to do a job. Parents of low-achieving students, on the other hand, tend to expect a lot, but give little positive recognition (Hermans et al., 1972). First-born children consistently demonstrate higher achievement motivation as well as higher affiliative tendencies because of the greater amount of parental attention given to them.

Although achievement motivation is directly correlated with other factors such as social class and intelligence, the general need for achievement can be changed with the proper help. For example, parents of low-achieving students who were given half-hour counseling sessions for 15 weeks reported a marked improvement in the achievement motivation of their sons and daughters (Gilmore, 1969). Also, adults encouraged to indulge in high-achievement fantasies, make positive plans, and get feedback about appropriate methods and goals experience a significant improvement in their achievement (McClelland, 1971).

Although the achievement motive seems to remain fairly stable across time, it does vary according to several factors. One of these is how the probability of success is perceived by a person. Another is how much the individual wants to succeed. A third factor is the sense of responsibility a person feels for his or her achievement. A fourth factor is the degree to which an individual derives satisfaction from a given incentive. Sometimes a fifth factor is suggested: whether the person is familiar with the specific means necessary to accomplish a goal. Motivation in a specific situation will vary according to a combination of such factors (Atkinson & Feather, 1966; McClelland, 1971). For example, if the probability of becoming a physician is felt to be low, then its incentive value may become even higher. Or, if it is very easy to get a job pumping gas at a service station, then failing at such a job will be doubly embarrassing. In other words, our achievement motivations vary somewhat not only from one person to another, but also from one situation to another.

There are actually two subpatterns at work in achievement motivation. One is the desire to approach success; the other is the desire to avoid failure. An individual motivated more by success tends to set more realistic goals of intermediate difficulty, thereby achieving success more often. But a person motivated by the desire to avoid failure tends to choose easy tasks with unrealistically low or high goals.

Matina Horner (1972) has pointed out a third pattern of achievement motivation—the avoidance of success—which is especially prevalent among women. It seems that the more highly feminine a woman's identity is, the more she will strive to avoid success and competition with males. Tresemer (1974) has challenged this, pointing out that many males are also motivated to avoid success. In recent years, however, fewer college women exhibit fear of success than was

---

MUST HIGH ACHIEVERS BE COMPETITIVE?

The cliché "Nice guys finish last" implies that you must be a highly competitive person to get ahead in our society. But is this always so?

Recent studies suggest not. In their research, Janet Spence and Robert Helmreich distinguished between three separate motives: *work orientation*—the desire to do a good job; *mastery*—the preference for challenging tasks; and *competitiveness*—the desire to win over others. They found that the highest achievers were those who were high in the work and mastery motives but low in the competitiveness motive. This pattern held true among college students who made the highest grades, scientists who made the greatest contributions, and business executives who made the highest salaries. They speculated that competitiveness may interfere with achievement because the desire to outdo our peers in prestige or money may diminish our interest in the task itself.

Janet Spence and Robert Helmreich, *Masculinity and Femininity* (Austin: University of Texas Press, 1979).

High achievers are motivated by the desire for mastery and success. (A.T.&T. Company Photo Center)

the case in the 1960s, while fear of success seems to have increased among men (Hoffman, 1977).

How much we're willing to risk to achieve a goal depends on the relative strength of our achievement motive in relation to our other motives. This is suggested by an experiment comparing the risk-taking tendencies of people high in achievement, affiliation, and power motives, respectively. When given an opportunity to play the game of roulette, those high in affiliation tended to shy away from competition by taking low risks, while those high in the power motive took high risks to get attention and recognition. The people rated highest in achievement motive took medium risks that gave them the best chances of actual success (McClelland & Watson, 1973). Individuals differing in these three types of motives probably tend to make similar choices in real life for the same reasons.

A GROWTH MODEL

So far we've been discussing physiological and psychological motives as if they were separate from each other. Actually they are not. We experience motives within our personality as a whole. As a result, we often act out of mixed motives. Our motives are also affected by other psychological processes such as perception, memory, and especially learning. Our surroundings also affect our motives. Then too, we sometimes seek stimulation and growth that increase rather than decrease our psychic tension. So we cannot do justice to an individual's motivational pattern as a whole on the basis of piecemeal scientific data.

Maslow (1970) holds that we must understand the individual's motivational pattern as a whole, making no sharp distinctions between biological tendencies and learned psychological ones. Since everything in our make-up is affected by learning and culture to some degree, even motives like hunger and sex are different in humans than in animals. Walter Cannon had said that once the basic homeostatic needs were met, the "priceless unessentials of life" could then be satisfied, but Maslow claims that psychologists have neglected studying this latter dimension of motivation. His view of motivation is meant to serve as a corrective to the predominant drive-reduction theory of motivation.

Survival and Growth Tendencies

Maslow agrees with psychologists like Goldstein and Rogers that the human organism exhibits a core biological tendency toward growth and the actualization of its potential as well as toward maintenance or survival. When survival motives such as hunger, security, affiliation, or achievement are unmet, we feel aroused to act in ways that reduce the tension and restore our psychic equilibrium. Maslow refers to this as *deficiency motivation,* but adds that it tends to distort our perception of reality, so that we are more apt to see what we "need" to see than what really is.

When growth motives such as the search for meaning, equality, and creative expression are unmet, we then act out of *growth motivation.* Unlike deficiency motivation, however, growth motivation sharpens rather than dulls our perception of social reality. For instance, a comparison of deficiency-motivated with growth-motivated people showed that the latter perceived reality more accurately, were more accepting of themselves and others, and were freer to concentrate on the real problems of the world (Maslow, 1970).

The main point here is that we cannot fully understand our motivational pattern as a whole without taking into account both kinds of motivation. Although our growth motives are not always as potent as our survival motives, they are no less important. In fact, it is the pursuit of our growth motives that often provides much of our sense of zest and meaning in life. While the deprivation of survival motives leads to the more familiar psychological illnesses such as the neuroses and psychoses, the blunting of growth motives may lead to equally incapacitating but more spiritual illnesses, such as apathy, cynicism, alienation, and despair.

A Hierarchy of Motives

Maslow claims these two types of motives are related in a hierarchical fashion, as seen in Figure 2-1. As our lower or survival motives become relatively satisfied, we become more aware of our higher or growth motives. Maslow (1968) views

FIGURE 2-1. Maslow's hierarchy of motives. The motives are arranged hierarchically from the bottom up according to how crucial the motive is for survival. The higher motives are experienced only to the degree that the more basic ones have been relatively satisfied. Diagram based on "A Theory of Human Motivation" in *Motivation and Personality*, 2nd edition, by Abraham H. Maslow. Copyright © 1970 by Abraham H. Maslow. Reprinted with permission of Harper & Row, Publishers, Inc.

these growth motives as equally important and therefore did not arrange them hierarchically. He also stresses that the growth motives manifest themselves after our survival motives are only relatively satisfied. In fact, he once estimated that the average person tends to be satisfied perhaps only 85 percent in terms of physiological needs, 70 percent in safety needs, 50 percent in love needs, 40 percent in esteem needs, and only 10 percent in terms of the self-actualization needs (1970).

The protests of labor groups in the early 1900s were understandable because they were seeking satisfaction of survival motives like food and security. But the student protests in the 1960s were not always so readily understood. More than one observer said of the students on campus or in Washington, "What are they complaining about? They never had it so good!" And indeed they hadn't. For the students active in the 1960s came largely from middle- and upper-middle-class homes. But it was precisely because they had satisfied their basic motives such as food, security, and affiliation that they felt motives such as freedom of speech, individuality, justice, and equality all the more keenly.

It is important to realize that Maslow's general hierarchy of motives varies somewhat from one person to another, depending on inborn differences, past experience, and so forth. For example, we've already pointed out how first-born children tend to have stronger achievement motives because of the greater attention they've received from their parents. In a similar way, individuals who have experienced rejection in their early lives will probably feel a stronger need for acceptance. A given person's hierarchy of motives will also vary from time to time because of the change that comes with satisfaction of motives, such as the lessened influence of the hunger motive after eating.

Resistance to Growth

If each of us has an inborn self-actualizing tendency, you may be asking "Why aren't people more fully actualized?" Maslow himself pondered this question and offered several possible explanations. First of all, our inner core of growth needs is relatively weak and undeveloped since we do not habitually live by our instincts. Accordingly, our growth tendencies are easily stifled by poor circumstances, making them hard to discover. Maslow also held that we may also have a minor countergrowth tendency. This may be seen as an energy-conserving tendency inherent in the human organism. It may be the result of acquired influences such as the inertia of habit or the fear of failing. Maslow favored the view that resistance to growth is mostly learned.

Maslow envisioned personal growth as more of a struggle between growth-fostering forces and growth-discouraging forces, such as the pains of growing, fear of the unfamiliar, and so forth. In many ways he felt that our society discourages growth by overvaluing safety and security. In contrast, he suggested that we minimize the attractions of security and maximize its dangers, such as boredom and stagnation. At the same time he felt we should emphasize the attractiveness of growth, while minimizing its dangers. Maslow repeatedly stressed that "growth is, *in itself,* a rewarding and exciting process," thereby overcoming much of our resistance to growth (1968, p. 30).

Finally, Maslow points out that even healthy, self-actualized people are not perfect human beings. In fact, their willingness to take risks and try new experiences often brings them additional problems. But, unlike neurotics who bring many of their own problems on themselves, the problems of healthy people tend to be existential or common to all people. In short, personal growth does not consist of the absence of tension or problems, but of the way people handle these within their lives as a whole.

Psychologists like Carl Rogers disagree with Maslow that we must have favorable conditions before our growth motives can emerge. According to Rogers, survival and growth tendencies always function together instead of hierarchically. Just think of the struggling artist who feels the urge to create more strongly than the need for security. Psychologist Salvatore Maddi also points to the countless examples of people who have been significantly creative in spite of deprived circumstances, such as Galileo, Van Gogh, and James Baldwin. In fact, Ernest Hemingway blamed his transition from a poor artist to an affluent writer for his later lack of creativity (Maddi, 1972). Maslow acknowledged that why affluence releases some people for growth while stunting others is somewhat of a mystery. As a result, Maslow (1967) suggested that a favorable environment is not enough to insure growth. There must also be sufficient personal motivation.

Individuals must have a *desire* to grow to offset the apathy and resistance to growth.

Maslow's view of self-actualization has been hailed as one of the greatest contributions to our understanding of motivation since Sigmund Freud. But some have complained that his theory remains too general and only tells us what self-actualization is, not how to achieve it. Maslow himself (1968) conceded that his work was meant to supplement rather than displace the dominant drive-reduction theory of motivation.

MOTIVES AND BEHAVIOR

Awareness of Motives

Much of the time we are only partly aware of our motives. Sometimes we act out of a hunch, with only a vague feeling of why we're doing what we do. At other times we act out of a mixture of motives, which can obscure a clear awareness of our intentions. Then too, the degree of awareness of our motives may vary from one behavior pattern to another. I may be quite aware of why I enjoy playing tennis, but can't understand why I don't achieve more in my career. Because of individual differences, some people may be more aware than others of why they behave the way they do. Generally speaking, however, the more integrated or whole we become, the more awareness we have of our motives.

The degree of ego involvement that a motive has also affects our awareness of it. When something has a *negative self-reference* and is highly threatening to us, we tend to repress it, unconsciously pushing it out of our awareness. For example, we may continue in an unpromising job, or an unsatisfying marriage saying it's a challenge to us, when the real reason may be that we are afraid to admit we've failed in such an important part of our lives. When a task has a more *positive self-reference*, we may invest ourselves in it more fully. For example, a man who never attended college may consistently strive to outperform his college-educated co-workers in order to prove himself. However, too much ego involvement of any type tends to blind us to our motives.

According to Freud, most motives remain unconscious because they are derived from unconscious instincts like sex and aggression. Thus, we forget many of our childhood experiences, such as the sexual fantasies associated with the Oedipal complex, because these become too embarrassing or painful to recall as we grow older. Motives that are not socially acceptable, like aggression or revenge, also tend to remain unconscious. For example, we may be pleased to see a competitor fail, but it's hard to admit this even to ourselves because of our obedience to social norms and the damage to our self-respect. Because so much of our unconscious motivation is unacceptable to us in Freud's view, he held that it is often expressed in irrational behavior. Everyday slips of the tongue or accidents may give away our unconscious motivation. Dreams and daydream fantasies of achieving fame may disclose something of our deeper aspirations to us. Neurotic symptoms, such as getting tired or having a headache when something unpleasant is asked of us, may also betray our unconscious motives. In short, Freud held that all the higher motives, such as learning, artistic creativity, or religious compassion, were sublimated expressions of our basic sexual instinct, so that all our motives shade off into unconscious ones (Freud, 1959).

While we often act out of unconscious motives, especially when we fall in love or overreact to personal criticism, such motives need not be derivations of sex or aggression. Psychologists now realize that our motivational life is also affected by other aspects of our make-up and environment. Accordingly, such influences as sex roles, circumstances, and life experiences play a larger role in our motivational lives than was previously recognized. Also, motives are more accessible to rational scrutiny and more subject to change than most people realize.

Changing Motives

Our motivational lives are generally a mixture of consistency and change. On the one hand, many motives exhibit a consistent pattern across the years. For example, a person high in achievement motive may be a lifelong achiever, though the object of that person's efforts may vary from one stage of life to another. On the other hand, a person's desire to achieve may be significantly strengthened because of some personal experience. For example, after becoming a world-class rowing champion, John B. Kelly was banned from England's Henley Royal Regatta because of his working-class background. Later, his son Jack Jr. won the Henley's Diamond Sculls trophy in 1947 and 1949, motivated in part by the desire to avenge his father's snub (reported by Rick Nichols in *The Philadelphia Inquirer,* April 3, 1982 p. 1D).

Satisfaction of a motive may also bring about a change in our motives. For example, an actress who has achieved fame and financial security may eventually become bored with just making movies. She may become more interested in taking on more challenging roles and making innovations in her field. Having satisfied those motives lower in Maslow's hierarchy of motives, she is freer to pursue the growth motives. In much the same way, each of us may find that our motives naturally change with maturity and life experiences. We may lose interest in activities that have been meaningful to us, whether out of satisfaction or boredom, and feel the need to take on newer, more challenging pursuits.

You may also continue an activity out of different motives. For example, you may take up the game of tennis mostly for the sake of mastery. But once you have learned to play reasonably well, you may continue playing tennis mostly for pleasure. In this case, you are motivated by intrinsic rewards, by something that is enjoyable in itself. In other instances, you may lose interest in something, such as your job, but continue doing it mostly for extrinsic rewards, such as money or security.

Ultimately, motivation is a highly personal matter. While we all share many motives such as eating and achievement, the intensity and priority of motives vary from one person to another. They also change from one period of our lives to another. Success or failure in a given endeavor may also strengthen or weaken a motive. Perhaps the most important thing to realize is that each of us has the potential to be highly motivated and growth oriented. When you are lacking in motivation, you may get valuable clues for becoming more highly motivated by assessing your life situation and reexamining your needs and interests. You might ask yourself: Am I in the situation I want to be in? If not, what must I do to get there? Am I doing what I really want to do? If not, why not follow your own interests? Tapping the rich resources of your own personal motivation usually leads to a more satisfying and successful life.

SUMMARY

We began this chapter by pointing out that the concept of motivation has to do with explaining behavior in terms of inner causes or motives.

Much of our motivation can be explained in terms of the drive-reduction model, which holds that we're moved to act mostly because of the tension of unmet needs. According to this view, we become aware of the imbalance of inner forces as a state of tension or a need, which in turn arouses us to seek appropriate gratification. Generally speaking, motivation refers to the inner conditions that energize and direct us to satisfy our needs. A particular motive such as the hunger motive refers to the more specific goal-directed activity of obtaining food.

We have classified motives along a continuum, with motives that are predominantly physiological toward one end and those that have more to do with our psychological well-being toward the other end. All motives, however, are affected to some degree by learning.

Physiological motives include hunger, thirst, the avoidance of pain and extreme stimuli, as well as sleep and dreams. We have included sex as a physiological motive, although it is probably more subject to learning and emotions than many of the other physiological motives.

Generally, psychological motives are less closely related to biological processes than physiological motives are, and thus are even more subject to learning. As a result, psychological motives tend to vary widely among different individuals. However, certain psychological motives are common to all of us, such as the striving for security, stimulation, affiliation, and achievement.

We've also pointed out that Maslow's growth model of motivation serves as a corrective and supplement to the drive-reduction model. In Maslow's view, we sometimes act to increase stimulation and tension, especially in the process of personal growth or self-actualization. However, he holds that our motives are related in a hierarchical manner, such that only as our survival needs are reasonably met do our growth needs become more apparent and urgent. We've also noted that each person's motivation varies considerably depending on personal experiences and individual differences.

Much of the time we're only partly aware of our motives, with the degree of awareness varying among different behavior patterns as well as individuals. According to Freud, many of our motives remain unconscious because they are associated with unacceptable experience. But we have also pointed out that many of our motives are more accessible to awareness and subject to change than was previously recognized.

QUESTIONS FOR SELF-REFLECTION

1. If you were making your own list of psychological motives, which ones would you add to those described in this chapter?
2. How important are social influences such as money and power in motivating people?
3. Do you ever have trouble knowing when you have had enough to eat or drink?
4. Does the amount of time you sleep each night remain the same or vary according to how you feel?
5. Could you live a normal, healthy existence without any direct gratification of your sexual needs?
6. Which is ordinarily the stronger influence for you, the motive for security or the motive for stimulation and change?
7. Do you tend to be more of a joiner or a loner?
8. Generally speaking, are you motivated more by the desire to achieve success or the desire to avoid failure?
9. If you were to picture yourself in terms of Maslow's hierarchy of motives, which motives would play a dominant role in your life?
10. How often do you do something without really knowing the reasons for your behavior?

EXERCISES

1. Distinguishing between basic needs and desires

Many times we say we *need* something, when it would be more accurate to say we *want* it. This exercise is designed to help you determine the extent to which a felt need is a basic one or more of an acquired desire.

Select a given need, such as your need for food. Then examine your eating behavior in light of Maslow's analysis of a basic need. In Maslow's (1970) view, a need may be considered basic when it fulfills the following characteristics:

a. Deprivation of the need fosters illness.
b. Gratification of the need prevents illness.
c. Gratification of the need restores health in a person who is sick.
d. The deprived person prefers gratification of this need over others when given a choice.
e. The need is not in a state of tension or privation in healthy persons.
f. A subjective feeling of lack or yearning is present when the need is unfulfilled.
g. Gratification of the need leads to a subjective sense of well-being.

Did you find that much of your need for food results from learned habits rather than biological necessity? If you like, you may apply the above criteria to other felt needs, such as your need for sleep, sex, security, achievement, new experience, and friends or socializing.

2. Determining your natural sleep length

This exercise is based on Wilse Webb's findings about natural sleep length as discussed in the text. You may recall that the way to tell if you are getting enough sleep is that you wake up spontaneously, feel well rested, and don't have to struggle through periods of sleepiness during the day. To find your own best sleep length, perform the following experiment.

During the first week go to bed one night at 5 AM and get up at 7 AM. Observe yourself all day to recognize the symptoms of not getting enough sleep. One night the next week go to bed at 3 AM and get up at 7 AM, and see how you feel. Then let yourself sleep two hours longer one night each successive week, until you wake up spontaneously and don't feel tired during the day. This is your natural sleep length.

Did you find that your natural sleep length corresponds to your regular sleeping habits? Or is it shorter or longer than you are accustomed to sleeping?

3. Seeking out stimulation or new experiences

Many times we become tired or disinterested in a given activity more from boredom than from excessive exertion. We may need more stimulation, novelty, or new experience to revitalize our experience. If you find yourself bored or in a rut in some aspect of your life, try some of the following suggestions:

Taste a food you've never tried.

If eating out, choose a new restaurant or dish.

Try some new sport or type of exercise.

Take up a new hobby or leisure activity.

Invite someone out socially you would like to know better.

Take a new course in a subject of interest.

Attend a workshop you're interested in.

See a film you're curious about but reluctant to attend.

You may add to this list by thinking up other suggestions of your own. Then try several of these suggestions and write down your reactions. Did you find that the stimulation of new experience enhances your enjoyment? Would you agree that variety is the spice of life?

4. Assessing your achievement motivation

Select a specific situation or aspect of your life in which you have a rather low level of achievement motivation. That is, you don't seem to be motivated or moved to accomplish much in a given activity. This could be a particular course in school, your studies as a whole, your job, or some sport. Then assess your achievement motivation by asking yourself the following questions:

What are your chances of succeeding?

How strongly do you want to succeed?

Do you feel responsible for the outcome?

Do you believe your ability is crucial?

Or do you believe it is mostly a matter of luck?

How important are circumstances?

How much do you enjoy what you're doing?

Do you have the needed skills to succeed?

If not, what are you doing about this?

A related issue is how much you are motivated by the desire to succeed or the attempt to avoid failure. Are you really making an honest effort to succeed? Or are you simply "going through the motions" to satisfy some requirement or authority?

Candid responses to all of the above questions may help you to understand why you are lacking in achievement motivation.

5. Taking a motivation inventory

This exercise is designed to help you evaluate and apply Maslow's hierarchy of motives to yourself.

Complete the following inventory. In each pair circle the *one* on which you presently spend more time and energy. There are no right or wrong answers. You should mark each according to *your own personal opinion.*

a. Providing for my physical comfort: adequate food, clothing, shelter, etc.

b. Pursuing hobbies that are fulfilling to me.

c. Pursuing hobbies that are fulfilling to me.

d. Keeping safe and secure so that no one can hurt me.

e. Cultivating close friends who think a lot of me.

f. Keeping safe and secure so that no one can hurt me.

g. Cultivating close friends who think a lot of me.

h. Pursuing hobbies that are fulfilling to me.

i. Providing for my physical comfort: adequate food, clothing, shelter, etc.

j. Cultivating close friends who think a lot of me.

k. Providing for my physical comfort: adequate food, clothing, shelter, etc.

l. Becoming a good person who is looked up to by others.

m. Becoming a good person who is looked up to by others.

n. Cultivating close friends who will think a lot of me.

o. Keeping safe and secure so that no one can hurt me.

p. Becoming a good person who is looked up to by others.

q. Providing for my physical comfort: adequate food, clothing, shelter, etc.

r. Keeping safe and secure so that one one can hurt me.

s. Becoming a good person who is looked up to by others.

t. Pursuing hobbies that are fulfilling to me.

As you can see, the inventory is composed of five recurring items. Each item measures one of Maslow's categories and is paired once with every other item. Your score for each of Maslow's motives is the number of times you circled that item.

The *self-actualization* activity appears in items B, C, H, and T. The *self-esteem* activity appears in items L, M, P, and S. The *love and belonging* activity appears in items E, G, J, and N. The *safety* activity appears in items D, F, O, and R. The *physiological* activity appears in items A, I, K, and Q.

Are your five motive scores an accurate picture of your personal motivational structures? Are you surprised at the results?

Look at your highest motive score. If Maslow's hierarchical principle is operating, motive scores on either side should decrease according to the sequence of his hierarchy. For example, the following scores confirm Maslow's hierarchical principle: AS-0, SE-4, LB-5, S-3, and P-2. The following scores would contradict the principle: SA-2, SE-1, LB-5, S-3, and P-4.[1]

RECOMMENDED READINGS

Bolles, R.C. *Theory of Motivation,* 2nd ed. New York: Harper & Row, 1975. An overview of motivation, including the various determinants of motivation.

Garfield, P. *Creative Dreaming.* New York: Ballantine, 1976 (paperback). The author tells how we can train ourselves to dream about matters that are bothering us.

Maslow, A.H. *Motivation and Personality,* 2nd. ed. New York: Harper & Row, 1970 (paperback). The classic statement of Maslow's views on motivation and self-actualization.

Spence, J. and R. Helmreich. *Masculinity and Femininity.* Austin: University of Texas Press, 1979 (paperback). An overview of sex differences, including the impact of sex roles on human motivation and behavior.

Webb, W.B. *Sleep: The Gentle Tyrant.* Englewood Cliffs, N.J.: Prentice-Hall, 1976 (paperback). A concise, readable explanation of sleep patterns by one of the leading researchers in the field.

Zuckerman, M. *Sensation Seeking.* New York: Halsted Press, 1979. A discussion of individual differences in people's sensation-seeking motive, including drug use, sports, and sexual behavior.

---

[1]From *Student's Guide for Contemporary Psychology and Effective Behavior* by William J. Gnagey. Copyright © 1974, 1970, 1963 by Scott, Foresman and Company. Reprinted by permission of the publishers.

Stress

3

Sometimes when we don't perform well, we say, "It's because of stress." Or when we have difficulty getting rid of a cold, we may say, "I'm under a lot of stress." Such remarks suggest that stress is a bad thing. But is it always harmful? Haven't you known people who deliberately seek out stress? They seem to thrive on stimulation. Achievement-oriented people and highly competitive individuals in particular often set even higher goals for themselves than expected by others, thereby increasing their levels of stress.

Knowing that stress often has harmful effects, how can we explain such individuals? Are they sick? Or are those who avoid the same stress somehow lacking in stress tolerance? There's no simple answer to such questions because stress does not affect everyone in the same way. So what is stress anyway? What are the conditions in which it may harm us or help us? How can we cope with stress more effectively? These are some of the questions we consider in this chapter.

THE SIGNIFICANCE OF STRESS

In recent years, we have heard a lot about stress, most of it bad. People complain about the stress in their jobs. They are quick to blame stress for whatever ails them. Workshops on stress management have sprung up almost everywhere. Clearly, stress is an important part of our lives. But just how many people really understand it?

What Is Stress?

In popular usage, stress is often spoken of as something external to us, such as being pressured to compete or having a demanding boss. Yet it is readily apparent that individuals respond to the same pressure differently, suggesting that our experience of stress also depends on our reaction to these external forces. Consequently, it seems best to include both the stimulus and response aspects of stress in our understanding of it. In this sense, stress is not simply something "out there" or "our reaction" to it, but the relationship between them. *Psychological stress* has to do with how we perceive and adapt to stressful forces and events.

Stress might be defined as *any adjustive demand that requires an adaptive response from us.* As such, stress is an inevitable part of life. Our bodies are under stress even when we're asleep. There are demands on our hearts to keep beating, on our brains to produce dreams, and especially on the regulatory systems to keep us in a balanced state. In fact, the only complete escape from stress is death.

Since stress is built into life itself, it's not so much whether we will experience stress or not, but what kind and how much. Ordinarily, when we say someone is under a lot of stress, we mean excessive, negative stress. But an intense pleasant occasion may also be stressful, such as a wedding or vacation.

For purposes of clarity some authors suggest that we use two different terms to distinguish the effects of stress on us (Bernard, 1968). The term *distress* would be reserved for the harmful effects of stress, such as excessive or unpleasant demands that drain our energy and make us more vulnerable to illness. The term *eustress* or "good" stress, on the other hand, would designate the stimulating, beneficial effects of stress.

You can readily appreciate why we cannot make a catalogue of the types of demands that would always be distressful or eustressful for everyone. For stress itself depends on the *relationship* between a particular person and a given demand. As you would suspect, there are wide individual differences in our needs for stress as well as our tolerance for it. The important points to keep in mind are that not all stress is bad, and that the same event affects individuals differently. Largely because of limited space, however, we will focus on the potentially harmful effects of stress and some of our common patterns of coping with it because that's what people most need to know about.

The Effects of Stress

Most of us are aware that the person under intense stress is more vulnerable to illness. There is an increasing amount of empirical support for this observation. But not all the stress that makes us more vulnerable to illness comes from negative or socially undesirable events. Most of it comes with the changes of everyday life events, such as getting engaged or married, moving, or changing jobs. Apparently, it is the *combined* effect of several of these events that intensifies our stress and predisposes us to illness.

Holmes and Rahe (1967) have constructed a Social-Readjustment Rating Scale (Table 3-1) that provides a graphic means of assessing the stress potential of various life events. Despite individual differences of age, sex, and race, Holmes and Rahe usually found a high percentage of agreement among the rankings of the various life events. The most important factor is the *total impact* of these life events, which in turn intensifies our need for adaptive responses. A total score of 150 to 199 life-change units (LCU) constitutes a mild life crisis. A score of 200 to 299 LCU constitutes a moderate crisis, and a score of 300 or more, a major crisis. As the number of LCU increases, the risk of illness becomes more certain. Interestingly enough, we continue to suffer from the effects of a stressful event for as long as a year afterwards.

A study of 2,500 officers and enlisted men aboard three U.S. Navy cruisers showed that in the first month of the cruise, men in the high-risk group (300 LCU or more) had nearly 90 percent more first illnesses than men in the low-risk group (150–199 LCU). And, for each month thereafter, the high-risk group continued to report more new illnesses than the other groups. Similar results have been reported for the relation between stress and football injuries, as well as the incidence of such illnesses as heart attacks, respiratory illnesses, skin and colon diseases, schizophrenia, and cancer (Holmes & Masuda, 1972). The particular kind of illness that strikes as a result of stress, of course, depends on an individual's physical make-up as well as the bacterial and viral agents present. But these studies show that we are more predisposed to becoming sick in some way when we have to cope with an excessive number of rapid changes. It would seem that such vigorous coping activity does tend to lower our resistance to disease.

Despite its usefulness, the life-events approach to stress has several limitations. In the first place, the particular selection of events may not be equally relevant for different groups of people, such as college students, blue-collar workers, and the elderly. Second, it does not take into account how individuals perceive and adapt to a given change. Furthermore, since the life-events approach is built around social change, it fails to include a great deal of stress that comes from chronic or repeated conditions, such as a boring job or an incompatible marriage (Lazarus, 1981).

TABLE 3-1. SOCIAL-READJUSTMENT RATING SCALE

Rank	Life Event	Mean Value
1	Death of spouse	100
2	Divorce	73
3	Marital separation	65
4	Jail term	63
5	Death of close family member	63
6	Personal injury or illness	53
7	Marriage	50
8	Fired at work	47
9	Marital reconciliation	45
10	Retirement	45
11	Change in health of family member	44
12	Pregnancy	40
13	Sex difficulties	39
14	Gain of new family member	39
15	Business readjustment	39
16	Change in financial state	38
17	Death of close friend	37
18	Change to different line of work	36
19	Change in number of arguments with spouse	35
20	Mortgage over $10,000	31
21	Foreclosure of mortgage or loan	30
22	Change in responsibilities at work	29
23	Son or daughter leaving home	29
24	Trouble with in-laws	29
25	Outstanding personal achievement	28
26	Wife begins or stops work	26
27	Begin or end school	26
28	Change in living conditions	25
29	Revision of personal habits	24
30	Trouble with boss	23
31	Change in work hours or conditions	20
32	Change in residence	20
33	Change in schools	20
34	Change in recreation	19
35	Change in church activities	19
36	Change in social activities	18
37	Mortgage or loan less than $10,000	17
38	Change in sleeping habits	16
39	Change in number of family get-togethers	15
40	Change in eating habits	15
41	Vacation	13
42	Christmas	12
43	Minor violations of the law	11

T.H. Holmes and R.H. Rahe, "Social Readjustment Rating Scale," *Journal of Psychosomatic Research,* vol. II, p. 216. © 1967, Pergamon Press, Ltd. Reprinted with permission.

Prolonged Stress

What happens to us when we experience intense stress over a prolonged period of time? According to Selye's General Adaptation Syndrome (1974), our reaction under stress occurs in three progressive stages: the alarm reaction, the stage of resistance, and the stage of exhaustion. Although Selye applies this model for psychosomatic symptoms, the processes leading to psychological breakdowns follow a similar pattern.

THE ALARM REACTION. This is our initial emergency response to the stress-provoking agents. At the physiological level of stress, this consists of complicated bodily and biochemical changes that result in similar symptoms regardless of the type of stressor. For this reason people with different illnesses often complain of common symptoms such as a fever, headache, aching muscles and joints, loss of appetite, and a generally tired feeling. When the stress is more directly psychological, the alarm response consists of a heightened sense of anxiety, which arouses and mobilizes our defenses. This usually makes us more apprehensive, unable to concentrate or sleep well, and generally upset. Defense mechanisms like rationalization or denial are frequently used at this stage. These are discussed later in the chapter.

THE STAGE OF RESISTANCE. This occurs when the body successfully adapts to prolonged stress. The symptoms of the alarm stage disappear and the bodily resistance rises above its normal level to cope with the continued stress. The price of this resistance includes increased secretions from various glands and organs of the body, a lowered resistance to infections, and what Selye has termed the "diseases of adaptation," such as ulcers or hypertension (1974). A chronically anxious or neurotic person with a rigid system of defenses or other coping devices is usually in this second stage of psychological stress.

THE STAGE OF EXHAUSTION. This stage may be reached if the stress continues. Bodily defenses break down, adaptation energy runs out, and the physical signs of the alarm reaction reappear. Since stress accentuates aging, the symptoms at this stage are similar to those of aging, except that the symptoms of exhaustion are more or less reversible with rest. However, continued stress at this stage, like aging, leads to death. When the prolonged stress is felt at the psychological level, there may be hallucinations, delusions, and other bizarre behavior characteristic of severely disturbed people. If this condition remains untreated, the individual tends to regress to the kind of apathetic behavior seen in psychotic patients institutionalized for many years—a kind of psychological death.

Social and Individual Factors

As with physiological stress, the combined effect of inner and outer factors determines our level of psychological stress. Although individuals and situations vary, some of the more important factors are as follows.

The importance of the combined effect of stressful events has already been mentioned in the studies of Holmes and others. Getting a divorce and then losing one's job would certainly be more stressful than dealing with either of these two events separately. The severity of the stress also varies with the situation. The death of a spouse is far more stressful than not having enough money to pay bills. The presence of threat of harm also increases stress. Thus, combat is more stressful than tennis. How sudden or unexpected an event is affects stress. Studies of surgical patients informed of the realistic threat and pain involved show that a moderate amount of anticipatory fear actually helps post-operative adjustment better than no fear (Janis, 1971). On the other hand, a long-standing stress, such as living with an alcoholic or a person with a severe behavior problem, may exact increasing wear and tear over the years. Being lonely also makes us more vulnerable to stress than having supportive friends or resources available to cope with the stress.

Individual factors that affect our experience of psychological stress are many and varied. According to one study, men with personality characteristics of intense drive, aggressiveness, ambition, competitiveness, and the pressure for

Sudden life-threatening events are especially stressful. (United Nations/Leo Siegel)

getting things done are two to three times more likely to have heart attacks in middle age than men who are equally competent but more easygoing (Friedman & Rosenman, 1974). How well we can cope with stress depends primarily on our intelligence, flexibility, and resourcefulness. The more an individual understands and approaches a stressful event on a problem-solving basis, the greater will be his or her chances of successfully coping with it. Self-esteem is also a vital factor. People with low self-esteem may find moderate criticism of their work highly threatening, while people with high self-esteem might find the same criticism helpful in improving their skills.

How people perceive a potentially stressful event also vitally affects their feelings of stress. A woman who has negative feelings about children is likely to find childrearing more stressful than does a woman who perceives it as a more positive experience. Finally, the tolerance for stress varies widely among individuals. High levels of chronic anxiety or poor physical health predispose us to low stress tolerance, while low levels of anxiety and good physical health maximize our tolerance to stress.

Each of us must discover our own optimal level of stress. This is especially necessary in our competitive culture with its emphasis on individual responsibility

DAILY HASSLES

Have you ever felt that it's the little things in life that get you down? Richard Lazarus and his colleagues (1981) found that daily hassles may have a greater effect on our moods and health than do the major misfortunes of life. Daily hassles arise from a number of sources, including incompatible relationships, momentary stressful situations, and the ripple effect of major life events. For example, the man who gets divorced may have to prepare his own meals for the first time, or the divorced woman may have to repair a leaky faucet. How we are affected by such daily hassles depends on a number of factors, such as the frequency, duration, and intensity of the event, as well as our personality and resources for coping with stress.

The Lazarus study indicated that people differed widely in what bothered them. Among college students, the most commonly reported hassles were anxiety over wasting time, meeting high standards, and being lonely. Middle-aged people were more likely to be bothered by economic concerns such as high prices. Health professionals felt they had too much to do, not enough time to do it, and trouble relaxing. Only three hassle items were common to all three groups: misplacing or losing things, physical appearance, and too many things to do.

If you were to make a list of your own personal hassles, what would it include? What are some of the little things that most annoy you? Do they bother others as much as you?

Richard S. Lazarus, "Little Hassles Can Be Hazardous to Health," *Psychology Today*, July 1981, p. 61. Copyright © 1981, Ziff-Davis Publishing Company.

and achievement. Our society bombards us daily with stimulation and excitement as a way of arousing our interest or our desire to buy something. Because overstimulation can be harmful, some people seem to prefer a vegetable existence protected from all kinds of situational stress. Others actually seek out stress because of their greater need for action and mastery. But most of us fall somewhere in between. Too little stress results in a boring and apathetic existence. Too much stress leads to undue wear and tear, making us more vulnerable to sickness and premature aging. Since there are great individual differences among us, it is important for each of us to find that optimal level of stress at which we function best.

TYPES OF PSYCHOLOGICAL STRESS

Since the human organism responds to stressful forces as a whole, we can distinguish but cannot separate the various forms of stress. A stress that is predominantly biological, such as a bacterial infection, may affect our emotions as well as our bodily defenses. Or a stress that is primarily psychological, such as the sense of frustration over a job failure, may also affect our physical well-being. Since we're primarily concerned with the process of personal adjustment, in the following pages we focus on the four main types of psychological stress: pressure, frustration, conflict, and anxiety, though they often occur together.

STRESS WITHOUT DISTRESS

When I entered medical school at the age of eighteen, I was so fascinated by the possibilities of research on life and disease that I used to get up at four o'clock in the morning to study in our garden until about six in the evening, with very few interruptions. My mother knew nothing about biological stress, but I still remember her telling me that this sort of thing could not be kept up for more than a couple of months and would undoubtedly precipitate a nervous breakdown. Now, at the age of sixty-seven, I still get up at four or five o'clock in the morning and still work until six at night, with few interruptions; and I am still perfectly happy leading this kind of life. No regrets. To combat the physical decay of senility, my only concession so far has been to set aside an hour a day to keep my muscles trim by swimming or by racing around the McGill campus on a bicycle at five in the morning.

From *Stress without Distress*, p. 97, by Hans Selye, M.D. Copyright © 1974 by Hans Selye, M.D. Reprinted by permission of J. B. Lippincott Company.

Pressure

We may experience pressure from inner or outer sources, or a combination of both. Personal ambitions are a common source of inner pressure, such as the highly ambitious executive who constantly pushes herself in hopes of becoming the president of her company. Sometimes the pressure to achieve our goals is intensified because of age or time limits, as in the case of the older student who feels he must finish school sooner to make up for the years he missed. All of us have felt the pressure of the inner "shoulds" and "oughts" of our conscience at one time or another. Sometimes we need this inner pressure to help us do our best. But some people make unduly harsh demands on themselves, resulting in self-defeating behaviors. An example would be the perfectionist who drops out of school rather than continue with mediocre grades.

A common pressure in a competitive society such as ours is the pressure to compete. We compete for just about everything, whether grades, jobs, or desirable marriage partners. If we fall short, we may feel even greater pressure to succeed the next time. Even when we do succeed, there is the constant pressure to stay ahead. Our everyday relationships with others, such as parents, employers, or friends, also make claims on us which constitute another type of pressure. There's also the pressure of meeting deadlines, whether taking an examination, submitting an application, or paying bills. Then too, some situations exert greater pressure than others, such as an air-traffic controller's job (see box).

Frustration

Frustration results from the blocking of our motives or goal-seeking behavior. It often occurs through the thwarting of an effort, such as when we are forced to wait when we are in a hurry. Frustration can also occur through the absence of an appropriate goal object, such as when we are hungry and have no food. Since frustration is so intimately connected with our motives, which vary from person to person, what frustrates me may not frustrate you, and vice versa. However, some conditions frustrate all of us at one time or another.

Delays are a common source of frustration. This is especially true for people living in a mechanized, time-conscious society such as ours. Every day we feel frustrated, waiting for the traffic light to change, waiting for people to get off the phone, trying to make ourselves understood clearly. The more urban and crowded our environment, the more frustration we're exposed to.

A certain degree of frustration is built into the process of growing up. Adolescents become physically mature and capable of sexual arousal before they are allowed gratification. They are expected to become independent, yet must depend on their parents to complete their studies. Then as they attain adult status, they're exposed to a flood of advertising that arouses their desires for things they can't afford. So frustration through delay is inherent in the process of living itself.

SOME JOBS ARE MORE STRESSFUL

One such job is that of air-traffic controller. At Chicago's O'Hare Airport, one of the busiest in the world, air-traffic controllers guide about 1900 planes in and out each day. During peak hours there's a takeoff or landing every 20 seconds, generating intense stress for the controllers.

Nearly two-thirds of the controllers, mostly in their late 20s and early 30s, either have ulcers or ulcer symptoms. Since 1970 more than 35 of them have been permanently removed for medical reasons, many of them under psychiatric care. Of the 94 controllers left, only 2 have been there longer than 10 years. Most don't last 5 years. They're burned out at 35 years of age.

A rapid turnover of personnel in such a pressurized job is understandable!

David Martindale, "Sweaty Palms in the Control Tower," *Psychology Today*, February 1977, pp. 71–75. Copyright © 1977, Ziff-Davis Publishing Company.

Waiting in line is a common source of frustration. (Marc P. Anderson)

Social obstacles also account for many of our frustrations. Failure is a prime example. In our competitive culture, when one person wins, another must lose. Such failure becomes doubly frustrating when we don't get another chance. If we anticipate an unpleasant surprise or frustration, however, such as a doctor telling us we must eat less if we want to lose weight, the experience may be less stressful than when it is unanticipated. Becoming adequately socialized involves learning to tolerate a fair amount of frustration from others, especially those in authoritative positions.

There are many different personal sources of frustration—for example, not having the abilities needed to achieve a goal. Lacking the commitment to school or a job makes us even more vulnerable to frustration. Lack of self-confidence may serve as an invisible barrier to carrying out our responsibilities in a satisfying way. Feelings of guilt may also corrode our enjoyment of sensual needs or self-expression. Any number of personal characteristics, such as our skin color or our sex, may frustrate us. Those things we cannot change may be especially frustrating.

Frustration often results in anger and aggressive behavior. While proponents of the frustration-aggression hypothesis originally held that frustration always led to aggression, more recently there is the realization that this is not necessarily the case. It depends on a number of factors. How strong are the frustrated motives and how many are there? How severe is the interference? And how well can this individual understand and tolerate frustration? The lower your tolerance for frustration, the more inclined you are to become aggressive.

Conflict

The psychological state of conflict exists when we are under pressure to respond simultaneously to two or more incompatible forces, like the conflicting urges to express or suppress sexuality or aggression. Now that individuals are expected to make more decisions for themselves, conflicts are an increasingly common source of stress.

In psychological studies, conflicts are usually classified according to the positive or negative values of the respective choices. When the choice has a positive goal, it is referred to as an *approach tendency;* when negative, it is called an *avoidance tendency.* As the goals become closer, both the approach and avoidance tendencies tend to become stronger, thus intensifying the stress. Characteristically, the avoidance tendency rises more sharply. For example, when a man and woman begin to get more serious about their relationship, the approach tendencies are usually stronger. But as they consider a long-term commitment to each other, both become more aware of the risks involved, and the avoidance tendency rises rapidly. It has been suggested that the engagement ring is often given at the point where the avoidance tendency tends to equal the approach tendency, for fear of breaking up. Even with couples who marry successfully, the presence of the avoidance tendency can be seen in the unduly nervous bride or groom on the day of the wedding.

Approach-approach conflicts are those in which you have to choose between two desirable alternatives. These conflicts are usually easily and quickly resolved, especially when the choices revolve around a minor issue such as "Which do you want for dinner—spaghetti or chow mein?" But, as the options involve more serious consequences or approach each other in value, decisions come more slowly. Deciding which of two colleges to attend or which of two jobs to take when both choices are equally promising can be frustrating.

Avoidance-avoidance conflicts occur whenever you are caught between undesirable alternatives. Since either choice involves unpleasant consequences, this type of conflict is much more difficult than approach-approach conflicts and usually takes more time and energy to resolve. For example, a student may be told that if he wants to avoid failing the course he will have to work harder than he ever has. Or a husband and wife may discover in their marriage counseling that if they want to avoid separation both will have to make some fundamental accommodations to the demands of the other. In both situations, the choices involve negative consequences of extra effort, or suffering from wounded pride, fear, or guilt. Small wonder that people tend to put off making such choices.

Approach-avoidance conflicts are those in which you feel both attracted and repelled by the same person or object. This is a more characteristic type of conflict and is encountered throughout life. It often involves the expression or control of basic motives or desires. For example, if your supervisor makes you angry about a personal matter you may feel like telling him off on the spot. On the approach side, if you express your feelings directly you may be able to clear the matter up right away. But previous experience may have shown you the value of avoidance, because expressing your anger directly risks antagonizing your supervisor and making your job more precarious.

The *double approach-avoidance* conflict is probably the most common type of all. Here, you are faced with a decision between two alternatives, both of which involve positive and negative consequences. For example, suppose a newly married couple is trying to decide whether to have children or not. If they do have children, the positive aspects are the gratification of bringing a new life into the world and helping a child to grow into maturity. The negative aspects include the added expense of children, the risk of damage to the couple's relationship, the interruption of the woman's career, along with the risk of being disappointed. Should they decide not to have children, they will have more freedom and resources to do as they wish in their social lives and careers. But they also risk being sorry later. In each case, either choice has positive and negative consequences that make a decision more agonizing. The most common pitfall in these double approach-avoidance conflicts is to vacillate between the alternatives without ever reaching a decision, deciding hastily on an irrational basis, or letting the decision be made for you—by not using contraceptives, for example.

Actual experience of conflict is rarely as clear-cut as this outline would imply. At times the same person behaves inconsistently, which can make the conflict more ambiguous. We may not be fully conscious of a conflict, though we give evidence of having one by overreacting to a situation. Frustration and anxiety inevitably accompany the more serious conflicts. In fact, it is precisely the frustration underlying a conflict and the anxiety over the consequences that make such choices so stressful.

Anxiety

You have a vague, uneasy feeling of impending danger. Your heart is pounding, your muscles are tense, and you break out in a cold sweat. You have the classic symptoms of anxiety. In the past there has been a tendency to regard anxiety as a negative type of stress. But today, psychologists regard it more as a normal part of life that can have a potentially helpful function, at least up to a point.

Essentially, anxiety functions as an alarm signal, warning us of imminent danger and arousing us to respond appropriately. For instance, when we read of all the chemical additives in our modern processed food, we may become apprehensive about the long-range effects on our physical health. But many of the things that make us anxious have to do with our psychological rather than physical security. For example, whenever you expect to have your work or behavior evaluated, you may become apprehensive. There's no danger to your physical safety, but you tend to feel anxious and self-protective. Thus, much of the stress of anxiety is learned and functions in relationship to feelings of security.

In mild to moderate doses anxiety may actually stimulate us to become more alert and responsive to a situation that warrants our attention. But in excessive amounts anxiety tends to overwhelm us and impair our performance. A common example would be our experience of test anxiety. Some studies have shown that anxiety may enhance test performance for some individuals, while interfering with the performance of others. *Facilitating anxiety* is positively related to academic aptitude as well as exam and course grades, while *debilitating anxiety* is associated with low aptitude and grades (Jewell, 1968). How does test anxiety affect you? Do you tend to work better under pressure? Or do you sometimes get so nervous that your mind goes blank?

Anxiety is commonly distinguished from fear. We feel fear when threatened by something specific and localized, such as a car out of control. But anxiety is a more subjective and generalized threat, such as the chronic worry of the graduate student that she will never get her degree, even though her grades are As and Bs. In this sense anxiety may well be more stressful than fear, because the threat is unknown and its effects more pervasive. Anxiety is also more cumulative in that it tends to constrict our awareness and impair our performance, which in turn makes us even more anxious and further hinders our performance. Anxiety as guilt over moral wrongdoing may be especially difficult to deal with when we feel there is little we can do to resolve it. For those plagued by high levels of chronic anxiety because of personal inadequacies, the situational stress of anxiety or fear only adds to the existing stress and needlessly usurps energy, lowering their resistance and causing premature aging.

SYMPTOM-REDUCING RESPONSES TO STRESS

Now that we've considered the significance and types of stress, what about our responses to it? There are two main types of responses to stress: those that reduce our awareness of stress or its symptoms and those that help us cope more directly with the sources of stress. Direct coping tends to be more conscious and deliberate and will be discussed in the next section. Here we focus on the more spontaneous reactions to stress, which alleviate some of the tension of stress but do not modify the overall stress situation. In short, they are symptom-reducing responses to stress. Included here are various defense mechanisms and other minor coping devices that are slightly more influenced by learning, such as talking, laughing, or crying under stress.

Defense Mechanisms

Early in life humans demonstrate spontaneous reactions to keep themselves from being overwhelmed by intense doses of psychological stress. These are commonly called defense mechanisms because they are used by the self (or *ego* in psychoanalytical terms) for protection from threat. Although these patterns are influenced by learning to some degree, they are largely automatic and spontaneous. Defense mechanisms are triggered by anxiety, but as we've seen, frustration and conflict are frequently involved as well. Defense mechanisms generally operate unconsciously, thereby protecting us automatically from sudden or excessive threat as well as from the painful awareness of its accompanying anxiety.

People under extreme stress often use defense mechanisms to gain relief from their emotional distress. Each of us uses defense mechanisms at one time or another; they are a part of normal life. But since these mechanisms include some degree of self-deception as well as distortion of reality, excessive reliance on them prevents personal growth.

Repression is the blocking of a threatening impulse or idea from entering our consciousness. Although we have little or no awareness of our repressed desires or ideas, they remain in the unconscious dimensions of our experience and will be expressed indirectly in our behavior. For example, a woman who has repressed her hostility against her supervisor for fear of losing her job may honestly say that she doesn't bear him any grudge. Yet she may frequently show up late for work or forget details that interfere with her effectiveness. She may also appear sullen and quiet around her supervisor, but sociable and pleasant with her co-workers. As a result, the buried hostility may become more apparent to others than to the person herself. In fact, we may suspect repression whenever people underreact to a situation that would normally arouse a threatening impulse, but at the same time show indirect evidence of that impulse in their behavior.

Repression brings some relief from the painful awareness of threat, but it also constricts our consciousness in ways that result in rigid, ineffective behavior. For example, repression may be one of the reasons that middle-aged parents or adults have trouble empathizing with turbulent adolescents. The older people have simply "forgotten" much of the emotional turmoil of their own youth. Nevertheless, some repression is a normal part of personal development and is used by all of us to some extent. It is the excessive use of repression that gives rise to habitually defensive behavior, as seen in people who are tense and guarded most of the time.

When we have a desire that arouses our anxiety, we may choose to consciously control it and express it only at appropriate times. This is known as *suppression* and tends to be a healthier process because it involves less self-deception and usurps less psychic energy than repression.

Denial is refusal to see or hear aspects of reality that are unpleasant or threatening to us. While repression is the blocking of our inner reality, denial is the refusal to acknowledge external, social reality. Confrontation with death, especially when it is unexpected, commonly evokes the response of denial. Suppose a friend were to say to you in a matter-of-fact way, "My mother died last night." You would probably marvel at his composure. Shouldn't he feel more grief?

POSITIVE ASPECTS OF DENIAL

Two psychiatrists at Massachusetts General Hospital observed that patients receiving intensive care in a coronary unit had beneficial effects from their tendency to deny the seriousness of their illness.

Three patterns of denial were observed. "Major" deniers stated unequivocally and persistently that they had no real fear of dying from their heart trouble. "Partial" deniers initially disclaimed any fear of their illness, but eventually admitted concern. "Minimal" deniers were not obviously fearful, but would admit to it if asked.

Although the patients were alike in terms of age, sex, and personality moods exhibited during their stay, the major deniers responded more positively to the electronic monitoring and had significantly higher survival rates. Out of the 50 patients in one study, not one major denier died during the study, while 2 of the partial deniers and 2 of the minimal deniers died. While the minimal deniers represented only 8 percent of the total sample, this type of patient contributed to 50 percent of the mortalities.

The psychiatrists concluded that when faced with a life-threatening illness, denial may be a constructive coping mechanism by which one affirms life. Interestingly enough, there were more major deniers among blue-collar workers, probably because admitting fear is more shameful to them than it was to more educated people.

T.P. Hackett and N.H. Cassem, "Psychological Reactions to Life-threatening Illness—Acute Myocardial Infarction," in H.S. Abram, ed., *Psychological Aspects of Stress* (Springfield, Ill.: Charles C Thomas, 1970), pp. 29–43.

Not necessarily at once. When you first hear of someone's death, especially someone you care about deeply, you are initially inclined to disbelief. "I just can't believe it," you might say. Then after a few hours or sometimes days, the reality of death sinks in, and you begin to feel a more profound sense of grief.

Rationalization is the attempt to justify unacceptable behavior in a rational and socially acceptable way. Unlike the more conscious process of lying, which involves deceiving others, rationalization involves self-deception. We try to convince ourselves as well as others of our good intentions when we rationalize.

We tend to rationalize whenever we do something wrong or experience disappointment or failure. For example, a student may explain cheating on an exam by saying, "That's the only way you can pass that stupid course!" Or another person may say, "Well, he asked for it," instead of apologizing for hurting a friend's feelings. A girl who has just been jilted may say, "I was getting bored with him anyway."

Since rationalization often contains some truth, it is not always easy to tell when someone is rationalizing or lying. However, when others question our rationalization and we become emotional or stubbornly refuse to admit any truth to their accusations, we must suspect rationalization. Rationalization helps to remove the disharmony of unpleasant conflicts in our minds, like trying to combine the idea of being a decent person with cheating on an exam. Justifying our behavior by minimizing unpleasant motives or behavior is less painful than admitting our guilt, hurts, and limitations—at least in the short run.

Reaction formation is the attempt to overcome unacceptable desires by adopting exaggerated feelings and behavior that are opposed to these desires. In this case, the basic repression is strengthened by a conscious attitude. In our society, feelings of hostility especially evoke reaction-formation tendencies as a way of making our behavior more socially acceptable. A person who characteristically avoids hostility through reaction-formation tendencies may be regarded by others as an exceptionally nice, loving person. "She never gets angry" is a remark often heard about such people. Those who know her better might add, "But when she does get mad, you'd better keep clear!" For behind the exaggerated loving behavior are hostile impulses, and when stress weakens the "front," some of the anger may burst through. But this doesn't necessarily mean that people aren't what they appear to be.

The key to the presence of reaction-formation tendencies lies in the exaggerated degree of conscious feelings and behavior. The overly orderly person may be covering up the tendency to be messy and dirty. The excessively gruff, swearing male may be hiding from his own tender feelings. The overly seductive male or excessively flirtatious female may be covering up deeply felt inadequacies about his or her sexuality. The compulsively cheerful person may be fighting off the sense of depression. But in all these instances the repressed desires find indirect expression in the people's behavior in one way or another, often to their own dismay.

Acting out involves relieving the tension of unacceptable impulses by expressing them directly or symbolically. People with inadequate self-control or a weakly developed conscience may choose acting out as the most convenient way to discharge their anxieties.

An adolescent struggling with feelings of independence toward parents who have sacrificed themselves for him may act out in moodiness, procrastination, and failure at school. Such negativistic behavior serves as an attempt, however unconsciously, at communicating underlying feelings of resentment toward parents or other adults. Acts of school vandalism may be expressions of the frustration and resentment associated with having to attend school. Also, delinquent behavior is sometimes a means of release from pent-up aggressive tendencies. Sexual promiscuity may be an attempt to find the acceptance not found at home.

A person who displays acting-out behavior will often say afterwards, "I don't know why I did that." This is an honest admission. For acting-out behavior helps a person achieve temporary relief from the painful awareness of unacceptable impulses, but does not lead to the self-insight needed for a satisfying resolution of the problem.

Fantasy involves relieving tensions through imaginary actions. However, not all our imaginative activity is defensive. The use of the imagination in daydreaming and make-believe play can enrich our world as much as novels and movies do. In fact, recent studies have shown that, just as we dream each night, so each of us indulges in daydreaming throughout the day, peaking about every 90 minutes (Singer, 1975). Our fantasy functions defensively, though, when it becomes excessive or is used as a substitute for reality.

One common type of fantasy can be seen in the conquering hero theme, in which the individual pictures himself or herself as some great person. During adolescence the contents of such fantasies frequently involve vocational success or relationships with the opposite sex. Another common type of fantasy is the suffering hero or martyr theme, in which we see ourselves as the victim of others. We may see ourselves as an underdog fighting against the established powers or as a seeker of truth misunderstood by the blind majority. By playing the innocent victim, we may avoid the sense of inferiority and gain sympathy rather than criticism from others.

Temporary excursions into the imagination may enrich our everyday lives, especially when we are bored with our present situation. But when we begin mistaking the imaginary for the real we are using our fantasy as a defense against the more painful aspects of ourselves that we've repressed. The extreme use of fantasy as a defense can be seen in psychotic people who live more in their fantasies than in social reality. A time-honored cliché runs, "Neurotics *dream* of castles in the air—psychotics *live* in them."

We have described each of these defense mechanisms separately, but they are often used in combination, as shown in Table 3-2. Although the particular defense mechanisms used may vary considerably depending upon the individual and the situation, certain patterns tend to be common. The defense mechanisms mentioned in Table 3-2 but not included in the text are defined in the glossary at the end of the book. You will probably recognize that most of us use these mechanisms at one time or another, especially when under intense stress. Defense mechanisms are spontaneous, unconscious ways of maintaining our sense of self-

TABLE 3-2. TYPICAL PATTERNS OF DEFENSE MECHANISMS

Stress	*Common Defense Mechanisms*
Failure	Rationalization, projection, compensation
Guilt	Rationalization, projection, undoing
Hostility	Fantasy, displacement, repression, reaction formation
Inferiority feelings	Identification, compensation, fantasy
Disappointment in love	Rationalization, fantasy, insulation
Personal limitations	Denial, fantasy, compensation
Forbidden sexual desires or behavior	Rationalization, projection, repression

From *Contemporary Psychology and Effective Behavior*, p. 139, by James C. Coleman and Constance L. Hammen. Copyright © 1974 by Scott, Foresman and Company. Reprinted by permission.

worth and adequacy in the face of threat; yet they involve self-deception and distortion of reality, so that a habitual use of them is self-defeating. They prevent us from growing.

Coping Devices for Minor Stress

In addition to defense mechanisms, there are a number of other ways we may allay minor stress. Karl Menninger (1963) suggests that we look at these as "coping devices for minor emergencies." Although these responses have been influenced by learning, they tend to operate automatically, though probably at a slightly higher level of awareness than the defense mechanisms. Which of these devices we use in a particular situation depends partly on the circumstances and partly on the suddenness and strength of the disturbance. But mostly the habitual patterns we've acquired in handling past stresses determine how we will react in a particular situation.

The comforts of *touch, food,* and *drink* are so familiar as to be taken for granted. We've all seen how a child will seek increasing physical contact with a parent as a way of gaining reassurance in the face of stress. Adults faced with sadness, sickness, or death also rely more on touching as a way of communicating concern at a time when words are often inadequate. The psychological value of food and drink at times of stress derives from their being substitutes for the primal food, the mother's breast, and their value as symbols of reassurance. When under pressure, some of us nibble or eat more, while others take a drink or a smoke. Still others seek out drugs, especially tranquilizers.

Laughing, crying, or *cursing* also have the effect of discharging tension. Have you ever noticed the loud, forced laughter of people just before they take an exam? Laughing at one's troubles can be cathartic, although hostile humor that puts one's self or others down is unhealthy. Crying it out comes naturally to children, who discharge their tensions rather spontaneously. Among adults, though, it has been more permissible for women than men to find release from stress through crying. But now more men are discovering that it's normal to cry. Traditionally, men have discharged their tensions more through cursing than crying.

Talking it out and *thinking it through* are probably the most common of all everyday devices for coping with stress. Finding someone who will listen to us is one of the most helpful things we can do when troubled. The more the other person simply listens and responds with empathy, rather than judgment or sympathy, the more we gain perspective on our problems. For we often don't know our own thoughts or feelings fully until we've expressed them. We also need time to think things through in the quietness of our own minds.

Working off tension in work or play affords a release from our pent-up energies, although this does not usually change the situation causing stress. Since our primary activities are moving and doing, it seems natural to use action to afford release from tension. Taking a walk, playing a vigorous game of tennis, or making something that will take our minds off our problems can all be excellent temporary ways to keep our sanity amid stress. Some people also seek out increased sexual activity as a way of displacing tension.

Each of us uses these devices at one time or another, possibly preferring some more than others. Some people are likely to blow off steam through verbal means. Others are more likely to work it off physically in work or play. Some accommodate stress through visceral means by eating, drinking, or emotional expression. Still others seek release through intellectual means, including daydreaming or meditation. You might ask yourself "Which way am I inclined?" Preferably, you should use the way that is most appropriate to you and your situation. The danger is in habitually adopting one of these strategies to the exclusion of the others. In so doing you will tend to rely on one of these devices in and of itself, whether it is appropriate to the external situation or not. In this way, the bottle becomes the alcoholic's best friend. Stress is no longer his problem. His problem now is his response to stress.

PROBLEM-SOLVING APPROACHES TO STRESS

Although each of us tends to use some of these coping devices at one time or another, there are better ways of managing stress. Unlike the unconscious and spontaneous responses that alleviate the symptoms of stress, the more effective approaches are highly conscious and deliberate. Essentially, they are learned, problem-solving approaches that help us to deal with stress directly. One such approach is to modify ourselves through increasing our tolerance for stress. Another consists of task-oriented responses aimed at modifying the stressful situation. A comprehensive approach to stress often involves both.

Increasing Stress Tolerance

Often all that is needed is a greater tolerance for stress. This may be defined as the degree and duration of stress we can tolerate without becoming irrational and disorganized. Or hypothetically, it's the point beyond which our thinking becomes irrational and our behavior inefficient. Understandably, this varies among individuals and from one situation to another for the same person. But each of us can learn to increase our tolerance for stress as suggested below.

Tolerance for pressure usually comes with greater experience and skill in a particular activity. For example, the first time you drove a car you probably felt very anxious and uncertain whether you would ever master driving. But with increased experience and skill, you probably learned how to drive with confidence even in heavy traffic. In a similar way, many persons who work in jobs with great pressure, such as surgeons and police, learn to perform well under stress because of greater experience and skill.

Another way of coping with pressure is to make realistic demands on yourself

Greater tolerance for pressure usually comes with experience and skill. (A.T.&T. Company Photo Center)

rather than unduly harsh ones. This is especially important in a competitive society. Whenever you succumb to the "success at any price" syndrome, you are putting yourself under unnecessary pressure. In contrast, when you can accept yourself and feel that your worth as a person is not totally dependent on your performance, then you can accept occasional acts of failure as an inevitable part of life. For almost everyone fails at something at one time or another. The important thing is how you handle the experience of failure. Do you automatically give up? Do you feel you have to blame someone or justify yourself? Or can you learn something from the experience of failure—about yourself and the skills needed to master the task at hand? Many outstanding people have become that way partly from the learning that came from earlier failures.

Frustration tolerance can be improved through such an obvious but often neglected means as being in good physical shape. Understanding the nature and source of frustration may also help you to avoid aggressive, self-defeating responses. Selecting appropriate tasks for your abilities and motivation is an important preventive measure. Adjusting your expectations to the task at hand is very important. Also, the newer and more complex the task, the more frustration you should be prepared for.

One of the most important ways of improving frustration tolerance is through achieving more independence—that is, through overcoming any undue dependence on other people. On the one hand, this involves growth in task-centered independence, which requires a wide range of abilities and skills in order to function autonomously. Each time we learn to drive a car, type, or cook a meal, we increase this type of independence, and thus our ability to adapt to stress.

Learning to delay gratification, up to a point at least, also helps us to tolerate frustration. But we must also learn how to grow in terms of emotional or relationship independence—in the ability to tolerate criticism, disappointment, and rejection at the hands of others. This is more difficult to achieve and requires higher self-esteem and emotional maturity. For example, a young man may feel independent in terms of having his own job and apartment, yet be emotionally devastated when his girl friend breaks off their relationship. Learning to tolerate frustration involves both types of independence. Since frustration is such an inevitable part of our urban and competitive society, a relatively high tolerance for frustration is a very important prerequisite for adult accomplishments and well-being.

Conflict tolerance begins with the awareness of conflict. Too often conflicts over basic drives such as sex or aggression remain unconscious and are resolved at the level of defense mechanisms. The more aware we become of a given conflict, however, the more we can approach it rationally and resolve it satisfactorily.

Since avoidance-avoidance conflicts involve the frustration of having to choose between undesirable alternatives, such as whether to make major repairs on our car or buy another one, they tend to remain unresolved. But in most instances procrastination only prolongs and aggravates the stress. When we realize this type of conflict is the most time-consuming and emotionally demanding, it may help us to reach a decision before we're forced to by circumstances.

The difficulty in approach-avoidance conflicts rises when an equilibrium is reached between the two opposing tendencies. At that point a person begins to vacillate, thus increasing the overall stress of the conflict. This is especially apparent with double approach-avoidance conflicts, in which both alternatives attract and repel. In this instance, the nearer in time one gets to goal A, the sharper the avoidance tendency becomes, so that one begins to doubt choice A. Then, as one turns to choice B, the same process occurs again. The result is that a person with a low conflict tolerance may fail to make any decision unless forced to, or may choose for an irrational reason such as emotional preference. For example, a young man tries to choose between a job that pays well but is not personally satisfying and another job that is more enjoyable but pays poorly. He may feel he's in a "damned if I do—damned if I don't" situation. On the other hand, a person with a high conflict tolerance may persist in examining both alternatives more rationally until he or she is able to reach an acceptable decision.

Anxiety tolerance refers to our ability to function while feeling threatened or anxious without sacrificing performance. There are many instances in everyday life when it is normal to feel anxious, especially in the face of an objective danger or threat. Getting ready for an important exam or competing for a good job are two examples. However, we mentioned earlier that while moderate anxiety may stimulate us to improve our performance, too much anxiety interferes with it. So it is important to ask, "Is my anxiety inappropriate to the risks involved?" "Am I more anxious than I was last time, or than others who have been in a similar situation?" If the answer to one or both questions is "yes," then your anxiety likely will interfere with your performance.

Since much of our anxious concern is over unknown dangers, one of the most effective ways of controlling anxiety is through acquiring more knowledge of the risks involved. More often than not relevant knowledge helps us to worry about the right things. Experience in a given task also helps us to achieve self-control and minimize the disruptive awareness of anxiety during a critical point in the task. For example, in one study, experienced parachutists felt their most intense anxiety early on the day they were scheduled to make a jump, but felt relatively little anxiety immediately before their jump (Epstein & Fenz, 1965). Thus, they maintained a high degree of self-control during the most critical point of their jump. Inexperienced parachutists, on the other hand, felt the most intense anxiety right before their jump, thereby risking greater interference of anxiety with their performance at the most critical time. It appears that when we face manageable threats, we may remain aware of anxiety as an incentive for improving performance. But when the danger becomes overwhelming, such as when we face a life-risking act or illness, then anxiety tolerance more appropriately calls for a suppression of anxiety as a means of achieving more self-control.

Task-Oriented Approaches

Task-oriented approaches are aimed at modifying the sources of stress, not simply our awareness of the symptoms of stress. Unlike the symptom-reducing responses, task-oriented approaches tend to be learned, problem-solving responses to stress. We employ them more deliberately. Three different types of task-oriented approaches will be considered: assertion, withdrawal, and compromise.

An *assertive approach* is generally the preferred way to manage stress whenever there is a reasonable possibility of success. Such an approach consists of direct attempts at modifying the stressful situation itself. Common examples would be returning a defective product to a store or manufacturer, or speaking up in response to an unreasonable request.

It is important to distinguish between assertiveness and aggressiveness. When people react to a stressful situation *aggressively*, they lash out blindly in a hostile, destructive way that usually aggravates the stress. In contrast, *assertiveness* has to do with expressing your rights and desires without infringing upon those of others. Assertiveness is a rational and constructive way of handling stress, which in turn tends to alleviate the stress involved. For example, a secretary who experienced a great deal of stress in her job became depressed and took out her frustrations by coming to the office late and putting off deadlines at work. After attending a workshop on assertiveness skills, however, she began to speak up. She told her boss how frustrated she became when he gave conflicting orders, such as wanting two different things typed at the same time. As often happens, her boss was not aware of the inconsistencies in his requests, and he promptly changed his ways, thereby allievating much of her stress.

As a general rule, it is advisable to resolve a stressful situation at the same level at which the problem is manifested, as in the example above. Only if that proves unsatisfactory, should you seek out the appropriate people higher in the chain of command. Going directly to a person's superiors without first exhausting attempts at communication with the person directly usually stiffens that person's resistance to a satisfactory solution.

Much of stress management consists of finding out the problem and fixing it. (Marc P. Anderson)

Often an assertive approach will include support from others. By sharing your frustrations with interested colleagues and friends, you may get a better grasp of the problem and discover alternative responses to it, as well as potential support. Joining appropriate action groups and using the resources of law are also becoming an integral part of handling stress assertively.

Withdrawal may be an appropriate response to stress, especially when a stressful situation cannot be successfully modified through assertiveness or compromise. Just the awareness that you can do something to minimize stress helps to reduce the stress. Animals trained to avoid shock by performing an escape response have shown significantly fewer stress symptoms such as ulcers than did their helpless partners who had no escape from the shock. Similarly, a person's belief that he or she can do something to avoid stress tends to reduce the actual emotional stress experienced (Weiss, 1972).

Withdrawal is neither good nor bad in itself. Much depends on how it is used. If someone habitually withdraws from stressful situations, that person may drift into a constricted lifestyle that prevents adequate adjustment or personal growth. On the other hand, the use of withdrawal as a *temporary* strategy may be a valuable means of coping with stress that has become overwhelming or detrimental to one's health. Some examples of temporary withdrawal would be students dropping out of school until they can earn more money, or marital partners agreeing to a separation while they seek counseling. When no suitable solution is forthcoming, despite the best efforts of the people involved, a permanent withdrawal may be more appropriate. An example would be the worker who actively looks for another job after getting no satisfaction from his or her supervisor.

HOW ASSERTIVE ARE YOU?

Assertiveness has to do with expressing your rights, thoughts, and feelings in a direct way without violating the rights of others.

Imagine yourself in each of the following situations. What would you say?

When your parents are giving unwanted advice

When a friend asks you for a loan

When you're being pressured to buy something

When refusing an unreasonable request

When interrupted while you're speaking

In the last situation, simply to keep quiet would be nonassertive. But to blurt out "Shut up!" would be aggressive or hurtful. Instead, an assertive response might be, "Excuse me. I'd like to finish what I was saying."

Ironically, the lack of assertiveness in everyday relationships produces more resentment and alienation in the long run than assertiveness. In contrast, assertive responses not only preserve your self-respect, but they also facilitate good communication, which is essential for mutually satisfying relationships.

Compromise is still another adaptive response to stress. In contrast to with-drawal, compromise allows us to remain in the stressful situation but in a less active way than with an assertive approach. Compromise is most likely to be used when one stressful agent holds a higher rank or authority than the other, or when both participants are at a standstill. The three most common types of compromise are conformity, negotiation, and substitution.

Conformity is a widely used response to stressful situations. Let's say you work as a buyer for a large corporation that has just ordered a more elaborate pro-cedure for purchasing, including much more paperwork and more signatures for approval. At the outset you detest the change. You may comply outwardly by adopting the new procedure even though you dislike it. Or you may conform to the new demands because you like your superiors and co-workers enough to accommodate to the added stress. Since jobs are not easy to get or hold, you may take the new procedures in stride and decide that changing your attitude is the most realistic approach, because endless strife and resentment may be more stressful than accommodation or outright assertion. The key question in any type of conformity response, however, is whether the price of the compro-mise is worth it.

Negotiation is a more active and promising way to achieve compromise in many situations of stress. Long used in the public areas of labor-management and political disputes, negotiation has now become more widely used at the inter-personal level among co-workers, marriage partners, and friends. Negotiation is preferable to conformity wherever possible because it involves mutual accom-modation among the participants.

Substitution is another way to achieve compromise where negotiation or con-formity is not appropriate. If a woman desires to resume her college education but has small children and cannot enroll full time, she may decide that the best alternative is to attend part time at a nearby community college. In this case, a substitute means was found to achieve the same goal. At other times, it may become necessary to choose a substitute goal. For example, the man who after several attempts is not admitted to medical school may choose some related vocational field in which there are more openings, such as pharmacy, physio-therapy, or paramedical training.

Compromise itself is neither good nor bad. Much depends on the relation between the satisfaction achieved and the price paid in the reduction of stress. Habitual compromise may bring more frustration and conflict than a more assertive approach. Too many people suffer in stale jobs or conflict-ridden mar-riages longer than necessary because compromise has become the easy way out. We need to take into account the long-range effects of compromise as well. A life of passive accommodation to undue stress may be more stressful than an assertive or avoidance approach.

In sum, stress management requires a positive, active approach to life. It entails learning how to accept stress and use it as a means of growth and ful-fillment. As we have seen, this approach relies on problem-solving skills as well as on the coping mechanisms for reducing the discomforts of stress. It also involves seasoned judgment as to the kinds of stress we handle best and, equally important, how much. If mastery is achieved, it is usually only after considerable trial and error. In the words of Hans Selye, we would do best to try to thrive on "stress without distress," whether our lifestyle is easy-going or is achievement oriented.

SUMMARY

Stress has been defined as any adjustive demand that requires an adaptive response from us. As such, it is neither good nor bad in itself but an inevitable part of our lives. How stress affects us depends on a combination of different factors, including the particular individual and his or her tolerance for stress. Even though we may adapt to severe or prolonged stress, the price is often a greater vulnerability to stress-related illnesses, such as ulcers or hypertension. Continued adaptation to severe stress may lead to the exhaustion of our adjustive capacities, with premature aging and sometimes psychological breakdown.

Although we experience stress as a whole, we have distinguished four main types of stress that are especially prevalent in psychological stress: pressure, frustration, conflict, and anxiety. Pressure may stem from inner demands or external ones, such as the pressure to compete. Frustration results from the thwarting of our motives, frequently through delays or because of social or personal obstacles. The experience of conflict comes about when we have to respond to two incompatible forces at the same time, with double approach-avoidance conflicts being the most common type. Anxiety is an unsettling feeling that serves to alert us to impending danger or threat, with mild doses of it stimulating us to improve our performance, while overwhelming doses disrupt it.

Our responses to stress can be classified under two main types: symptom-reducing responses, which essentially reduce our awareness of stress, and problem-solving approaches, which are aimed at modifying the sources of stress.

Among the former responses, defense mechanisms are common ways of reducing the tension of stress. Essentially, these are unconscious, automatic responses that enable us to function in the face of threat with little or no awareness of it. Some defense mechanisms commonly employed are repression, denial, rationalization, reaction-formation, acting-out, and fantasy. In addition, there are other symptom-reducing responses that operate at a slightly more conscious level, such as talking over a stressful experience, laughing it off, or working it off. All of these responses have a temporary, limited value in reducing the tension of stress.

In contrast, problem-solving approaches are more conscious, deliberate ways of coping with the stress itself. These may consist of attempts to modify ourselves by increasing our tolerance for stress. Or they may consist of task-oriented responses aimed at modifying the overall stress situation. Whenever possible, it is preferable to adopt an assertive approach, dealing with people or problem situations directly. However, in some instances it may be more appropriate to withdraw or adopt one of several strategies of compromise, such as conformity, negotiation, or substitution. Just the awareness that we can do something to reduce stress may itself help to diminish the experience of stress.

QUESTIONS FOR SELF-REFLECTION

1. In what ways do you seek out stress as a desirable influence in your life?
2. What types of experiences produce the most undesirable stress in your life?
3. Whenever you have undergone a period of severe or prolonged stress, were you aware of some of the stress reactions described in Selye's general adaptation syndrome?
4. What are some of the influences in modern society that increase our feelings of relative deprivation?
5. Which people or situations make you feel the most anxious?
6. Do you habitually use some defense mechanisms more than others? If so, which ones?
7. Which of the coping devices for reducing the tension of stress do you use most often?
8. What steps could you take to increase your own tolerance of stress?
9. Think of some stressful situations in which you have adopted either a withdrawal or compromise approach. What would have happened if you had used an assertive approach instead?

EXERCISES

1. Taking inventory of your stress

Use the Social-Readjustment Rating Scale presented earlier in the chapter to assess the significant changes in your life during the past year. Since your aim is to assess the stress in your overall life situation as realistically as possible, you may have to add points for events not included in the rating scale. For example, if you have experienced stressful events not listed specifically in the rating scale, try to assign a numerical value by comparing them to a similar event in the rating scale. Suppose you have broken off a steady relationship with a friend of the opposite sex. You could assign this a value of 65, comparing it to the emotional stress of a marital separation. Or you could assign it a lesser value, like change in the number of arguments with spouse at 35 points. When in doubt use your own judgment.

Add up all your points to arrive at a total LCU score. Which stress level does your score represent—mild, moderate, or major? When you think back over the past year, does your level of physical health and personal functioning reflect this stress level?

As a variation of this exercise, think back to some period of your life in which you were sick more frequently than usual. Then, using the same procedure, assess your level of stress in the year preceding the sickness or hard-luck period. Does your score on the Rating Scale support your life experience or not?

2. Reactions to frustration

How would you react to the following frustrations?

You put money in a food machine but nothing comes out.

Someone who has promised to meet you fails to show up.

Your car won't start before class.

You receive an average test grade after studying harder than usual.

You lose your wallet or purse.

No matter how much you explain your problem, someone in authority can't understand you.

You're late and can't find your car keys.

Select a recent situation in which you experienced significant frustration, and tell how you reacted to your frustration. How well do you think you coped with this situation?

3. Use of defense mechanisms

Look back at Table 3-2 on typical patterns of defense mechanisms. Now think of several experiences you have had for each of the stressful situations listed in the left-hand column. How did you react to those experiences? For example, think of several situations in which you experienced some sort of failure. How did you react? Did your response include some rationalizing? Or did you blame someone else, thus projecting your guilt? Do you find that certain defense mechanisms are rather commonly employed for given types of stress?

4. Conflict resolution

Draw a line down the middle of an $8\frac{1}{2} \times 11$ sheet of paper. Label one column CONFLICTS RESOLVED EASILY and the other CONFLICTS RESOLVED WITH DIFFICULTY.

Think back and recall eight to ten conflict situations you have had to resolve in one way or the other. Try to think of an equal number of situations in which you made a decision rather easily and in which you came to some kind of resolution only with difficulty. Jot down each situation in the appropriate column with several words of identification *before* reading the rest of this exercise.

Now go back and code each conflict situation in terms of whether it was primarily an approach-approach conflict (choice between two equally attractive options), an avoidance-avoidance conflict (choice between two unattractive options), or an approach-avoidance conflict in which you simultaneously were attracted and repelled by one or more courses of action.

Experimentation has shown that individuals judge the approach-approach conflicts easier and take less time resolving them than avoidance-avoidance or approach-avoidance conflicts. Did you find that more of your easily resolved conflicts were the approach-approach type? Conversely, did you also find that more of your difficult conflicts were of the avoidance-avoidance and approach-avoidance types?

5. Frustration tolerance

Since frustration is an inevitable part of our lives in an urban, competitive society, a relatively high tolerance for frustration is necessary for adult accomplishments and a sense of well-being.

With an eye toward increasing your tolerance for frustration, how would you answer the following questions?

When frustrated, do you continue making the same unproductive response? Or do you stop and try to understand the nature and source of your frustration?

Do you try to accomplish too much too soon? Or do you adjust your expectations to the task and situation at hand?

Do you tend to act impulsively? Or can you work for delayed gratification?

Are you heavily dependent on others to get things done? Or do you have a wide range of skills yourself?

When things are going badly do you tend to give up? Or do you continue doing the best you can despite the odds?

Are you easily disillusioned when people disappoint you? Or can you accomplish things in the face of disappointment, criticism, and occasional failure?

6. Managing stress assertively

As you may recall, an assertive approach to stress aims at modifying the stressful situation itself. A common example would be taking a defective product back to the store.

Select some stressful situation that you managed in an assertive way. After describing the situation, tell what you did and how it turned out. If you can't recall such a situation, think of a similar experience that you wished you had approached more assertively. Then tell how it turned out and how you feel about it. Would you agree that an assertive approach to stress is usually preferable?

7. Reducing stress through negotiation

Negotiation is an increasingly valuable means of reducing stress because it involves mutual accommodation. Common examples would be an employer and worker reaching a compromise agreement in regard to overtime work, or two marriage partners settling a dispute to their mutual satisfaction.

Select some stressful situation in which you used some kind of negotiation. Then describe the situation, what you did, and how it turned out. How satisfactory was the solution? Would you agree that negotiation is a valuable means of stress management?

RECOMMENDED READINGS

Dudley, D.L. and E. Welke. *How to Survive Being Alive.* New York: New American Library, 1979 (paperback). Shows how we can use the Life Change Scale to predict and cope more effectively with stress.

Friedman, M. and R.H. Rosenman. *Type A Behavior and Your Heart.* New York: Fawcett, 1981 (paperback). Explains how individual differences in personality are related to the likelihood of a heart attack.

Mascia, M.F. and S.R. Aronson. *The Stress Management Workbook.* Englewood Cliffs, N.J.: Prentice-Hall, 1981 (paperback). Contains numerous scales and tests to help you identify and manage stress in your life.

Pelletier, K.R. *Mind as Healer Mind as Slayer.* New York: Delta, 1977 (paperback). Analyzes the role of stress in sickness and health, and includes suggested techniques for preventing stress-related diseases.

Ulene, A. and J. Fried. *Feeling Fine.* New York: St. Martins, 1977. A gynecologist (specialist in female physiology) explains how stress manifests itself in various parts of the body; especially valuable for women.

Welch, I.D., D.C. Medeiros, and G.A. Tate. *Beyond Burnout.* Englewood Cliffs, N.J.: Prentice-Hall, 1981 (paperback). A discussion of the causes and symptoms of burnout together with practical suggestions for curing it.

Emotions

4

In hopes of compiling a dictionary of emotions, Joel Davitz asked other psychologists to explain what they meant by various emotional labels such as anger. But he soon found himself confused by the jargon of psychologists. When he turned to nonpsychologists, however, he became more encouraged. "The conversations changed dramatically. For the most part, people were quite clear about what they meant by various emotional labels, and while they did not always communicate with the verbal grace and precision of my fellow psychologists, they frequently gave rather rich and dramatic definitions of the emotional words they used" (Davitz, 1970, p. 251). It became evident to Davitz that when people say "I feel happy" or "I feel sad," they are expressing something very important about themselves.

Perhaps you have noticed how often people refer to their emotions in explaining their behavior. Workers fail to show up, saying, "I don't feel like working." Students cut classes, saying, "I don't feel like going to class." Couples break up, explaining, "We're not in love anymore." It seems that emotions or feelings (we tend to use these two terms interchangeably) are a meaningful part of our lives. Sometimes they interfere with our thinking, leading us to act in irrational and self-defeating ways. Yet they also add meaning and zest to our lives.

But just what are emotions? How much should we express or control them? And what about handling the troublesome emotions such as anxiety, anger, and guilt? These are some of the issues covered in this chapter.

WHAT ARE EMOTIONS?

As Davitz's remarks imply, this is not an easy question to answer. Part of the difficulty lies in the personal, subjective nature of emotions. Despite this, psychologists have taken an increasing interest in studying emotion, accumulating an impressive amount of scientific knowledge along the way. Yet they lack a single, unifying theory of emotion that adequately integrates all their findings. Many psychologists, however, would agree that what we call an emotion includes several components: physiological changes, including bodily sensations; a subjective awareness and meaningful interpretation of these sensations; and a high probability that such awareness will be expressed in overt behavior. The various theories of emotion differ mainly in the priority given to each of these components. But each theory tends to include these components in one way or the other (Arnold, 1970).

Essentially, an emotion is a complex state of awareness involving inner sensations and outer expressions that has the power to motivate us to act. In fact, the word *emotion* comes from a Latin term which means to "move out," indicating its basic arousal function. Charles Darwin (1872) early argued that emotions are largely inherited responses of arousal that have a survival value in evolution. Just as the frightened deer runs for its life, so the fearful person becomes more cautious and watchful for his or her life. In both instances, emotions serve to awaken and mobilize us for defense. But exactly how do emotions do this?

Bodily Sensations

One of the earliest theories held that a person's perception of an external stimulus automatically aroused bodily changes, such as the reflexive muscle contractions that draw us back from an electrical shock. Then, as an aftereffect, we feel these sensations consciously as emotion. Later investigators located the source of emotions in the central nervous system. But there is no single, simple brain center of the emotions. Instead, emotions involve an intricate network of physiological changes that both our minds and bodies contribute to. It is more accurate to say that we feel and act simultaneously. Once a stimulus is perceived through the sense organs, the nerve impulses pass through the brain centers, where they split. Some impulses go to the cortex, where the stimulus is perceived and emotions are felt. Other impulses go to the muscles, where bodily changes and behavior occur.

An interesting result of neurological studies is the discovery that we can control some of our emotions by manipulating certain sensations. For example, since the brain acts selectively in regard to incoming messages, we can control the emotion of pain by blocking the gates that allow pain signals to pass from the afflicted body area to the brain, as in acupuncture, or by counteracting the pain signals through electrical stimulation (Wang, 1977).

Interpreted Sensations

Proponents of cognitive theories of emotion point out that emotions are more than sensations. They are interpreted sensations. The bodily arousal of sensations furnishes the *intensity* of an emotion, but its *quality* or *meaning* for us is determined by relevant mental components.

A series of experiments by Stanley Schachter and Jerome Singer (1962) have shown how our conscious experience of emotions depends very much on what we think and how we interact with others when emotionally aroused. In the Schachter-Singer studies, people were told that the experimenter was interested in seeing the visual effects of "Suproxin," a fictional drug. Those in the experimental group actually received injections of epinephrine, which produces effects similar to those of the sympathetic nervous system, an increase in the heart rate, blood pressure, palpitations, and flushing of the face. Those in the control group were given a placebo injection of saline solution, which produces no physiological arousal. In one experimental subgroup, people were told about the actual effects of epinephrine. In another experimental subgroup, the people were told to expect symptoms other than those produced by the epinephrine, such as a slight headache, itching, and numbness. People in a third group were told nothing about what effects to anticipate.

All the people were then told they would have to wait 20 minutes until the drug had taken effect and their vision would be analyzed. During this waiting period, each person was exposed to a person believed to be waiting for an injection but who was actually a stooge in the experiment. Some people were exposed to a "happy" stooge who was instructed to behave in a euphoric way by running around, shooting baskets with wads of paper, throwing paper airplanes, and asking the subjects to join in the fun. Other people were exposed to an "angry" stooge, who expressed bitterness, behaved aggressively, and made insulting remarks. The experimenters wanted to know if the stooges' behavior affected the way the people felt when they were emotionally aroused.

The investigators found that the two groups of subjects, who were misinformed (those told to expect false symptoms) or ignorant (those told nothing) were highly susceptible to the influence of the stooges' behavior. People in these groups tended to act happy when the stooge acted happy and angry when the stooge acted angry. In contrast, those who had been told the actual effects of epinephrine were less likely to be affected by the stooges' behavior.

Studies such as these suggest that our emotions depend on our expectations and perceptions of others as well as physiological arousal. Our mental set and social setting furnish important cues that help us interpret our bodily sensations. In short, learning plays a significant role in what we actually feel, which has tremendous implications for regulating our emotions.

However, you should be aware of a bias toward the cognitive approach in psychology. One survey found that while most introductory textbooks in psychology endorse the cognitive view of emotions despite the lack of conclusive evidence for it, few recognize the alternative "nativistic" view that emotions are inborn (Hogan & Schroeder, 1981). At least one major researcher, Carroll Izard (1977), has attempted to integrate the evolutionary basis of emotions and the learned, environmental factors into a more comprehensive model of emotions. While we shall emphasize the cognitive approach in this chapter—mostly because of its practical implication that we can do something about our emotions—you should be aware that in the final analysis emotions are probably a complex mixture of inborn physiological and learned factors.

Adaptive Responses

The cognitive approach to emotion helps to explain how emotions influence behavior. Cognitive theorists maintain that, immediately after a person perceives a stimulus, there is an intuitive appraisal of it as well (Arnold, 1970). In turn, this judgment of a stimulus as good or bad furnishes cues for our response. Just as the primitive emotional responses of animals incline them toward "fight or flight" responses, so our emotions predispose us to certain courses of action, such as approach or avoidance.

For example, suppose someone bumps into you so hard that you fall down, and it is clearly not accidental. How do you feel? Chances are that if you are larger or more powerful than the other person, you'll feel angry. Anger is our intuitive response of "fight," usually experienced in situations where we judge we have some control. But suppose you are smaller or less powerful than the other person. You're more likely to feel fear. For fear is our intuitive "flight" response, usually experienced where we feel relatively helpless. In both instances, the emotion you feel furnishes an immediate cue to your appropriate response. In this sense, emotions play an important function in our lives. They predispose us toward adaptive responses that enhance our chances for survival.

Another adaptive function of emotions is to strengthen the social ties between individuals and groups. Just as human reproduction is aided by the intensely pleasurable feelings of sexual intercourse, so our life together in groups is strengthened by emotional bonds. Stirrings of romantic love attract individuals to each other. Tender feelings of parental love help parents care for their children. Positive feelings of attachment and identification help socialize the growing child. Negative emotions also serve an important function. The emotional responses of anger, anxiety, jealousy, and grief serve to make the disruption of social relationships undesirable.

To sum up what we know about emotions: Emotions involve *bodily sensations*, including complex neurological processes in the brain. But emotions are more than sensations; they are *interpreted sensations*. How we think and perceive the world around us affects what we actually feel. Furthermore, the process of interpreting our inner sensations includes intuitive appraisals or judgments of the stimulus, which in turn furnishes cues for our behavior. The result is that emotions serve to arouse and motivate us to behave in *adaptive ways* toward our environment and toward each other.

AWARENESS OF OUR EMOTIONS

Maybe you've had the experience of coming out of a meeting and having someone ask you, "How do you feel about what we were talking about? I mean, what's your gut reaction?" Chances are the other person isn't interested in what you think as much as in how you feel. And there's some wisdom in this. For emotions are a kind of barometer of our inner world. Like the sensations of touch or sight, emotions of pain or pleasure provide us with an intuitive kind of knowledge about ourselves at a glance. Emotions are the personally colored meanings that an event has for us. When we know a person's feelings, we know something about that person.

Intensity of Arousal

Suppose you find you have to miss your best friend's party because of a previous engagement. You probably feel keenly disappointed. But if you lose a button off your coat, you feel only mild annoyance. In each instance the intensity of your emotions indicates how much you're affected by the event. Whenever we feel strong emotions, we know automatically that our needs and desires are intensely affected in some way. This intense emotional reaction serves to arouse or motivate us to action. But when we feel little or no emotion, we know that our needs and desires are not noticeably affected, and little or nothing is demanded of us. We're not "emotionally involved."

Emotions are a barometer of the inner world. (Ken Karp/Sirovich Senior Center)

Marked awareness of our emotions indicates significant change in our inner motivational state, depending on how our needs and satisfactions are affected by the world around us. Ordinarily, we become so accustomed to the usual ups and downs in our subjective experience that we aren't always aware of our emotions. As with body temperature, we become more aware of our emotions when they change, either in intensity or meaning. Even then, some people experience their emotions more intensely than others. The intensity of our emotions is probably influenced by hereditary factors, such as the characteristics of our nervous system and glands. Age is also a factor. Children and adolescents seem to feel their emotions more intensely than older people. But our habitual level of emotions is also influenced by our learning experiences. Individuals who grow up among people who are highly emotional and express their feelings freely will probably experience their emotions more strongly than those who were raised in less demonstrative families.

Personal Meaning

While the intensity of emotional arousal tells us how much we're affected, it is the personal meaning of our arousal that tells us in what way we're affected. In general, the pleasant emotions such as joy, ecstasy, and love accompany the satisfaction of our needs and desires, while the unpleasant emotions such as fear, anger, and jealousy accompany interference or deprivation. In other words, the personal significance an emotion has for us tells us which kind of change is occurring in our inner motivational state and in turn provides us with intuitive cues for an appropriate response to the stimuli around us. Whenever we feel pleasant emotions, we're inclined toward an approach response, but whenever we feel unpleasant emotions, we tend to adopt some sort of avoidance response. These two types of emotional meanings—the pleasant and the unpleasant—constitute our basic emotions. All the other separate emotions that we learn on the way to becoming an adult are differentiated forms and mixtures of these two basic kinds, with all their varying intensities.

At this point you may be asking, "Just how many emotions are there?" We really don't know the answer to this question, largely because our emotions include so many subjective factors and individual differences. However, psychologists who study emotion have made up lists of certain basic emotions, which may help us to understand our specific emotions. Even here it is best to conceive of a particular emotion as a *mixture* of the various intensities of arousal and basic types of meaning. For example, look at Plutchik's model of emotions (Figure 4-1). Each section of the cone represents a specific emotion. The horizontal dimension refers to the type of emotional meaning, and the vertical dimension refers to the intensity of arousal. The eight basic types of emotional meaning are arranged around the top of the cone according to how similar or different they are in relation to each other. Positive emotions are ecstasy, acceptance, and

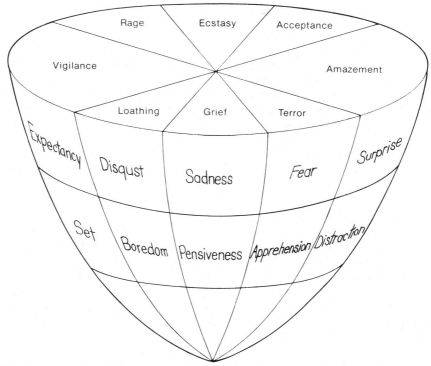

FIGURE 4.1 A multidimensional model of the emotions. R. Plutchik, *Emotion.* (Homewood, Ill.: Learning Systems Company, 1975), p. 19. Reprinted by permission of the publishers.

amazement. Negative emotions are rage, vigilance, loathing, grief, and terror. Some emotions are so different from each other that they are polar extremes or opposites, such as ecstacy and grief. The vertical dimension represents the difference among emotions according to their intensity. Notice that the feeling of pensiveness is less intense than grief, but has a similar meaning for us.

You can also imagine mixing these basic emotions in the same manner as mixing the primary colors. For example, college students asked to name the mixtures of primary emotions gave responses such as: "Joy plus acceptance equals love; friendliness. Expectancy plus anger equals aggressiveness. Acceptance plus fear equals submission; modesty. Sadness plus expectancy equals pessimism" (Plutchik, 1975, p. 19). You can easily see how many different emotions you could list. But the fact that each of us tends to label similar feelings somewhat differently because of past experience, tradition, and different degrees of awareness also complicates the accurate classification of emotions.

Momentary Experience

It is important to realize that emotions reflect momentary experience. We experience many emotional ups and downs throughout the day as a result of the changes in our subjective experience, needs, and satisfactions. It is a common mistake, however, to feel that our emotions at any moment will be permanent. This is especially true when we feel intense emotions such as anger, fear, or compassion. Haven't you done something in haste because you were emotionally aroused, only to regret it later? Sometimes we stick with our course of action, rather than admitting that we acted too "emotionally." A child may be wiser in this respect. A child may say, "I hate you," only to return a short time later with an affectionate, "Would you read me a story?" Children seem to realize that emotions are momentary and show little fear or embarrassment when laughter easily takes the place of tears. Knowing this as adults can help us to experience and express our emotions more fully at the moment, realizing that our emotions may change.

When emotions persist over a longer period of time, we refer to them as *moods*. But even our moods are relatively temporary and tend to change with a good night's sleep or a visit with a friend in a different mood. When our moods resist change without sufficient reason in our circumstances, we may begin to suspect the presence of pathological factors, which may be either physical or psychological.

EXPRESSION AND CONTROL OF EMOTIONS

Whenever you hear a baby screaming for food or cooing with satisfaction after finishing a meal, you realize that babies have no trouble expressing their emotions. The baby's uninhibited display of feeling attracts the attention of those who can relieve its discomfort. However, such uncontrolled emotion puts an unreasonable amount of stress on the baby's caretakers, and, as the baby's nervous and glandular systems mature, it is soon taught better control. The result is that the growing child continues to experience emotions, but often stops showing them openly. In so doing, the child risks adopting the hypocrisy and characteristic masks of our adult society. In fact, overcontrol poses our biggest problem in expressing emotions.

Repression

The most common form of overcontrol is *repression*. As discussed in the previous chapter on stress, repression is an automatic, unconscious process. In repression, the self denies its awareness of a feeling that, if consciously admitted, would be highly threatening. But a certain degree of self-deception is also involved, in that while the person has little or no awareness of the threat or anxiety, he or she continues unconsciously to experience the stress of the unresolved emotions.

As a result, it is often easier to recognize the manifestations of repressed emotions in others than in ourselves. An omission of something in a person's speech, thoughts, feelings, or behavior that would ordinarily be expected under the circumstances is a classic sign of repressed emotions. So is selective recall of the past. We tend to forget those things that are highly threatening to us, such as an embarrassing failure. Chronic tension of a muscle, such as a stiff neck or a twitching face muscle, is an easily observable sign of repression. Behavior contradictory to one's verbal messages is another sign of repressed emotion. The

---

EMOTIONAL MOODS

A *mood* is a generalized emotional state that lasts over a period of time—hours or even days. It is a temporary disposition toward certain behaviors and private feelings.

A number of specific moods have been identified, such as being elated, sad, tense, or apathetic, to name a few. But we may experience more than one mood at a time, as in the happy but tearful bride, the tired but happy worker, or the well-controlled thrill seeker who is also frightened.

We may manipulate our moods to some extent through the use of alcohol or drugs. The names "uppers" and "downers" appropriately suggest that we may alter the direction of our moods more than their precise effects, which depend on many factors.

What causes our moods? A dreary day? A chance meeting with an old friend? Physiological factors? Actually any of these and often a combination of factors may be the cause.

It has long been known that women experience fairly regular mood changes related to the menstrual cycle and hormone levels. It has been estimated that about two-thirds of all women experience some of the effects of premenstrual tension, such as headaches, mild irritation, depression, and decline in attentiveness. But there are wide individual variations among women. Furthermore, the negative moods and symptoms associated with menstruation are actually more evenly distributed over the entire month than was previously believed. Women are more likely to attribute such discomforts to their menstrual cycle largely because of the negative cultural beliefs about menstruation.

Our moods also show interesting patterns with the rise and fall of our body temperature during a 24-hour period (biorhythms). Some people tend to be more active and to perform better in the morning, but become more susceptible to irritation as the day proceeds. Others tend to be slow and grouchy in the morning, but hit their peak later in the afternoon or evening.

Are you aware of your own pattern of moods? If you keep track of them over an extended period of time, you may be able to learn something valuable about yourself. Once you discover how your moods affect you, it is easier to make allowances or modify your judgment or behavior.

boy who continues crushing a paper cup with his hand while denying any hostility is expressing mixed signals of his feelings. So is the girl with tight, revealing clothes and flirtatious mannerisms who disclaims any intentions of being seductive. The refusal to consider any motive for behavior other than the ones admitted is usually a reliable sign of repression. The common feature in all these behaviors is the person's *lack of awareness* of his or her true feelings, as well as a *refusal* to examine them.

Suppression

Emotions are often suppressed instead of being repressed. In *suppression*, people are usually conscious of their emotions, but deliberately control rather than express them. In general, suppression is a healthier way of handling feelings than repression. But the habitual suppression of emotion may lead to many of the undersirable effects of repression. In addition, chronic suppression of feelings interferes with rational, problem-solving behavior. When people have unexpressed feelings that are smoldering within, they cannot concentrate. They may not be able to study, work, or even play. Also, feelings that are chronically suppressed may erupt in explosive behavior in ways that worsen the problem. In short, chronic suppression may be just as unhealthy as repression.

Verbal Expression

If you suddenly become angry, frightened, or ecstatic, you probably do not think through what you want to say before you say it. But reason does play an important part in the healthy expression of emotions. We usually make a distinction between reason and emotion, but this is a relative and in some ways a false distinction. We've already indicated that emotions contain cognitive elements of interpretation and appraisal. Conversely, thinking also involves nonrational processes, such as imagination, imagery, memory, and intuition, in addition to abstract reason. Although we can mentally distinguish between our thinking and emotions, actually we think and feel as a whole person. So it should not be surprising that we need a certain degree of rational control to identify and express our emotions verbally. Expressing your emotions "from the hip," so to speak, tends to be more of an impulsive and irresponsible act than an honest one. Learning to express your emotions effectively involves a healthy balance between spontaneous expression and deliberate, rational control.

We may begin by expressing our everyday feelings more frequently. Many times we feel an emotion only on the surface, such as when we're pleasantly surprised with an invitation or gift. Why not share that feeling? The more you articulate your safe feelings, the more you grow in your awareness of them and ability to express them. Then when you experience an emotion more deeply, like intense anger or disgust, you may find it easier to know what you're feeling and the risk involved in expressing it. More often than not, it's a risk worth taking. Expressing your emotions openly clears the air and usually helps more than it hurts the situation. This is especially true when we respond more to behavior than to the personality of others, as suggested in recent child-rearing and human relations techniques.

Sharing our feelings with an attentive person also helps us to clarify them. For we often aren't fully certain what we're feeling until we've expressed it and hear how others respond. Even negative feedback may help test the strength of our emotional convictions. Frequently, all we need is more practice in sharing our feelings in order to become emotionally articulate and to say what we feel accurately. When we feel secure in our intimate relationships with friends, spouses, and co-workers, we're inclined to do this naturally. But when we're unable to express ourselves, we may find a counselor or psychotherapist helpful in learning to express our emotions more openly. For it is not so much what we feel as how we express it that counts.

"OWNING" OUR EMOTIONS

When we're not sufficiently aware of our emotions, we often attribute them to others. We say to someone, "Your performance was not good," instead of "I didn't like it." Or we say, "Don't count on me," instead of "I don't feel interested." Such expressions don't tell others how we feel. We fail to "own" our emotions.

Such "you" messages tend to distort our communication with others. They tend to judge, name-call, accuse, approve, and disapprove of others, prematurely judging them, putting them on the defensive, and cutting off communication.

You and I can communicate ourselves more effectively to others by "owning" our feelings and expressing ourselves in "I" messages. In an "I" message, we express our own feelings toward another person or situation. In this way, the other person does not feel prematurely judged and remains more open to what we really have to say or ask of him or her.

Tom Gordon says that an "I" message is especially effective in modifying another person's behavior that is troublesome for us. Such an "I" message ideally includes three things: a *nonjudgmental description* of the other's troublesome behavior, the *tangible effects* on me, and how I *feel* about it.

For example, suppose a friend repeatedly borrows things from me and doesn't return them. Instead of saying, "You're inconsiderate," I might say, "When you borrow something without returning it, I often need it, and then I get very annoyed." My friend may still take offense, but he is more likely to say, "I didn't realize I was inconveniencing you. I'm glad you spoke up"

Thomas Gordon, *Parent Effectiveness Training* (New York: Peter H. Wyden, 1970), pp. 115-120.

Facial and Bodily Expressions

Emotions are usually communicated through nonverbal as well as verbal means. Body movement, vocalization, and especially facial expression may be strong indicators of what a person is feeling. It is interesting to note that certain common emotional expressions appear in blind children who have never seen a laughing or mourning face (Eibl-Eibesfeldt, 1970). Furthermore, cross-cultural studies using photographs of posed facial expressions have also shown a moderate agreement on some emotions among judges from countries such as Brazil, Japan, and the United States. The best agreement was found for expressions of happiness, anger, and fear. Less agreement was found for sadness and disgust (Ekman, Sorenson, & Friesen, 1969).

As you would expect, it is difficult to separate the learned from the unlearned components of our emotional expressions. However, Ekman and Friesen (1971) suggest that facial expressions of emotion among different groups of people vary according to three factors: the same stimulus may evoke different emotions in different cultures; cultures have varying expectations as to which emotions are to be controlled and which expressed; and the consequences of emotions vary in different cultures. Whenever the facial expression is ambiguous, knowing the social setting or environment helps make the meaning clearer.

Most of us find some emotions easier to express than others. People usually have no trouble expressing love, fear, happiness, and determination. But disgust, contempt, and suffering are more difficult to express (Thompson & Meltzer, 1964). In one study most people could express at best only two out of the following six emotions with any degree of accuracy: anger, fear, seductiveness,

Facial expressions reveal what a person is feeling. (Irene Springer)

SMILING

Do you ever smile when you are alone? Probably not nearly as often as when you are with others, according to recent studies. Robert Kraut and Robert Johnson and their students spent several hundred hours observing bowlers in the bowling alleys of Ithaca, New York. They found that while about one third of the bowlers smiled to themselves when they scored a strike or a spare, they were even more likely to smile when they were looking at or talking with others. Similar results were observed in other settings. While people smile more frequently on nice days than bad ones, they are much more likely to smile while greeting or conversing with others.

It appears that social smiling serves as a means of communication and probably evolved from the tendency among primates to smile when signaling friendship or appeasement to others.

Robert Kraut and Robert Johnson, "Social and Emotional Messages of Smiling: An Ethological Approach," *Journal of Personality and Social Psychology*, 39(1979), 9, 1539–1553.

indifference, happiness, and sadness. One girl appeared angry regardless of the emotion she was expressing, while another appeared seductive in most of her expressions (Beier, 1974). It appears that we often misinform others of our emotions and must learn how to communicate nonverbally as well as verbally.

Women generally express their emotions more readily than men, and they engage in more nonverbal expressions such as hugging, kissing, and touching. According to one survey, two-thirds of the women said they often hugged their female friends, but an even larger number of men reported that they rarely or never hugged their friends of the same sex. Since children learn such patterns almost incidentally, it is not surprising that these same parents reported a similar pattern of emotional expressions among their children and adolescents. That is, daughters regularly hugged their girl friends, but boys rarely hugged their same-sex friends. Although nine out of ten of the fathers wanted to communicate their emotions to their children and felt it was "good for men to cry," few of them did so in practice. When offered a set of situations in which intense emotions were expressed, in every instance except one fewer men than women reported crying. The only exception was anger. At least until recently, it has been more acceptable for men to express anger (Roberts, Kline, & Gagnon, 1978). Today, however, with greater openness and expressiveness acceptable among both sexes, these patterns are gradually changing. More men are willing to show tears in public, while more women are able to express anger. What sort of parental modeling were you exposed to in your home? What about yourself?

Women also tend to be better than men in understanding nonverbal cues in emotional expression (Rosenthal et al., 1974). One explanation offered is that women's traditional role as mother demands an ability to interpret bodily expressions of emotion. Another is that women have been oppressed, and oppressed people tend to become more skillful in interpreting subtle communication as a means of survival. However, the study also showed that men in the helping professions, such as psychiatrists, psychologists, teachers, and social workers, as well as actors, artists, and designers, scored as high as the women did. The study also showed that sensitivity to nonverbal cues of emotion increases with age and experience. It seems that our ability to interpret the nonverbal expressions of emotion depends more on our experience in doing so than on our sex.

HANDLING TROUBLESOME EMOTIONS

As important as emotions are, they're sometimes troublesome. For instance, strong feelings tend to interfere with our ability to think clearly and perform well. In general, the more complex the task, the greater the interference. For example, intense feelings of anxiety may greatly disrupt your studying for an exam, but will not affect your ability to find your way to the classroom. At other times, emotions become a problem when they urge us in a direction at odds with our deliberate, rational judgments, like deciding to be more patient with your children, but becoming angry the first time they disobey. Some emotions are more potentially troublesome than others. They are harder to ignore or control and demand more experience and skill in handling effectively. Several of the more troublesome emotions are considered here in detail.

Anxiety

Anxiety is a basic troublemaker for almost everyone. Anxiety is an unpleasant, foreboding feeling that something bad is about to happen. It tends to be a vague, subjective awareness of a threat not too clearly perceived. Fear, a related emotion, refers to a more specific and objective danger. People usually know what they are afraid of and what to do about it. But the anxious individual senses danger without being clear about what it is or what to do about it. Often fear and anxiety are experienced together. A graduate student highly anxious about getting his degree may become intensely fearful of his dissertation oral exam. Worry refers to still another form of anxiety. People tend to worry about future events, especially those they are emotionally involved in and whose outcome they are uncertain about. But many worries never materialize precisely because they are anxieties.

Anxiety in its many forms tends to function as an emotional alarm signal, warning the individual of threat or imminent danger. There are many instances in a normal life when anxiety or fear is appropriate. For example, an airport worker once opened the door of a plane's cargo compartment and saw a lion walking around loose. His intense feeling of fear led him to close the door with lightning speed. At other times, we may feel threatened where there is little real danger. In fact, many of the things we feel anxious about pose little threat to our physical survival, but are mostly threats to some value in our self-system. People suffering from a chronic sense of anxiety are hindered in several ways. Constant anxiety syphons off energy by keeping the body mobilized for action where none is needed. Then too, chronic anxiety constricts our perceptions and tends to make us more rigid in our behavior. Individuals plagued by constant anxiety also tend to worry about things that never happen, thereby robbing themselves of much of the enjoyment of life.

Since anxiety is a highly unpleasant feeling, each of us has some built-in devices for minimizing this emotion, as discussed in the chapter on stress and defense mechanisms. But a healthier way of handling your anxiety is to become more aware of the feeling itself and find out what it is that threatens you. You can be alert for the signs of anxiety, such as the pounding heart, tensing of the muscles, the dry throat or mouth, and the cold sweat. When you realize you feel anxious, you might ask yourself: Why do I feel anxious? Am I facing a realistic threat? An unrealistic one? Can I do anything about this threat?

For example, suppose each time you speak out in class or any public place, your mouth becomes dry, your voice begins trembling, and you become so rattled you can't think or express yourself clearly. One student who became aware of

Anxiety is a troublesome emotion for almost everyone. (A.T.&T. Company Photo Center)

this behavior reasoned that she was afraid of making herself look foolish and of being criticized. Yet, she was an A student in the class. With the help of one of the college counselors, she began sharing her opinions with individual classmates. Then she began speaking up in small groups in the class. Later she began to speak up more in the class discussions. By thinking out her question or response somewhat ahead of time, she found that she could express herself despite feelings of anxiety. Furthermore, each time she spoke out and found that she was not criticized, she gradually felt less anxiety and learned to speak out in public with more confidence.

Anxiety and fear do not always have negative effects. Fear that leads to a sense of preparation and caution in the face of a realistic danger may be helpful. A moderate sense of anxiety may also facilitate preparation for an exam or important performance. Often there are instances in which anxiety can serve as a means of growth. Whenever you confront the difficult choices about which college to attend, which vocation to select, or whom to marry, you tend to become anxious—and understandably so. It's tempting to escape from such anxiety through indecision, compliance, or one of many kinds of diversions, such as sex, drugs, or alcohol. Having the courage instead to face up to these inevitable anxieties of life, to make decisions and to abide by their consequences without blaming others can further our personal growth.

Anger

Anger is another troublemaker that plagues each of us at one time or another. Anger refers to a feeling of extreme displeasure, usually brought about by interference with our needs or desires. Rage is uncontrolled anger. Hostility, hate, and aggression may include varying degrees of the feeling of anger, but also imply some harmful intent or action as well. The ability to experience anger, like anxiety, is a biological endowment. Anger helps to arouse us to lash out, control, or fight the object occasioning the anger. In anxiety, we tend to feel helpless and adopt a flight response, but in anger we sense more possibilities of control, warranting a fight or attack response.

Overcontrol of anger is a characteristic problem for many people in our society. Children soon learn that if they express anger they risk losing the love of their parents and other significant persons. So they cease to express anger openly, which may cause more trouble later on. Perhaps you have heard someone you would normally expect to react with anger say instead, "It's not worth getting mad over," or "I refuse to get angry."

Whenever you repress your anger, you also lose control over its effects. But repressed anger, like repressed anxiety, manifests itself in many ways. The businessman who habitually makes others wait to see him for office appointments may harbor a secret resentment toward his clients. Whenever we feel obligated to do something we really don't want to, we may find ourselves making foolish mistakes that mar our performance. We may also take repressed anger out on

> I was angry with my friend:
> I told my wrath, my wrath did end.
> I was angry with my foe:
> I told it not, my wrath did grow.
>
> William Blake, from "A Poison Tree"

ourselves. Sullen, depressed, or suicidal individuals tend to have a lot of repressed anger. Repressed anger is also an important factor in many physical symptoms, such as high blood pressure, some headaches (or "hate-aches"), and various types of ulcers, especially ulcerative colitis.

Learning to handle anger more positively begins with the recognition that anger is a perfectly normal human emotion. Everyone gets mad at times. We're especially inclined to become angry with those we love, since they can disappoint and hurt us the most. Furthermore, some anger is pretty much inevitable in the give and take of all human relationships, especially in a society where individuals are encouraged to be assertive and competitive. And if it's normal for you to get angry, how about others? Do you take expressions of anger toward you as vicious personal attacks? Or do you realize that in most instances angry people are trying to communicate something to you? In fact, the healthier you become, the more you will give up the notion that everyone must love and appreciate you at all times.

IS THIS YOU?

Do you avoid little blow-ups until you face a much-dreaded major blow-up?

What is your time lapse between getting angry and feeling angry and between feeling anger and showing anger? Are you shortening the lapse and getting healthier?

Are you fully aware that anger is not the same as sustained hostility and hatred?

Are you aware that your anger will not kill anyone, and that no one's anger will kill you?

Do you save anger for enemies only? Why aren't you as good to your friends?

Are you aware that healthy anger functions in the service of real closeness?

Are you aware that people can feel loving and make love after a fight because an emotional traffic jam has been cleared?

Do you remember that anger is not forever?

Theodore Isaac Rubin, M.D., *The Angry Book* (New York: Macmillan Publishing Company, Inc., 1969), pp 203-223. Copyright © 1969 by Dr. Theodore Isaac Rubin. Adapted by permission of Macmillan Publishing Company, Inc.

It is also very important to learn how to express anger in a direct and constructive manner. Some parents teach their children (best by example) to express their angry feelings directly in a nonviolent way. Whether you've learned to do this already or not, verbalizing your anger spontaneously is desirable whenever this is appropriate. Don't be afraid to use the nonverbal expressions of anger as well, such as an increased volume, pitch, and rate of speaking as well as appropriate gestures. It all helps to communicate your emotions clearly. Feeling anger often arouses you to constructive change you would not have attempted otherwise. At other times, it may be best to use your anger to work out the most appropriate strategy of action before expressing yourself verbally. As with emotions in general, it is best to adopt a healthy balance of spontaneous expression and deliberate rational control with anger.

Guilt

Guilt can also be a troublesome emotion at any age. We feel a sense of guilt when we have violated our conscience, our internalized standards of good and bad. This sense of guilt is a mixture of remorse, self-reproach, and apprehension (anxiety) over the fear of punishment.

Children acquire their conscience and the capacity for guilt in their preschool years, before they are capable of rational understanding, so the childhood conscience functions to control behavior emotionally and automatically. It is largely the internalized voice of parental authority. Whenever we feel guilt from violating the dictates of our childhood conscience, it tends to be an excessively harsh and self-punishing sense of guilt. This kind of guilt tends to reinforce the individual's sense of dependency on authority and the need for love. As a child grows into adolescence and becomes more capable of rational and deliberate self-control, the sense of guilt should appropriately reflect a more adult conscience.

Adults tend to revise the contents of their conscience in keeping with their own sense of values and standards of right and wrong. The sense of guilt from this adult conscience functions more as a positive, socializing force than as an excessively inhibiting one. Such guilt tends to be more appropriate to the wrongdoing, more accessible to reason and control, as well as less harsh and punitive than childhood guilt. Our conscience lets us know that we have done something wrong and need to make atonement to remedy the wrong done. It reminds us of our personal responsibility and thus functions to make us more independent of authority and the need for love. Someone with a strong conscience usually becomes aware of a sense of guilt in a direct, intuitive way. Those in whom an adult conscience is less well developed, however, may experience more of the indirect signs of guilt, such as the habitual tendency to apologize (saying "I'm sorry"), the tendency to be excessively critical or blame others or themselves, or the need to constantly engage in good works to make themselves acceptable to others.

Since the values of our adult conscience tend to supersede rather than entirely displace the dictates of the earlier childhood conscience, sometimes our sense of guilt may reflect the violations of our childhood conscience. In such instances we feel guilty even though we have done nothing wrong by our adult standards. For example, merely expressing justified anger or just talking with a policeman or authority figure would make us feel guilty. But to stop expressing our anger or avoid all authority figures because of this inappropriate guilt would be to continue childish, dependent behavior.

Sometimes we encounter a person with a chronically guilty conscience. Such people have usually repressed much of their guilt, especially from their childhood conscience, so that they exhibit what Freud called "unconscious guilt" (Freud, 1957). These individuals tend to act in a guilty manner while being unaware of guilt feelings. Such people frequently tend to be unduly critical of others or themselves. When something goes wrong, they feel strongly that someone should be blamed. They may become accident-prone and hurt themselves more frequently than the average person. At times, such people may display provocative behavior that invites punishment. For example, a boy may engage in behavior that tests the limits of acceptability, such as insulting a policeman or breaking the windows in the local high school. Or a girl may become provocative in a sexual manner by behaving in a promiscuous way that invites censure. In such cases, the individual doesn't feel guilty because of any wrongdoing as much as he or she acts wrongly because of an unconscious sense of guilt. Guilt in these instances serves as a form of self-punishment. When punished, the individual may protest loudly, but may inwardly feel a strange sense of relief. Such self-defeating behavior will probably continue until the person becomes more fully aware of his or her guilt and resolves the childhood notions that gave rise to it.

It should be apparent at this point that the emotional sense of guilt in moderate doses is both normal and necessary. Being aware of your guilt helps you to take the necessary steps in modifying your behavior accordingly. The positive purpose of guilt is self-correction, not self-punishment. A sense of guilt over disappointing others may serve to modify your behavior better than just saying "I'm sorry" all the time. A healthy sense of guilt over sex may serve to ward off the danger of an unwanted pregnancy or of using a person for your own satisfaction. Guilt in the positive, healthy sense serves to facilitate free, independent behavior by making people accept personal responsibility. The person of high self-esteem tends to take the appropriate steps to resolve his or her sense of guilt, as, for example, when a coach offers an apology to a player he has cursed at during a critical point in the game. Guilt in this instance serves to maintain the integrity of our social relationships as well as our own self-respect. As with anxiety, one of the worst things is to have too much guilt. But worse still is to have no guilt at all.

There are many other problem emotions we could discuss, such as jealousy, depression, loneliness, and bereavement, to name a few. But actually, any emotion can become troublesome, depending on the individual and the situation.

Interestingly enough, psychologists tend to give disproportionate attention to negative emotions. One study of 172 psychology textbooks written during the past 85 years revealed that unpleasant emotions are discussed twice as much as pleasant ones (Carlson, 1966). In contrast, an analysis of representative literary works including poetry, fiction, and plays showed that almost three-fourths of the references to emotions were to pleasant emotions (Lindauer, 1968). It's an interesting contrast. It may be that psychologists are overly concerned with our problems. Or could it be that the positive emotions are harder to study? Do we find them less interesting to read about? In any event, as a partial corrective, let's now look briefly at the emotional aspects of love.

Love

Our focus here is on the emotional aspects of love, even though the experience of love encompasses more than emotion as we will discuss in the chapter on love and marriage. Even at this level, love is a complex emotion frequently reported by people engaged in such diverse activities as sexual or religious behavior. Although love is not an emergency emotion like anxiety or anger, it does serve an adaptive function as a bond for social relationships.

Love motivates us to form attachments with each other. Strong emotions usually accompany our needs for attachment and the satisfaction of these needs.

For this reason we often speak of love as a desire or need, on the one hand, and as acceptance or a blissful state, on the other hand.

One of the most familiar forms of love is romantic love, which may be defined as a strong emotional arousal and attraction toward another person, together with a need for the physical presence and support of the other person, caring, and intimate sharing (Rubin, 1973). We often resort to the metaphor of heat or flame when speaking of romantic love; we may feel filled with a warm flush or as if we are going to burst. Folklore suggests that romantic love is uncontrollable—we *"fall* in love"—and that love is a mixture of ecstasy and suffering—"true love never runs smooth."

Studies based on cognitive theory suggest that any type of physiological arousal may be interpreted as love in the proper context, especially in the presence of an attractive person of the opposite sex. One such study included men crossing two types of bridges—one a rickety bridge swaying in the wind several hundred feet above a rocky canyon, the other a solid structure just a few feet above a shallow stream. An attractive young woman approached the men as they were crossing either bridge, asking them if they would participate in a study on the effect of scenic attraction on creative expression. As expected, the researchers found that the men approached on the fear-arousing bridge were more sexually aroused than the men on the solid bridge. They were also much more likely to telephone the woman afterwards, supposedly to get more information about the study. In short, the arousal of fear served to heighten feelings of love and attraction (Dutton & Aron, 1974). Similarly, the arousal of loneliness, frustration, anger, and sexual desire may all deepen the passion of love under certain conditions.

It is largely because of the emotional aspects of love that what is felt to be

Feelings of love reflect joy and acceptance. (A.T.&T. Company Photo Center)

love at the moment may in retrospect be regarded as infatuation—shallow or fleeting love. The emotional aspects of love may also help to explain the diminished intensity of genuine love over time. This can be seen in a study of 45 couples at a large college, which included 15 couples in love, 15 couples who were friends but not in love, and another 15 couples who were friends but didn't date or were not in love. Feelings of love rarely remained the same; they either increased or decreased with time. Self-reported feelings of love generally tended to decrease over the six-month period of the study, with the sharpest declines being registered by those couples who were most in love at the outset (Pam, 1970).

Love as an emotion not only moves us to form relationships with others; it also serves to maintain and strengthen those relationships. That is, feelings of love may express fulfillment of our needs for belonging. When asked to explain the emotion of love as fulfillment, people have said that it is the experience of acceptance coupled with joy or pleasure. And this held true regardless of whether the relationship involved two opposite-sexed adults, two friends, or mother and child (Plutchik, 1975). To feel loved is to feel accepted as a person. To love is to accept another as a person. Since love is more than an emotion, however, to be in a love relationship does not mean that we will always feel the emotion of love. But when felt, the emotional aspects of love as acceptance serve to strengthen the relationship.

SUMMARY

We began this chapter by defining emotion as a complex state of awareness involving inner sensations and outer expressions that has the power of motivating us to act.

The cognitive theory of emotions implies that our feelings are affected by our expectations and surroundings and thus are largely learned responses. Generally, emotions serve the purpose of arousing us to respond to our environment in adaptive ways, as well as strengthening our social ties with others.

Emotions also serve as a kind of barometer of our inner world. The intensity of arousal discloses the magnitude of change in our motivational state, while the personal meaning of our emotions indicates what type of change is occurring, whether toward satisfaction or deprivation. Although our emotions provide useful cues for responding to others, it is important to recognize that they are momentary expressions of our subjective experience and therefore subject to change. According to Plutchik's model, the specific emotions we feel tend to represent mixtures of various types as well as different intensities of certain primary emotions such as grief and ecstasy.

At times our emotions become troublesome for us, especially when they interfere with our judgment or performance. Some emotions are more potentially troublesome than others, such as anxiety, anger, guilt, and love. Although mild doses of anxiety may arouse as in the face of danger, more intense anxiety leads us to act in defensive and self-defeating ways. Since we tend to overcontrol anger, expressing it in an appropriate manner may help us to act in a more constructive way. While childish, irrational guilt feelings serve to reinforce self-punitive and dependent behavior, a healthy, adult sense of guilt may lead us to act in a more responsible, independent way. In coping with the emotional aspects of love, it is good to remember that the term *love* is associated with many different meanings and intensities of love, ranging from a need or desire to a state of satisfaction.

QUESTIONS FOR SELF-REFLECTION

1. How often do you refer to your feelings to explain your behavior?
2. Can you think of some specific occasions when your expectations and surroundings definitely affected the emotions you felt?
3. How much attention do you give to your emotions in making a decision? Should decisions be entirely rational?
4. Do others refer to you as a moody person?
5. How do you express your feelings—frequently and easily or only occasionally and with difficulty?
6. Which feelings do you find the hardest to express—anger, love, disgust, joy, or compassion?
7. When you are having trouble expressing your emotions verbally, which nonverbal expressions tend to give away your true feelings?
8. How do you usually handle anxiety—through defense mechanisms like rationalization or through awareness of the threat and appropriate growth?
9. When it comes to anger, do you tend to either blow up early or hold it in too long?
10. Do you recognize any of the signs of unconscious guilt in your everyday behavior, such as the tendency to blame someone else or yourself, self-righteousness, unexplained accidents or failure, or provocative behavior?
11. When you experience strong feelings of love for someone, is it mostly a longing to receive affection or give it? Or is it both?

EXERCISES

1. Expressing your emotions effectively

This exercise is designed to give you experience in expressing your emotions in a direct, nonjudgmental way, as described in the box on "owning" our emotions. Please reread the box on page 89 before continuing.

Take an $8^{1}/_{2} \times 11$ sheet of paper and turn it sideways. Make four columns as follows:

Situation	Description of behavior	Tangible effects on me	How I feel about it

Then, using the following situations, write out a complete "I message" by composing each part of the "I message" under the three respective columns. After you have finished, compare your completed "I messages" with those in the answer key.

Situation 1. You've just had to call a friend to get back a book loaned earlier in order to study for a test.

Situation 2. Your date keeps you waiting every time you get ready to go out, but you've run out of patience.

Situation 3. Each time you suggest ways to improve things at work, a co-worker starts criticizing before you finish explaining your point.

Situation 4. A friend has a habit of offering you extra tickets to concerts at the last minute, but feels offended that you rarely accept them.

Situation 5. Your instructor has just handed back an essay test with a C grade without any comments or explanations for your grade.

After you have completed the first part of the exercise, compare your three-part "I messages" with these suggestions:

Situation 1. Whenever you don't bring my book back in time to study for a test, I resent loaning it to you.

Situation 2. Each time you show up late, I feel so annoyed that it's hard to enjoy our time together.

Situation 3. When you start criticizing me before hearing what I have to say, I feel frustrated and like not even trying to help.

Situation 4. When you offer me tickets at the last minute, it usually conflicts with something else I've already planned, and I regret you didn't let me know sooner.

Situation 5. Getting a test back without any explanation for my grade doesn't tell me what I did right or wrong, and I feel frustrated as to how to improve. (Gordon, 1972)[1]

2. Listening for others' feelings

People tend to communicate their emotions or feelings as part of an overall message. Many times the feelings are obscured by the verbal labels or code used to express them.

This exercise is designed to help you cut through to the essential message being expressed, especially the meanings or feelings.

Take an $8^1/_2 \times 11$ sheet of paper and make two headings as shown on p. 103. Then for each example in the left-hand column, write single words or short phrases in the answer column that might sum up the message or feelings being expressed. Ask yourself, "What is the sender trying to tell me?"

[1]Adapted from Dr. Thomas Gordon's participant notebook *Human Effectiveness Training* (Solana Beach, Ca.: Effectiveness Training, Inc., 1972). Reprinted by permission of publishers.

Other Person Says	*Message or Feelings Expressed*

a. I've had it up to here with your excuses.

b. Okay, I apologized. What more do you want me to do?

c. I couldn't do another paper at this point if I tried.

d. You want to check my answer?

e. I shouldn't have treated her that way.

f. Can't you wait until after the weekend to take up our projects? I've got another test on Friday too.

g. He seems to do everything well, even though he hasn't had as much experience as I have.

h. I can't figure those people out. Maybe we should stop trying to satisfy them.

i. I'll never help her again, not a single word of thanks for all that I did for her.

j. We could try again, but frankly I don't think it's worth it.

After you have completed the right-hand column, compare your answers with the suggested ones listed below. Give yourself credit if you captured the main message, whether you used exactly the same words below or not. What percentage of the messages did you perceive accurately?

a. exasperated, wants results

b. feels enough has been said

c. feels worn out, exhausted

d. unsure of self, wants assurance

e. feels regret, guilt

f. pressured for time, overloaded

g. admiration, envy

h. feels discouraged, would like to quit

i. bitter, resentful

j. skeptical, doubtful.[2]

[2]Adapted from Dr. Thomas Gordon's participant notebook *Human Effectiveness Training* (Solana Beach, Ca.: Effectiveness Training, Inc., 1972). Reprinted by permission of publishers.

3. Identifying the emotion of anxiety

In order to better understand your experience of a particular emotion such as anxiety, ask yourself the following questions. Writing down your answers will further help you to recognize and understand your experience of anxiety.

Which types of situations make you anxious?

Are there some types of persons who make you more anxious than others?

Do your own expectations contribute to your anxiety?

How do you know when you are getting anxious? Are there bodily changes that occur?

What words do you use to express your feelings of anxiety? Can you express your feelings readily?

Is your anxiety appropriate to the situation that aroused it or not? Do you tend to overreact or underreact to threatening situations?

How does anxiety affect your performance? Does it stimulate you to do well or does it tend to interfere with your performance?

For additional exercises, you may want to take some of the other basic emotions described in the chapter such as anger, guilt, or love. Perhaps there are other emotions that are especially troublesome for you.

4. Labeling the intensity of your emotions

You'll recall from the drawing of Plutchik's three-dimensional model of emotions that each of the basic emotions varies in strength, ranging from maximum intensity at the top of Figure 4-1 to minimal intensity at the bottom or apex of the cone.

One of the reasons we have trouble in expressing and recognizing emotions is that we tend to use different words to express varying intensities of the same basic emotion. This exercise is designed to help you recognize some of the words commonly associated with different intensities of the same basic emotion.

Select one of the basic emotions mentioned by Plutchik, such as grief. Then write down as many different words as you can to express grief, ranging from the most intense grief to the least intense. For convenience, place the most intense grief at the top of the page and least intense at the bottom. Where would you place the following words on your list: depressed, sad, despondent, despair, feeling blue, gloomy, sorrow, miserable, desolate, below par, pensive, and so forth? How many other words can you think of to express grief? Do you think people use these words consistently or not? Does the social situation affect the particular label we put on our feelings?

5. Recognizing nonverbal cues of emotional expression

Select several of the basic emotions, such as anger, joy, jealousy, and so forth. Then write down the nonverbal cues commonly associated with these emotions. For example, some nonverbal cues associated with anger are as follows:

Nonverbal Cues	*Anger*
facial expressions	frowning, tense, red-faced
tone of voice	loud, rising pitch
eye contact	narrowing eyes, staring
body posture	taut, arms astride waist or folded in defiance
	pointed finger, clenched fist
gestures	not too close
spatial distance	no touching or aggressive contact like pushing
touching or not	

Are there individual differences in expressing these emotions? Are there any characteristic cues used by your father? Mother? Spouse or best friends? Yourself?

Is it easier to recognize nonverbal cues when you know someone well?

You might also discuss your results with other students. Do you find more agreement on some emotions than others? Which nonverbal cues are the most helpful in detecting emotions? Are there any differences among males or females or age groups in recognizing nonverbal cues?

6. Charades—a group exercise for recognizing nonverbal cues of emotions

Many of you have probably played charades already—a guessing game based on nonverbally acting out words. The main difference in this exercise is that all the words should designate emotions.

First, divide up the group or class into teams of five or six members each. Then have each team meet as a group to think of a half dozen or so emotions to be acted out by the other teams. Try to think up emotions that will be challenging to act out but not so difficult that hardly anyone would ever think of them. It's best to use emotions commonly expressed in everyday life. Write down each emotion on a separate slip of paper, folding the paper to protect the secrecy of your choices.

Then, have the teams exchange their slips of paper so that each team will be acting out choices selected by another team. Nobody is to look at the individual selections until the game begins.

The game is played by having one member of a team at a time draw a piece of paper from the selections previously drawn by his or her team. After a few seconds of deliberation, the individual attempts to act out nonverbally the emotion written on the piece of paper. The object is to have his or her own team guess the appropriate emotion within a set time limit, usually about three minutes. Each team wins one point for every correct guess.

Rotate the teams in order, so that one individual from each team acts out an emotion before starting with the first team again. Continue until all individuals have had a chance to act out an emotion, or if time is limited, an equal number of individuals from each team have performed.

The team that accumulates the most points is the winner. How do you account for the winning team? Were there some persons who were especially perceptive in detecting nonverbal cues? Were there any differences among the sexes? Were age or experience involved?

RECOMMENDED READINGS

Burns, D., M.D. *Feeling Good.* New York: William Morrow and Company, Inc., 1980. A cognitive approach, full of diagnostic aids and practical strategies for overcoming depression.

Gaylin, W., M.D. *Feelings.* New York: Harper & Row, 1979. A clear explanation of why we feel the way we do, as well as how to cope with our emotions and use them to our advantage.

May, R. *The Meaning of Anxiety,* rev. ed. New York: Washington Square Press, 1979 (paperback). Lucid descriptions of the various theories of anxiety together with numerous case studies demonstrating anxiety.

Phillips, D. and R. Judd. *How to Fall Out of Love* New York: Popular Library, 1980 (paperback). Practical techniques for overcoming unsatisfying or impossible love affairs.

Rubin, T. I. *The Angry Book.* New York: Collier Books, 1975 (paperback). A down-to-earth account of how to handle anger by a well-known psychoanalyst, with 103 questions designed as self-help exercises.

Wood, J. *How Do You Feel?* Englewood Cliffs, N.J.: Prentice-Hall, 1974 (paperback). First-person accounts of what it's like to feel about 30 different emotions, including hurt, joy, boredom, love, sadness, and so forth.

Self-Concept

The self-concept, or the way I see myself, is central to my awareness and behavior. When I say someone is tall or short, I usually mean taller or shorter than myself. The self-concept also serves as the basis for evaluating our own experience. Whatever is consistent with the sense of self is readily accepted, even though it may be painful, while that which is inconsistent is resisted. For example a student with low self-esteem might find it easier to accept a C on a test rather than an A. Although the higher grade may be more desirable, it would also evoke all kinds of self-justifications to make it congruent with the student's poor self-image, such as, "The teacher must be an easy grader," "It's probably a mistake," or "I was lucky."

As you can see, the sense of self is an important part of our personal make-up. In fact, it is such an intimate part of our subjective experience that it is difficult to investigate. Yet therapists and researchers alike attest to the importance of the self-concept in everyday behavior.

In the first half of this chapter, we will explain what the self-concept is and how it functions. Then in the latter two sections we will focus more on how the self-concept changes in the course of social interaction and personal growth.

WHAT IS THE SELF-CONCEPT?

Essentially, self-concept is the overall way I see myself. As such, it is composed of all those perceptions of "I" and "me" together with the feelings, values, and beliefs associated with them.

Actually, what we call the self-concept is more of a collection of selves rather than a static thing. It includes hundreds of self-perceptions in varying degrees of clarity and intensity that we have acquired in our experience, mostly with others. Because these self-perceptions exhibit a certain consistency or organizing pattern as a whole, we refer to them collectively as a self-concept. But our self-concept is more of a mental construct or "theory" we use to explain how these self-perceptions function in our experience (Epstein, 1973). People with only a fragmented, incoherent view of themselves—such as those who are emotionally disturbed—may wonder about who they are and behave in a highly inconsistent manner from one time to the next. In contrast, those who have achieved a desirable integration of their various selves may feel a clearer sense of personal identity and behave in a more dependable manner.

It is somewhat arbitrary how many different selves we care to distinguish. If I wanted to make an exhaustive list of myself, I might start off by naming my sensual self, my loving self, my impish self, and so forth. At a more general level, however, some of the more common distinctions include: the self I see myself to be *(subjective self)*; the awareness of my body *(body image)*; the self I'd like to be *(ideal self)*, and the way I feel others see me *(social self)*. Since this last one will be dealt with in a later section, let's focus here on the first three.

The Subjective Self

This is the way I see myself. It is the self I think I am. It is composed of highly personal self-images. Since it is so private, each of us is an expert on our subjective self—however realistic or unrealistic our perception may be.

Our subjective self is made up of the many self-perceptions we have acquired growing up, especially in our formative years. It is mostly influenced by the way we are seen and treated by significant others, especially by our parents. When we are young and impressionable, we tend to internalize what they think of us, their judgments and expectations, and regard ourselves accordingly. For example, I knew a mother who resented having to take care of her children and was constantly yelling at them, "Don't do that, stupid!" "What's wrong with you?" "You're going to be the death of me yet." Can you imagine how her children felt about themselves after years of repeated exposure to such remarks? Are you surprised that they were troublemakers at home and at school?

Fortunately, we tend to revise our self-images through later experience with others, especially with our friends, teachers, and spouses. One girl who suffered from a low opinion of herself, partly because of overly critical parents, began seeing herself in a new way at adolescence. Through doing more things on her own and sharing with her friends, she began appreciating her good points and acquired a more positive view of herself. She even got to the point of being able to shrug off her parents' sarcastic remarks, much to her parents' amazement.

Body Image

One of the earliest and most important sources of self-perception is our body image. This is the way we see our body. It includes not only what we see reflected in the mirror, but also the way we experience our bodies. Seymour Fisher (1973) has pointed out that there is no more fascinating sight than the image of our own body reflected back at us from the mirror. We are attracted to it in a half-embarrassed but emotionally involved way. A photograph of ourselves usually arouses intense curiosity about "How do I look?"

Since the body has been identified in Western society with our animal nature, many people have difficulty accepting their bodies. They remain oblivious to its feelings and insensitive to its needs. Part of the reason may be our custom of concealing much of the body in clothing. Even without clothes, it is difficult to know what much of our body looks like without a mirror, much less feel it is an intimate part of "me." Adolescents in particular tend to be unhappy with their

It's important to feel good about the way you look. (Irene Springer)

bodies, with complaints about their physical appearance often topping their list of dissatisfactions. It is unusual to find teen-agers who don't feel they are too short or too tall, too fat or too thin, regardless of their actual physical appearance.

How acceptable our body image is depends partly on social and cultural influences. In American society, the ideal body varies somewhat for men and women. Generally, men aim to be tall and large, whereas women want to be slim with large breasts. The more nearly their bodily dimensions approximate the respective body ideals, the more readily individuals like their body image (Jourard & Landsman, 1980).

The meaning of body image also differs for each sex. Women are generally more concerned with attractiveness or the social appeal of their appearance. Men, however, emphasize physical competence or what they can do with their bodies as a means of influencing the environment (Lerner, Orlos, & Knapp, 1976). Although both sexes agree on the importance of many body characteristics, especially the general appearance and face, there are also some notable differences (see Table 5-1). Women generally rate the shape of the legs and hips more important than men do, whereas the men tend to place more importance on the neck and width of shoulders (Lerner & Karabenick, 1974).

What about those whose bodies differ markedly from the cultural ideal? Are they doomed to dislike their body image? Not necessarily. Normally, individuals modify the cultural ideal to accommodate the realities of their own body image, thus enhancing the probability of accepting their own bodies. The current trend toward appreciating each person's individuality and uniqueness also may help each of us feel good about our bodies.

The Ideal Self

This is the self I'd like to be, including my aspirations, moral ideals, and values.

According to the psychoanalytic view, we are not fully aware of our ideal self because we have acquired much of it through identifying with parental demands and prohibitions during the formative years of childhood. Accordingly, many of the "shoulds" and "should nots" of our conscience represent unconscious and unrealistic demands that may keep us from growing up. An example would be the perfectionistic student who feels he must make all As or he will not be a worthwhile person. I once knew a very competent but rigid graduate student who told all his friends that he would kill himself if he ever received a B in any of his courses. When he eventually made a B, he stopped short of taking his life, but he managed to make himself and everyone else around him miserable for months after that. Interestingly, many students who succeed in taking their lives make better than average grades but suffer from unrealistically high expectations of themselves.

Ordinarily, we think of having to change our self-image and behavior to

TABLE 5-1. THE IMPORTANCE OF SELECTED BODY CHARACTERISTICS FOR PHYSICAL ATTRACTIVENESS, BASED ON SELF-RATINGS OF COLLEGE STUDENTS

Body Characteristics	Female's Own Importance	Male's Own Importance
General appearance	1.3	1.5
Face	1.4	1.5
Facial complexion	1.6	1.8
Distribution of weight	1.7	2.0
Body build	1.7	1.9
Teeth	1.9	2.0
Eyes	1.9	2.4
Shape of legs	2.2	2.8
Hips	2.2	2.8
Hair texture	2.3	2.3
Waist	2.3	2.4
Chest	2.4	2.6
Nose	2.4	2.4
Mouth	2.4	2.4
Profile	2.5	2.3
Thighs	2.5	2.9
Height	2.9	2.7
Chin	3.1	2.8
Arms	3.1	3.0
Hair color	3.2	3.2
Neck	3.2	2.8
Width of shoulders	3.4	2.9
Ears	3.9	3.5
Ankles	4.1	4.2

R.M. Lerner and S.A. Karabenick, "Physical Attractiveness, Body Attitudes, and Self-concept in Late Adolescents," *Journal of Youth and Adolescence*, 3 (1974), 311.

Scores range between 1 (very important) and 5 (very unimportant).

conform more to our ideal self. Indeed, there is some evidence that our ideal self remains more consistent across time than our subjective self (Wylie, 1974). But when our aspirations prove to be excessive or unrealistic, it may be more appropriate for us to modify our ideal self as a way of furthering our growth and self-esteem. Fortunately, we tend to modify many of the dictates of our ideal self with experience so that they represent self-chosen values that express in a healthy, adult way what we expect of ourselves. Accordingly, our ideal self may serve as an incentive for us to do our best, as with the student who puts forth his or her best effort in hopes of entering medical school. But when we fail to live up to our ideal self, it is healthy to feel we have a choice either to redouble our efforts to achieve our aspirations or to modify them in the direction of more fruitful incentives.

CHARACTERISTICS OF THE SELF-CONCEPT

At this point, it should be clear that the overall self-concept, including our body image and ideal self, does not *do* anything—at least not directly. Instead, our self-concept is an acceptable self-awareness that we've accumulated about ourselves. Yet it exerts a powerful influence on everything we do as an active self. That is, our self-concept affects our actions indirectly, through its formative influence on us as causal agents.

Essentially, the self-concept functions as a filter through which everything we see or hear passes. In this way, the self-concept exerts a selective influence on our experience, so that we tend to perceive, judge, and even act in ways that will be consistent with our existing self-concept. Consequently, the self-concept exercises a circular, self-perpetuating influence on us, supporting the existing beliefs we have about ourselves. Let us now look in more detail at how this selective influence works.

Selective Perception

In Carl Rogers's view (1961), when we experience something consistent with both our direct, sensory reactions and our learned self-concept, then our experience tends to be accurately labeled (or "symbolized") and admitted fully into our conscious awareness. Such perceptions comprise the core of our self-concept and are visualized in Figure 5-1 by the shaded area where these two circles overlap. Experiences that are *not* consistent both with our sensory reactions and our self-concept are perceived more selectively. They are either distorted or denied to awareness.

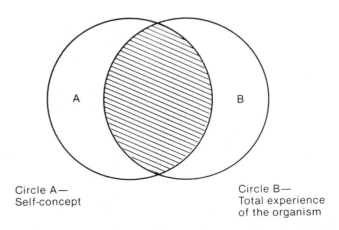

Circle A—
Self-concept

Circle B—
Total experience
of the organism

FIGURE 5-1. The interaction of the self-concept and the environment. From Carl R. Rogers, *Client-centered Therapy* (Boston: Houghton Mifflin, 1951), p. 526. Reprinted by permission of the publishers.

When we experience something that is consistent with our self-concept but is not confirmed by our own sensory reactions, we perceive and label such experiences in a distorted fashion, as if they were part of us. Such experiences are visualized by the area in Circle A outside the shaded area. They are primarily part of our learned self-concept. For example, suppose a girl influenced by the stereotyped sex-roles in our society believes herself to be inept in math. Each time she works with numbers, she indeed does poorly. But she readily assimilates such experiences of failure because they are consistent with her existing self-concept. Here the self-concept distorts her actual experience, so that she actually believes she is no good in math, even though that distorted perception of herself is not valid.

Some experiences that are not consistent with our learned self-concept are perceived as too threatening and are not even recognized as self-experiences. Consequently, they are not accurately perceived or labeled, but are denied to awareness, either in part or in whole. Here, denial is roughly comparable to the concept of repression in Freudian terms and refers to an unconscious exclusion of experience because of the threat associated with it. Such experiences are visualized in the diagram by the area in Circle B outside the shaded area.

Suppose a woman who believes she is no good at math is required to take two semesters of math as a part of her major studies. She may begin the course with a determination to do well, accompanied by a vague fear that she won't. At first she works hard and even discovers to her surprise that she enjoys the precision of mathematical thinking. Then she receives the grade on her first test. It's a 96! "Me doing well in math? How can this be? Maybe the instructor made a mistake in grading the papers. Maybe he likes me or feels sorry for me. It's probably dumb luck. It won't happen again." Like the rest of us, she will probably rely on a variety of such self-justifying mechanisms to make this experience acceptable to her existing self-concept. In doing so she also denies her actual experience of success, and thereby fails to discover her personal potential for math. In the final section of this chapter, we will take another look at how this same woman might change her self-concept to accommodate her newly discovered ability in math.

Self-esteem

Another way in which the self-concept affects our experience selectively is through our self-esteem. Essentially, *self-esteem* is the way we feel about ourselves, the extent to which we value or admire ourselves. It is the sense of personal worth we associate with our self-concept. Understandably, this varies from time to time, depending on all kinds of influences—such as achievements, treatment by others, and even body image, as explained in the boxed material on p. 114.

Psychologists say that we also have a *global esteem,* or a characteristic level of esteem that remains somewhat consistent from day to day. A major reason for this is that our esteem depends largely on the self-judgments we make in light of our ideal self, which remains rather consistent across time. Thus people with low esteem may continue to belittle themselves despite outward success, while people with high esteem may bounce back from outward failures with little time spent in blame or self-pity.

Self-esteem is related to so many aspects of life that it is difficult to make generalizations about cause and effect, though some evidence is suggestive. Such influences as social class, religion, ethnic group, and traumatic experiences in childhood are only weakly related to self-esteem (Coopersmith, 1967). One of the most important factors is the amount of parental attention and acceptance experienced in growing up. High-esteem individuals tend to come from homes in which the parents have expressed a great deal of acceptance and relied on democratic methods of child rearing. Low-esteem individuals usually have been exposed to more parental criticism and rejection, as well as to coercive methods of discipline (Graybill, 1978). Self-esteem is also influenced by a variety of other factors, including sex role. One study of women undergraduates at six prestigious colleges in the Northeast found that women generally had lower self-esteem and lower aspirations than men, even though their grades were about the same (Monteiro, 1978).

BODY IMAGE AND SELF-ESTEEM

A sample of 2,000 questionnaires on body image was drawn from over 62,000 *Psychology Today* readers for detailed analysis, with the resulting sample approximating the national population in regard to sex and age. The sample was evenly divided between men and women. About half the respondents were 24 years of age or younger, about one-fourth of them were between 25 and 44 years of age, and the rest were 45 years of age or older.

The results showed that for both sexes body image is strongly related to self-esteem. Only 11 percent of those with a below-average body image (compared to 50 percent of those with an above-average body image) had an above-average level of self-esteem. An examination of the links between satisfaction with the various body parts and self-esteem showed that for both sexes, the face makes the difference. People who are satisfied with their faces are more self-confident.

For males, the body part that had the second strongest impact on self-esteem was the chest; for females, the second most important factor was the mid-torso area, reflecting their worry about weight. Satisfaction with sex organs or torso was not significantly related to self-esteem for men or women. This provides further evidence that the importance of penis size and breast size is exaggerated in this society; the respondents paid little attention to size of sex organs. A woman's self-esteem relates to her feeling pretty and slim; a man's self-esteem relates to being handsome and having a muscular chest.

Most psychologists have overlooked the connection between body image and self-esteem. Obviously, body image is only one component of self-esteem; a person's assessment of his or her abilities and other attributes is equally important. Some respondents felt that other sources of self-esteem supersede the relevance of body image. Looks don't matter, runs this view, since I'm bright/talented/charming or whatever.

Of course, one trouble with survey findings is that we cannot determine cause and effect. A positive body image may increase a person's self-esteem. Or basic self-esteem may lead a person to feel good about his or her body. The readers themselves disagreed on what causes what.

Self-esteem—the general feeling that we are competent and confident—spills over into other areas of personality. Respondents who have above average positive body images also consider themselves to be more likable, assertive, conscientious, and even more intelligent than the "average person." For example, of those who rate their body images as above average, 69 percent also indicate that they're more likable than the average person, compared to 40 percent of those who rate their body images below average. People who are happy with their bodies may actually be more assertive and likable than those who have negative body images. Or at least they *think* they are.

In Comparison with the "Average" Person, Respondent Feels More	Body Image Is		
	Above Average	Average	Below Average
Likable	69	54	40
Intelligent	86	75	69
Assertive	60	45	30

Ellen Berscheid, Elaine Walster, and George Bohrnstedt, "The Happy American Body: A Survey Report," *Psychology Today*, November 1973, pp 119–123 and 126–131. Copyright © 1973 Ziff-Davis Publishing Company.

A Self-fulfilling Prophecy

Although our characteristic self-esteem changes somewhat with experience, it also tends to function in a circular fashion. That is, we tend to judge ourselves selectively in relation to our ideal self. Then we tend to act according to the way we feel about ourselves, so that our self-esteem serves as a kind of self-fulfilling prophecy. As a result, our achievements often reflect our self-esteem more than our actual abilities.

For example, in one study males of equal intelligence were selected from the lowest and highest fourth of their class. The high-achieving boys had consistently higher self-esteem than the boys of low achievement. As a result, the high achievers felt less anxious and defensive about criticism of their work and freer to pursue their own interests. But the low achievers felt more anxious and defensive about their work, as well as more inhibited in following their own interests (Coopersmith, 1967). Here, in the case of the low achievers, you can see how a person's existing self-esteem may outweigh intelligence, so that he or she achieves not what is possible but what is consistent with the poor self-image.

Persons with low esteem are also more prone to other difficulties, such as an unstable self-identity. For example, Rosenberg (1965) found that low-esteem persons were four times more likely than those with high esteem to have unstable self-images. Low-esteem individuals were also more likely to suffer from various psychosomatic symptoms, such as anxiety, nervousness, insomnia, headaches, nail biting, and heart palpitations (Howard and Kubis, 1964). Conversely, those with high esteem were much less likely to suffer from such symptoms (Rosenberg, 1965).

Our sense of self-worth also affects the way we relate to others. Not surprisingly, low-esteem persons tend to feel awkward and uneasy in social situations and will go to any lengths to avoid embarrassment. They are so in need of approval that they are more inclined to like someone who is accepting and affectionate than a person of higher esteem would be. As a result, low-esteem people tend to be more easily persuaded and prone to conformity (Aronson, 1980). Yet such people also have more difficulty in accepting the affection they crave. It appears that even though you don't like yourself, you still expect others to treat you accordingly, as if to verify your negative self-concept (Jacobs, Berscheid, & Walster, 1971).

At times, people of low esteem may become quite popular with others. But such popularity has been found to be more positively related to behavioral signs of self-assurance, such as confidence and forthrightness, than to favorable self-attitudes (Coopersmith, 1967). It seems that low-esteem persons are so in need of approval that they more readily accommodate themselves to the needs of others to gain acceptance. But inwardly they dislike themselves for giving in to others too much.

Interestingly enough, people of high esteem tend to perceive themselves as even more popular than persons of low esteem (Kimble & Helmreich, 1972). But the high-esteem person displays a need for social approval for different reasons. If you like yourself, you naturally tend to expect others to do likewise. You'll be disappointed if they don't, but chances are you will not be crushed. In other words, in the case of high-esteem people, popularity tends to reflect self-acceptance, while for low-esteem people, it tends to be more of a compensatory social acceptance gained at the price of self-acceptance.

To sum up, self-concept affects behavior indirectly by providing a filter of acceptable self-awareness through which we see or hear everything we experience. As such, the self-concept characteristically fosters selective perception and circular, self-perpetuating tendencies on our part, so that we tend to think and act in ways consistent with our existing beliefs about ourselves. In this way our self-concept provides us with a stable sense of personal identity. But it does so at a price—namely, our tendency to resist changes in our self-perception, even when those changes would be to our advantage.

SELF AND SOCIAL INFLUENCE

So far we've described the self-concept in terms of its characteristic self-perpetuating tendencies, sometimes called its *central tendencies*. From such a description you may have the impression that self-concept doesn't change very much. Unfortunately, that's how psychologists have tended to view the self-concept too, and it's partly true. But it's not the whole story.

Just think for a minute. How many people do you know who are highly consistent in their behavior? Probably not many, and they may not even be the healthiest people. Actually, few if any of us attain the degree of self-consistency deemed so desirable by psychologists. Parents make conflicting demands, and the lessons of early life are more chaotic than consistent. Consequently, all of us have a fair degree of inconsistency in our make-up. But that doesn't necessarily make us neurotic. Fortunately, today more psychologists are recognizing that inconsistency has a positive value too. In fact, inconsistency in our self-concept is not only inevitable, but may be desirable for coping with a many-sided world such as ours. For inconsistency implies that our self-concept may be more flexible and changeable than we've realized.

Our Social Selves

Much of the inconsistency in our self-make-up derives from our experience as "social animals," as Aristotle once put it. Each time we meet another person, we're influenced by that person's attitudes and behavior toward us. As a result, we tend to modify our behavior to be accepted, and in the process we alter our self-perceptions as well. From what we've said about the self-perpetuating tendencies of the self-concept, it's obvious that we don't change everything about ourselves. What we change are those self-perceptions most accessible to social influences, or our social selves. These include all those self-perceptions organized around our social roles (or what others expect of us), as well as how others treat us.

"A man has as many different social selves as there are distinct groups of persons about whose opinion he cares," said William James (1890). Indeed, it is more appropriate to use the plural term *selves*. Unlike the central core of self-perceptions, which are more resistant to change, our social selves are more flexible and change more readily. In fact, the ease with which our social selves are influenced by a particular situation probably accounts for the widely varied findings in different research studies on the self-concept.

On the positive side, our capacity to have many social selves encourages us to develop different facets of our potential. Each time you try a new leisure activity or job or acquire a new friend, you are satisfying different needs and interests. For example, look at one man's description of his interests and experience: "Active in dancing, guitar playing, scuba diving, tennis, and local

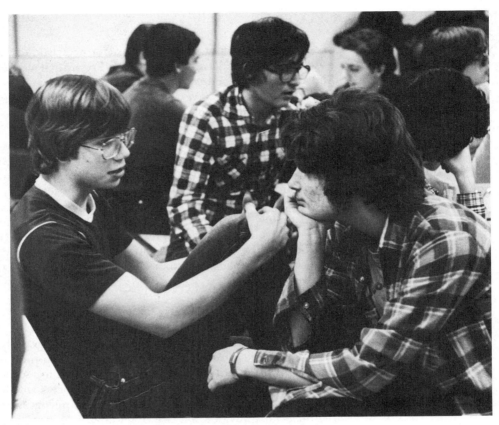

Each friend brings out a different part of us. (Ken Karp)

historical society. Past experience in teaching, oceanography, and mental hospital work." Does this sound like a wishy-washy dabbler? Actually, it's the description of a highly reputable clinical psychologist who discovered his life's work partly through trying these different activities. Occasionally someone will say, "I like so many different kinds of people, they wouldn't mix well if they met in one room." Perhaps you've felt like this. Do you also realize that each of them brings out a slightly different aspect of yourself, making you a richer and more interesting person?

Sometimes, however, we engage in so many different roles that we may wonder who we really are. This is the negative side of our multiple selves and does represent a threat to our personal identity. It's a problem for everyone who lives in a pluralistic society, and it's especially acute for adolescents in the process of redefining their roles. An adolescent's parents expect one thing, friends another, and teachers and employers still another. Trying to please them all may lead to a certain amount of identity confusion. Although there are wide variations among individuals, this tendency toward identity confusion tends to peak in the middle of the adolescent years (Horrocks, 1976). Usually, the decisions adolescents make about college, jobs, and marriage tend to crystallize their sense of personal identity somewhat, so that they are less plagued by identity confusion as they grow up. But in a complex, rapidly changing society such as ours, we all experience a certain degree of uncertainty about our identity throughout our lives as a reflection of our culture and time.

Changing Our Social Selves

So far we've been describing our social selves as a function of the give-and-take of everyday life. But how about the possibilities for changing our social selves by manipulating social influences? The relative ease with which this can be done has been illustrated in a number of experimental studies.

THE CHANGEABLE SELF

There is some evidence that rapid technological and social change affects the fundamental way we perceive and understand ourselves. At least this is what Louis Zurcher found in his study using the Kuhn and McPartland Twenty Statements test. In this open-ended, relatively unstructured procedure, each student is asked to answer the question "Who am I?" twenty times. The answers are then scored according to several basic categories.

During the 1950s, Zurcher found that students gave answers that predominantly identified their selves with a social role or institutional status. For example, students tended to define themselves by saying, "I am a student," "I am a female," or "I am an American." Such responses indicated that their personal identity was largely a social identity, closely linked with existing social roles and institutions. The prevalence of such statements in the 1950s reflected the relatively stable and widely accepted social order of that time.

During the 1970s, however, Zurcher discovered that students tended to give a different type of response. Now the prevalent responses reflected a self-concept *not* closely identified with social roles or institutions. For example, students tended to describe themselves in more personal statements, such as "I am happy," "I am searching," or "I am a frustrated person." Such statements reflected a self-concept based more on personal characteristics and relatively "situation-free," compared to the typical self-concept of the 1950s. The prevalence of such statements has been interpreted as a sign that contemporary students are more at home with constant change and may sometimes deliberately seek change.

Zurcher suggests that such a changeable or mutable self may be a more functional mode of self-concept for coping with the accelerated change in our contemporary society.

Louis A. Zurcher, Jr., *The Mutable Self* (Beverly Hills, Ca.: Sage Publications, 1977), Chap. 2.

In one study, for example, a clinical trainee interviewed female college students. After asking each student a variety of questions about her background, the interviewer asked 60 questions about how each woman saw herself. Each time a student gave a positive self-evaluation, the interviewer expressed subtle signs of approval, such as smiling and occasionally agreeing verbally. Each time a student gave a negative self-evaluation, the interviewer disapproved by shaking her head, frowning, or verbally disagreeing. As a result, the students' self-evaluations became more positive—significantly more than those in the control group, who received no feedback. These and other studies have shown how self-concept can be significantly altered by substituting persons of different status, sex, or behavior for the influential others in the environment (Gergen, 1971, 1972).

The realization that our self-concept is affected by social influences heightens the importance of the choices we make. Once we have chosen a school, a job, or friends, we're shaped in turn by the people associated with our choice. Are there people and circumstances that discourage or stifle us? We should avoid them when possible. Are there others that bring out the best in us and help us to grow and actualize ourselves? Perhaps we should seek them out more often. In both instances, we can change our self-concept by modifying the social influences that affect us. It would be foolish to think we can change everything about ourselves in this way. But it's a reminder that there are more possibilities for change and growth than we may be utilizing.

CHANGES IN THE SELF-CONCEPT

The images we have of ourselves change to some extent during the normal course of everyday living. In some instances, more positive self-images may come from deliberate efforts at change—such as education, growth groups, and psychotherapy. In other instances, our self-concept changes as a byproduct of our achievements or interaction with friends. Or, as we pointed out in the section on social selves, we may begin acting in a new way and find that it changes our beliefs about ourselves as well. Carol Tavris (1982) points out the irony that self-improvement is like happiness in that it is often found in the course of looking for something else. Completing a degree, finding a new job, or deepening a friendship may bring unforeseen changes in our self-confidence as well.

The Search for Self-identity

Changes in self-image are especially apparent during the physical changes of puberty and the subsequent search for self-identity. According to Erik Erikson (1968), the main task of adolescence is the achievement of a sense of personal identity based on physical and sexual maturity. Identity here refers not just to personal uniqueness, but also to the degree of consistency within our self-concept, such as the unity of our personal self and social roles, past and present identities, and so forth.

A series of interviews with high school and college students showed a definite tendency for them to see themselves as more distinct individuals as they got older. But they also saw a definite connection between what they had been in the past and what they were in the present, with a slightly weaker relationship to what they expected to become in the future. At least a third of them perceived their selves as having an "unchanging core" (Guardo & Bohan, 1973).

People's success in achieving a sense of identity may be seen in the commitments they have made, especially in terms of a vocation and friends. We can distinguish four different statuses of identity and achievement, from the most to the least successful: (1) *identity achievement* refers to those who have resolved their identity crisis and have made definite commitments, such as the woman who has entered law school and is planning to get married soon; (2) *moratorium status* can be seen in those who are actively struggling to find out who they are but have been delayed in their search, such as the young man who just has switched from a pre-med to an engineering major because he likes his engineering studies better; (3) *foreclosure status* includes those who make premature commitments without much real thought or struggle on their part, such as the young man who goes into his father's business and marries his childhood girlfriend; (4) *identity diffusion* status includes those who haven't really faced up to the search for identity, such as the drifters or the perennial playboys or playgirls (Marcia, 1966). Following the disenchantment of the 1960s, Orlofsky and others (1973) identified a fifth category—*alienated achievement;* people in this category are relatively healthy individuals who are actively engaged in finding their place in society, but who remain uncommitted to conventional occupations and lifestyles.

Of course, individuals may change their identity status with experience and personal growth. For example, Waterman and Waterman (1971) found that 75 percent of students in their first year of college changed their identity status either in terms of their vocation or preferred groups, implying that high school identities are highly tentative. By the senior year of college, more students were found in the achievement status, with fewer still struggling to make a vocational choice (moratorium) and fewer holding unexamined values (foreclosures). Even then, 16 percent of the seniors were seen as identity diffusers, suggesting that the college environment doesn't necessarily help everyone to find himself or herself (Waterman, Geary, & Waterman, 1974).

Individuals who have achieved a sense of identity tend to score high on measures of ego identity and have a sense of self-esteem that is less vulnerable to negative evaluation by others. In contrast, foreclosures tend to be highly dependent and vulnerable to negative influence from others. Those identified as moratoriums generally exhibit the highest levels of anxiety, giving evidence of an active struggle to define themselves. Identity diffusers tend to be disorganized and drifting, though they are not necessarily sick in a clinical sense (Marcia, 1966).

Another condition that facilitates favorable changes in our self-concept is understanding and acceptance from others. Carl Rogers points out that the more empathetically we are understood and the more unconditionally we are accepted, the freer we are to explore and revise our self-concept (1961). Although Rogers's description of how individuals change their self-concepts is drawn from his extensive experience in client-centered psychotherapy, it applies to some extent to personal growth in any context—whether in friendship, marriage, career, or therapy. Generally, people move away from other-directedness and characteristics they dislike about themselves toward more self-direction and greater self-acceptance.

Away from Other-directedness

This is characteristic mostly of the early stages of self-revision. Through years of dependency and socialization, each of us has acquired many perceptions of ourselves that we actually dislike. Yet because of social pressure and the desire to be accepted, we often continue to be the same. This results in a certain degree of self-alienation. As a result, the early stages of revising our self-concept are characterized by increasing awareness and dissatisfaction with those aspects of ourselves we dislike. This may help to explain the characteristic negativism of early adolescence and the prevalence of complaints and self-disparagement so often seen in the early stages of psychotherapy.

For example, one woman reported that she had always felt she had to be good to satisfy her father. She told her therapist how hard she had tried to earn her father's acceptance, and how discouraging it had been. Even though she tried meeting his demands, each time he would make another, and another. It became a sort of endless demand. In the process she had become overly submissive and false to her own desires. She had not really wanted

to be that kind of person. I find it's not a good way to be, but yet I think I've had a sort of belief that that's the way you have *to be if you intend to be thought a lot of and loved. And yet who would* want *to love somebody who was that sort of wishy-washy person. . . . At least I wouldn't want to be loved by the kind of person who'd love a door mat!* (Rogers, 1961)

The disdain in her voice as well as in her words made it clear to her therapist that this person had already begun moving away from a self that had been designed to please other people.

Toward Greater Self-direction

Self-direction characterizes the more positive stages of revising your self-concept. At this stage, you take greater responsibility for yourself and decide what activities and behaviors are meaningful for you and which are not. As strange as it sounds, such autonomy is a bit frightening, and clients in therapy move toward it rather cautiously at first. They say things like, "I feel vulnerable," or "I'm not sure I'm doing the right thing." More often than not they also feel new sources of strength surging up from within—a sobering but exciting experience. They do not always make sound choices. But by learning to live with the consequences of their decisions rather than blaming somebody else, they grow in their ability to direct their own lives.

An increasing trust in yourself is an integral part of greater self-direction. Like an artist who has only an intuitive sense of what he or she wants to create, a person growing in autonomy learns to become more resourceful and self-reliant. This doesn't mean just doing things independently. It also means being able to absorb criticism and rejection without devastation because you believe in yourself. Trusting yourself also means that you approach your future with confidence, even though you don't profess to know the "answer" at the moment.

Time and again in my clients, I have seen simple people become significant and creative in their own spheres, as they have developed more trust of the processes going on within themselves, and have dared to feel their own feelings, live by values which they discover within, and express themselves in their own unique ways (Rogers, 1961).

Greater self-acceptance involves more openness to your own experience as well as greater congruence between your self-concept and ideal self. As clients progress in the kind of *client-centered therapy* Rogers describes, they become more aware of and comfortable with the complexity of their feelings and needs, including conflicting desires. They may feel anger and love toward the same person. Or they may feel excited but fearful about moving to another job. But realizing that overall experience and self-concepts are inherently complex and changing, they learn to feel more at home with themselves in spite of these conflicts.

The growth of self-acceptance includes greater congruence between self-concept and actual experience. For example, remember the young woman we spoke of earlier who continued to believe she was no good in math despite her improved performance? Let's say she finishes both math courses with As and gets a job working with computers. If she continues to grow in self-acceptance, chances are that she will eventually see herself more positively, in a way that more accurately reflects her real ability in math.

One of the surest signs of self-acceptance is greater openness and acceptance of others. "As a client moves toward being able to accept his own experience, he also moves toward the acceptance of the experience of others. He values and appreciates both his own experience and that of others for what it is" (Rogers, 1961, p. 174). In the company of such people, others also tend to feel more comfortable and freer to be themselves.

As you can see, changing your self-concept may be unsettling at times. It involves moving away from some of the familiar self-images acquired in your formative years. It also involves perceiving yourself in new and different ways, especially as a self-directed person. There is no detailed guide to assure that you are doing the right thing. Familiarity with the general pattern of personal growth, as suggested in the preceding pages, may be helpful. Feedback from others may serve as a useful mirror. Increased self-awareness also may be helpful up to a point. But it is optimal rather than constant or excessive self-awareness that is desirable. Most important of all, learn to trust *yourself*. Be open to your own experience.

SUMMARY

The self-concept consists of all of our perceptions of "I" and "me" together with the feelings, values, and beliefs associated with them. Although it is arbitrary how many different selves we care to distinguish within the self-concept, we specifically discussed the subjective self, body image, ideal self, and the social self.

Once formed, the self-concept functions as a filter that exerts a circular, self-perpetuating influence on our experience. We perceive ourselves and the world around us selectively, so that much of our experience is distorted to fit our self-concept or denied to awareness because it is too threatening to our self-concept. Our sense of self-esteem or self-worth also tends to function in this circular way, predisposing us to act and judge ourselves in ways consistent with our self-concept—as a self-fulfilling prophecy.

In addition to the stable core of the self, our overall self-concept includes many self-images organized around our social roles and interactions with others, or our social selves. Experimental studies suggest that by altering the social influences that shape our social selves, we may also change our self-concept to a greater extent than previously realized.

Our self-concepts also change as a normal part of growing up. Such changes are especially evident during the physical changes of puberty and the search for self-identity throughout adolescence. Progressive gains in identity achievement during these years are usually accompanied by a more stable and positive self-image.

Other changes in our self-concept demand more deliberate, self-conscious efforts, such as those experienced in psychotherapy. According to Carl Rogers, individuals experiencing personal growth tend to modify their self-concepts away from blindly pleasing and conforming to others, toward greater self-direction, self-trust, and self-acceptance. Although such changes may be unsettling at times, they are often necessary as a part of acquiring greater independence and self-fulfillment.

QUESTIONS FOR SELF-REFLECTION

1. What words would you use to describe your self-image?
2. How would you characterize your ideal self?
3. How do you feel about your body image?
4. Do your achievements sometimes reflect your self-esteem more than your abilities?
5. Has your social self changed in the past several years? If so, in what ways?
6. Which of Erikson's identity statuses—achievement, moratorium, foreclosure, or confusion—best characterizes your own search for self-identity during the high school and college years?
7. How would you rate your characteristic self-esteem?
8. Would you agree that the greater your self-acceptance, the more you can accept others?
9. In what ways, if any, are you still dependent on the approval of others?
10. To what extent have you become a self-directed person?

EXERCISES

1. An exercise in self-awareness

When people unexpectedly see themselves in a mirror, they often fail to recognize themselves. Or they become critical of what they see. It's as if they have little awareness of themselves as they really are.

Select a place where you have privacy and try the following exercises. Stand in front of a full-length mirror and observe yourself for a few minutes. What do you notice most? Is your posture relaxed or tense? What about your face? Are you frowning or smiling? Do you notice anything about your physical presence you are not ordinarily aware of?

You might also read or speak into a tape recorder for a few minutes. Do you like what you hear? Does listening to yourself make you more aware of how you sound?

You can also ask yourself these same questions while looking at old photographs of yourself or reading a letter or paper you've written some time ago.

Many people avoid things like mirrors and tape recorders or seeing their own pictures because they feel it makes them more self-critical. Did you find this so? Or did your increased self-awareness also make you aware of your good points? Why do you think increased self-awareness often leads to self-criticism?

2. Seeing yourself as others see you

It's common knowledge that others perceive us differently than we perceive ourselves. Sometimes we would rather not know what others think about us for fear it will be critical. Yet feedback from others often confirms our strengths as well as our weaknesses.

Take an $8^{1}/_{2} \times 11$ sheet of paper and label two columns with the words *Strengths* and *Weaknesses*. Then jot down phrases that you think represent your main strengths and weaknesses, listing an equal number of each. Try to be as honest as you can about both.

Ask several of your friends to do the same thing on the basis of how they see you. Try to select individuals who know you fairly well, but are not so close they would have difficulty taking part in this exercise. Then compare lists. How much agreement do you find? Is there more agreement regarding your strengths or weaknesses? Were there any surprises?

3. Body image and self-esteem

Reread the boxed material on the relationship between body image and self-esteem. Then apply the material to yourself.

In regard to how you feel about your body, how would you estimate your own body image—above average, average, or below average? How would you estimate your self-esteem—above average, average, or below average?

When you compare your body-image and self-esteem ratings, are they about the same? Or is one higher than the other? If so, which one? Does your body image help raise your self-esteem, or is it the other way around?

Do you agree that your feelings about your face are the most important part of accepting your body? If you are a male, do you consider your chest the next most important part of your body? If you are a female, do you consider your mid-torso area the next most important part of your body? Or are you also concerned about other parts of your body peculiar to your own physical appearance?

It has been observed that physical appearance tends to be more important for self-esteem among females than males. If you compare your answers with others in the class, is there any evidence for this? Or do you think this difference is becoming less important today?

4. Identifying your social selves

This exercise is based on William James's observation that we have as many different social selves as there are people whose opinion we care about.

Select five or six people you associate with regularly. Then try to identify which aspects of yourself are most readily expressed when you're with these people. As you write the name of each person on a piece of paper, jot down some of the activities you do with that person, the interests shared, and some of your feelings and attitudes toward the person. For example, a handyman once admitted, "I just dread going to that man's house because he always wants something I can't do." It seems the man referred to was an overly demanding, manipulative person who made others feel inferior.

Do you find that you feel and behave a bit differently with different people? How free do you feel with the people you selected? Do some of them make you feel you must live up to their expectations? Are there others who make you feel comfortable enough to be yourself? How do you think you influence others?

5. Your ideal self

How would you characterize your ideal self? Can you identify some of the "shoulds" and "should nots" you've acquired from your family? How about those values you have chosen for your own ideals? Write down some of your dominant values. What values do you hold as a result of identifying with teachers, mentors, or heroes? What kind of person are you striving to become? Jot down some of the traits that best characterize your ideal self.

Are you aware of any perfectionistic tendencies in yourself? Do you feel that everything must be "just right"? Do you find yourself expending more energy than is warranted in accomplishing tasks? Remember that perfectionism differs from a genuine desire for mastery and achievement in that perfectionism derives from self-belittlement, so that despite your accomplishments you constantly feel "I am not good enough. I must do better." Are you bothered by this feeling? Or can you genuinely enjoy your accomplishments despite certain imperfections?

While much of the improvement in self-esteem comes from changing our self-images to conform to our ideal self, we also need to modify unrealistic aspects of our ideal self as well.

6. Measuring the correlation between your self-concept and ideal self[1]

One of the key points in the self theory of Carl Rogers is that well-adjusted people have a self-image that corresponds rather closely to reality. That is, they tend to see themselves as they really are. Maladjusted people, on the other hand, have images of themselves that do not match their true feelings and the actual nature of their experiences.

It has also been found that normal people are reasonably satisfied with themselves; there is a fairly close correspondence between their self-images and their ideal images.

---

[1]This exercise is based on material from the Study Guide with Programmed Units and Learning Objectives to accompany Kagan and Havemann's *Psychology: An Introduction*, 3rd ed., by Robert B. McCall and Ernest Havemann. © 1976 by Harcourt Brace Jovanovich, Inc. Reprinted by permission of the publishers.

People with personality problems, on the other hand, tend to show little or no similarity between what they think they are and what they would like to be. In other words, they tend to be quite dissatisfied with their images of themselves.

In this connection, you can perform an informal experiment that will give you at least a rough idea of the relationship between what you think you are and what you would like to be.[2] Reproduce the items below and cut them into the sixteen rectangles indicated by the lines. Shuffle them, put them on a desk or table in random order, and then arrange them in a line from left to right. At the extreme left, place the statement that you think

I usually manage to stay even tempered. A	I consider myself a leader. I
I spend too much time daydreaming. B	I am a shy person. J
I am a very likable person. C	I am physically attractive. K
I have to admit that I am rather selfish. D	I often feel blue and discouraged. L
I can work as hard as anybody when I want to. E	I am more intelligent than most people. M
I have a hard time standing up for myself. F	I worry about what other people think of me. N
Nothing frightens me. G	I have a good sense of humor. O
I often feel tense around other people. H	I wouldn't be above cheating. P

[2]This exercise is based on J. M. Butler and G. V. Haigh, "Changes in the Relation between Self-concepts and Ideal Concepts Consequent upon Client-centered Counseling, in C. R. Rogers, and R. F. Dymond, eds., *Psychotherapy and Personality Change: Coordinated Studies in the Client-centered Approach* (Chicago: University of Chicago Press, 1954), pp. 55–76.

describes you best. At the extreme right, place the statement that you think is most untrue about you. In between, arrange the remaining cards in the order ranging from most true to least true. When you have finished, use Table 5-2 to write down the order of the cards as you have arranged them, from 1 at the extreme left to 16 at the extreme right; do this under "Rank on list 1."

Next reshuffle the cards, place them in front of you again, and this time arrange them in an order that best describes not what you are but what you would like to be. Put the statement that you wish were most true of you at the extreme left, the one you wish

TABLE 5-2

Card	Rank on List 1	Rank on List 2	Difference in Rank	Difference Squared
A				
B				
C				
D				
E				
F				
G				
H				
I				
J				
K				
L				
M				
N				
O				
P				
Total of differences				
Total of squared differences				

$$\text{Correlation coefficient} = 1 - \frac{(\text{Total of squared differences})}{680} = \underline{\qquad}$$

were least true of you at the extreme right. When you have completed this pattern of what you would like to be, use Table 5-2 to write down the order of the cards as you have arranged them under "Rank on list 2."

For a rough measure of how your self-image differs from your ideal image, note the difference in the rank of each card from list 1 to list 2, disregarding whether it ranked higher on list 1 or list 2. For example if card A was 6 on list 1 and 8 on list 2, the difference is 2; if card A was 8 on list 1 and 6 on list 2, the difference is also 2. Total the differences. The smaller the total, the greater is the correspondence between what you think you are and what you would like to be.

The average person usually shows a total difference of between about 50 and 60. A difference as low as 35 shows a rather rare correspondence between self-image and ideal image. A score of more than 75 indicates a rather low correspondence. However, if you score 75 or even higher, do not leap to the conclusion that you are suffering from a personality problem. On a short and informal test such as this, many factors can influence the result. The exercise is designed only to cast some light on the Rogers theory, not to diagnose personality.

By doing a little further arithmetic, you can get a more accurate measure. For each card, square the number found in the column showing difference in rank, and enter the square in the column called "Difference squared." Then total the numbers you have just placed in this column. Divide the total by 680, and subtract the answer from 1.

What you have just done is compute a *coefficient of correlation,* which is a statistical measure of the relationship between two factors. In the study on which this exercise is based, the correlation between self-image and ideal image for subjects who had never sought psychotherapy was .58. For subjects who were seeking treatment for personality problems, the correlation was zero, but it rose to .34 after they received psychotherapy. However, the original study and this informal exercise differ in important ways, and the results are not completely comparable. Moreover, it must again be pointed out that the experiment is not intended as a diagnosis of personality, and a zero or even a minus correlation is not to be considered alarming.

RECOMMENDED READINGS

Fisher, S. *Body Consciousness.* Englewood Cliffs, N.J.: Prentice-Hall, 1973 (paperback). A brief but informed view of the role body feelings play in the development of our personalities, written by a leading researcher in the field.

Gergen, K. J. *The Concept of Self.* New York: Holt, Rinehart and Winston, 1971 (paperback). An overview of research and theory on the self-concept in nontechnical terms. A very good introduction to the subject.

Hamacheck, D. E. *Encounters with the Self,* 2nd ed. New York: Holt, Rinehart and Winston, 1978 (paperback). A collection of readings on the self as experienced in growth and learning.

Prather, H. *Notes to Myself.* Lafayette, Ca.: Real People Press, 1970. A personal diary showing how one man maintains his self-concept from day to day.

Rogers, C. R. *On Becoming A Person.* Boston: Houghton Mifflin, 1961 (paperback). One of Rogers's best-known works on the meaning and process of self-discovery.

Schaffer, K. F. *Sex-Role Issues in Mental Health.* Reading, Mass.: Addison-Wesley, 1980 (paperback). An overview of sex-role issues in the areas of family, career, achievement, therapy, and social issues.

Zurcher, L. A. *The Mutable Self.* Beverly Hills, Ca.: Sage, 1977 (paperback). Explains how our personal identity and self-concept are affected by life in a rapidly changing society.

Interpersonal Relationships

6

UNDERSTANDING RELATIONSHIPS
  social or fair-exchange model
  transactional analysis model

BEGINNING RELATIONSHIPS
  impression formation
  interpersonal attraction

ROLE RELATIONSHIPS
  role model
  role adequacy and conflict
  authenticity in role relationships

INTIMATE, PERSONAL RELATIONSHIPS
  mutual self-disclosure
  personal compatibility
  mutual accommodation

INTIMACY AND GROWTH

SUMMARY

"No man is an Island, entire of itself," wrote John Donne. Instead, we are deeply affected by other people. Without them we are overwhelmed with feelings of desolation, as reported by solitary prisoners and shipwrecked sailors. With them even the frustrations and sorrows of life become more bearable. It is in our moments of intimacy with others that we come to feel most at home in the world.

There are times when our relationships with others get us down. Other people annoy us, they disappoint us, and sometimes they betray us. Yet, no matter to what lengths we go to avoid them, whether living like a hermit or working with "things," the big problems in life inevitably turn out to be people problems. And conversely, some of life's greatest satisfactions stem from our relationships with friends and lovers. It probably comes as no surprise that young people and adults alike consistently put the importance of personal relationships at the top of their values (Bachman & Johnston, 1979).

We will begin by taking a look at some of the different ways of understanding relationships. Then most of the chapter will deal with the three different levels of relationships according to personal involvement: beginning relationships, role relationships, and intimate relationships.

UNDERSTANDING RELATIONSHIPS

We do not relate to people in a vacuum. Instead, we approach each other with certain expectations and associations acquired from past experience. One of the things we learn is that there are different ways of relating to others, such as a business-like exchange with a sales clerk or a more intimate sharing of ourselves with a friend. Psychologists contend that there are fundamentally different ways of understanding the meaning of human relationships, sometimes referred to as *models of interpersonal relationships*. We will explore two of these models in the following pages: the social or fair-exchange model and the transactional analysis model. In a later section we will also take a look at the role model. While none of these models will explain all our relationships, awareness of them may help us become more aware of the varying meanings and implications of everyday relationships.

Social or Fair-exchange Model

According to this model, the purpose of interpersonal relationships is the mutual satisfaction of needs. Proponents of this view refer to it in terms of *exchange theory* (Thibaut & Kelley, 1959), *reciprocity theory* (Altman & Taylor, 1973), or *equity theory* (Walster, Berscheid, & Walster, 1973). Whatever the label, you will notice the similarity to economic theory. Initially, people tend to react negatively to the idea of comparing human relationships to economic transactions. But Erich Fromm says, "While a great deal of lip service is paid to the religious ideal of love of one's neighbor, our relations are actually determined, at their best, by the principle of *fairness*" (1956, p. 129). That is, we tend to relate to others in such a way that each of us will receive a fair exchange of what we put into a relationship and what we get out of it. Some of the key terms in this approach are described in the following paragraphs.

REWARDS.   A reward is any and all gains from a relationship that have positive value. Rewards range from rather obvious benefits like food, sex, or money to the more complex ones like recognition and approval. Understandably, what one person finds rewarding, another may not, so that there are wide individual differences as to what constitutes a reward. Also the reward value of a given behavior may change over time. For example, a complimentary remark provides more reward to a beginning guitarist than to a professional.

COSTS.   Any loss incurred in a relationship that has negative value is called a cost. This may consist of the degree of emotional investment or the amount of time and energy it takes to keep up a relationship. Or it may take the form of disappointment in the other's response. Like rewards, what constitutes a cost depends on many factors, such as the individual, the time, and the overall context of a relationship. From time to time we may let a promising relationship with another person drop because it demands too much to keep up.

THE DIFFERENCE BETWEEN REWARDS AND COSTS. When the rewards of a relationship outweigh the costs incurred, we may speak of a relationship as being very rewarding. When the costs outweigh the rewards, then we may refer to a relationship as being unfair. According to this view, we attempt to get out of unfair relationships, such as those with a friend who is always taking advantage of us or an employer who expects too much from us. Each of us seeks to maximize our rewards and minimize our losses, although the principle of fair exchange implies that we also accommodate ourselves to others. The result is that we often seek to do things that are mutually satisfying to both partners. Naturally, what constitutes a reward, a cost, or a fair exchange depends on many subjective influences as well as objective factors.

As in economic theory, we must also keep an eye on the marketplace as a whole. That is, the availability of competing relationships must be kept in mind. If an outside partner offers you more satisfactions with less demands on you than your current "steady," then such a person poses a real threat to your present relationship. In this way, the fair-exchange approach may explain why many satisfying relationships break up because an even more satisfying one is available at less cost. It may also help to explain why many *un*satisfying relationships continue because the individuals fail to see a more promising partner on the horizon.

Transactional Analysis Model

Game theory provides still another model of relationships. According to this view, relationships are best understood as a combination of inner *ego states* and external *transactions*. Major proponents of this view, such as Berne (1964) and Harris (1967), hold that most of our relationships consist of game-type transactions that prevent the more desirable experience of intimacy. Let's briefly examine three of the main concepts of this view; ego states, transactions, and games.

An *ego state* is a concept we use to describe a coherent system of inner feelings and perceptions that are manifested in related behavior patterns. It can be detected in words, voice inflection, facial expressions, bodily gestures, and posture. Individual personality is understood in terms of three such states: Child, Parent, and Adult.

The *Child ego state* comprises all the desires and feelings that come naturally to most of us, with a further distinction between the natural Child and the adaptive or socialized Child state.

The *Parent ego state* consists of all those perceptions, attitudes, and behavior patterns we take in from outside sources while growing up, especially from our parents. The nurturing Parent inclines us toward encouraging and supportive behavior, while the critical Parent tends toward controlling repressive behavior.

The *Adult ego state* includes mostly the rational, reality-oriented processes by which we use information from all sources to regulate our behavior. Although the Adult state would appear to be the most socially desirable, all three ego states are essential. The functioning of a given ego state becomes undesirable only inasmuch as it disturbs the healthy balance of the whole personality—for example, if it dominates and restricts a relationship.

A *transaction* is an exchange between individuals that involves a stimulus and a response between specific ego states of those individuals. Transactions may be

THE YES, BUT GAME

This is a common game in which one person presents a problem and then proceeds to shoot down all suggestions offered. Although the transactions may appear to be between the Adult ego states (shown in the solid lines below), there is also an ulterior transaction between the Child of the sender and the Parent of the responder (broken lines).

A Person who plays YES, BUT does so to maintain the position that "authorities aren't going to tell me anything" or "parents are stupid." Such a person may have had parents who tried to supply all the answers or never gave any, resulting in the child's reaction against receiving answers from others. In this case, the Child of the sender attempts to gain the upper hand over the Parent of the responder by rejecting all suggestions. The game is likely to be YES, BUT if a leader asks the group how to proceed and then rejects all proposals, or if a friend asks your help with a problem and then rejects all your suggestions.

If you think you're unwittingly becoming involved in a game of YES, BUT, you can decline to play by not offering suggestions. Instead, keep to your Adult state by saying something like, "Well, it looks like none of my ideas are acceptable, so I guess I can't be helpful to you." After all, it takes two to play a game.

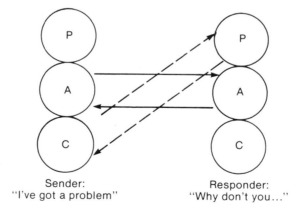

Sender:
"I've got a problem"

Responder:
"Why don't you..."

YES, BUT...

From Dorothy Jongeward and Muriel James, *Winning with People* (Reading, Mass.: Addison-Wesley, 1973), p. 75. Reprinted with the permission of the publishers.

complimentary, crossed, or *ulterior.* When only two ego states are involved, one from each person, the transaction lines are parallel, and communication usually proceeds smoothly. However, when the lines of communication between ego states are crossed or not parallel, a breakdown in communication may result. Ulterior transactions involve communication between two or more ego states at the same time, involving hidden payoffs in addition to the exchange apparent on the surface.

While there are several different types of transactions—ranging from the rituals of "Hello, how are you?" to the more complicated activities of school, work, or family—most of our relationships consist of game-type transactions. A *game* is essentially a relationship with ulterior transactions resulting in a hidden payoff for both parties. Although the term *game* implies an element of calculation, most games are played with little or no awareness of the dynamics involved. Moreover, games are not necessarily undesirable. There are good games, where the ulterior payoff is positive and benefits both parties. But, all games prevent interpersonal intimacy, which is the most mutually satisfying transaction of all. Berne (1964) described a number of different types of games, including sexual games, marital games, party games, and life games (see box).

Each of these models brings out a different aspect of our everyday relationships. The exchange model reminds us that we tend to expect a fair return on what we have invested in our relationships with others. The transactional model highlights the complexity of communication involved in our relationships, especially how we manipulate each other in predictable ways to get what we want.

In addition to the different ways of understanding relationships, we can also distinguish various levels of relationships, from the superficial to the more intimate. In the following sections, we will look at three different levels of relationships according to the degree of personal involvement: beginning relationships; superficial or role relationships; and intimate, personal relationships. Ordinarily, relationships progress through these levels sequentially, sometimes reaching the level of intimacy. But more often relationships remain at the first two levels, or sometimes dissolve completely. We'll look at each of these types of relationships in more detail in the next three sections of this chapter.

BEGINNING RELATIONSHIPS

When you first meet someone, you tend to form a definite impression of that person. Although you may not know exactly why you feel the way you do, studies have shown that you tend to form impressions on the basis of the following general principles.

Impression Formation

Characteristically, we tend to form extensive impressions of other people on the basis of very little information about them. Perhaps this stems from our need to know in order to be ready to respond. But whatever the reason, we make definite judgments about someone after meeting that person for only a few minutes. Unless we have strong evidence to the contrary, we generally think a person has the characteristics we expect him or her to have. What we hear about someone from others tends to sway our impression one way or the other.

When we first meet a person, we notice things like the sex, age, race, physical appearance, and dress of that person. Although we judge mostly by what a person says and does, we also rely on other cues, such as eye contact. Generally, we are more favorably impressed with someone who maintains some eye contact with us, though a constant stare or outright avoidance of eye contact affects us negatively. The emotional judgment we make regarding the warmth or coldness of a person also affects our overall impression, with warm people generally being seen to possess more desirable qualities.

Unfortunately, our impressions are sometimes marred by stereotypes or false generalizations. That is, we tend to attribute identical characteristics to people with surface similarities, regardless of the actual differences between them. For example, there's a tendency to see all people wearing glasses as more intelligent, industrious, and reliable than those not wearing glasses (Manz & Lueck, 1968). Also, men with beards tend to be viewed as more masculine, mature, self-confident, and liberal than clean-shaven men, with men having moustaches and goatees falling somewhere between (Pellegrini, 1973).

More often than not, first impressions of others are positive, sometimes referred to as the *leniency effect* (Sears & Whitney, 1973). For some reason negative impressions are more specific than positive ones, so that we may know exactly why we don't like someone, but may be uncertain why we do.

Many of our initial impressions of others turn out to be reasonably correct, which is fortunate, since first impressions tend to be lasting. When they are mistaken, however, it may be because of any of the following factors:

Perhaps the most common cause of wrong impressions is the *lack of sufficient knowledge*. We simply don't have enough facts to justify the impression we're forming on an emotional basis.

Another factor that predisposes us toward mistaken impressions is the strong tendency toward *assumed similarity*: thinking that other people are pretty much like we are. For this reason we tend to be more accurate in judging those who are more like us than unlike us.

We're also misled by *false cues*, mistaking a woman's friendliness for a sexual invitation, or a man's silence as a mark of strong character.

Stereotypes also contribute to false impressions, such as the belief that blondes are more feminine but less intelligent than brunettes.

A frequent source of mistaken impressions is the tendency toward *logical error*, by which we assume that because a person has one trait, that person will have the others usually associated with this trait. For example, attractive people are usually judged to be more intelligent and successful than unattractive people.

Finally, there are the *halo* and *devil* effects. When we like someone, we tend to view everything that person does favorably (halo effect). And conversely, when we dislike a person, that person can do no good in our eyes (devil effect).

Interpersonal Attraction

Many of our impressions are formed simply by observing others. As we begin interacting with people, however, we acquire even stronger feelings of like or dislike toward them. Such feelings may seem fickle at the time, but actually they are affected by a number of predictable factors, including the following.

Physical proximity is especially important in the beginning stages of a relationship. We are more likely to be attracted to someone who lives near us, attends the same school, or works at the same company we do. The reason is that physical nearness facilitates greater interaction with others, which in turn generally increases our liking for them (Saegert, Swamp, & Zajonc, 1973). However, when there are conflicting interests and personalities, greater familiarity may breed contempt rather than attraction, as reflected in the fact that a large percentage of murder victims are killed by their own spouses.

How *similar* people are to us also heightens their attractiveness to us. Whenever we meet people who are like us in terms of beliefs, attitudes, or social background, we tend to be more attracted to them than to someone who is less like us. For example, Byrne (1961) found that the more similar the attitudes between two people, the greater the attraction between them. Furthermore, the more important an attitude or belief is to us, the greater the attraction when we find someone who also shares that attitude or belief. Similarity of personal characteristics also increases our liking for others, but this varies more widely among different situations and is less predictable than similarity of social backgrounds.

One explanation of why we are more attracted to people who are like us comes from Leon Festinger's *social comparison theory* (1957). According to this view, when standards of physical reality become uncertain, we rely more on social reality or other people to compare ourselves with. In doing so we are more likely to select people who are similar to ourselves, thereby confirming our opinions and diminishing our anxiety.

Mutual liking is another powerful force in interpersonal attraction. That is, not only do we like people who are like us, we also like those who *like* us too. However, when we feel that others are insincere in their expressions of approval or compliments, we feel uncomfortable rather than attracted. In contrast, the more sincere and discerning we feel the person is who likes us, the more we like that person (Mettee, 1971a, 1971b). As important as mutual liking is for interpersonal attraction, the relative gain or loss of liking from others can also serve as a key factor. When someone *increases* their liking for us, we tend to like that person more than we like people who have liked us all along. And conversely, if someone *decreases* their liking for us, we tend to dislike that person more than those who have disliked us from the start (Aronson, 1980).

Attractive people are judged more favorably, even on characteristics that have nothing to do with attractiveness. (Marc P. Anderson)

Physical attraction is obviously an important factor in our liking another person. Common sense suggests that all of us are more attracted to someone who possesses physical attractiveness. So it probably comes as no surprise that some studies on computer dating have found that most people prefer the most attractive partner available (Walster et al., 1966). However, other studies have disclosed that we are physically attracted to other people according to a *matching hypothesis.* For example, in one study the more physically attractive a person was rated by a panel of judges, the more that person preferred a partner who had a similar degree of physical attractiveness. It may be that all of us would like the most attractive partner possible, but from fear of rejection we settle for someone more like us (Berscheid et al., 1971). Additional support for this idea comes from the finding that couples who were going steady or engaged showed more similarity in physical attractiveness than randomly matched couples (Murstein, 1972).

DON'T THE GIRLS GET PRETTIER AT CLOSING TIME!

An equal number of men and women at several bars within walking distance of a university were approached at three different times—9 PM, 10:30 PM, and midnight—shortly before closing time on a Thursday evening. Each patron was asked to rate both the same-sex and opposite-sex individuals in the bar on a scale from 1 (least attractive) to 10 (most attractive). As the graph indicates, the attractiveness of opposite-sex persons increased significantly between 10:30 PM and midnight.

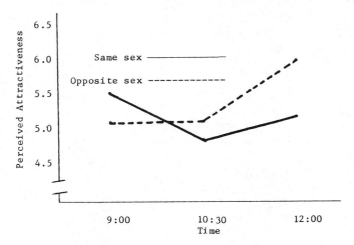

While the effect of alcohol on the evaluation of attractiveness cannot be ruled out, the results were explained mostly on the basis of *reactance theory;* that is, with decreased time to make a decision, the alternatives become more attractive. Since many individuals go to the bar to pick up a partner, the potential opposite-sex partners look increasingly attractive toward closing time. Or as singer Mickey Gilley expressed it, "All the girls get prettier at closing time; they all get to look like movie stars."

From James W. Pennebaker, Mary Anne Dyer, R. Scott Caulkins, Debra Lynn Litowitz, Phillip L. Ackerman, Douglas B. Anderson, and Kevin M. McGraw, "Don't the Girls Get Prettier at Closing Time: A Country and Western Application to Psychology," *Personality and Social Psychology Bulletin,* 1979, 5, 1, 122–125. © 1979 The Society for Personality and Social Psychology, Inc., with the permission of Sage Publications, Inc.

The role that physical attractiveness plays in our overall interpersonal attraction varies according to individuals, sex, and cultural standards. However, a typical finding is that males are attracted to females on the basis of physical attractiveness and sex appeal, while females are attracted to males more on the basis of personality characteristics and accomplishments than physical appearance (Morse, Gruzen, & Reis, 1973). A similar bias can be seen in a computer dating service ad that invited applications from successful men and attractive women.

ROLE RELATIONSHIPS

While we are initially drawn to others on the basis of certain impressions and feelings of attraction, the type of relationship we form with them depends heavily on social roles, or expected behavior. The key term here is *appropriateness*. What is the appropriate thing to do in this relationship? As soon as we meet someone new, each of us is busy intuitively defining our relationship with that person. We're figuring out what to talk about, what is expected of us, what we can ask of the other person, and so forth. Studies have shown that the uncertainty in verbal expressions during this initial phase of meeting decreases as each person receives feedback from the other (Lalljee & Cook, 1973). Presumably, such feedback helps each person to get a clearer idea of the relationship and to structure it accordingly.

Sometimes we initiate relationships primarily on the basis of role behavior, such as when we hand our money to a bank teller who may be a total stranger to us personally. Here we trust others because of their roles and our past experience with people in these roles. Even here, however, we may show a subtle preference for one teller over another, depending on the kind of impressions and attraction we feel toward such persons. But at this level we are dealing primarily with role relationships.

Role Model

Essentially, a *role* is the expected behavior associated with a given position or status in society. Originally, the term *role* came from the theater, where it refers to the player's script or lines. Just as actors learn their roles for a play from a script, so each of us learns how to function as members of society through all kinds of life scripts—written and oral.

Roles make it possible to socialize humans even before they are capable of fully understanding or controlling their behavior rationally. For example, from the moment of birth on, each of us learns an appropriate sex role through all kinds of input, both obvious and subtle. The name we're given, the clothes we wear, the types of activity we're encouraged to do—all teach us how to act appropriately as males or females. We continue learning many other roles throughout life as well, such as how to act as a teen-ager, student, worker, leader, husband, wife—all of which enable us to interact with a wide variety of persons in an appropriate way.

Roles also tend to be modified with time, with such changes being especially evident today in the area of sex roles. While people have mistakenly assumed that much of the behavior expected of males and females was *inherent* in their respective biological make-ups, we are discovering that many of these behaviors are primarily *learned* and can be modified. An example would be the degree of assertiveness acceptable among females. While speaking up and expressing yourself forthrightly has been generally regarded as "unfeminine" in the past, such behavior is not only encouraged today but is also being taught as an integral part of becoming an effective person for both sexes.

Role Adequacy and Conflict

As we mentioned earlier, the key term in role relationships is appropriateness, or acting the way you are "supposed to act." As long as people fulfill the various role demands made on them, things may go smoothly. But sometimes people do not fulfill their roles adequately. Individuals may be either unwilling or unable to do this, such as the worker who refuses to follow orders or the student who does not turn in work on time. If such behavior continues, a role relationship may be terminated. From time to time, persons differ in their expectations of each other and may experience a clash of roles. An example would be a wife who expects to get help with the household chores upon taking a job outside the home, while the husband may expect her to continue doing everything she was doing before in addition to the job. This couple must resolve such differences in their role expectations or they will continue to experience friction in their marriage.

In a complex society such as ours, we must also learn how to handle many different roles and shift easily from one to another. Think of all the different roles you fulfill in a given day. At home you may relate to others as a son or daughter, or perhaps as husband or wife. At school you shift into the role of a student, both with classmates and teachers. If you work, you may fulfill still another set of expectations, often with a change of dress. Sometimes you may experience a conflict between these various roles, such as being asked to work overtime at your job just before an important exam at school. In such instances, you may discover that role expectations are not inflexible. An understanding teacher may allow you to take the test later, or an interested boss may allow you to exchange work assignments with someone else. If not, you may have to choose which role demands will affect you the most negatively if left unmet.

Authenticity in Role Relationships

Sometimes people have the impression that role relationships are inherently unnatural or phony. This probably stems from the erroneous notion that we consciously act out our roles—which we don't. When we are spontaneously active in a role, we usually have little awareness of it. It seems the natural thing to do. Part of the reason is that we learn such roles gradually over a long period of time. Also, we personalize our roles so that they become an integral part of our self-identity, as we pointed out in the chapter on self-concept. But role relationships do pose certain pitfalls or dangers for us.

One danger is *overidentifying* with a role, or investing more of ourselves in a role than is appropriate for it. An example would be an actress who, in an effort to project herself into a character she is playing for a movie, overidentifies with that role. She may fall in love with the director, perhaps marry him, and generally live out the role of the character she is playing. After the filming is over, however, she may begin identifying with another role for a different movie, perhaps divorcing the director of the earlier movie in the process. Such a person lacks a sufficient degree of personal identity to distinguish between the core of her self and her roles. Other examples would be the professor who constantly "lectures" even out of the classroom, or the physician who treats his family and friends "like patients."

An opposite danger lies in investing too little of ourselves in a role. Here we pretend to be in a role without being sufficiently committed to it. An example would be a man who has a sales job but hates selling. Such a person may feel that selling requires lying and manipulating customers. Yet he may inwardly hate himself for doing this type of work, perhaps drowning his self-hatred in excessive drinking. This person is being inauthentic in his role (Jourard & Landsman, 1980). In contrast, a person who is authentic in a sales role might enjoy dealing with people and regard selling as a way of helping people satisfy their needs. Such a person might also realize the value of respecting his customers and allowing them to make up their own minds, rather than manipulating them. The result would probably be a more satisfying fit between person and role. As you can see, being authentic in a role depends more on attitude and commitment to that role than the role itself.

Being authentic in a role has a lot to do with your attitude toward that role. (Irene Springer)

Another danger of role relationships derives from the changes in society itself. We are living in a time of increasing change and mobility. As a result, we have a greater number of social contacts than in the past, providing us with a broader scope for developing our interests and personalities. But at the same time, most of these relationships tend to be of short duration with less emotional depth or intimacy. In other words, most of our everyday interactions are primarily role-type relationships, whether we recognize them as such or not. Consequently, a person may be very active with other people while inwardly feeling lonely, if not alienated. An example would be the executive who serves on many boards but has few close friends.

Often what is needed is not more relationships but more emotionally satisfying ones. In fact, healthy people not only desire but need some intimate, personal relationships in which they can share themselves more spontaneously and deeply than in role relationships. While such relationships pose a greater risk of disappointment and hurt, they also help us grow more fully as a person, along with the greater emotional satisfaction this brings.

INTIMATE, PERSONAL RELATIONSHIPS

According to typical dictionary definitions, *intimacy* refers to an informal, warm relationship between two friends or lovers resulting from a long period of association. Yet this is not always the case. For haven't you felt very intimate with someone you haven't known very long, such as a person you've shared a lot with at a party? On the other hand, you've probably known some people a long time without ever feeling close to them. It seems intimacy has more to do with the *quality* of a relationship than with the duration of our contacts with others, though there is usually a positive association between the two.

Intimacy refers to a close personal attachment to another person, in which the partners share their innermost thoughts and feelings. It is no accident that intimacy is often synonymous with sexual intimacy, because sexual intercourse ordinarily involves close contact between two people. But we may experience interpersonal intimacy without sexual intercourse, as in same-sexed friendships and therapist-patient relationships. On the other hand, two people can engage in sexual intercourse with very little emotional involvement, as in a casual sex affair. However, even when we achieve personal intimacy with our friends, lovers, or marriage partners, these periods usually alternate with role relationships.

How we describe intimacy depends partly on the various models of relationships discussed earlier in the chapter. In the fair-exchange model, intimacy refers primarily to an uncalculated mutuality, with each partner spontaneously giving and receiving in a way that is satisfying to both. According to the transactional analysis model, intimacy involves loving, game-free transactions with others, with a minimum of manipulation between partners. On the basis of the role model, we would expect personal relationships to involve rich, open communication between partners and a deep emotional investment in their relationship surpassing role expectations.

There are several conditions that are generally associated with interpersonal intimacy: (1) mutual self-disclosure, (2) personal compatibility, and (3) mutual accommodation between partners.

Mutual Self-Disclosure

Mutual self-disclosure has to do with two or more people voluntarily sharing their innermost thoughts and feelings. As long as it is appropriate to the relationship, mutual self-disclosure usually brings about greater intimacy. With people we've just met, however, a low to medium self-disclosure tends to evoke a similar response from others. But a high self-disclosure is more likely to meet with a negative response (Rubin, 1973). Even with friends, disclosing a lot about yourself too quickly or pushing another person to do the same puts a damper on the relationship. Altman and Taylor (1973) suggest that a hasty self-disclosure generally leads to an "easy in, easy out" syndrome, with partners expecting rapid deterioration and dissolving of their relationship. This may occur when two people experience a high degree of intimacy in a relatively short period of time, say during a weekend together. In such instances, one or both partners may pull back a bit in order to feel more secure in the relationship.

Mutual self-disclosure is most likely to occur within existing intimate relationships, such as with friends, spouses, or other family members. Sidney Jourard (1971) found that unmarried people tend to disclose themselves more freely to their mothers than to their fathers, probably because of the nurturant role associated with women. Young women engaged in self-disclosure about equally with their girl friends as with their mothers, but less so with their boy friends. Young men kept both parents about equally informed, but disclosed even more to their male friends. As expected, married people disclosed more easily with their spouses than anyone else. The less happily married a couple is, however, the less willing the partners are to share themselves with each other.

One of the most important factors in mutual self-disclosure is the act of self-disclosure itself. That is, you are more likely to disclose yourself to people who have disclosed themselves to you. Maximum self-disclosure occurs when both partners disclose a lot about themselves and also ask for information about the other person at increasingly intimate levels (Sermat & Smyth, 1973). For example, one woman said, "A casual friend became much closer after she shared a highly confidential matter about her marriage. I shared some personal experiences about a similar matter in my own marriage. Since then, we've been much closer friends."

Such an exchange also illustrates the importance of *trust* in self-disclosure and intimacy. When someone reveals herself to you, this is likely to be interpreted as an act of trust and liking for you. After all, she has made herself vulnerable to you by sharing things not ordinarily revealed to others. Rather than retaining such confidential knowledge as a relative power advantage over her, it is natural for you to respond with a similar degree of trust and self-disclosure, thereby demonstrating that her confidence and trust are well placed (Rubin, 1973).

Most people find that it is easier to talk about some things than about others. Relatively safe topics are information about our work, interests, tastes, avocational activities, and, to a lesser extent, politics and religion. On the other hand, we are more reluctant to share the details of our financial affairs and personal feelings about ourselves, especially our sex life (Jourard, 1971).

Perhaps you are wondering about the sharing of secrets—information restricted to certain people. But secrets, too, it seems, are mostly for telling. Being able to tell secrets to a friend is one reason for having them. The sharing of secrets generally makes both participants feel closer to each other, with the two most common themes of secrets among college-aged students being sex and failure (Hillix, Harari, and Mohr, 1979).

It is not always easy to know what to share and what not to share, since this depends largely on the particular people involved, the nature of their relationship, and how such disclosure might affect their relationship. In speaking about the limits of intimacy, Morton Hunt (1980) tells of a young man in his late 30s who told his wife about a brief sex affair he'd had while out of town several months earlier. The man said he felt no emotional attachment to the other woman and would be able to control his impulses in the future. Furthermore, he said that he felt better for having shared this secret with his wife, and believed it would bring them closer together. But he was wrong. Ever since that night, his wife has found herself plagued with doubts about her own attractiveness to her husband and wonders what he is doing when out of town.

As long as mutual self-disclosure meets with acceptance, not necessarily approval, it increases trust and intimacy among everyone involved. In turn, such intimacy leads to greater mutual self-disclosure, so that self-disclosure, trust, and intimacy are all closely related. Not surprisingly, "having an intimate talk" is usually ranked at the top of the most common activities friends engage in, especially women friends (Parlee et al., 1979).

Personal Compatibility

The more two people disclose themselves to each other, the greater fondness they feel for each other. Much of the reason has to do with their discovery of similar interests and experiences, as well as the act of sharing itself. But it is also true that progressive self-disclosure inevitably reveals areas of difference and conflict, so that a key issue eventually becomes how compatible two people are.

A major basis of personal compatibility is similarity of background, with people who have grown up in similar cultural, social, and educational backgrounds having much in common. Similarity of personal interests, temperament, and values is also important, though less consistently found in lasting friendships and marriages. Recent studies of friendship show that more and more people are reporting friendships that cut across all sorts of social boundaries. In a *Psychology Today* survey of friendship consisting of a majority of young adults, about half of the respondents said they had at least one close friend of a different racial, ethnic, or religious background. At the same time, more than half of

---

LONELINESS

Almost everyone is lonely at times. Yet this familiar feeling arises less out of circumstances themselves than out of how we interpret them. Consequently, we may be alone without being lonely, but lonely while surrounded by friends.

Studies by Carin Rubinstein, Phillip Shaver, and Letitia Anne Peplau (1982) have shown that loneliness is essentially a state of mind that results from the mismatch between our actual life and some desired state. Interviews with people of all ages have shown that young people in the 18-to-25-year-old group suffer the most from loneliness. The reason is the sharp discrepancy between their search for intimacy and the failure to find it. Loneliness declines steadily with age, so that older people in the 70-plus age group complain the least of loneliness though they spend the most time alone.

Contrary to popular assumptions, frequent moving around has little to do with loneliness. Apparently, people who move a lot learn quickly how to make new friends. The loneliest people in all age groups tend to be those who were the most dissatisfied with their lives as a whole, including their marriages or love affairs and their sex lives. A critical factor was having lost a parent through divorce at an early age. The earlier the age of the individual at the time of the parent's divorce, the more susceptible he or she was to loneliness. People with unhappy childhoods may grow up with a more guarded personality that makes it difficult for them to get close to others.

Loneliness doesn't feel the same to everyone. A large number of people feel desperate, helpless, and abandoned. Others experience a milder kind of loneliness, the kind you feel when you find yourself alone unexpectedly on Saturday night. Still others experience their loneliness in terms of feeling unattractive and sad. The most lonely people react to their mood by passive means, such as crying, sleeping, or watching TV. But people who are only mildly or rarely lonely prefer to adopt more active strategies, such as working, reading, or calling or visiting a friend.

Since loneliness is a subjective experience occasioned both by personal and by situational factors, it helps to correctly understand the precipitating factors and take appropriate action. It may also help to realize that solitude need not lead to loneliness. As a matter of fact, people with high self-esteem and close friends are *more* likely than those without such friends to enjoy being alone at times.

Carin Rubinstein, Phillip Shaver, and Letitia Anne Peplau, "Loneliness," in Nathaniel Jackson, ed., *Personal Growth and Behavior* 82/83. (Guilford, Conn.: The Dushkin Publishing Group, Inc., 1982), pp. 151–157.

them said that most of their close friends were of the same sex (Parlee et al., 1979). All too often, people run around with friends who share all of their activities or values, making for boring friendships. In contrast, one young woman said, "I like doing different things with different people. It makes life more interesting."

The idea that people are attracted to those who are different in personal make-up is expressed in Robert Winch's (1971) concept of *complementarity*, popularly known as the idea that "opposites attract." According to this view, each person acting out of his or her needs simultaneously complements or satisfies the needs of the other person. For example a highly sociable person will become friends with a quite introverted person; in this instance, each complements the other's personal traits. Complementarity probably plays a more important role in the later stages of a relationship, especially in long-term friendships and marriages. Also complementarity may apply more to specific traits than to personality as a whole. In one study, when student nurses were asked whether they preferred a roommate who was similar or different in terms of dominance, most indicated a preference for someone similar to themselves. Yet it was found that the most stable relationships were those between roommates who were complementary in dominance (Bermann & Miller, 1967).

In many instances, compatibility may be based on an intricate mixture of similarities and complementary differences that are not always apparent to the

Personal compatibility and conflict are not mutually exclusive. (Teri Leigh Stratford)

partners themselves. Yet no matter how compatible two people are, a certain amount of difference, if not conflict, is inevitable in intimate relationships. The important matter is how such differences are handled. When differences are ignored, the partners may experience the symptoms of covert conflict, such as boredom with the relationship, consistent irritation, or dissatisfaction with each other without explanation. Or the partners may criticize, nag, or become easily angered without sufficient cause.

Sometimes close friends or marriage partners avoid conflict for fear it will end their relationship. Yet when differences or conflict mean the end of a friendship or love relationship, it probably wasn't much of a relationship to begin with. On the other hand, when both persons care deeply about each other, a healthy conflict may leave their friendship or marriage even stronger. In fact, we would expect two persons who have worked together to resolve their differences to appreciate each other even more than they would otherwise. A lot depends on how partners handle their differences, as we will discuss more fully in the chapter on marriage.

Mutual Accommodation

One of the most distinctive characteristics of intimate relationships, whether between friends or lovers, is the deep emotional investment partners have in their relationship. On the one hand, this leads to a great deal of caring and willingness to help each other. But it also leads partners to expect a lot from each other. These expectations in turn often set the stage for misunderstanding and conflict unless both persons engage in a certain amount of mutual accommodation.

Accommodation begins with the attempt to understand the other person's viewpoint. Essentially this involves *empathy,* or experiencing another's attitudes or feelings through your own imaginative awareness. Empathy means trying to understand someone in terms of his or her own frame of awareness, "as if" you were in that person's place. Even though this doesn't mean you necessarily agree with the other person, there is always the danger that empathizing with a friend's feelings will be mistaken for agreement with his or her position.

This danger emphasizes the importance of communicating empathy effectively. For we must not only have an empathetic attitude, but we must also implement this attitude in our words and behavior toward the other person. As psychotherapists have long realized, such implementing involves specific skills, such as learning how to listen actively to another person's feelings and responding in a non-judgmental manner, as discussed in the chapter on emotions. Such empathetic understanding creates a climate of trust and acceptance in which individuals feel less defensive and freer to express themselves as they are. As Carl Rogers says, "When someone understands how it feels and seems to me, without wanting to analyze or judge me, then I can blossom and grow in that climate" (1971, p. 90).

Although it is easier to empathize with someone who is similar or compatible with us (Stotland & Dunn, 1963), empathy is even more important in trying to understand someone who is quite different from us. Examples would be two friends who repeatedly misunderstand each other because of differences in their social or cultural backgrounds, or lovers and marriage partners who disagree because of conflicting sex-role expectations.

Sometimes it is not enough for partners to understand each other; they must also change to accommodate each other's needs and desires as well. The old cliché that every successful relationship involves a 50-50 effort on the part of both parties implies that the norm of accommodation is fairness, as discussed earlier in this chapter. But Erich Fromm (1956) insists that as intimacy develops into true love, it involves more than fairness. It means an unconditional giving of ourselves, with each person putting forth a 100 percent effort. Even though friends and lovers rarely attain this ideal fully, it is important that both partners be equally committed to maintaining and enhancing their relationship. Otherwise, the one who is the most emotionally involved tends to suffer unfairly in the relationship, such as the wife who continues being faithful to her husband despite his "playing around with other women." When a couple that was highly successful in their professional partnership as well as in their married life was asked to give their secret of success, both partners agreed, "We respect each other. We both know how to give and take."

One of the most demanding aspects of any deep, personal relationship is adjusting to another person's style of intimacy. For each of us tends to experience and express deep emotional caring and love in somewhat different ways. For example, John Lee (1974) observed that there are different styles of loving common in man-woman relationships. Whereas some individuals plunge into relationships with intense passion and intimacy, others desire to let relationships develop more gradually. Some persons have trouble putting their feelings into words and prefer to express their love in overt actions. But others may express their emotions more readily in words, while hesitating to become involved physically. Also, some individuals pay more attention to the balance of payoffs in their relationships, while others are more intuitive and generous in their love.

You can just imagine the possible misunderstanding between two persons with different styles of loving. For example, a more erotic lover who thrives on sexual intimacy might push for early sexual involvement, while a less emotional person who views sex as an intimate self-revelation might prefer postponing sex until later in the relationship. Without much understanding and accommodation, such a couple may drift into a one-sided affair or decide to terminate their relationship completely.

John Lee found no unqualified examples of the *agape* style of loving (named for the generous, unselfish love found in all the great religions). But he did find half a dozen or so couples whose relationship came close to this altruistic type of love. Such individuals felt intense emotion for their partners, but without the exclusive absorption with each other and jealousy so often seen in romantic love.

FRIENDSHIP

Youth and adults agree that friendship is one of the most important things in life.

Friendship is a unique type of relationship in that it grows out of free choice rather than necessity. While friendship may develop within other roles such as co-workers, it usually transcends social roles and has its own inner rationale, which is to foster feelings of warmth, trust, and affection between two people (Parlee et al., 1979).

There are all kinds of friends. You may have "work" friends to share coffee-breaks with, or "activity" friends to play tennis with. You may also have "favor" friends who will loan you a book. But many of these people may never be very close to you. In fact, most people can readily distinguish between their casual friends and their close friends.

The most frequent activity among close friends is simply having an intimate talk. A close friend is someone you can share your most intimate thoughts, feelings, and secrets with in an atmosphere of trust. As you might expect, the two most important qualities of a friend are loyalty and the ability to keep a confidence. Warmth, affection, and supportiveness are also highly desirable in a friend. Most people feel their friendships are reciprocal. So if you want to have friends, you have to be a good friend who listens, supports, and above all, keeps confidences. When in need, many people would turn to a friend before their family. A lasting friendship depends more on the quality of the relationship rather than the frequency of getting together. Conversely, when a friendship ends, it is usually because one person feels betrayed, or the partners have grown apart in their interests and views (Parlee et al., 1979).

There is a trend toward more opposite-sex friendships among adolescents and adults alike. Yet many adults feel that friendship with the opposite sex is different from same-sex friendship. The major reason is that sexual tensions may complicate the relationship. Another reason may be the different meaning of friendship to men and women. Men tend to avoid close intimate relationships, preferring casual friends for sharing activities or exchanging favors. Women, on the other hand, prefer more emotionally involved relationships, with an intimate sharing of feelings.

As we move away from the stereotyped notions of male and female in our society, how do you think this will affect the pattern of friendships between men and women?

Mary Brown Parlee and the editors of *Psychology Today*, October 1979, pp. 43–54, 113.

They also seemed to find the act of loving itself so fulfilling that reciprocity in their relationship became almost irrelevant.

INTIMACY AND GROWTH

Ideally, an intimate relationship helps both partners grow more fully as persons. The affection and trust between them provides a safe, accepting atmosphere in which both can share and affirm themselves at increasingly deeper levels of their personalities. The satisfaction of their basic needs for security and acceptance, in Maslow's terms, frees them to actualize themselves in terms of their higher, growth needs. At some time or another, each of us has probably had this experience of spontaneously wanting to reach out and try new things in the companionship and warmth of a friend or lover. Yet such experiences of healthy intimacy and growth occur less frequently than we would desire.

More often, intimacy leads to growth through facing and resolving the conflicts and problems that come with close personal relationships. For no matter how compatible two people are, their intimate disclosures and expectations inevitably bring out certain differences and conflicts. Furthermore, the more emotionally committed persons become to their relationship, the more likely they are to make claims and demands on their partner, which in turn generates a certain amount of conflict. When growth occurs, the stimulus to change comes not so much through spontaneous growth, as through a challenge or demand for change in order to maintain the relationship. For example, if one person experiences a restricted social life because of a partner's abuse of alcohol or drugs, he or she might say, "Either you change your ways, or I'm not going out with you anymore." While the anxiety and self-doubt of such an encounter might threaten the future of their relationship, the emotional bond between them might also provide an added incentive to change. Close friends or couples who have experienced such growth will often say things like, "It wasn't easy," or "We had to work at it"—suggesting that growth often comes only after meeting and resolving conflicts at a deeply personal level.

Sometimes intimacy results in one-sided changes or the avoidance of change. Rather than going through all the trouble of facing and reconciling differences, some individuals attempt to manipulate change in the other person. One example would be the husband who uses money or physical power to get his own way, or the wife who uses the children or sex to get her way. Either way, manipulation undermines true intimacy. Sometimes one partner may change a great deal more than the other, such as a woman who continues to learn and grow in school, while her friend stays home doing the same old things. They may find themselves drifting apart with the realization that "we don't have much in common anymore." Since one-sided change often disrupts the balance of close relationships, some partners seem to settle down to a nonthreatening but growth-resistant relationship. A common example would be the married couple with a stable but "empty" marriage.

The simplest way to initiate change in a personal relationship is to ask one's partner to change. The response to such a request is often, "I didn't realize this was a problem for you; why didn't you ask me sooner?" But sometimes individuals hesitate to ask for a number of reasons. One is the fear of being rejected. Another reason is the desire to avoid conflict or the added obligations that go with changes in any relationship. Then too, a person may underestimate his or her partner's capacity to change.

A major reason why intimate relationships do not always result in personal growth has to do with the unresolved needs for dependency and security on the part of one or both persons involved. While some individuals take out their dependency needs in alcohol or drugs, others seek emotional gratification through emotional attachment to other people. This is especially true of middle-class people who have been reared to expect emotional gratification in exclusive one-to-one relationships. Finding so little in their everyday contacts, some individuals enter into what Stanton Peele and Archie Brodsky (1974) call "addictive relationships." Here, two people become so emotionally involved and preoccupied with their relationship they they cut off everything else. They let go of all other interests, activities, or persons that would interfere with their sense of security with each other. They tend to resent any change or growth in the other, which makes their break-up more traumatic. Like those addicted to alcohol or drugs, such individuals need increasingly larger doses of security to satisfy their dependency, with the break-up of their relationship resulting in an agonizing feeling of inner emptiness.

In contrast, individuals in mature love relationships feel a desire to grow and expand through their relationship. They welcome change and involvement in their partner as a way of adding to the growth and richness of the relationship. In actuality, however, Peele and Brodsky recognize that most intimate relationships are neither extremely addictive nor mature love relationships, but combine characteristics of both. In the final analysis, each of us must assess the health or maturity of our personal relationships by asking such questions as the following:

Are both of us improved by this relationship?
Does this relationship stimulate each of us to change and grow in a desirable direction?
Do both of us maintain other interests and meaningful relationships outside this one?
If lovers, are we also friends?
Does each of us have a need to give as well as to receive love?
Can we experience intimacy without giving up our individuality?
Does each of us feel worthwhile as a person apart from this relationship?

Answers to questions like these may help each partner to untangle some of the intricacies that differentiate addictive from mature personal relationships.

SUMMARY

We began this chapter with a consideration of the different ways of understanding human relationships, with each model bringing out the different meanings implicit in everyday relationships. The exchange model emphasizes the importance of getting a fair return on what we have invested in our relationships. The transactional analysis model reminds us of the complexity of interpersonal transactions and how we tend to manipulate each other to get what we want.

We have also distinguished several levels of relationships according to the degree of personal involvement, including beginning relationships, role relationships, and intimate, personal relationships.

We tend to enter into a relationship with another person on the basis of certain impressions and feelings of attraction toward that person. Although most of these initial impressions are reasonably accurate, they may be mistaken because of faulty evaluations. How much we are attracted to another person is influenced by a number of factors, especially physical proximity, similarity of social backgrounds or personalities, how much the other person likes us, and physical attraction.

Many of our relationships are shaped by roles or the expected behavior we've learned as an integral part of becoming socialized. A key problem is learning how to fulfill many different types of roles. There is also the danger of investing too much or too little of ourselves, such that individuals may become inauthentic in their roles. Although most of our everyday contacts remain at the level of role relationships, healthy people not only desire but also need closer relationships in which they can share themselves more deeply.

Intimate, personal relationships involve mutual self-disclosure between the partners, with certain patterns evident for appropriate self-disclosure. Although we tend to disclose ourselves more readily with people who are compatible with us, intimacy tends to bring out both similarities and differences between individuals. The latter emphasizes the importance of mutual accommodation in personal relationships, with a need for each partner to understand and change in order to maintain and enhance their relationship.

Intimate relationships may lead persons to grow individually as well as in their relationship. But more often intimacy facilitates growth through partners' facing and resolving the conflicts that inevitably come with intimacy. A major reason why individuals fail to grow through intimate involvements has to do with their unresolved needs for dependency and security, as in addictive versus mature love relationships.

QUESTIONS FOR SELF-REFLECTION

1. Do you put as much of yourself into your relationships as you get out of them?
2. Are you aware of any game-type transactions you commonly engage in?
3. Do you judge others by first impressions too quickly?
4. What type of first impression do you make on others? Have you ever asked to find out?
5. What attracted you to your friends? Similar interests? Other factors?
6. Do you feel less at home in some roles more than others? Which ones?
7. Which people do you feel most comfortable disclosing personal information to? Is such disclosure mutual?
8. Does that relationship ever involve any discussion of differences or conflicts?
9. How do you tell the difference between a true friend and someone you have more of a role relationship with?
10. Would you say your current intimate relationships are basically growth-facilitating or dependent, addictive relationships?

EXERCISES

1. Impression formation

This is a group or class exercise on how we judge people, and especially our use of stereotypes.

Have your instructor ask for four or five volunteers who will conduct the exercise. The main idea of the exercise is to have the class match anonymous blackboard descriptions of the volunteers with the actual individuals themselves. The volunteers or presenters should plan their part before the class presentation. During the planning, they should agree upon six to ten categories to describe each one to the class, such as: college major, career aspirations, favorite sport, hobbies, outstanding high school achievement, favorite musical group, Hollywood actor or actress each would most want to date.

When the class is ready, have the presenters write the list of descriptive phrases for each presenter on a separate blackboard space. Then ask the class to match up presenters with the blackboard descriptions. This is usually done by a process of informal verbal consensus. Generally, there is a fair amount of disagreement and changing of minds, accompanied by much laughter, before the final choices are reached. After the class choices are agreed upon, have each presenter stand in front of the blackboard description selected by the class.

Then have the presenters change their positions so that each one stands in front of his or her actual blackboard description. A crucial part of the exercise is the discussion of the class choices. Have the presenters ask various individuals in the class why they had a certain impression about a given presenter. The class discussion usually reveals how we tend to judge people on the basis of various stereotypes.

2. Interpersonal attraction

Think of five or six friends of both sexes; then examine your attraction to them on the basis of the following factors.

Using the categories below, check each factor that you think applies to these friendship relationships. For example, you may feel you became friends with Brian mostly because you shared classes your first semester and also seemed personally compatible. On the other hand, you may feel that your friendship with Nancy grew out of your similarity in social backgrounds, belonging to the same church, and the fact that she has increased her liking for you with time.

Basis of attraction
  Physical proximity

  Similar social background

  Similar personality characteristics

  Physical attraction

  Mutual liking

  Increased liking for you

As you look over your completed list, do some factors seem consistently more important than others? Was physical proximity more important in the beginning of your relationships?

Does similarity in social background seem to count in most of your relationships? Are there also other factors that do not appear in the above list? What does this exercise tell you about the way you are attracted to others?

3. Conflict management

This exercise is designed to increase your awareness of how you handle conflicts.

Select one of your relationships with a close friend of either sex. Then examine the way you handle disagreement and conflict with this friend. Ask yourself the following questions:

Which way do you handle conflicts?

Do you tend to avoid disagreements?

Do you usually give in to the other person?

Or do you try to get your way?

Which strategy do you use in dealing with conflicts?

Do you attack the problem rather than the person?

Do you express yourself as clearly and directly as possible?

Do you stick to the main point?

Are you willing to engage in mutual accommodation?

You might also look at the way your parents handle conflicts. How does your father handle disagreement and anger? How does your mother? How do they handle disagreements in family matters? How similar is your approach to theirs?

4. Exercise on self-disclosure

Complete Table 6-1, indicating the degree of your self-disclosure on the various topics and target persons.

Look over your completed table and compare your results with the findings on self-disclosure discussed in this chapter. Ask yourself such questions as the following:

Which persons do I disclose the most to? Which persons the least?

What topics do I talk about more readily? The least readily?

Do I disclose more to same-sex than opposite-sex friends? Or is it the other way around?

If married, do I disclose more to my spouse than friends or parents?

How can I account for my pattern of self-disclosure?

Are liking and disclosure to others closely related?

5. Friendship

Select two or three of your closest friendships and look at them in relation to the material on friendship in this chapter.

TABLE 6-1

	Father	Mother	Husband-Wife	Same-sex friend	Opposite-sex friend	Other	
Attitudes							**Key**
Interests							0—no disclosure
School							1—low disclosure
Work							2—medium disclosure
Money							3—high disclosure
Personality							
Interpersonal							
Sex							
Body-health							

Are most or all of your closest friends your own sex?

What personal qualities are most important in your friend?

Do you share intimate feelings as well as factual information with each other?

Which kinds of activities do you engage in with your friends?

Are your friendships reciprocal?

Do you get together frequently? Or is it the quality of the relationship that keeps the friendship alive?

Most people believe that friendships enhance and offer relief from the other emotional roles we play. Would you agree? You might find it interesting to write a short paragraph telling what your friends mean to you and why you need close friends.

6. Intimacy and growth

Select a few of your closest relationships with friends or lovers, and take a look at how these relationships affect your growth as an individual and in the relationship. Write down your reactions to the following questions:

Are both of us improved by this relationship?

Does this relationship stimulate each of us to change and grow in a desirable direction?

Do both of us maintain other interests and meaningful relationships outside this one?

If lovers, are we also friends?

Does each of us have a need to give as well as to receive love?

Can we experience intimacy without giving up our individuality?

Does each of us feel worthwhile as a person apart from this relationship?

You will probably find that most of your intimate relationships are neither extremely healthy nor dependent and addictive, but a combination of both. Hopefully, this exercise will help you become more aware of the differences between these two types of relationships.

RECOMMENDED READINGS

Brain, R. *Friends and Lovers.* New York: Basic Books, 1977 (paperback). Drawing on friendship patterns in many cultures, the author points out the need and value of friendship in contrast to the preoccupation with romantic love and sex.

Fromm, E. *The Art of Loving.* New York: Harper & Row, 1974 (paperback). A short, insightful account of the varied meanings of love by one of the foremost psychoanalysts of our time.

Kleinke, C. L. *First Impressions.* Englewood Cliffs, N.J.: Prentice-Hall, 1975 (paperback). An informed guide to the factors that influence our first impressions of others, such as looks, eye contact, body language, and verbal exchange.

Ramey, J. W. *Intimate Friendships.* Englewood Cliffs, N.J.: Prentice-Hall, 1976 (paperback). Explains how close primary relationships function in our lives.

Rubinstein, C. and P. Shaver. *What It Means to Be Lonely.* New York: Delacorte Press, 1982. An in-depth understanding of loneliness based on the authors' research findings.

Sager, C. J. and B. Hunt. *Intimate Partners.* New York: McGraw-Hill, 1979. Explores the hidden patterns in love relationships.

Zimbardo, P. G. *Shyness.* Reading, Mass.: Addison-Wesley, 1977 (paperback). An examination of shyness in relation to the cultural forces that produce it, with suggestions for overcoming it.

Sex Roles and Sexuality

7

SEX ROLES
    male and female
    stereotyped sex roles
    changing sex roles

SEXUAL MOTIVATION
    contributing factors
    characteristic sex drives
    sexual arousal
    sex differences

SEXUAL BEHAVIOR
    masturbation
    petting
    premarital intercourse
    other sexual behaviors

CHANGING ATTITUDES TOWARD SEX
    greater personal choice in sex
    acceptance of premarital sex
    emphasis on sexual fulfillment

SUMMARY

Even though our biological sex, or gender, is genetically determined at the moment of conception, much of our sexual identity and behavior is learned. Through the way we are treated and taught, we come to see ourselves as male or female and act accordingly. However, the inherent differences between the sexes have been exaggerated by stereotyped notions, such as that of the sexually driven male and the passive, reluctant female, making for misunderstanding between the sexes. Then too, until recently, much of sexual behavior has been shrouded in secrecy and learned through the most unreliable sources, such as friends, anecdotes, or pornographic books and movies. As a result, our understanding of sex is obscured by many half-truths and outright falsehoods.

But it doesn't have to be this way. Today there is more openness and honesty about sexual interests, as well as much more reliable information available. And there is a growing awareness that sex is more than simply a mechanical means of reproduction or source of pleasure. It is also a vital way that men and women relate to each other as persons and fulfill their own potential. It is with this in mind that we begin our discussion of sex, which will include the influence of sex roles, sexual arousal and desire, sexual behavior, and changing attitudes toward sex.

SEX ROLES

Much of your sexual identity, from the way you dress to the way you feel about yourself as a sexual being, results from sex roles—social expectations concerning appropriate behavior for males and females. Since sex roles are based on learning as well as on biological considerations, they vary from one culture to another. Yet within a given society sex roles often appear to be relatively fixed, with negative labeling and impaired well-being resulting for those who deviate too far from the prescribed sex roles. This section deals with how our lives are shaped by sex roles, especially the restrictive influence of stereotyped sex roles and the growing concern for more flexible ones.

Male and Female

From the moment of birth, infants are classified as male or female on the basis of biological sex differences. They are also given a name and treated in a manner appropriate to their sex. Yet much of this treatment is based on cultural expectations rather than on biological make-up. Nevertheless, by the time you and I reach adolescence we take many of the differences between the sexes as unalterable facts of existence, rather than as learned differences. We simply assume members of each sex are naturally inclined toward their respective sex-role expectations.

The core of the prescribed female sex role currently includes an emphasis on: (1) marriage and having children; (2) reliance on a male provider, both in taking the man's name and in sharing his income; (3) nurturing behavior, both in mothering children and in caring for the aged and helpless; (4) physical attractiveness and beauty; and (5) a ban on direct expression of aggression and power striving (Keller, 1974).

Similarly, the core of the prescribed male sex role includes an emphasis on: (1) vocational identity; (2) being a provider and protector of women; (3) physical strength and accomplishment; (4) a high degree of control over emotion, with the exception of anger; and (5) strong bonds with others, but the avoidance of emotional intimacy with other men or boys (Pleck, 1976).

While differences between the sexes need not mean one is superior to the other, many believe that sex roles in Western society contain an implicit male bias. For example, when married men and women under 40 were asked what sex child they would prefer, twice as many of them indicated they preferred having a boy as a girl, with the preference for a boy especially marked among the men (Hoffman, 1977). Boys are also given greater opportunities in their development, as seen in the furnishings of their rooms. While girls' rooms tend to have more floral furnishings and dolls, boys' rooms have more animal furnishings, educational toys, athletic equipment, art supplies, and vehicles (Rheingold & Cook, 1975).

Furthermore, a greater number of desirable personality traits are assigned to men than to women. Men are more likely to be characterized as active, competitive, aggressive, dominant, independent, and self-confident, while women are likely to be described as more gentle, neat, emotional, expressive, sensitive, and tactful than men (Broverman et al., 1972). Men are also more likely than women to be evaluated favorably. In one study, over 600 students of both sexes rated male and female players on videotapes on intelligence and likability. The results showed that male players were judged to be more intelligent and likable than female players in every condition. While medium assertiveness was associated with the highest levels of perceived intelligence for both sexes, high assertiveness resulted in higher ratings of intelligence for men, but lower ratings of intelligence for women (Lao et al., 1975).

Stereotyped Sex Roles

Much of the negative impact of sex roles is due to *stereotyped* sex roles—widely held generalizations about the characteristics of males and females. Actually, stereotypes are *over*generalizations that exaggerate the real differences between the sexes and minimize the differences within each sex group. While some stereotypes are based on real differences, such as men are more aggressive than women, these differences are usually exaggerated beyond the evidence. Other stereotypes are false from their inception, such as the notion that men are superior to women in intelligence, which has no basis in fact (Schaffer, 1980).

One of the difficulties with sex-role stereotypes is that they encourage us to think about ourselves and others in a way that ignores individual differences. Just think of the many men and women whose psychological make-up differs from their respective stereotypes who are considered normal, if not healthy, by their peers. Think of men in the helping professions who stress acceptance and empathy, just the opposite of the male ideals of aggressiveness and competitiveness. Or think of women in the professions or business world who excel in a competitive environment. Consider also men who care little or nothing for typical male pursuits such as sports or hunting, and who readily share with their wives in household and child-rearing responsibilities. And consider women who care little or nothing about housekeeping or mothering, preferring pursuits that would normally be considered masculine. Of course, there are many men and women who combine stereotyped sex characteristics with those that are not characteristic of their sex. The point is that the actual behaviors of both sexes exhibit a wider range of appropriate behaviors than those implied in the sex stereotypes.

Stereotyped sex roles are also self-defeating. In the first place, the discrepancy between stereotyped sex roles and a person's actual psychological make-up creates feelings of inadequacy and inferiority among many people. Think of the negative consequences in the lives of women who inhibit their need for achievement and assertiveness, or men who inhibit their emotions, especially the tender affections of compassion and empathy. In the second place, even those who successfully identify with the respective sex-role stereotypes become less adaptable as a result. The stereotyped female who becomes overly dependent on her husband, who has never worked outside the home, who equates her personal worth with her physical attractiveness, or who becomes overly involved emotionally with her family is a highly vulnerable person. In a similar way, the stereotyped male who overidentifies with work and making money for his sense of personal worth, who remains alienated from his feelings, and who remains distant in his relationships with others is an equally vulnerable person. In short, stereotyped sex roles are overly restrictive and maladaptive for both sexes.

Changing Sex Roles

Greater awareness of how stereotyped sex roles affect behavior has brought about an increased concern for more flexible sex roles. Such concern is most evident among those who are young, college-educated (especially women), and single or divorced. There is a growing realization that flexible sex roles may be more adaptive for both sexes. Sandra Bem (1974,1975) has proposed the term *androgyny* (from *andros,* meaning man, and *gyne,* meaning woman) for the ability to combine the desirable traits from both sex roles. Thus, a psychologically androgynous woman can be assertive, forceful, and self-reliant, or gentle, compassionate, and dependent, depending on what is appropriate to the occasion. Similarly, an androgynous man may be affectionate, empathetic, and loving when so desired, or dominant, independent, and willing to take a stand, depending on what is appropriate to a given situation.

Androgynous people are more independent and have a wider range of abilities than those with stereotyped male or female identities, giving them greater ability to adapt to different situations (Bem, 1975). In contrast, people with stereotyped sex identities are more likely to avoid situations involving inappropriate sex-role behavior, even if the rewards are less (Bem & Lenney, 1976). Androgynous people of both sexes also exhibit the highest level of self-esteem in high school and college, followed in order by those with a masculine, feminine, or undifferentiated sexual identity (Spence & Helmreich, 1978).

A study of interpersonal attraction found that androgynous people are the most attractive on both platonic and romantic measures of liking, while those with undifferentiated sexual identities were the least popular. However, there was one notable exception. While men preferred androgynous women for friends, they wanted women with more feminine qualities for romantic partners (Kulik & Harackiewicz, 1979).

Because of the male bias in stereotyped sex roles, much of the concern for more flexible sex roles has been evident among women. Letty Pogrebin (1980) has noted that feminist parents often find it easier to understand the implications of nonsexist child rearing for their daughters than for their sons. While they support nontraditional interests and activities for their daughters, they become concerned if their sons are not sufficiently competitive or if they express an

The concern for more flexible sex roles is especially evident among young women. (A.T.&T. Company Photo Center)

interest in the arts. Such observations have led Joseph Pleck (1981) to note that when today's daughters reach womanhood in the 1990s, they will be faced with a generation of males raised largely with traditional notions of masculinity. Consequently, Pleck holds that the concern for more flexible sex roles should apply equally to both sexes. He feels there is no special need, however, to encourage men and women to take different roles, since their biological differences will be expressed with a minimum of help from parents and educators. This does not mean we have to make men and women the same. Rather, we can cease striving so hard to make them different. Would you agree?

SEXUAL MOTIVATION

Nowhere is the pervasive influence of stereotyped sex roles felt more keenly than in regard to the sex drive. It has been said somewhat humorously that when it comes to sex, men are like ever-ready flashlight batteries, while women are like the old-fashioned telephones that had to be cranked up before they would operate. But we are discovering that such stereotyped notions of the sexually potent male and the passive, reluctant female are highly misleading. The actual similarities and differences in sexuality among men and women are more complex, as we will see in the following pages.

Contributing Factors

Because our biological drives are shaped by cultural factors, the felt need for sex derives from a unique blend of inborn and learned influences, as we discussed in Chapter 2. As a result, sexual motivation is rather complex and is influenced by many psychological and social factors, some of which are closer to our awareness than others. The following overview of sexual motivation may help you get a better idea of the range of factors that influence sexual desire.

First of all, the tendency toward a low, medium, or high sexual arousability is thought to be controlled by our genes. When questioned about various aspects of their sex lives, such as the frequency of masturbation or age of first intercourse with the opposite sex, identical twins almost always give similar answers, while fraternal twins, more like brothers and sisters, do not. At the same time, the degree to which our inborn propensity for sexual arousal is developed depends greatly on other influences, such as environmental stimuli, or pleasurable and unpleasurable experiences (Goldstein, 1976).

Sexual motivation is dependent to some extent on hormonal levels. A male's sexual responsiveness is especially influenced by the biological level of testosterone, the most powerful male sex hormone, with higher levels of testosterone being found in males during and immediately after intercourse (Fox, 1972). Conversely, males who have been castrated (had their testes removed) or who have low levels of testosterone exhibit greatly reduced sex drives. Testosterone also plays a key role in female sexuality. While the female sex hormone estrogen aids intercourse by increasing the lubrication and flexibility of the vagina, it is testosterone that actually increases the sensitivity of the clitoris and enhances sexual desire (Bardwick, 1971). However, since sexual motivation is influenced by the combined effect of several hormones as well as by learned, emotional factors, it is difficult to determine the exact influence of sex hormones on sexual behavior at any given time. For example, while the most common peaks in sexual activity among women occur just before menstruation, when testosterone levels are relatively high, and during the midpoint of the menstrual cycle, at the time of ovulation, these peaks are not universal. Many women who report peaks in sexual activity do not show consistent variations, and some women report no cyclical pattern of sexual activity at all, suggesting that hormones are often outweighed by psychological and social factors (Weidiger, 1976).

Various parts of our nervous system also stimulate and inhibit sexual responsiveness in a variety of ways. Whenever I ask students to name the main sex organ, they invariably (and correctly) point to their heads, because of the importance of the brain and central nervous system in sexual desire. We're all familiar with how erotic thoughts or feelings may lead to sexual arousal. We may be equally familiar with how easily sexual arousal can be triggered through stimulation of the various senses, such as touch, sight, hearing, smell, or taste— a topic that will be discussed in a later section. The tendency toward a slow, medium, or fast sexual arousal is also affected by the make-up of our nervous system, with a wide range of individual differences in both sexes.

Many of the particular cues that we find sexually arousing come from learning and from our acquired associations with sex. That is, we may become sexually aroused while viewing a romantic scene on film because we associate that with the pleasure of genital stimulation. In a similar way, we may become conditioned to a whole class of stimuli, such as erotic touching, fragrant scents, provocative dress, music, dancing, and semidarkness. The degree to which our previous sexual and social experiences have been pleasant and unpleasant may also serve to arouse or inhibit us sexually on future occasions.

Sexual motivation is also affected by age, as seen in the relatively intense sex drive following puberty and the gradual decrease with age, especially after middle age. Part of the reason may be the general slowing down of our system, including lower levels of sex hormones and less acute sensory reactions. But sexual motivation also varies widely depending on sexual activity. Men who remain sexually active retain greater sensitivity in the penis than males who are less active (Newman, 1970). Furthermore, sexually active couples report less decline in their sex lives with age than those who are less active.

Cultural values and practices also affect our sexual motivation. For instance, some people are stimulated by sex in direct proportion to how illicit it is. The more forbidden sex is, whether among young teenagers or in extramarital affairs, the more titillation the partners find in it. On the other hand, some educators believe that a less repressive society might help put sex in a better perspective by removing the risk and thrill of doing something wrong. Yet, the transition to greater freedom in sexual matters in our society has brought about a preoccupation with sex, making it difficult for many people to simply accept and enjoy sex in its proper perspective.

Sexual motivation is also affected by a variety of other environmental influences, such as nutrition, disease, seasons, temperature, and aphrodisiacs. Stress is also an important factor. Since stress activates the adrenal glands, which secrete small amounts of both sex hormones, it can increase sexual arousal. But it can also inhibit sexual desire. We've all known people who sought out sex before or during stressful periods in their lives, while others have experienced diminished sex desires under the same stress.

Characteristic Sex Drives

One of the widely recognized differences between men and women is their characteristic sexual responsiveness. In men, sex tends to be focused more on the genitals, but in women sex is more diffused and tied in with psychological and social influences. In part this is related to the different sexual functions in men and women. Male sexuality depends primarily on the penis, so that, from early puberty on, the penis becomes the focus of sexual interest and activity. But females have a more inclusive sexual function with a more complex anatomy. As a result, female sexuality includes at least three types of sexual behavior involving two persons: intercourse and orgasm, labor and childbirth, and nursing. While the conventional view of childbirth has emphasized the painful aspects of this experience, recent studies have shown many similarities between natural childbirth and sexual orgasm, for example, in facial expressions, physical changes, and sensory and emotional responses. Women themselves have reported feeling sensations similar to orgasm. Furthermore, mothers who breastfeed their babies have reported a higher level of sexual interest and an increased desire to return to intercourse with their husbands (Newton, 1971). In short, it appears that there is a close association between all these experiences because they are an integral part of a woman's sexual make-up and function.

Another reason for the characteristic differences in male and female sexuality is bound up with our interest and attitudes toward the genitals. The fact that the male penis is plainly visible and the female clitoris is hidden affects how readily each sex discovers the pleasures of masturbation or genital stimulation. Furthermore, males and females tend to learn about masturbation in different ways. Males are more likely to hear about masturbation from others, possibly through observing other males doing it. Females, however, tend to exchange such information less freely and must frequently discover the pleasures of masturbation for themselves. They are more apt to acquire negative associations with their genitals because of menstruation and the threat of pregnancy. As a result, females don't associate pleasure with their genitals to the same degree males do and characteristically engage in less masturbation (Hite, 1976).

When Kinsey (1953) found that the peak sex drives of males occurred during their late teens but that of females not until their late thirties, many people assumed this was a biological fact. But we are now discovering that women are experiencing their peak sexual desires at increasingly earlier ages, suggesting that much of this disparity between the sexes is the result of learning, rather than biology. For example, in response to the question whether or not females have an inherently weaker capacity for sex, a nationwide survey of adolescent girls aged 13–19 showed that two-thirds of them felt that girls enjoy sex just as much as boys. Only 1 out of 10 believed that girls have less capacity for sexual satisfaction than boys (Hunt, 1974). Actually, there seems to be no evidence that the female sex drive is any less intense or "animalistic" than the male's, only that society has demanded that females express their desires according to prevailing stereotypes of appropriate female behavior (Laws & Schwartz, 1977).

The difficulty of comparing the characteristic sex drives of men and women is also compounded by individual differences in both sexes. Today there is a greater appreciation of the variation in sexual desire, expression, and lifestyle among both males and females, making automatic assumptions and labels about the sexes obsolete. In some cases, as Masters and Johnson (1970) have observed, a woman's sexual responsiveness may surpass that of a man, but this also varies more widely among women and with a particular woman at different times. Furthermore, men and women are attracted to each other and sexually aroused in different ways.

Sexual Arousal

Sexual arousal, the level of excitement at a particular moment, varies considerably among individuals as well as between men and women. As we've already mentioned, your tendency toward a low, medium, or high level of arousal depends partly on your own physical make-up. But even more important are your actual experiences of sexual arousal and how pleasant or unpleasant these have been.

A primary means of sexual arousal is the stimulation of our erogenous zones, those parts of the skin that result in sexual arousal when they are stroked. Since physical touching produces pleasurable sensations, almost any portion of our bodies may become an erogenous zone through the association of pleasure and sexual arousal. However, some parts of our bodies are naturally more sensitive than others, resulting in a wide consensus as to our most erogenous zones, as shown in Table 7-1. Except for the genitals, females generally report their breasts as the most erotic zone, while males rate their thighs as the most sexually sensitive part of their bodies.

Another important means of sexual arousal is *foreplay,* or physical contact for the purpose of increasing readiness for intercourse. The most frequently used

TABLE 7-1. PRIMARY EROTIC ZONES EXCLUDING GENITALS

Zone	Males, %	Females, %
Back	4.9	4.3
Breasts	4.9	36.5
Chest	4.6	0.24
Ears	7.0	8.1
Lips	10.0	6.0
Neck	4.6	6.5
Stomach	5.2	6.7
Thighs	31.5	14.2
Other	6.1	3.4

Bernard Goldstein, *Human Sexuality* (New York: McGraw-Hill, 1976), p. 130. Reprinted by permission of the publishers.

Results obtained from a questionnaire given to 370 males and 417 females.

foreplay is some type of general body contact, like hugging or caressing. Simple kissing and tongue kissing occur somewhat less frequently. Although kissing is universally practiced among Americans, it is not nearly so common in many parts of the world as manual manipulation or oral contact with the genitals (Goldstein, 1976). Manual stimulation of the female breasts is also a common means of arousal, with three women observed by Masters and Johnson (1966) being able to reach orgasm by breast stimulation alone.

Of course, handling the genitals is probably the most exciting form of foreplay. For males, handling the penis brings the greatest arousal, with the adjacent scrotum considerably less sensitive though still responsive to caressing. The greater complexity of the female's sexuality furnishes several erogenous areas. The main source of sexual excitement in women is the clitoris, with many women preferring clitoral stimulation to orgasm over vaginal intercourse (Hite, 1976). However, since the female genital area includes an intricate network of nerves, blood vessels, tissue, and muscles surrounding and extending within the vaginal opening, women may be sexually aroused by a wide variety of erogenous stimulation of the surface tissues and vaginal opening as well as of the clitoral shaft itself. Other higher excitable areas are the lips of the vagina and the *mons veneris* or fatty tissue underlying the pubic hair at the top of the vulva.

The time spent in foreplay varies considerably among cultures. The Trob-

NAMING THE SEX ORGANS

Men and women may experience difficulties communicating with each other because they grow up speaking about sex in two different languages.

Almost two hundred college students in the Midwest were asked to write the word or phrase they used to describe the male and female sex organs and sexual intercourse in four different contexts: with others of the same sex, spouse or lover, mixed company, and parents. The results showed that men used a greater variety of terms and varied them more with different listeners. With most people, men were inclined to use slang expressions for the genitals, such as "pussy" or "dick." They also tended to use aggressive or active terms for sexual intercourse. Women were more likely to stick to clinical terms for the genitals, such as "vagina" and "penis." They were more apt to use the phrase "making love" for sexual intercourse, while men used this phrase mostly when speaking with a spouse or lover. Women had learned fewer terms for the genitals and had a more difficult time talking about their own genitals than had men (Sanders & Robinson, 1979).

Another study showed that women were also more likely to have learned euphemistic nicknames for their genitals from their parents such as "bunny," "pocketbook," or "Christmas," which might easily become confusing when the meaning of these words changes in another context (Gartrell & Mosbacher, 1979).

One of the implications of such findings is that parents should be encouraged to teach children the correct anatomical names for genitals so that they will view their sex organs as an equally acceptable part of their bodies as their fingers and toes.

rianders of Eastern Melanesia may spend up to several hours in complex foreplay, while the Lapchaus of the Himalayas engage in a minimum of foreplay (Goldstein, 1976). People in the United States show great variation, both in the duration and the complexity of their foreplay. Even though different studies have yielded contrasting results, there is some evidence that up to 20 to 25 minutes of foreplay increases the woman's chances of reaching orgasm (Gebhard, 1966). Attitude is even more important than the time spent in foreplay. The typical American male tends to work at it with such determination that foreplay ceases to be leisurely and mutually enjoyable. The woman is more likely to say, "take it easy—be a little more playful," which is just one of the differences in the way men and women are sexually aroused. With a proper attitude and sufficient time, foreplay can be a satisfying activity, whether it leads to intercourse or not.

Sex Differences

Many observers have found that men are more readily aroused than women are by such devices as erotic pictures. A common explanation for this is that women have greater inhibitions about sex because of social restraint. As an example, one of the recurring fantasies experienced by normal, healthy women is being overpowered or forced to surrender sexually (Hariton, 1973). Earlier psychoanalytically oriented psychiatrists and psychologists often interpreted this as an indication of female masochism, but today it is more likely to be interpreted as the result of the social suppression of female sexuality. Such feelings as those expressed in rape fantasies are more likely rooted in a woman's anxiety and guilt about wanting sex, and occur more frequently among women from conservative backgrounds.

Actually, Heiman (1975) found that women may be as readily aroused sexually as men; they may simply have more trouble admitting it. With the changing attitudes toward sex in general and women in particular, we sometimes find little or no difference between men and women in response to erotic pictures and stories (Izard & Caplan, 1974). In fact, when a woman feels more comfortable about her sexuality, say, after marriage, such differences may disappear. At least one study of happily married couples has already found that women were aroused by erotic pictures even more than men were (Mann, Sidman, & Starr, 1971).

Another explanation for the differences in sexual arousal between men and women has to do with sex-role learning. Early in childhood males learn to think in more abstract terms and become more activity oriented. Females learn to think more in personal terms, becoming more emotional and relationship oriented. As you would expect, such differences in sexual identity inevitably show up in the way men and women become sexually aroused. For example, men and women respond to pornographic material differently. A man tends to lift the woman out of the picture and fantasize about her privately, while a woman tends to project herself into the picture and imagine herself in the woman's place. As a result, many women are more aroused by a romantic story or a scene of tender expression between men and women than by a picture of a nude male (Gould, 1975).

To sum up, it seems that the characteristic sex drives and arousal patterns of men and women have been shaped in different ways by our cultural patterns. Generally speaking, men tend to emphasize genital satisfaction, while women tend to value loving relationships over genital pleasure. With the personal growth of individuals as well as the influence of women's liberation, however, people of both sexes are outgrowing many of these learned sexual differences. As a result, women are becoming more readily aroused and expressing greater enjoyment of genital sexuality, while men are learning that sex can be even more enjoyable within the context of loving, humane relationships with women.

SEXUAL BEHAVIOR

Although many people agree that our attitudes toward sex are changing, there is less consensus about changes in our sexual behavior. Some people believe there is simply more talk about sex rather than an increased frequency of sexual behaviors. Actually, a great deal depends on *what* specific behavior we are talking about, as well as *which* individual and *how* recently. In this section some of the general patterns of sexual behavior in regard to masturbation, petting, premarital intercourse, and homosexuality are described. But you should keep in mind that the sexual behavior of individuals often varies greatly from one person to another.

Masturbation

One of the earliest sexual behaviors we engage in is masturbation. Essentially, this is the act of manipulating our sex organs to produce pleasure, without the help of another person. Despite the greater openness about sex, some people still worry about how much they can masturbate without harming themselves. Perhaps they haven't heard the old story about the boy who when caught masturbating by his aunt was told it would make him blind, to which he replied, "Then I'll just do it until I need glasses!" Despite such notions there is clinical evidence that we can indulge in frequent masturbation without harm. Raboch (1969) reports on a Nazi experiment in which 21 males were forced to masturbate every 3 hours day and night for 21 months, without any evidence of physical or sexual disorder being found.

The incidence of masturbation has remained fairly consistent among males in the last 25 years, while there has been a moderate increase in masturbation among females. In Kinsey's surveys (1948, 1953) 92 percent of the males and 30 percent of the females had engaged in masturbation by late adolescence.

Later studies have shown that almost all males and from one-half to two-thirds of females have masturbated to orgasm by late adolescence (Hunt, 1974; Diepold & Young, 1979). Experts differ in their explanations of the lower incidence of masturbation among females. Bardwick (1971) argues that females may masturbate less partly because of the relative insensitivity of the inner two-thirds of the vagina, while the clitoris, though more sensitive, is relatively inaccessible. Others point to the greater influence of learned inhibitions against masturbation among females. Support for this view can be seen in the higher incidence of masturbation among married women who have achieved greater acceptance of genital stimulation. In one study, three-fourths of the married women reported masturbating since marriage, with 3 out of 10 of them doing so often (Levin & Levin, 1975).

Individuals of both sexes fantasize during masturbation and, to a lesser extent, use erotic pictures and stories to heighten sexual arousal during masturbation. While fantasies may sometimes involve improbable feats and partners, in most instances the overwhelming majority of both sexes fantasize about sex within a context of affection (Miller & Simon, 1980). Specific techniques of masturbation vary among individuals. Men commonly grasp the penile shaft with one hand and use up-and-down motions with varying pressures and tempos to achieve orgasm. Although women enjoy a greater variety of techniques, a common method is to stimulate the clitoral area with circular, back-and-forth or up-and-down movements of the hand, touching the glans or end of the clitoral shaft only indirectly or lightly, Contrary to pornographic accounts, few women use vaginal insertion, whether their fingers or phallic-shaped objects, to produce orgasm (Crooks & Baur, 1980).

Masturbation is now regarded as a normal part of sexual life, with the majority of men and women, married and unmarried, masturbating on occasion. People may masturbate for any number of reasons, not the least of which is the pleasure of arousal and orgasm. Some people also find masturbation a valuable means of self-exploration. Self-stimulation is often helpful for men experimenting with their response pattern to achieve ejaculatory control and for preorgasmic women learning to have orgasms. Masturbation is also commonly used as a substitute when a sexual partner is not available. Furthermore, the continuation of masturbation within a committed relationship is not necessarily an indication of a problem. According to a survey of married couples in their twenties and thirties, 72 percent of the husbands and 68 percent of the wives masturbated, with an average of twice and once per month respectively (Hunt, 1974).

Probably the greatest change in masturbation practice is the reduced anxiety and guilt associated with it. At the same time, some people may worry about whether they do it too frequently. A survey of students using the University of Chicago Student Mental Health Clinic showed that 25 percent of them feared they masturbated too frequently (Winer et al., 1977). It also appears that many people still have misgivings about achieving pleasure through self-stimulation.

Perhaps this can be explained by the fact that the adventure, stimulation, and closeness of a love relationship that accompany intercourse are missing in masturbation.

Petting

Petting refers to erotic caressing and fondling of another person, which may or may not culminate in orgasm. Youth in every generation has engaged in petting, though the word for it changes periodically. Even the word "petting" may be in the process of being replaced by other terms, such as "making out." The latter term appears to have different connotations for different ages, however, with younger adolescents using it for kissing and the older ones for heavy petting and intercourse.

Young people are beginning to pet at increasingly earlier ages and are more apt to engage in heavy petting than in previous eras. Generally they proceed from hand holding and kissing to light petting, which consists of touching, hugging, and caressing, to more advanced levels. Heavy petting may include handling the girl's breasts and fondling the pubic area or the sex organs of either sex—sometimes to the point of orgasm. "How far to go" sometimes becomes an issue, with the classic contest consisting of males proceeding as far as possible and females attempting to go only as far as is "respectable." The acceptance of heavy petting can be seen in a study of college students that showed that 80 percent of the males and 70 percent of the females had engaged in heavy petting at one time or another (King et al., 1977).

Heavy petting is more likely to occur between people who are going steady or are engaged and is least likely to occur between partners who have little affection for each other (Kaats & Davis, 1970). Yet with the rise of recreational sex, or sex for pleasure, more individuals of both sexes admit to heavy petting with someone they don't really love, especially among those exhibiting a liberal lifestyle in regard to sex (Peplau, Rubin, & Hill, 1977). Heavy petting also has its dangers when it leads to a level of sexual arousal that is not mutual. According to one study, about one-half of the university females reported having been victims of some form of sexual aggression in a dating situation, ranging from kissing to intercourse with violence, with one-fourth of the incidents involving forcible intercourse (Kanin & Parcell, 1977).

Many individuals overlook the value of petting itself, seeing it only as a prelude to intercourse. Yet petting may serve as a means of learning about our own bodily and emotional reactions, as well as how to pleasurably stimulate another person. It also serves as a valuable means of communication and sharing between two people when intercourse is not possible or not desirable. As it is, too many people rush through the petting stage of their sexual development and arrive at intercourse without really acquiring the skills or satisfactions that can be learned from petting. Those people, whom Sorensen refers to as "advanced beginners," have developed their petting activities to a point where they achieve

Touching, hugging, and kissing are valuable means of communication apart from sexual intercourse. (Ken Karp)

a great deal of mutual satisfaction through petting without intercourse. They tend to report a level of mutuality that may surpass that achieved by those who engage in routine intercourse (Sorensen, 1973). It is a lesson many adults could benefit from. For example, Masters and Johnson (1970) suggest that couples having sexual problems temporarily refrain from intercourse. They are told to practice exchanging tender caressing and various sensual pleasures as a way of establishing an overall relationship of intimacy. Only after this climate of closeness has been achieved does intercourse bring deep satisfaction.

Premarital Intercourse

There has been a significant increase in premarital intercourse since the 1950s, especially among middle-class youth and females. One reason has been the growing acceptance of premarital sex among many segments of our society. Another reason is the greater availability of "the pill" and other contraceptives. Yet a third reason is the longer period between puberty and marriage, with an earlier sexual maturation, on the one hand, and a later age of marriage, on the other.

INTROVERTS, EXTROVERTS AND SEX

Marked differences have been found in the sexual behavior of people classified as introverts or extroverts according to the Eysenck Personality Inventory. Extroverts of both sexes tend to masturbate less and engage in more petting and intercourse than introverts. In addition, it was also found that male extroverts tend to have sex with more partners than male introverts, while female extroverts experience orgasm twice as frequently as female introverts.

UNMARRIED GERMAN COLLEGE STUDENTS

	Males		Females	
	Extroverts	*Introverts*	*Extroverts*	*Introverts*
Masturbation	72%	86%	39%	47%
Petting	78	57	76	62
Intercourse	77	47	71	42
Long sex play	28	21	18	21
Cunnilingus	64	52	69	58
Fellatio	69	53	61	53
More than three different positions in intercourse	26	10	13	12

Adapted from H.J. Eysenck "Introverts, Extroverts, and Sex," *Psychology Today*, January 1971, pp. 49–51, 82. Copyright © 1971, Ziff-Davis Publishing Company.

It is difficult to talk about specific percentages of young people who have engaged in premarital intercourse because of the many variables involved. As mentioned at the beginning of this section, much depends on *which* individual, *what* region of the country, *which* social class, and *how* recently. For instance, while young people are beginning sexual intercourse at an earlier age than in the past, this too depends on social-class factors. Women with only a high school education tend to have their first intercourse at an average age of 16, while those who graduate from college begin somewhat later, at an average age of 18 (Levin & Levin, 1975). Among all social classes, however, there is a tendency for the frequency of premarital intercourse to rise with age. Surveys of a cross-section of teenagers, including both blacks and whites, have shown that at age 17, a little under half of the girls and a little over half of the boys have ever engaged in intercourse before marriage. By age 19, over two-thirds of the girls and over three-fourths of the boys report premarital sexual experience (Zelnik & Kantner, 1980). A number of studies, however, now indicate little or no disparity between the proportion of boys and girls reporting premarital sex (Miller & Simon, 1980).

At the same time, it is important to make due allowance for exaggerated notions of sexual intercourse because of the widespread acceptance of premarital intercourse. As one authority so aptly put it, "Today's adolescent has not had as much sex as he says he has, while a generation ago he probably had more sex than he admitted to" (Godenne, 1974, p. 67). A good example of this can be seen in a study of the discrepancy between perceived and actual accounts of intercourse among young people. Collins (1974) found that while women expected 66 percent of their peers to have sexual intercourse when going steady, only 28 percent of them reported actually doing so. At the same time, men expected 91 percent of their peers to have intercourse when engaged, though only 45 percent of them reported this. Such exaggerated notions of sexual intimacy undoubtedly increase the pressure to conform to peer expectations at a time when individuals are especially susceptible to such conformity. Consequently, some individuals may engage in sexual intercourse before they are really ready or desirous of it, mostly because they feel "it's the thing to do."

The majority of young people feel that they should have some kind of loving relationship or mutual commitment before engaging in sexual intercourse. Although partners often kiss on the first or second date, heavy petting and intercourse usually come later in the relationship. Typically, more men than women report having engaged in intercourse on the first date, with 10 percent of the men compared to only 2 percent of the women admitting to this in one study (Collins, 1974). Despite the preference for sex with love, however, there is an increased acceptance of sex as a pleasurable experience in itself, though more so among males than females. In a survey of several hundred college students, 70 percent of the women and 79 percent of the men admitted that "Love enriches sexual relations but is not necessary for enjoyment" (Crooks & Baur, 1980, p. 142). Only a relatively small percentage of students, 30 percent of the women and 12 percent of the men, felt that sex was either not enjoyable or totally inappropriate without love.

The relationship between love and sex appears to be more closely related for women than men. For example, in one study, women reported greater love for their boyfriends if they had engaged in sex, with the love scores being especially high for those whose first sexual experience was with their current boyfriend. The same study found no such relationship between love and sex for men. One possible explanation for this may be the persistence of the double standard in sex, which makes it more acceptable for men to engage in casual sex than for women. As a result, women may tend to rationalize their actions by deciding they must be in love (Peplau, Rubin, & Hill, 1977).

How does premarital sex affect a relationship? As you will notice in Table 7-2, immediate reactions to one's first intercourse vary according to sex. Males generally report more positive reactions than females. But the relatively greater emotional involvement of females in the relationship may partly explain their somewhat more negative response to their first intercourse. Apparently, many of them felt pressured into it and were uncertain how it would affect their

TABLE 7-2. ADOLESCENTS' IMMEDIATE REACTIONS TO THEIR FIRST INTERCOURSE*

	All	Boys	Girls
Excited	37%	46%	26%
Afraid	37	17	63
Happy	35	42	26
Satisfied	33	43	20
Thrilled	30	43	13
Curious	26	23	30
Joyful	23	31	12
Mature	23	29	14
Fulfilled	20	29	8
Worried	20	9	35
Guilty	17	3	36
Embarrassed	17	7	31
Tired	15	15	14
Relieved	14	19	8
Sorry	12	1	25
Hurt	11	0	25
Powerful	9	15	1
Foolish	8	7	9
Used	7	0	16
Disappointed	6	3	10
Raped	3	0	6

Table 510 from *Adolescent Sexuality in Contemporary America* by Robert C. Sorensen, Copyright © 1972, 1973 by Robert C. Sorensen. Reprinted by permission of Harper & Row, Publishers, Inc.

Percentages add up to more than 100 percent because most respondents reported more than one reaction.

relationship with their boyfriends. Females did report more positive reactions to subsequent experiences of intercourse, so there was no real difference between the guilt felt by males or females as a whole. As a matter of fact, half of all the adolescents in Sorenson's study said they were glad they had engaged in intercourse and felt that it had strengthened their relationship. Yet it is interesting to note that more than three times as many girls as boys wished they had waited until they were older before having sex (Sorensen, 1973).

At least one study of college students showed that sexual intercourse had no systematic effect on the future of a couple's relationship. Couples who had intercourse were no more or less likely to stay together than those who had not engaged in sex. As in Sorenson's study, many individuals of both sexes felt intercourse had strengthened their relationship. But others felt their love for each other would have been just as strong or stronger without sex (Peplau, Rubin, & Hill, 1977).

Other Sexual Behaviors

With all the erotic magazines and pornography available to the public today, it is evident that masturbation, petting, and intercourse are not the only forms of sexual behavior being practiced. There are also many others. Here we consider the two that are most common: oral-genital sex and homosexual behavior.

Since oral-genital sex stimulation was considered taboo even among married couples in Kinsey's time, he found that only 20 percent of high-school-educated and 60 percent of college-educated couples admitted having experienced oral-genital sex (Kinsey, 1948, 1953). Since that time, the *Psychology Today* questionnaire has shown that about 35 to 40 percent of both sexes, married and unmarried, reported practicing this type of sexual stimulation *regularly*, with another 10 percent expressing a desire to try it (Athanasiou, Shaver, & Tavris, 1970). Furthermore, Hunt's survey (1974) found that 90 percent of the married couples under 25 years of age—regardless of educational level—had practiced oral-genital sex. The growing acceptability of this practice reminds us that normal or even healthy sexual behavior depends more on the mutual satisfaction of both participants within the bounds of good taste than on the particular nature of the act itself.

Homosexual behavior is another matter of concern, with many people considering this abnormal. Yet the concern about homosexuality often overshadows the amount of homosexual activity that actually occurs. While Sorensen (1973) found that about one-fourth of the 13-to-19-year olds had experienced sexual advances by someone of the opposite sex (twice as many boys as girls), only 11 percent of the boys and 6 percent of the girls reported having at least one homosexual experience. Similar studies of college students have found that about 10 percent of the males and 5 percent of the females reported at least one homosexual experience (Hunt, 1974). In most cases, homosexual experimentation is a passing phase of sexual development and does not lead to a lifelong preference for homosexuality. Also, there are other situations in which people engage in transitory homosexual behavior, as in same-sex boarding schools and prisons, with individuals resuming heterosexual relationships when the opportunity is once again available.

It should be clear that engaging in homosexual behavior does not make one a homosexual. Instead, it may be helpful to distinguish between sexual behavior and sexual orientation. An informed estimate is that only about 2 percent of the men and 1 percent of the women adopt an exclusively homosexual orientation. About 75 percent of the men and 85 percent of the women are exclusively heterosexual, with roughly 23 percent of the men and 14 percent of the women reporting both types of experiences (Crooks & Baur, 1980). However, some gay rights advocates estimate that the actual number of predominately homosexual people is 10 percent of the population, with the higher estimate based on the assumption that many people conceal their sexual orientation because of social pressure (*Time*, Sept. 8, 1975).

Many individuals who exhibit strong homosexual tendencies do not conform to the popular stereotypes of the "effeminate" male or "butch" female homosexual. In addition, many homosexuals marry and have children. Actually, in their attitudes toward sex, male and female homosexuals tend to resemble their heterosexual counterparts more than they do each other. For example, female homosexuals (sometimes called "lesbians") often value the emotional, rather than the sexual, aspects of their relationships with women, while male homosexuals, like male heterosexuals, tend to put more emphasis on genital activity. Consequently, there is a tendency for females to value long-term relationships, while males tend to separate sex from affection and have a greater number of sex partners (Bell & Weinberg, 1978). However, these patterns are not universal, with some men desiring a strong emotional relationship before becoming sexually involved.

Much of the difficulty lies with the way homosexuals are treated by society. In fact, some authorities go so far as to say that it is our attitude toward homosexuals that causes their deviance (Myrick, 1974). Although this appears to be overstating the case, more and more studies are finding that there is little or no difference between homosexuals and heterosexuals in terms of general psychopathology (Hyde & Rosenberg, 1976).

According to one national survey, well over half the population supports the civil rights of homosexuals, though a considerably smaller percentage of the public accepts them in role-model positions such as teaching or the ministry

---

WHAT IS YOUR ATTITUDE TOWARD HOMOSEXUALITY?

The following homophobic scale has been developed to identify homophobia, or the excessive fear of homosexuality. To assess your own attitude, answer *yes* or *no* to indicate your agreement or disagreement with the following statements. The key to interpreting your responses can be found on page 186.

1. Homosexuals should be locked up to protect society.
2. It would be upsetting for me to find out I was alone with a homosexual.
3. Homosexuals should be allowed to hold government positions.
4. I would not want to be a member of an organization that had any homosexuals in its membership.
5. I find the thought of homosexual acts disgusting.
6. If laws against homosexuality were eliminated, the proportion of homosexuals in the population would probably remain the same.
7. A homosexual could be a good President of the United States.
8. I would be afraid for a child of mine to have a teacher who was homosexual.
9. If a homosexual sat next to me on a bus, I would get nervous.

K. Smith, "The Homophobic Scale," in G. Weinberg, *Society and The Healthy Homosexual* (New York: Anchor, 1973), pp. 129–130. St. Martin's Press. Inc. Copyright © 1972 by George Weinberg.

(*Time*, Nov. 21, 1977). While few mental health professionals advocate homosexuality as an adaptive way of life in our heterosexually oriented society, homosexuals are increasingly accepted as normal individuals.

CHANGING ATTITUDES TOWARD SEX

The discussion of homosexuality underlines the importance of our changing attitudes toward sex. Generally, attitudes toward sex are becoming more liberal, with at least two-thirds of the people in one national survey agreeing that it's better to have more openness about things like premarital sex and homosexuality (*Time*, Nov. 21, 1977). Sometimes these changes are loosely referred to as a *sexual revolution*. But after an extensive study of sexual behavior, Hunt (1974) sees them as an extension of the trend toward *sexual liberation*, without a radical break in those cultural values linking sex to love, marriage, and family life. Three changing attitudes that are especially significant are a greater freedom of personal choice in sex, a growing acceptance of sex outside marriage, and an emphasis on sexual fulfillment.

Greater Personal Choice in Sex

More individuals now feel that what they do in regard to sex is their own business. This partly reflects the high value people now place on privacy in their lives. It also reflects their questioning and challenging the conventional approach that measures the morality of our sexual behavior by conformity to one set standard. In a more positive sense, individuals are claiming their freedom of choice in sex as part of their personal freedom in a democratic society. Just as people are free to practice the religion or support the political party of their choice, so they must be free to practice whatever forms of sexuality they desire as long as others are not harmed.

Such personal freedom may provide an opportunity for individuals to develop their own sense of values in sexual matters and thus facilitate personal growth. Sorensen holds that it is this positive use of freedom, rather than the disregard of social values that adolescents have in mind when they insist on doing what they want to do regardless of what society thinks. Many of the adolescents in Sorensen's study felt they had already worked out their own sense of values, though they did not feel what was right for them was necessarily right for others (1973). But such a relativistic approach inevitably makes a greater demand on one's personal maturity than conformity with a set standard, generating a certain amount of uncertainty. In one national study, two-thirds of those under 25 years of age reported they were either uncertain or confused about right and wrong in sexual matters (*Time*, Nov. 21, 1977). The implication is that many young people could benefit from more guidance on the ethical aspects of sex, as long as such instruction encourages the development of personal choices and values.

Greater freedom of choice in sex also carries with it a greater personal responsibility. Freedom implies the responsibility not to act in a compulsive or degrading way or exploit another person. It also implies that you are accountable for the consequences of your behavior. For example, unwanted pregnancy is one potentially serious problem. In Sorensen's study, 55 percent of the adolescents reported that they used no means of birth control during their first intercourse, though a larger percentage did so in subsequent experiences. Their reasons for not doing so suggest that young people need more education in this area. For example, a third of them said they didn't know where to get birth control devices. Some of them felt using such devices would spoil the spontaneity of the act or would force them to acknowledge wanting to have intercourse when they had not fully accepted this. Others cited the lessened stigma of having a child out of wedlock or the greater availability of abortion (Sorensen, 1973). When Sol Gordon asked a group of 300 pregnant high school girls why they became pregnant, not one of them said they really wanted to. Some of their reasons for not using birth control devices included the belief that you couldn't get pregnant the first time you had sex or while standing up. Others used contraceptives such as vaginal foam improperly, as a douche—afterwards (Gordon, 1977).

All things considered, the fact that individuals are initiating intercourse at earlier ages and marrying at later ages implies a greater need for individuals to become more responsible in their use of contraceptives if sexual freedom is to be used positively for personal growth.

Acceptance of Premarital Sex

There is an increased acceptance of premarital sex today. While this is ordinarily taken to mean greater acceptance of sexual intercourse among young people *before* marriage, it also includes acceptance of intercourse among single adults. The proportion of people flatly disapproving of premarital intercourse has been falling steadily in recent decades, though the figures vary from one study to another. Among students at a Southern university, only 20 and 21 percent of males and females respectively expressed disapproval of premarital intercourse (King et al., 1977). A similar survey among students at an upstate university in New York showed that while 26 percent of the males and 47 percent of the females objected to premarital sex primarily for physical satisfaction, only 3 percent of the males and 11 percent of the females objected to premarital intercourse when the couple was in love (Rogers, 1981).

The increasing acceptance of sexual intercourse apart from marriage means that the motives and consequences of sexual behavior become as important as the behavior itself. Then the relevant questions become: Is the desire for sex mutual and voluntary? Does the act of intercourse strengthen or impoverish your relationship with another person? Will having sex harm either partner emotionally or in any other way? Of course, the difficulty with such questions

The motives and consequences of sexual behavior have become as important as the behavior itself. (Teri Leigh Stratford)

is that they cannot be answered authoritatively by anyone. Ultimately, they must be asked and answered by the partners themselves. Obviously, this leaves the way open for individuals to justify their feelings of the moment, to do what they want to do and call it right. But it also opens the way for individuals to examine their attitudes and their relationships in a way that may promote personal growth rather than just blind conformity.

Essentially, the acceptability of premarital sex depends on how meaningful and mutual it is to the partners themselves. For many couples, this means being in love or going steady, though both sexes realize that their love may not necessarily be lasting. Among students at the upstate New York university cited above, 79 percent of the women and 87 percent of the men either strongly approved or approved of premarital sexual intercourse when the couple are in love. At the same time, there is an increased acceptance of the pleasure ethic, with some couples feeling it is appropriate to engage in sexual intercourse mostly for pleasure, provided it is mutually agreeable and satisfying. While 31 percent of the women and 35 percent of the men in the same university approved of premarital sex for physical satisfaction, only 1 percent of the women and 3 percent of the men strongly approved of this, suggesting that the pleasurable ethic is not as firmly established among young people as popularly believed (Rogers, 1981).

Despite the acceptance of premarital sex, guilt still plays a significant role in sexual behavior, with church-going youth most likely to feel guilty about premarital sex (Gunderson & McCrary, 1979). Others who engage in premarital intercourse don't always feel good about it. Among the youth using the University

VIRGINS—A NEGLECTED MINORITY?

To hear some people talk, there are very few virgins left among today's youth. But the facts tell another story.

Even though the actual figures vary from one study to another, approximately half the adolescents are still virgins by their senior year in high school. While the percentage of virgins drops with increasing age, especially during the first two years of college, conservative estimates indicate that at least 2 out of 10 college seniors remain virgins (Jessor & Jessor, 1975; Miller & Simon, 1980). At the same time, many young people hesitate to admit their virginity because of social pressure. As one girl aptly said, "My older sister says she used to lie to her friends and say she was a virgin to protect her reputation. It is just the opposite for me. I lie to my friends claiming I'm not a virgin" (Crooks & Baur, 1980, p. 397).

Reports from single people of all ages show that 22 percent of the men and 21 percent of the women have never had intercourse. Yet, interestingly enough, only 1 and 2 percent of these men and women, respectively, think their peers are also virgins (Shaver & Freedman, 1976). Apparently, each virgin feels he or she is a minority of one.

Virgins may be a valuable minority. There is some evidence that adolescent virgins of both sexes experience less conflicts and enjoy better communication with their parents than nonvirgins do (Sorensen, 1973). Some researchers have also found greater predicted marital happiness for female virgins than nonvirgins. But the reasons have less to do with the fact of virginity itself than the nonsexual personality characteristics of virgins, such as greater personal stability, more conventional values, and stronger moral convictions (Shope, 1975).

Sorensen also found that many of the adolescent virgins of both sexes were that way by choice—either because they felt they were not ready for sex or had not found a suitable partner. It is a reminder that virginity is often an autonomous decision that warrants respect in an age characterized by obsessive and often premature sexual activity.

of Chicago Student Mental Health Clinic, 20 percent reported that their current sexual experiences were making them feel guilty, 12 percent said they had intercourse with those they didn't want to, 12 percent felt they were promiscuous, 10 percent avoided sex because it made them feel guilty, and 6 percent avoided sex out of fear (Winer et al., 1977).

A related issue has to do with whether premarital sex is equally acceptable for women as well as for men. While younger adolescents often adhere to a double standard in which both sexes expect greater sexual experience among males, there is less disagreement on this issue with increasing age (Sorensen, 1973). Even though you will usually find a larger percentage of men than women sanctioning premarital intercourse in the surveys cited above, you may also notice that the difference between the sexes is not large, suggesting that we are evolving toward a single standard in sex. Yet Pietropinto and Simenauer (1977) found that one-third of the men in their survey still want to marry a virgin. Also men who approve of premarital sex for women do so mostly when sex is accompanied by affection or commitment, but not when done primarily for pleasure.

It seems that society is moving toward a more egalitarian standard of sex, but we have a way to go. At present, more young women are taking responsibility for their own sex lives and insisting on greater options than in the past. No doubt this growing sexual liberation will accelerate the movement toward a single standard. Meanwhile, the single standard is more evident among those of both sexes with a liberal sexual lifestyle, who are not only more likely to engage in premarital sex but also derive greater satisfaction and less guilt from it than those holding moderate or traditional sexual values (Peplau, Rubin, & Hill, 1977).

Emphasis on Sexual Fulfillment

Another shift in attitudes is toward greater emphasis on sexual fulfillment. This includes an increasing awareness that sex is not just for reproduction. Sex is also a means of expressing our love for each other as well as a source of intense pleasure. Sometimes, we experience all three of these aspects of sex simultaneously, or in succession, or even separately. But all three aspects of sex are integral parts of our sexual fulfillment.

The emphasis on sexual fulfillment may facilitate personal growth in a number of ways. Unmarried couples may express their love in sexually satisfying ways without feeling they have to rush into marriage to make sex legitimate. Married couples may feel less obligation to have children to justify their marriage. Instead, they can take advantage of a wider range of birth control devices and make a more deliberate decision whether to have children or not. Furthermore, everyone may experience a wider variety of sexual pleasures than before without feeling they are doing something wrong. With greater acceptance of sexuality, we may acquire more understanding of it, as well as more techniques and resources for fulfilling our sexual potential.

A major pitfall in the pursuit of sexual fulfillment, however, is an undue emphasis on sexual performance. When people become overconcerned about performing adequately in sex, they experience new sources of anxiety. Their preoccupation with technique and achieving orgasm often results in mechanical, joyless sex. In short, the pursuit of sexual fulfillment apart from loving relationships becomes self-defeating. As a result, more professionals are suggesting that we need to integrate love and sex even at the level of sexual competence, not to mention healthy relationships. Or as Sol Gordon puts it, "*Love* is part of competence. Caring for another human being, not exploiting another human being, not being exploited, that's part of competence, that's what we can teach" (1977, p. 13).

As mentioned earlier, women have traditionally shown more concern about the relation of love and sex than men have. But Pietropinto and Simenauer (1977) point out that men are not necessarily the insensitive creatures they have been portrayed to be. More than one-third of the men in their study believe that love is the most important thing in the world, with another third admitting that love is essential for sex or makes it better. Both sexes are coming to see that through our sexual encounters, we learn something about ourselves as persons. One of the most valuable lessons of all is that loving, humane relationships are essential for sexual fulfillment. Ultimately, sex cannot be separated from overall relationships and personal growth.

SUMMARY

Many of our attitudes and behaviors are shaped by sex roles—the cultural expectations concerning the appropriate behavior for males and females. We pointed out how the male bias in Western sex roles and stereotyped sex roles exaggerate the differences between the sexes, with negative effects especially evident among women. The concern for more flexible sex roles, which arose out of dissatisfaction with the stereotyped female sex role, promises not only greater adaptability among individuals of both sexes, but also better communication and cooperation between males and females.

The pervasive influence of sex roles can also be seen in sexual motivation, or the urge for sexual activity. Although the sex drive is affected by many factors, ranging from biological to cultural influences, the characteristic male emphasis on genital satisfaction and female emphasis on relationship-oriented sex is thought to be largely the result of sex-role influences. Consequently, the growth toward a mutually gratifying sex life generally requires that women become more accepting of genital sex and that men integrate genital sex into more loving, humane relationships with women.

We also discussed changing patterns of sexual behavior. Probably the two major changes in regard to masturbation have been the increasing incidence of masturbation among women and the diminished sense of guilt associated with this practice among both sexes. Although there has been an increase in more intimate forms of petting, often to the point of orgasm or as a prelude to intercourse, young people tend to overlook the value of petting as a meaningful form of communication in itself. While the increase in premarital sexual intercourse occurs mostly among partners who have established a close relationship, a significant minority of both sexes also seek out sex primarily for pleasure.

We also pointed out that the concern about homosexuality exceeds the amount of homosexual activity, with only a relatively small percentage of individuals adopting an exclusively homosexual orientation.

Attitudes toward sex are generally becoming more liberal and include a desire for greater personal freedom of choice in sex, acceptance of sex outside marriage, and more emphasis on sexual fulfillment. The extent to which these attitudes may lead to increased sexual fulfillment or problems, however, depends largely on how well we integrate sex into a humane, loving way of relating to others, as well as into our personal growth as a whole.

QUESTIONS FOR SELF-REFLECTION

1. What do you usually mean when you use the term *sex*? An act, a set of attitudes, or biological differences?

2. How do you feel toward stereotyped males or females? Do you feel admiration, envy, or contempt?

3. In what ways could you benefit from adopting a more androgynous sex role?

4. It has been said that there are no sexually unresponsive women, only inept lovers. Would you agree or disagree?

5. Have you ever stopped to think that masturbation is a more widely practiced form of sexual gratification than sexual intercourse?

6. Must physical touching and pleasuring always lead to sexual intercourse?

7. What makes you suspect someone of being homosexual? How accepting of such individuals are you?

8. Do you think sexual practices have become more liberal in recent years, or just talked about more openly?

9. At what age should we encourage individuals to practice freedom of choice in sexual matters?

10. Do you think having sexual intercourse primarily for pleasure will become more acceptable in the future?

EXERCISES

1. Sex role identity

This is an exercise to assess your own sex-role identity, based on the male and female sex-role characteristics described earlier in the chapter. Under the heading "Sex Roles" on page 160 you will find five characteristics for the female sex role and five characteristics for the male sex role. After you have reviewed all ten characteristics, try as honestly as you can to select those five traits that are most characteristic of you, regardless of which sex they are associated with.

Now analyze your list of personal characteristics. Are practically all of them associated with your own sex? Are most of them associated with the opposite sex? Or does your list include a mixture of characteristics from both sex roles?

How do you account for your own sex-role identity? Do either or both of your parents seem to have a stereotyped sex-role identity? Does either parent have several characteristics normally found in the opposite sex? If so, which one? Or are your parents more of an androgynous blend of sex-role characteristics from both sexes? Are you comfortable with your own sex-role identity? If not, which characteristics would you most like to change? Would you agree that androgynous people of both sexes are better able to cope with the diverse demands of our society?

2. Sexual concerns

Think over some of the concerns, difficulties, or worries you have about sex, and write one or two of them on a 3 × 5 card without identifying yourself. Then have someone collect the cards and give them to the instructor. Have the instructor read each card, make a brief comment on each question, and ask for other comments or responses from the class.

I have found it helpful to collect the cards ahead of the class session at which I read the cards, thus giving me an opportunity to better understand and respond to each question. Classes usually find this an interesting and helpful session.

3. Sexual attitudes and information

Invite someone with a special expertise or viewpoint in the area of sex to speak to your class. This could be a person who works with an organization such as Planned Parenthood or a center for rape counseling. Or it could be a representative from an organization that advocates some special viewpoint such as gay rights, swingers' groups, or nudist camps. Students often gain new information and have their stereotypes challenged by visiting speakers. The goal of such a visit would be to learn more about the topic, whether you agree with the speaker or not.

Films are another source of information and stimulation. Have each member of the class attend an erotic movie of his or her own choice, and then share the reactions in class. Or arrange to have an erotic, educational film shown in class, allowing time for class discussion afterwards.

4. Attitudes toward homosexuality

Indicate your agreement or disagreement with the statements on the homophobic scale presented earlier in the chapter. Then refer to the key for interpreting your responses below. For purposes of evaluation, you may assign one point for each *yes* answer to statements 1, 2, 4, 5, 8, and 9, and for each *no* answer to statements 3, 6, and 7. The greater the number of points, the more apprehensive or anxious you are about homosexuality. How would you interpret your score? Are you fairly comfortable around homosexuals? Or are you quite apprehensive about them? Is your attitude based on past experiences with homosexuals, or mostly ignorance and fear?

You may want to administer this scale to a group of people such as your class. Have each person calculate his or her own score as explained above. Then calculate an average score for the entire group by adding all the individual scores and dividing by the number of people. In this way, individuals may get some idea of how their attitudes are related to others' attitudes, which you could then use as a basis of a class discussion. But it is important to keep in mind this is an *exercise,* not a test.

Key to the homophobic scale

(*Yes* responses to statements 1, 2, 4, 5, 8, and 9, and *no* responses to statements 3, 6, and 7 indicate homophobic attitudes.)

5. Erogenous zones

Take the list of erogenous zones presented in Table 7-1 and rank them from 1 to 8 according to which of these zones when stimulated gives you the most sexual arousal, which the second most arousal, and so forth. If you want to add other zones to the list, such as feet, simply include these under "others" as item 9. Is your list similar to that in the book? Or is it quite different? How do you account for these differences? Have your past experiences been a factor?

You can also do this as a class exercise. In this case have class members write down on 3 × 5 cards which *one* erogenous zone (except the genitals) when stimulated gives them the *most* sexual arousal. Then collect the cards and make a simple numerical count of the responses for each erogenous zone or, better still, calculate the percentage of responses that match each erogenous zone. How does your list compare to that presented in the book?

6. Sharing sexual fantasies

Each of us has sexual fantasies from time to time, though we rarely share them with others. Such fantasies may be enjoyable in themselves or may be used to enhance arousal during masturbation or sexual intercourse.

If you are married or sexually active with someone you feel secure with, try sharing some of your sexual fantasies with your partner. It is generally helpful if such sharing is mutual rather than unilateral. It is usually wise to begin with mild fantasies that can help desensitize fears and embarrassment and enable you to judge the impact of such sharing on your partner and yourself. It is also best to avoid sharing fantasies that would shock your partner or that involve lovers that may be threatening to the relationship.

Another way of doing this exercise is to have each person in class write one of his or her sexual fantasies on a 3 × 5 card, and have the cards collected. Then have the instructor or some designated person to read each fantasy aloud and invite class reaction.

7. Defining sex terms

So much sex talk is done in slang terms or in an off-color way that most people never learn the proper terms for sex matters, much less their meaning. This exercise is designed to increase your vocabulary of proper sex terms and to speak about sex in a more objective, matter-of-fact way. Essentially, this is a word game along the lines of the old-fashioned spelling bee, with the focus on sex terms.

Divide the class into two or more teams, preferably by having individuals count out 1, 2, 1, 2, until everyone is on a team. Then have your instructor take some authoritative guide of sexual terms and quiz individuals on each team alternately. A good source containing several hundred such terms is Bernard Goldstein's *Human Sexuality* (New York: McGraw-Hill, 1976).

Each person should be asked to write the term on the blackboard and then briefly explain it. You might give 1 point for each term correctly spelled and 2 points for each correct definition. Whenever a person begins laughing or smirking while spelling or explaining a term, 1 point is deducted from his or her team's score.

While this exercise is meant to be fun, it also points up the need for us to learn how to use correct terms for sexual matters in a more natural, matter-of-fact way. One of the reasons people remain ignorant about sex is their embarrassment in talking about it.

RECOMMENDED READINGS

Boston Women's Health Collective. *Our Bodies, Ourselves,* rev. ed. New York: Simon & Schuster, 1976 (paperback). An informed, practical guide to all aspects of female sexuality.

Comfort, A., ed. *More Joy of Sex.* New York: Simon & Schuster, 1975 (paperback). An anthology on the variety of lovemaking, illustrated with tasteful art.

Crooks, R. and K. Baur. *Our Sexuality.* Menlo Park, Calif.: The Benjamin/Cummings Publishing Company, 1980. A well-rounded and readable text on human sexuality, with selected drawings and photographs.

Goldstein, B. *Human Sexuality.* New York: McGraw-Hill, 1976 (paperback). An overview of human sexuality with in-depth information, line drawings, and an extensive glossary of sex terms.

Gordon, S. and R. Libby. *Sexuality Today and Tomorrow.* North Scituate, Mass.: Duxbury Press, 1976 (paperback). A lucid and practical guide to responsible sexuality among young people.

Hite, S. *The Hite Report.* New York: Dell, 1976 (paperback). Contains detailed comments from 3,000 women of all ages on a variety of sexual matters from clitoral stimulation to lesbianism.

McCarthy, B. W. and E. J. McCarthy. *Sex and Satisfaction after 30.* Englewood Cliffs, N.J.: Prentice-Hall, 1981 (paperback). An exploration of sexual fulfillment during the middle years of marriage.

Pietropinto, A. and J. Simenauer. *Beyond the Male Myth.* New York: Quadrangle, 1977. A lively rubuttal to the stereotyped view of males as aggressive and insensitive in sexual matters, based on a national survey of over 4,000 men.

Love and Marriage

Marriage has this peculiar characteristic, observed Ralph Waldo Emerson—"those out want to get in," while "those in want to get out."

It is just as true today as when Emerson said it over one hundred years ago. Approximately 95 percent of all individuals eventually get married, down only a few points from the idyllic 1950s. And college and noncollege youth alike say that the most important thing in life is having a good marriage and family life (Bachman & Johnston, 1979). Apparently, the anticipated satisfactions of marriage outweigh its problems, and achieving lasting intimacy with someone of the other sex remains a major life goal for most people.

At the same time, the divorce rate has risen dramatically in the past few decades, with two out of every three marriages now ending in divorce. It has been estimated that about half of all the children born since the late 1970s will spend part of their lives with only one parent. As a result, there has been an increasing concern among the helping professions to find new ways to improve marriage and family life and to curtail hasty divorces.

We will begin by taking a look at how individuals choose a marriage partner. We will also discuss the types of marital relationships plus selected issues in marital adjustment and growth. Then the important topic of divorce and marriage will be dealt with, as well as alternatives to marriage.

CHOOSING A MATE

While it may not be apparent why someone decides to marry this person rather than that one, some reasons are more common than others. Ordinarily, people like to feel that they are in love with their future partner. Now that marriage is no longer required for economic survival or for the satisfaction of sexual needs, love has become the prevailing rationale for getting married and staying married. Even upper-class couples and royalty, who frequently marry as much for social reasons as for personal motives, prefer marriages based on love.

Love

In everyday terms, love can mean anything from the expression of tender affection for someone to a passionate attachment to another person. The experience of love also varies according to the object of love, such as the love between parent and child, friends, or lovers.

People seem to have little difficulty recognizing love as it relates to their own experience. When college students were asked whether they knew what love was, 90 percent of the women and 84 percent of the men were either certain or thought they knew what love is. Love is usually equated with romantic love and means a strong emotional attachment to a person of the opposite sex, a tendency to idealize that person, as well as a marked sexual attraction to this person (Kephart, 1977). There is also a widespread folklore about romantic love, including the following notions: Love is uncontrollable, like "falling in love." Love is fated, predestined, or "meant to be." Love transcends all social barriers so that "all you need is love." Love is also irrational or "blind." It involves a mixture of ecstasy and suffering such that "true love never runs smooth" or "it's too good to be true."

Psychologists are apt to explain the emotional intensity and irrationality of romantic love in terms of the unconscious aspects of our experience. A Freudian psychologist may explain falling in love in terms of finding someone who resembles our mother or father image. Carl Jung contends that each of us has an unconscious psychic image of the opposite sex. Ordinarily, we are not aware of this until we meet someone of the opposite sex who closely resembles it. When this happens, especially in love at first sight, the psychic image may be projected onto someone of the opposite sex without sufficient regard for what the other person is really like. Frequently, the result is misunderstanding and bitter disappointment. Jung said, "You see that girl, or at least a good imitation of your type, and instantly you get the seizure; you are caught. And afterward you may discover that it was a hell of a mistake" (Jung, in Evans, 1976, p. 282). For this reason, psychologists warn of the dangers of romantic love. Yet empirical studies have failed to show a strong positive relationship between romanticism and maladjustment (Spanier, 1972). In fact, just the opposite seems to be the case. When college students were asked how they had been affected by their experience of love, including infatuation (short-lived affairs), 70 percent or more of both sexes acknowledged that their experience of love had made them a happier person (Kephart, 1977).

Nevertheless, as many songs and novels attest, love is more often sought than found. According to Erich Fromm in his classic book *The Art of Loving* (1956), much of the trouble is that people are preoccupied with being loved instead of loving. When people say they want love, they often mean something to help them overcome their loneliness or feelings of emptiness. Consequently, feelings of love may mask loneliness and dependency or other unmet childhood needs. This may be the reason that romantic love is strongest during courtship and the early stages of marriage but then declines steadily afterwards (Bell, 1975). In contrast, mature love is based on self-love and the ability to give as well as to receive love. Loving relationships are normally achieved only through personal maturity and considerable give and take in intimate relationships. It is probably love in this latter sense that people have in mind when they say that love is the most important quality in their marriage. Here, love is taken to mean emotional closeness, sexual attraction, and personal compatibility with their partner (Tavris & Jayaratne, 1976). When couples fail to transform romantic love into mature love, they often end up with an "empty" marriage or a devitalized relationship, as discussed later in this chapter.

Do Likes or Opposites Attract?

Many of the reasons two people become attracted to each other have already been discussed under interpersonal attraction. You may recall the importance of proximity, or two people being in the same class in school or same work setting, how frequently they see each other, how physically attracted to each other they are, and how mutual their attraction is. Another important factor has to do with compatibility, or how like or unlike two people are in their personal make-up and backgrounds.

Similarity of social characteristics remains one of the most reliable predictors of attraction and a lasting marriage relationship. That is, we tend to be most compatible with someone who comes from the same background as ourselves in terms of income, social class, educational level, race, and religion. Even though more people are marrying across these boundaries, they remain in the minority (Kephart, 1977). Yet people seem to be paying less attention to such factors. According to a *Redbook Magazine* survey of married women, only 4 percent of them felt similarity of backgrounds was important for marriage, while one-third of them felt it was unimportant (Tavris & Jayaratne, 1976). Much of the change in attitude has to do with living in a mobile, individualistic society. While initially this affords people greater freedom in the selection of a marriage partner, it also exposes them to greater dangers of incompatibility later in the relationship as the partners increasingly engage in the mutual accommodation so necessary in marriage.

Similarity of personal characteristics such as attitudes and interests is considerably less reliable as a predictor of attraction and marital success. Yet it is important. For instance, it has been shown that couples with a high degree of similarity in such matters as physical attractiveness, self-esteem, sex drive, and neurotic tendencies move toward marriage faster than do other couples (Murstein, 1971). Which characteristics attract two people, of course, depends largely on what each person considers important and this varies according to individual and sex differences. Apparently, men are more attracted to women with similar attitudes on sex, while women are more attracted to men with similar attitudes on religion (Touhey, 1972). Also, men tend to be attracted to women on the basis of physical attractiveness and sex appeal, while women are more attracted to men on the basis of personal characteristics such as intelligence, self-confidence, and successfulness (Morse, Gruzen, & Reis, 1973; Tavris, 1977).

The romantic notion that opposites attract has already been discussed in relation to the theory of complementary needs (Winch, 1971). According to this view, as you will recall, individuals tend to select marriage partners whose need patterns complement their own, making for mutual gratification. For example, an achievement-oriented person will tend to marry an easy-going person who admires achievement and success. Or an outgoing "life of the party" person will marry a shy, introverted mate. At the same time, the very qualities that complement each other's personality may become the basis of conflicts when things are not going well. Consequently, there seems to be more support for opposites being attracted on specific traits such as dominance, as discussed in Chapter 6. Furthermore, an attraction based on complementarity often involves unconscious factors that are difficult to verify, though these may be more apparent in a clinical assessment of a couple's relationship during marriage or family therapy. While healthy marriage relationships may combine varying degrees of similarity and complementarity, it is more important that both partners have the ability to change and adapt to each other's needs as they grow in their relationship. Interestingly, Goodman (1976) found that people with low self-esteem are more likely to marry to complement their needs, while those with high self-esteem are more likely to marry someone with high esteem like themselves.

A Rational or Emotional Choice?

Because romantic love is so subjective and unpredictable, it is sometimes suggested that we should encourage couples to judge their compatibility by more rational means. Yet it would be a mistake to ignore our feelings as much as it would be to rely on them exclusively. For our emotions tell us something about our intuitive, unconscious response to others. Actually, we need to use our heart as well as our head, and take both emotional and rational influences into consideration in making a wise decision about marriage. This is one of the reasons why couples who become better acquainted during their dating and courtship have a much better chance for a happy marriage than those who rush into marriage (Udry, 1974).

Interestingly enough, the stereotypes of the rational male in control of his feelings and the highly emotional female are misleading. Rubin (1973) found that men actually scored higher than women on scales measuring romanticism. And Combs and Kenkel (1966) found that women were more demanding and less satisfied with their computer-matched dates than men. It may be that women experience more romantic attachments during early adolescence than men. But, as they approach marriageable age, women tend to gain better control of their romantic feelings and make more realistic choices than men—mostly because of their greater investment in the marriage relationship.

What about couples who live together before marriage? How does this affect both their decision to marry and the marriage itself? While it may be too early to tell, some evidence is suggestive. According to one comparison of cohabiting couples and other dating couples, there is little difference regarding the decision to eventually marry someone, with cohabiting couples only slightly less inclined to marry than other couples, and little or no difference in regard to the decision to marry their current partner. Women were slightly more likely to marry their partner when living together than when not. But there was no difference in the likelihood that men planned to marry their partner among cohabiting and non-cohabiting couples. Cohabiting couples did move toward marriage more quickly and were less likely to go through the rituals of traditional marriage, such as taking a honeymoon. Once married, however, there was no reported difference in marital satisfaction among couples who had lived together and those who had not (Risman et al., 1981).

THE MARRIAGE RELATIONSHIP

Despite the risks of marriage, more than 9 out of 10 people eventually marry, most of them in their twenties. While many couples, especially among the college-educated people, may wait longer before marrying than in previous decades, the delay in marriage has been exaggerated. The main reason is that while the median age of all marriages has been rising in recent years, it has been vitally affected by the increasing rate of divorce and remarriage among young people. In contrast, the median age for *first* marriage has remained remarkably stable, at about 21 for women and 23 for men (U.S. Bureau of the Census, 1981). The biggest change has been in the goals of marriage.

Goals in Marriage

People now are more apt to marry for companionship and the satisfaction of psychological needs than for economic and social needs.

The main reason people marry is to find companionship. When 75,000 married women were asked about the importance of various qualities of married life, their top three choices were love, respect, and friendship in that order, all having to do with the relationship aspects of marriage (Tavris & Jayaratne, 1976). Companionship provides marriage partners with an emotional "home base" to see them through the ups and downs of life. During the days of the Stalinist terror in Russia, many couples felt that it was the openness and supportiveness in their marriage that helped them keep their sanity (Mace, 1975).

Individuals are also putting a higher priority on the fulfillment of psychological needs, rather than on the traditional needs of financial security or having

Both men and women are looking for companionship in marriage. (Teri Leigh Stratford)

children. For example, many young couples are no longer willing to sacrifice to give their children the "best" or stay in an unhappy marriage for the sake of the children (Yankelovich, Skelly, & White, 1977). Instead, marriage is seen as a means of personal fulfillment and growth. To a large extent, this reflects the affluence and changing values of society in which actualization needs have taken precedence over maintenance needs.

Another important goal is greater flexibility and openness in marriage. This includes such diverse matters as more flexible family roles, two-career families, commuting couples, and greater honesty and authenticity in marriage. Yet, the attainment of these goals often exacts a price neither partner has fully anticipated. Good communication especially remains a stumbling block for many couples, mostly because, like love, it is something easier to desire than to achieve.

The quality of the marriage relationship has now become more important than its permanence. In part, this reflects the growing belief among Americans that personal happiness is a right rather than a luxury. Consequently, couples tend to expect more from their marriages than in the past and are more likely to end an unhappy marriage than their parents were. This has led some couples to formalize their expectations and claims on each other in marriage contracts and to negotiate their differences with an eye toward maximizing mutual happiness.

Although these values are important to most people, not all couples are able to achieve them in the same way and in the same degree. As a result, there are different types of marriage relationships.

Types of Marriage Relationships

William Lederer and Don Jackson (1968) have classified marriages according to two dimensions: satisfactory/unsatisfactory and stable/unstable. They say that most intact marriages are probably of the satisfactory/unstable type, in which there is a strong commitment to the marriage despite occasional stress, disappointments, and quarrels. On the other hand, most couples that end up in marriage counseling or divorce have an unsatisfactory/unstable relationship, characterized by continuing conflict and mutual destructiveness.

One of the most widely known typologies of the marriage relationship comes from a study by Cuber and Harroff (1965). After interviewing over one hundred couples who had been married for over ten years and had never seriously considered divorce, they classified couples according to one or more of the following types.

The *conflict-habituated* relationship is typical of couples who have fallen into a habit of nagging and quarreling. It has become a way of life for them, so that they are constantly finding something to disagree about. Yet it is the stimulation of their differences and conflicts that holds these couples together, sometimes aided by a satisfactory sex life.

The *devitalized* relationship is characteristic of couples who at one time may have been in love, enjoyed sex, and had a close identification with each other. But they have drifted into an empty marriage and stay together mostly because of their children or their community standing. Interestingly enough, many of these couples do not feel especially unhappy, but think it is natural for married life to be dull and routine after the excitement of the earlier years has passed. Unfortunately, this is probably the most common type of marriage.

Couples who have a *passive-congenial* relationship are similar to the devitalized couples, except their relationship has been this way from the beginning. Often such couples have entered marriage in a calculating, unemotional way, viewing marriage more as a social and economic arrangement than a personal relationship. As with the devitalized couples, there is little emotional involvement, resulting in less overt conflict but also less personal satisfaction in marriage. Actually, the partners are more resigned than committed to each other.

All of these types are really different forms of the *utilitarian* marriage, with the emphasis on role rather than personal relationships. In contrast, the last two types are forms of the *intrinsic* marriage, in which the marriage relationship itself is of central importance.

The *vital* relationship is one in which the partners are bound together primarily by their personal relationship with each other. There is much mutual concern with satisfying each other's psychological needs and the sharing of many activities. In fact, the process of sharing takes precedence over the content of any specific instance of sharing. Each person retains a strong personal identity. There is honest and open communication between partners, and when there are conflicts, they tend to be about really important matters and are settled rather quickly. This is the most satisfying type of marriage, but unfortunately it is also the least common.

The *total* relationship is much like the vital marriage except more so. Here, couples become "one flesh." They engage in total togetherness, allowing for a minimum of private experience or conflict. Unlike the devitalized relationship, however, agreement is usually for the sake of the relationship itself, rather than for peace at any price. This type of marriage is exceedingly rare. But then one might pose the question, "Just how desirable is this type of marriage anyway?"

Do you know couples who fit into one or more of these categories? George and Nena O'Neill found many examples of these types of marriages in their own research with couples (1976). Actually, it may be hard to tell unless you know a couple well. Sociologist Richard Udry contends that most Americans "do not know what happens after marriage" (1974). Instead, friends, relatives, and sometimes children see mostly what couples want them to see. The unfortunate result is that many young couples enter marriage with only the vaguest notion of what is actually involved in the relationship aspects of marriage. Yet, this aspect of marriage holds the greatest potential for marital happiness.

Happiness Is a Satisfying Relationship

How happy a couple feels depends directly on their satisfaction in the relationship aspects of their marriage. For example, a landmark study of American mental health showed that those who are very happy in their marriage are more likely to stress the relationship aspects of their marriage, while those less happy rely more on role relationships or the situational aspects of marriage. It seems that when you are happy in the marriage relationship, you're happy despite day-to-day disappointments in your surroundings. But when you are not happy in your marriage relationship, then you tend to look for happiness more in your children, job, or material things. True happiness, though, is a satisfying relationship with your spouse. Interestingly, married respondents reported greater satisfaction with their marriages in the late 1970s than in the 1950s. But happily married couples are also more willing to admit conflict or resentment in their marriages today. It appears that much of the rise in marital happiness comes from the increased emphasis on the relationship aspects of married life and the growing tendency for dissatisfied couples to divorce (Veroff, Douvan, & Kulka, 1981).

Women tend to value the relationship aspects of marriage more highly than men. According to one study, the top three sources of happiness for married women were love, marriage, and their partner's happiness, while the corresponding rankings for men were personal growth, love, and marriage. When all the respondents currently in love were questioned, only about half reported that they and their partners loved each other equally. The rest, more women than men, were on the giving end of an unequal love affair (Shaver & Freedman, 1976).

Findings like these have prompted Jessie Bernard to say that women have been reared to need men and close relationships so much that they will cling to marriage regardless of its costs. But she asks, "Does the satisfaction of these needs for love and companionship have to extort such excessive costs?" (1972, p. 53). On the one hand, the greater investment of women in their marriage relationships leads married women to report higher happiness than single women, but, on the other hand, they also complain of more marital unhappiness than their husbands. In one study, however, the paradox of the happily married woman who complains a lot was found mostly among housewives. Married women employed outside the home were both happier than single women and had fewer psychological problems than housewives (Shaver & Freedman, 1976).

We should also point out that while men are generally more satisfied with their marriages than women are, both sexes are increasingly apt to judge by the same criteria, especially regarding the importance of the relationship aspects of marriage. Consequently, the quality of marital happiness tends to differ more in degree than in kind between spouses today (Rhyne, 1981).

MARITAL ADJUSTMENT AND GROWTH

To desire a satisfying marriage relationship is one thing; to achieve it is another. Unfortunately, the various myths of marriage incline us to expect the impossible. For example, one person cannot satisfy all our needs. Then too, couples tend to gloss over important issues during their courtship and the early stages of their marriage. Moreover, most couples do not prepare themselves with the communication and interpersonal skills needed for marriage. Most of them are too busy getting a license, planning their marriage ceremony and reception, finding a place to live, and setting up housekeeping. But later on, as the glow of the early months of marriage wears off, the couple settles down to the more central task of marriage—learning how to adjust to each other.

Role Adjustments

It is usually easier to adjust to someone who comes from a similar background. For one thing, we have already learned many of the same marital roles or the behavior expected of us in marriage. This is one reason why the similarity of social backgrounds is such a good predictor of marital success. It is also why individuals who marry from mixed backgrounds—whether in social class, religion, race, or even intact or broken homes—face a greater risk in their marriage. For they enter marriage with greater differences, many of which they may become aware of only after they have begun living together. However, the statistical association between background factors and marital success is not absolute, nor is it binding on an individual marriage. A couple who have everything going for them may fail disastrously in their marriage, while another couple with everything against them may achieve a highly satisfactory relationship. But these are exceptions to the rule. Actually, a great deal depends on the individuals involved, how personally compatible they are, and the intangible qualities they bring to the marriage, especially their motivation to make their marriage work.

How much a husband and wife agree or disagree in regard to their respective roles becomes a very important area of marital adjustment for many couples. For example, a man may see himself as a good husband because he earns a good salary, though his wife may feel it is important that he take more time with the children or do more things with her. A woman may feel she fulfills the sexual demands made by her husband by having intercourse so many times a week, while her husband may feel dissatisfied because of her passivity. To achieve satisfaction in marriage, both partners must continue readjusting their understanding of what they can reasonably expect of each other in their respective roles.

Much of the adjustment in marriage comes from adapting to newer, emerging roles in marriage. One of the most important of these is the greater flexibility in the respective role expectations between husbands and wives, with more sharing of roles between partners. For example, more wives are now sharing the provider role by working outside the home, while husbands are sharing more

There is more sharing of roles between marriage partners today. (Teri Leigh Stratford)

in rearing the children and performing routine chores around the house. Decision making has also become more democratic. For example, there's a tendency for the person with the greatest competency or available time to be responsible for a given task, like paying the bills. Another change is the growing responsibility of the husband for helping his wife achieve sexual satisfaction, thereby ensuring greater mutuality in sex. There is also more emphasis on the relationship aspects of marriage, including better communication, discussion of problems, and a more therapeutic, supportive role for both partners (Bell, 1975).

It seems that Swedish couples share household chores more evenly than American couples do, but their practice lags considerably behind their ideology. In the majority of Swedish marriages, women do most of the cooking, laundry, and cleaning. Only in a minority of cases do husbands share or do most of the chores, such as bedmaking, dishes, and food shopping. At the same time, younger couples share more evenly than do older couples, suggesting that the trend is toward greater role sharing (Haas, 1981).

One difficulty with sharing roles is that each partner tends to want greater rewards at no additional cost. For example, a husband may want his wife to work to help pay the bills, but may still expect her to continue doing all the things she did around the house before taking a job. In turn, a working wife may want to keep most of her earnings and may expect her husband to help out more around the house. It is interesting, in this regard, that many professional women are engaging more in role expansion than in role sharing. That is, despite working outside the home, they continue to regard housework chores as their own. One explanation may be their need to demonstrate that a professional woman can be just as good a wife as a nonworking wife (Yogev, 1981). In due time, though, women employed outside the home may need to redefine their roles more realistically, including more role sharing and mutual accommodation.

Many individuals continue adhering to the more conventional, fixed husband-and-wife roles, especially those with less education or in blue-collar jobs. In these instances there is less concern with the emerging goals of interpersonal intimacy, democratic decision making, and mutuality of sexual satisfaction (Bell, 1975). There is also some evidence that couples who maintain strong kinship ties with those outside their marriage tend to follow more conventional roles. In-laws have a way of exerting pressure as well as fulfilling recreational needs of young married couples, thus restricting their roles to traditional patterns.

Communication and Conflict

One of the most important areas of marital adjustment is learning to communicate effectively with your partner. One study disclosed that happily married couples, compared to unhappily married couples, had not only more communication but also better communication. They talked about a wider range of subjects, conveyed more understanding of what they heard, showed more sensitivity to each other's feelings, and supplemented their verbal communication with more nonverbal signals as well. In contrast, unhappily married couples often compounded their problems with faulty communication, such as expressing their feelings indirectly and vaguely rather than directly, not conveying a clear, complete, or sufficiently forceful message, and failing to get valuable feedback from their partners (Navran, 1967).

The same applies to nonverbal communication. Happily married couples seem to have no trouble understanding each partner's emotional messages, while dissatisfied couples distort such messages in a negative way. Husbands are especially likely to misunderstand a wife's emotional messages in an unhappy marriage (Gottman & Porterfield, 1981).

Some degree of conflict is inevitable in such an intimate relationship as marriage. The most common conflicts involve a breakdown in communication, loss of shared goals, or sexual incompatibility, all of which pertain to the marriage relationship itself. Other problems frequently involve money, children, infidelity, or in-laws. Sometimes recurring conflicts that do not reach a solution may be more symptomatic of an underlying power struggle in the marriage relationship than the matter at hand. Such power struggles are more likely to occur in marriages in which both partners are highly competitive or in which one spouse is dominant and the other is submissive. Couples sharing power more or less equally experience fewer conflicts and greater satisfaction in marriage (Tavris & Jayaratne, 1976). The least satisfying to both partners is the female-dominated relationship (Peplau, Rubin, & Hill, 1976).

A crucial part of communication is the management of conflict. Couples tend to adopt one of two general styles of handling conflict: either *engagement* in which they meet their differences in a variety of ways, or *avoidance,* in which they deny them (Rausch, 1974). Interestingly, 80 percent of the couples who seek out training for conflict management do so because they have avoided conflicts (Bach & Wyden, 1969). Apparently the emotional void or empty marriage experienced by such couples is more intolerable than the prospect of facing conflict. In fact, a marriage counselor, David Mace, says, "It would not be too much to say that interpersonal conflict, far from being an extraneous element in modern marriage, actually represents the raw material out of which an effective marital partnership has to be shaped" (1975, p. 9).

It is not so much whether couples experience conflicts but how they handle them that makes the difference in marriage. According to an extensive survey of married women, those who were the most satisfied with their marriage readily admitted having disagreements and conflict but felt they had learned how to handle these in an agreeable manner (Tavris & Jayaratne, 1976). One of the main difficulties couples have is "fighting dirty" in which the partners not only destroy their intimacy, but often the relationship itself. After appropriate training in conflict management, however, many couples learn how to handle their conflicts in a way that promotes intimacy rather than alienation.

Although Bach and Wyden (1969) distinguish between the rational methods of handling conflict and the more destructive "kitchen sink" or "Virginia Woolf" type fighting, there are dangers in using the leveling or catharsis view of handling aggression. For example, in a study of husband-wife conflicts, Straus (1975) found that, as the verbal aggression increases, physical aggression also increases dramatically, suggesting a point of diminishing returns for airing complaints openly.

A fairly common conflict that baffles many couples is fighting to avoid intimacy. This tends to occur when one or both partners feel temporarily engulfed by their closeness. The fight then serves the unconscious purpose of creating optimal distance between the partners. The one who needs more distance in order to feel comfortable in the relationship often starts the fight. Interestingly enough, such fights tend to occur over "nothing" and are especially apt to occur after a satisfying experience such as lovemaking. Seasoned couples may come to regard such fights as a warning signal for temporary relief from closeness so that they may preserve a more lasting intimacy (Bach & Wyden, 1969).

Sex in Marriage

A quarrel may sometimes end in the bedroom. For there is a strong positive association between a couple's satisfaction in their marriage and their sexual life. It seems impossible to tell which one influences the other more. In fact, each aspect of marriage is equally effective in predicting the other ten years later (Dentler & Pineo, 1960).

A fairly common concern among couples is the discrepancy between the husband's and wife's desire for sexual intercourse and the satisfaction each derives from it. Compared to their wives, husbands characteristically desire intercourse more frequently, achieve orgasm more regularly, and report enjoying sex more than their wives (Fisher, 1973). Both the desire for sex and the satisfaction experienced varies more widely among women than men, as well as with a particular woman from time to time (Masters & Johnson, 1966). At the same time, there appears to be greater mutuality of sexual satisfaction among the better-educated couples, with over half of the middle-class couples enjoying intercourse equally—roughly twice the number of lower-class couples (Rainwater, 1965). Generally, the more frequently intercourse leads to orgasm, the more a woman enjoys her sex life (Levin, 1975). But this often does not occur when the man reaches orgasm first or fails to provide effective manual or oral stimulation for his wife.

Although Masters and Johnson have shown the existence of one kind of physiological orgasm in women, they did note a subjective difference between orgasm achieved through clitoral or vaginal stimulation. Women reported that a clitorally stimulated orgasm is more locally intense and sharper, while orgasm achieved through penile-vaginal intercourse is more diffused throughout the genital area and body and more satisfying psychologically. Furthermore, while Hite (1976) found that no more than a fourth of her respondents achieved orgasm through intercourse alone, 87 percent said they enjoyed intercourse because of the feelings of closeness and security associated with it.

Common problems for husbands are premature ejaculation and impotency, or the inability to achieve or sustain an erection. Although traditionally most men have not been bothered by impotency until they reach 45 or 50 years of age, more younger men are experiencing this problem. Much of the reason has to do with the man's increased anxiety over performing well, especially satisfying his wife's heightened desire for enjoyable sex. Boredom from unlimited sex or sex with the same partner over the years may also contribute to impotency, though this usually vanishes upon taking another sex partner. The most common complaints among women are slowness in becoming aroused and trouble achieving orgasm (Shaver & Freedman, 1976). Husbands can be more effective in arousing their wives by encouraging them to vocalize their preferences more freely. Also, both partners may find it helpful to get a better understanding of the fourfold sexual response cycle—defined as the excitement, plateau, orgasm, and resolution phases—as well as the need for variation in lovemaking (Masters & Johnson, 1966). Probably most helpful of all is an attitude of love and sensitivity with a healthy acceptance of sensuality on the part of both partners.

Couples tend to engage in intercourse less frequently the longer they remain married. This generally leads to diminished satisfaction with their sex life, but not greatly so. For example, one study found that 67 percent of the couples married 10 years or more described their sex life as "good or very good," compared to 82 percent of newly married couples. Actually, much depends on the particular couple. Sexually satisfying marriages tend to remain that way, while sexually lukewarm marriages tend to turn even cooler (Levin, 1975). Despite the preoccupation of Americans with the frequency of intercourse, though, it appears that overall happiness in sex depends more on its quality, or what it means to the couple, than its frequency (Shaver & Freedman, 1976).

While the great majority of husbands and wives restrict sexual intercourse to their marriage partners, marital infidelity has been on the increase since the 1960s. When men become involved with someone else, women are apt to believe it is because of the quest for sexual variety, thus reinforcing their image of men as "sexual animals." But when women stray outside the relationship, men tend to feel their partners are seeking greater love and affection or commitment, reflecting their view of women as "marriage-oriented." Among both sexes, however, suspicion of a partner's sexual involvement with someone else often reflects an underlying fear that their own sexual attractiveness is inadequate (White, 1981).

Traditionally, the double standard in sex has permitted husbands to engage in sex outside of marriage more frequently than wives, but that too is changing. Today more women are engaging in extramarital sex. Marital infidelity is especially common among women who have engaged in premarital intercourse and who work outside the home. Working women are twice as likely as housewives to have sex outside of marriage. Although women who participate in extramarital sex tend to be dissatisfied with marriages more frequently than are other wives, the difference is not striking. Furthermore, a small minority of wives who engage in extramarital sex report enjoying their marriage, including their sex life, suggesting that some of the motivation for extramarital sex may be experimental or recreational rather than from dissatisfaction or for retaliation (Levin, 1975).

The appeal of extramarital sex arises partly because the novelty and excitement of sex wears off the longer a couple lives together. Yet, as Masters and Johnson point out in *The Pleasure Bond* (1974), the satisfaction and commitment a couple enjoys in their relationship may actually strengthen their overall bond of pleasure, which can compensate somewhat for the loss of sensual excitement.

Changes with the Length of Marriage

It is not uncommon to hear married couples say, "Our marriage is different today than it was ten or fifteen years ago." Some couples feel they have grown closer together, while others feel they have drifted apart. But few will deny that their marriage has changed with the years.

One of the most consistent changes is a decrease in marital happiness, especially after the first few years of marriage. Roger Gould (1978) found that after the first several years, couples were usually less convinced that their marriage was a good thing. Instead, both partners were increasingly concerned about being accepted for "the person that I am" in the marriage. Much of this can be explained by the inevitable transition from romantic love to the everyday reality of living together. As both partners become more aware of their need to adjust to each other as they are rather than as they wish each other to be, they are generally less satisfied in their marriage.

Changes in marital satisfaction are also affected by such things as the presence

---

WHAT ABOUT HAVING CHILDREN?

Until recently, married couples were expected to have children. But in the last decade, the option of not having children has become more acceptable. Generally, a couple will postpone having children until they make the postponement final (Veevers, 1973).

More couples are waiting until their late twenties and early thirties to have their first child. Interviews with parents who had their first child early or late disclosed advantages and disadvantages to both patterns. Parents who waited mentioned having a chance to solidify their marriage and career before having a child. Those who had their children early cited the advantage of being able to grow up with their children and avoid a conflict with their career development later on (Daniels & Weingarten, 1981).

Couples are having fewer children as well. According to a 1980 Gallup Poll, over half of the public now prefers the two-child family. Only one in six individuals favors having four or more children, down from the one in two persons in the late 1960s. The most frequent reasons given for not having children include family expenses, squabbling children, lack of privacy, and overpopulation (Fleming, 1975).

Having children also has a great impact on the parents' marriage. Parents derive many satisfactions from rearing children, including a greater sense of purpose and responsibility, as well as affection and fun. But rearing children also brings financial burdens, difficulties balancing work and family, and less time to spend with each other. Consequently, couples generally report lessened marital satisfaction with the duration of marriage. Yet as children grow up and leave home, many couples report renewed levels of happiness, as shown in the figure below.

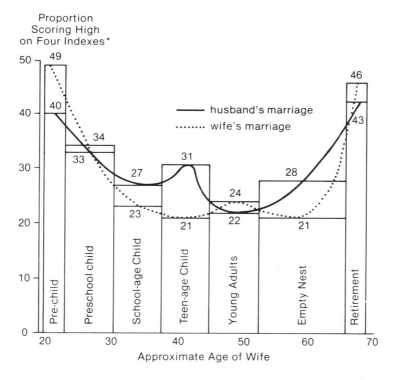

general marital satisfaction; positive companionship; satisfaction with present stage in the life cycle; and absence of negative feeling

From Boyd C. Rollins and Harold Feldman, "Marital Satisfaction over the Family Life Cycle," *Journal of Marriage and the Family*, 32 (February 1970), pp. 20–28. Copyright © 1970 by the National Council on Family Relations. Reprinted by permission.

of children, the number of children and their ages, and the duration of marriage. Studies of many married couples have shown the following typical pattern of marital satisfaction. Generally, there is a high degree of marital happiness in the first two years, followed by a sharp decline between the second and eighth year, with a strong rebound about the ninth or tenth year of marriage. The ebb and flow of marital satisfaction continues, with low points just before the end of the second decade of marriage (too many teenagers?) and just before the twenty-fifth anniversary. Those who were still together at their fiftieth anniversary, however, reported levels of marital happiness as high as the first two years of marriage (Greeley, 1981).

Over the course of time, the average marriage in our society tends to become devitalized, with less love expressed between spouses but also with fewer problems. Marriage partners usually speak to each other less often, exchange less information, provide less self-disclosure, engage in more fault-finding, and have a less accurate understanding of each other. In short, the partners tend to grow apart. Husbands tend to become more preoccupied with their career than with their home life. And once the children have left home, wives tend to seek more outside fulfillment (Swensen, Eskew, & Kohlhepp, 1981).

Fortunately, there are many exceptions to these patterns. In the study just described, for example, individuals who remained open to each other and grew together expressed more love in their retirement years than earlier in the marriage. As you can tell, much depends on the particular couple. How about the couples you know? Or if you are married, how about you and your spouse?

DIVORCE AND REMARRIAGE

Now that the success of a marriage is judged more by the happiness it brings than how long it lasts, people are less likely to remain in empty marriages. You need only look at the dramatic rise in the divorce rate. According to the U.S. Census Bureau, 1 out of 5 marriages ended in divorce in 1930, compared to 1 out of 3 in 1960. Today, the divorce rate is 2 out of every 3 marriages. The divorce rate tends to be higher among people who marry in their teens, after only a brief courtship, and who come from an unhappy or broken home. Divorce rates are also higher among those from lower educational and socioeconomic backgrounds and those who don't belong to a church or synagogue.

Marriages that end in divorce are generally short-lived. A significant number of separations occur in the first few years following the marriage. Because of legal procedures, however, the average elapsed time from the marriage to the divorce is about six years (Kephart, 1977). At the same time, many separations come only after a long, anguished process of mutual alienation, sometimes after the children have grown up and left home.

Causes of Divorce

Although it is practically impossible to pinpoint the real causes of any divorce, the official grounds for divorce given by couples are suggestive. One study comparing the counseling records of 600 couples applying for divorce found that wives cited twice as many complaints as their husbands. Wives were more likely to mention physical and mental cruelty and problems of money or drinking, while husbands more frequently mentioned cruelty, neglect of the home and children, infidelity, and sexual incompatibility. There were also social class differences. Lower-class couples showed more concern with money and physical behavior, while middle-class couples expressed more concern with psychological and emotional satisfactions (Levinger, 1966).

The rising divorce rate probably tells us as much about the changing expectations of marriage as it does about marital instability. Couples today expect more from their marriages than couples did in the past. This is especially true for highly educated and professional couples, who are more inclined to expect psychological fulfillment in their marriage and to seek a divorce when it is missing. Those with less education and blue-collar jobs are more likely to remain in an unhappy marriage (Landis, 1975).

Breakdown in communication and loss of shared goals are two of the most common problems in marriage. (Teri Leigh Stratford)

The Divorce Experience

Getting a divorce is usually a complex crisis because several things are happening at once. Bohannan (1975) has identified 6 of these overlapping experiences common to almost everyone's experience of divorce, although they may occur in different order and with varying intensities from couple to couple.

The *emotional divorce* is most likely to occur first. The partners tend to withdraw emotionally from each other, or to coexist with a great deal of mutual antagonism. The cold-war atmosphere of this emotional divorce often does more damage to the children than the physical, legal divorce that follows.

The *legal divorce* is necessary if the individuals ever want to remarry. In most states couples may divorce only if there are sufficient grounds for divorce, such as mental or physical cruelty, adultery, or the abuse of alcohol or drugs. Because many of our existing divorce laws punish the "guilty" partner, and reward the "innocent" party, some states are now providing for a "no fault" divorce based on mutual incompatibility. Most states also allow for divorce after a specified period of physical separation. Either way, the legal aspects of divorce are not only expensive but emotionally exhausting as well.

The *economic divorce* deals with the settlement of property and money. Although alimony ("giving food") has traditionally been granted to wives, it may now be given to the partner of either sex with the lesser income or not given at all. As long they are physically and financially able, however, fathers are generally responsible for child support payments until their children become of legal age.

The *coparental divorce* has to do with custody of the children and visitation rights. The courts tend to follow the principle of "the best interests of the child," which has meant that custody has been automatically given to the wife. More husbands today are now receiving custody, however. The partner who is not granted physical and legal custody of the children is usually granted certain visitation rights.

The *community divorce* comes in the form of disapproval and rejection by friends and acquaintances. The increasing number of divorces as well as the special groups now being formed for divorced people help to alleviate much of the loneliness and ostracism that inevitably accompanies divorce.

The *psychic divorce* is almost always the last and the most difficult part of divorce. It consists of separating one's self from the influence of one's partner and becoming an autonomous social being again. It is also potentially one of the most constructive aspects of divorce in which the individual may experience much personal growth.

Remarriage

Despite the agony of divorce, four out of five divorced people eventually remarry. They wait an average of three years before doing so and usually choose August rather than June for their wedding. More men than women remarry, and usually within a shorter period of time. The average age of remarried men is 35 years of age, and 30 years for remarried women. In most instances, a divorced person marries another divorced person, probably because they share similar experiences and motivation.

Unfortunately, the percentage of second marriages that end in divorce is even higher than that for first marriages. Remarriages last an average of only six years in contrast to seven years for first marriages. However, the percentage of second marriages that end in divorce decreases as one goes up the socioeconomic ladder. Apparently, middle- and upper-class people are not only more likely to seek a divorce when they are unhappily married; they are also more inclined to work harder at their second marriages (Westoff, 1975).

Jesse Bernard (1971) found that 80 to 90 percent of remarried people rated their second marriages anywhere from satisfactory to extremely satisfactory. Part of the reason is having had greater experience of living with another person. However, greater personal maturity also plays a significant part with successfully remarried persons often saying, "I've learned a lot about myself too." Support for both points can be seen in a study that found that people who remarry late in life have a much better chance of success, with only 6 out of 100 reporting marital failure, compared to the 33 out of 100 in first marriages (McKain, 1969).

CHILDREN OF DIVORCE

It has been predicted that by 1990, one-third of all 18-year-olds will have experienced the divorce of their parents (Glick, 1979). How will they be affected by divorce?

In an attempt to answer this, researchers interviewed parents and children of 60 families, then interviewed them 18 months later, and again after five years. They found children of all ages had a sense of anger, loneliness, and sadness. Younger children who are unable to understand divorce tend to blame themselves for the divorce, feeling they were being punished for being bad. While adolescents were less likely to blame themselves, they were especially vulnerable to being coerced to take sides with one parent. Adolescents were also more apt to hide their hurt feelings, prolonging their adjustment to the divorce. By the end of the first year and a half, most of the children and adolescents had adjusted reasonably well to their new home situation. But a disturbing number of them remained intensely dissatisfied even after five years (Wallerstein & Kelly, 1980).

The effects of divorce are not all bad. Some studies suggest that children of divorce may suffer less anguish and maladjustment than those growing up in homes with intact but conflict-ridden marriages (Bane, 1979). Moreover, because of their situation, children of divorced parents may become more responsible and self-reliant at an earlier age. At the same time, it is true that children of divorce are more likely to get divorced themselves, probably because they have learned that divorce is a solution to marital conflict (Pope & Mueller, 1979).

ALTERNATIVES TO MARRIAGE

Although the majority of people continue to marry in the traditional manner, a larger proportion of people choose either to remain single or to seek an alternative type of partnership. These alternatives, in turn, tend to modify rather than displace traditional marriage.

Being Single

Remaining single no longer carries the stigma it used to have. Instead, there is greater recognition that the reasons for being single may be as varied as those for getting married. A person may not have found a suitable marriage partner, or wants to put career above marriage, or desires greater freedom than is inherent in the commitment to marriage. As a result, being single has become a more acceptable style of life.

Actually, there are so many types of singles that it is difficult to talk about them as a group. There are a small number of people who never get married. There are a much larger number of people who are divorced, many of whom will remarry. Most of the singles in their 20s and 30s will eventually marry, while many of the middle-aged singles will not. There are also the older people who become single because of the death of their spouses, who will be discussed in a later chapter. One could easily designate still other types of singles, such as the gay singles, the lone artists, and the eccentrics, to name just a few.

Younger singles may have to contend with the pressure from their parents about getting married, as well as with their own reaction to that pressure, such as annoyance, resentment, or guilt. Then too, they may have to resist the special pressures of living up to the "swinging singles" lifestyle or succumbing to the loneliness of being single. They may also find it awkward to socialize with their married friends. Actually, single people tend to find their happiness in different ways than do married people. Singles of both sexes are more likely to find fulfillment in their friends and social lives, jobs, love affairs, and recognition and success in their careers (Shaver & Freedman, 1976). They also face special dangers, with people who live alone being especially susceptible to serious illnesses and premature death (Lynch, 1979).

All in all, there are advantages to being single as well as to getting married. Generally, singles have more privacy and peace, more time for entertaining, traveling, and relaxing, and greater freedom and opportunities to live their lives as they please. Married people, on the other hand, may, but not necessarily, have more companionship, more help sharing the work, the security of having someone else to look after them, and the satisfactions of having children and seeing them grow (Edwards & Hoover, 1980). Since being single has become a more acceptable lifestyle for people at any age, each of us now has more freedom to choose either way.

Living Together

Cohabitation or living together has become an increasingly accepted alternative to marriage, especially among college and graduate students as well as other young adults. According to a study of cohabiting couples at Cornell University (Macklin, 1974), most of them had drifted into that arrangement gradually. Only one-fourth of them had deliberately planned it that way. The majority of students living together continued to maintain a place of their own, mostly for occasional privacy or to avoid an unpleasant confrontation with their parents. When asked to check the most important reason why they chose to live with someone, the majority of cohabitants picked "emotional attachment to each other" most frequently, with other reasons being security, companionship, enjoyment, and convenience.

Students living together experienced many of the same problems of married couples, such as discrepancy of sexual interests, fear of pregnancy, and occasional failure to reach orgasm. The most common emotional problem was overinvolvement in the relationship, with too little opportunity to engage in outside relationships. Despite their problems, more than 90 percent of the cohabitants at Cornell felt that their experience of living together was successful, pleasurable, and maturing. Most of them viewed living together as an opportunity to experience a total relationship with another person without the binding commitment of marriage, rather than as a trial marriage. Similar findings can be seen in another study in which two-thirds of those living together were unsure of their original motives, with over half of them not knowing if they would marry in the future (Arafat & Yorburg, 1976).

Further understanding about the experience of living together comes from a two-year study of college students that compared cohabiting couples with other dating couples. About one-fourth of the dating couples were currently living together. Cohabiting couples were less likely to participate in religious organizations and held more liberal attitudes in regard to many matters. But, surprisingly, there were more complaints about male dominance among cohabiting couples than among noncohabiting couples. Generally, couples living together enjoyed greater satisfaction in their relationship with each other, with men being especially satisfied in regard to the sexual aspects of the relationship. Cohabiting couples also reported more intimacy, both in more frequent interaction and in closer relationships than did other dating couples. Yet there was no significant difference between cohabiting and noncohabiting couples in regard to the rates of break-up, marriage, or eventual marital satisfaction. Cohabiting couples who eventually married did move toward marriage in a shorter period of time than did other dating couples, and engaged in fewer rituals of traditional marriage, such as taking a honeymoon. Apparently, the practice of living together influences the development of the dating relationship more than it poses a threat to the institution of marriage itself (Risman et al., 1981).

Other Alternatives

Although trial marriage has been practiced among the Peruvian Indians for four centuries, it sounded like a novel idea when Margaret Mead (1971) proposed a two-step trial marriage in the 1960s. The first step would be "individual marriage," marked by a simple ceremony, no children, and easy divorce. The second step, "parental marriage," would include children and the financial responsibility for them and would be more difficult to enter and terminate. Others, like family therapist Virginia Satir (1967), have suggested that couples have renewable five-year contracts. In both instances, marriage would be based on a real commitment, but there would be greater flexibility for ending relationships that turn sour.

Multilateral or *group marriages* consist of three or more people who consider themselves married to one another. Although group marriages are relatively rare, ten such groups have been observed by Joan Constantine and Larry Constantine (1970). These groups were distinguished from other social groups and cooperative households by the more intimate and affectionate bonds between their members and the fact that acceptance of new members was usually by unanimous rather than majority decision. Although such an arrangement promises both sexual variety as well as security, the attempts to find an acceptable system for rotating sexual partners constantly jeopardized most of these marriages. Homosexual relations were usually permitted, but were not encouraged. The group marriages studied lasted an average of a year and a half, partly because of social disapproval as well as the more complex accommodations necessary to sustain such arrangements.

Communes include three or more people who wish to share a given style of life, with or without marriage. Since the attachment between two people often undermines their commitment to the larger community, many communes permit but do not encourage marriage.

Individuals who join a *nonutopian commune* are generally seeking a sense of community, but do not want to be radically different from other members of society. One study of fifteen middle-class communes found that they were characteristically small, with an average of eight people. Each individual usually had his or her own bedroom, though living and dining quarters were shared. Everyone shared responsibilities for the children (who usually shared rooms), but the major responsibility for them rested with the biological parents. Most people retained their own incomes and private property, but were assessed a regular fee for their food, housing, and utilities. Although sex and physical privacy were not found to be major problems, psychological privacy was, as when one member made a demand that was difficult to refuse without incurring resentment on the part of the others (Bradford & Klevansky, 1975).

Those who join a *utopian commune,* sometimes called a counterculture commune, not only seek a different life but one that they feel is better than that offered by traditional marriage and society. While nineteenth-century communes were often based on ideas, especially religious beliefs, most twentieth-century

Many communes permit but do not encourage marriage. (United Nations/John Robaton)

communes are founded on psychological gratifications and a sense of community without substantial political or religious beliefs (Kanter, 1972). Utopian communes vary widely in regard to their arrangements for personal freedom, property, sex, and children. Like the successful nineteenth-century communes, the more durable twentieth-century ones tend either to adopt a relatively permissive policy toward sex or prohibit it entirely. One of the most stable of these communes, Twin Oaks of Virginia, permits but does not encourage two-person marriages, but most individuals do not bother to marry. Members at Twin Oaks have private rooms and respect each other's personal freedom, but otherwise share work, property, sex, children, and a commitment to their community (Kinkade, 1973).

With so many alternatives to choose from, will marriage as we know it survive in the next century? Most likely, yes. In fact, Jessie Bernard (1972) says we should stop asking about the future of marriage and start talking about "marriage in the future." Most couples will continue to marry, but they will have more options to choose from. We can't predict what all these options will be. Nor do we have any guarantee that marriages in the future will be any happier than those of today. We can hope that marriage will be more fulfilling to both partners, as well as more adaptive to society.

SUMMARY

Choosing a marriage partner culminates a process that begins in the dating practices and love affairs of the high school years. Generally, individuals prefer partners with similar social characteristics and, to a lesser extent, similar personal characteristics. In most instances, the choice of a marriage partner includes both rational and emotional factors. The better acquainted two persons become before marriage, the better their chances for marital success.

Individuals are now more likely to marry for personal satisfactions than for economic necessity, having children, or conformity to social and legal custom. Despite the heightened expectations of the relationship aspects of marriage, most marriages can be classified in terms of a utilitarian type marriage in which couples relate to each other mostly in terms of role behaviors. Only a minority of couples achieve the more desirable intrinsic type marriage, in which couples find the relationship aspect of their marriage more central and satisfying.

Married couples must learn to adjust to each other in terms of their marriage roles, communication, sex life, as well as the changes in their relationship with the passing years. It is important that husbands and wives agree on their respective roles in marriage, though there is now greater flexibility in role expectations and sharing of roles between marriage partners. A very important part of communication in marriage is the management of conflicts, with disagreements leading either to greater intimacy or alienation, depending on how they are handled. There is also a positive association between marital satisfaction and sexual fulfillment, so that each of these aspects of a couple's marriage vitally affects the other. Although the longer a couple lives together the less romantic attachment they feel for each other, the loss of romantic feeling is often replaced by love as mutuality among compatible couples.

The divorce rate has increased dramatically in recent years, though the real causes of divorce probably reflect the increased expectations of marriage as much as its instability.

There are now more acceptable alternatives to traditional marriage for those who choose to do otherwise. These include a diversity of lifestyles among various types of singles, cohabitation or living together without marriage, group marriage, and communes.

Despite the shortcomings and alternatives to traditional marriage, it is predicted that the great majority of people will continue to marry in the future, but they will have more options and types of marriage to choose from.

QUESTIONS FOR SELF-REFLECTION

1. What is your own personal view about whether likes or opposites attract? What are your reasons for holding this view?

2. To what extent can computer matching help us make a wiser selection of a marriage partner?

3. Why is companionship such an important part of marriage today?

4. Which type of marital relationship described by Cuber and Harroff do you think applies to your parents' marriage? To your own relationship?

5. How do you feel about David Mace's observation that conflict is the raw material out of which a satisfying marriage relationship is shaped?

6. How much truth is there to the old adage that men tend to give love for sex, while women tend to give sex for love?

7. Why do you suppose the divorce rate is so high for those who marry under 18 years of age?

8. Based on your own conversations with divorced people, what is the hardest part of getting divorced?

9. How would you account for the fact that married people tend to live longer than singles of either sex?

10. What are the advantages and disadvantages of Margaret Mead's proposal of a trial marriage?

EXERCISES

1. Writing a personal ad

Suppose you were to write a personal ad about yourself for the classified section of a magazine devoted to introducing singles. How would you describe yourself? How would you describe the kind of person you are looking for? Which personal qualities and interests would you emphasize?

Write your ad in the form of a short paragraph, no more than five or six lines. If others in the class are interested in writing such an ad, you could distribute the list of ads and have each person indicate which two or three ads he or she would be most interested in answering. Try to keep the exercise on an informal level without overinterpreting the results.

2. Romantic love

You may recall that most students feel their experiences of romantic love, including infatuation or short-lived affairs, have made them a happier person. Would you agree? Have your experiences of being in love made you a happier, more loving person? Or have they made you cautious about becoming involved in love relationships?

Write a page or so, based on your own love affairs, telling what you have learned about being in love and about your own capacity for intimate relationships. How do you tell the difference between "real love" and infatuation or "shallow, foolish" love affairs?

3. Qualities desired in a mate

Make a list of some personal qualities you would like in a marriage partner. You might list a dozen such qualities, and then go back and check the three most important ones. Write a short paragraph telling why you think these three qualities are the most important.

You might do the same for personal qualities you would not like in a marriage partner. Again, list a dozen such qualities, and then check the three most important ones. Why do you think these qualities are undesirable? Writing out your explanations may help to clarify your expectations regarding prospective marriage partners.

4. Qualities you offer to a prospective mate

Make a list of the major personal strengths and weaknesses you would bring to a marriage relationship. What are the three most desirable qualities you have to offer? What are some of your less desirable qualities that might affect the marriage?

If you are going steady with someone or if you are married, you might ask your partner to add to your list. Try to list more desirable qualities than undesirable ones.

5. Type of marriage relationship

If you are married, which of Cuber and Harroff's types of marital relationships does your marriage most resemble? Write a paragraph or so explaining your choice.

If you are unmarried but are involved in a love relationship or living with someone of the opposite sex, you might apply the same exercise to this relationship.

Another possibility is to interview several married couples you know well, and have both partners tell you which type of marital relationship their marriage most resembles. Ask them to explain their choice.

6. Conflict management

If you are married or are presently involved in a love relationship, write a page or so describing how you and your partner handle conflict in the relationship. Use the following questions as a guide.

Have you experienced some disagreement or conflict? How often does this occur?

Do you tend to acknowledge conflict openly, or do you engage in skirmishes such as nagging, criticism, or dissatisfaction with the other person?

When conflicts are acknowledged openly, how do you tend to deal with them?

Do you attack the problem rather than the person?

Do both of you express yourselves clearly?

Do you stick with the main point or digress a lot?

How do you usually resolve a conflict?

Does one partner get his/her way more than the other?

Or do you tend to compromise or make mutual accommodations?

7. The divorce experience

If you have gone through a separation or divorce, write up your experience. To what extent did you experience the six overlapping phases of divorce described in this chapter? How has the divorce experience influenced your desire to remarry?

If you came from a home with divorced parents, you might write up your experience telling how you have been affected by your parents' divorce. How has your experience influenced your outlook on marriage? On divorce?

8. Cohabitation

If you are currently living with someone of the opposite sex or have had such an experience, write a page or so telling what you learned from this experience. To what extent is your experience similar to that of cohabitating couples described in this chapter? Did cohabitation include serious plans for marriage? What are some of the values of cohabitation? The hazards? Would you recommend this experience to others?

RECOMMENDED READINGS

Bernard, J. *The Future of Marriage.* New York: World, 1972. A positive look at the shape of marriage in the coming years by a leading sociologist in the field.

Branden, N. *The Psychology of Romantic Love.* New York: Bantam, 1981 (paperback). A psychologist gives a positive interpretation of romantic love, including the conditions in which it grows and dies.

Krantzier, M. *Creative Marriage.* New York: McGraw-Hill, 1981. A lucid, down-to-earth guide for improving marriage in the 1980s.

Libby, R. W. and R. N. Whitehurst. *Marriage and Alternatives.* Glenview, Ill.: Scott, Foresman, 1977 (paperback). An exploration of intimate relationships, including the alternatives to traditional marriage.

Masters, W. H. and V. E. Johnson. *The Pleasure Bond.* Boston: Little, Brown, 1974 (paperback). Two well-known leaders in the field of sex research and therapy point out the importance of the man-woman relationship in improving sexual satisfaction in marriage.

Rogers, C. R. *Becoming Partners.* New York: Delacorte Press, 1972 (Delta paperback, 1973). A look at the possibilities and pitfalls of the man-woman relationships by the founder of client-centered therapy.

Weiss, R. S. *Marital Separation.* New York: Basic Books, 1977 (paperback). A helpful overview of the process of marital separation and divorce.

Work and Leisure

9

Most of us spend about forty years of our lives working. But how do we feel toward our work? How do our jobs affect us?

After asking such questions of people all over the country, Studs Terkel concluded that "those we call ordinary are aware of a sense of personal worth—or more often a lack of it—in the work they do" (1972, p. xxiv). Good or bad, it seems that work is a central part of our lives and helps to determine how we feel about ourselves.

This chapter examines some of the changing attitudes toward work, the process of choosing a vocation, and the importance of finding a vocation that is compatible with your interests and abilities. Job satisfaction, women in the work force, and changing jobs are also dealt with, as well as the importance of leisure.

CHANGING ATTITUDES TOWARD WORK

The old Puritan notion that work is not only necessary for survival but also a virtue in itself continues to shape our attitudes. This American work ethic is so deeply embedded in our cultural values that we take it for granted. Many of the underlying themes of the work ethic as described by Daniel Yankelovich (1974a) are easily recognizable. One is the idea that being a "good provider" is the most important characteristic of a "real man." Another theme is that making a living is the way to "stand on your own two feet." Work brings money, freedom, and independence. Still another theme is that hard work leads to success, with the payoff of owning your own home, raising a family, and enjoying the good things in life. There's also the theme of self-respect. We still feel that our sense of personal worth is tied up with our achievements in the world of work. To work at something and do it well makes us feel good about ourselves.

At the same time, people's attitudes toward work are changing. People today expect more from their jobs than simply earning a living. In terms of Abraham Maslow's hierarchy of needs, as work meets people's basic needs, such as job security, satisfactory wages, and safety on the job, they become more aware of their higher needs. Consequently, we pay increasing attention to the psychological satisfactions of work, especially work that is interesting and fulfilling.

The Declining Value of Work

It would be a mistake to conclude that the old work ethic is completely dead, as can be seen in a *Psychology Today* survey of work attitudes. The findings of that study are especially important in that the majority of respondents were young (two-thirds were under 34 years of age) and college-educated, and half were women. The results showed that more than half of the respondents felt that hard work makes you a better person. More than three-fourths of them felt that people who were capable of working but chose not to were a drain on society (Renwick & Lawler, 1978).

At the same time, a comparison of early with later surveys indicates significant changes in people's attitudes toward work. One of the most important changes has been the sharp drop in the number of college students who believe "hard work always pays off." In the mid 1960s, Yankelovich (1974b) found that 72 percent of the students agreed with this view. But by the early 1970s, that number had fallen by almost half, with just 40 percent agreeing with the statement. Realizing that college students do not always reflect the views of the rest of society, Yankelovich also conducted surveys of the general public. His findings showed a shift in the same direction, but with a less drastic change. Whereas in the late 1960s a 58 percent majority of the public believed that "hard work always pays off," by the late 1970s only a 43 percent minority felt this way (Yankelovich, 1981).

Such responses indicate a significant shift in Americans' attitudes toward work.

Some people have become disillusioned about work and their chances of sharing in its rewards. Yet the majority of people, especially college-educated people in general and young people in particular, still believe they can win success if they work hard by the old rules, though they are more apt to question whether the old rules are worth the bother. Even more significant, though, is the change in what people want out of their jobs. It seems that many workers, both young and old, are now seeking more psychological satisfaction in their work (Yankelovich, 1981).

What Do People Look for in a Job?

You might say that what a person looks for in a job all depends on the person. And there's some truth to this. But Daniel Yankelovich (1974b) found a remarkable consensus of responses to this question among a cross-section of workers, including blue-collar and white-collar workers and professionals. The two most frequently given responses were "interesting work" and having "friendly, helpful co-workers," with each response given by 70 percent of the workers. Close behind were two additional answers having to do with meaningful work—namely, the "opportunity to use your mind" and "work results you can see"—given by 65 and 62 percent of the workers respectively. While good pay ranked fifth on the average (given by 62 percent of all the workers), blue-collar workers placed a greater emphasis on money, and professionals put less emphasis on money, with white-collar workers falling in between.

Similar results were found in a survey of college freshmen, class of '83. When asked to rate what was most important for job satisfaction, the top five criteria were in descending order: interesting to do, uses skills and abilities, good chances for advancement, secure future, and tangible results. Good pay ranked eighth. Noncollege youth gave similar responses except that they put more importance on money; good pay ranked fifth (Bachman & Johnston, 1979).

Respondents in a *Psychology Today* survey that included mostly young adult and college-educated workers made a sharp distinction between what they *liked* about their jobs and what they thought was most *important* about work in general. As indicated in Table 9-1, the most satisfying aspects of work have to do with the interpersonal atmosphere of work, such as the friendliness of fellow workers, the opportunity to participate in work decisions, and the respect you receive from people you work with. On the other hand, the most important aspects of work have to do with personal growth or self-actualization, including chances to do things that make you feel good about yourself, to do worthwhile things, and to learn new things.

Is self-actualization even more important than money? When respondents were pressed on the issue of whether they would accept a higher paying job that was less interesting, almost two-thirds said they were unwilling. On the other hand, almost half (46 percent) of the respondents would not accept a more interesting job if it paid less than their existing job. However, almost as many

TABLE 9-1. WHAT PEOPLE LOOK FOR IN A JOB

	Importance	Satisfaction
Chances to do something that makes you feel good about yourself	1	8
Chances to accomplish something worthwhile	2	6
Chances to learn new things	3	10
Opportunity to develop your skills and abilities	4	12
Amount of freedom you have on the job	5	2
Chances to do things you do best	6	11
The resources to do your job	7	9
The respect you receive from people you work with	8	3
Amount of information you get on job performance	9	17
Chances to take part in making decisions	10	14
Amount of job security you have	11	5
The amount of pay you get	12	16
Way you are treated by people you work with	13	4
Friendliness of people you work with	14	1
Amount of praise you get for job well done	15	15
The amount of fringe benefits you get	16	7
Chances for getting a promotion	17	18
Physical surroundings of your job	18	13

Adapted from Patricia Renwick, Edward Lawler, and the *Psychology Today* staff, "What You Really Want from Your Job," *Psychology Today*, May 1978, p. 56.

Respondents were asked, "How satisfied are you with each of the following aspects of your job? And how important to you is each one?" Based on the averages of their responses, items were ranked from 1 (most important or most satisfying) to 18 (least important or least satisfying).

respondents (41 percent) were willing to make such a tradeoff. Those least willing to take a pay cut were divorced women (55 percent), married men (49 percent), widows (47 percent) and women living with someone (47 percent), in that order (Renwick & Lawler, 1978).

Psychological Functions of Work

Despite what people say about having to work for a living, it may be obvious by now that hardly anyone works for money alone. Surveys show that most people would continue working even if they had enough money to live comfortably the rest of their lives (Renwick & Lawler, 1978). The truth is, work fulfills the following important psychological and social needs.

SENSE OF PERSONAL FULFILLMENT.   People need to feel they are growing, learning new skills, and accomplishing something worthwhile. When this feeling is lacking, they may change to a job that promises more fulfillment or tangible results. For example, an action-oriented individual may leave a desk job to work in sales or construction. Even people who have earned a lot of money do not necessarily reduce the time and energy spent at their jobs, largely because of a need for achievement and mastery (Morgan, 1972).

PERSONAL IDENTITY.   People tend to identify with what they are doing. How often have you heard individuals introduce themselves by saying, "I work for IBM" or "I'm a nurse"? Studs Terkel (1972) found that people working in dull, mechanical jobs often feel they have become just a "machine" or a "robot." On the other hand, people engaged in challenging and fulfilling jobs in the arts or professions often feel a sense of purpose in their lives, probably as a result of the work they are doing.

PREVENTION OF BOREDOM.   Although most of us are reluctant to admit it, we work partly to avoid being bored. If you scoff at this, just talk with someone who has been out of work for a long time because of unemployment, sickness, or retirement. Even people who are forced to take an early retirement, such as police and military personnel, often take another job to prevent boredom.

SERVING OTHERS.   While helping others occupies a lower priority than personal fulfillment for most people, over a third of the respondents in one national survey listed "work that is socially useful" as one of the things they looked for in a job (Yankelovich, 1974b). Many people who do volunteer work in hospitals or prisons or who continue in lower paying jobs, such as teaching or the ministry, do so largely because of the sense of fulfillment they get from helping others.

STATUS AND APPROVAL.   Occupation is one of the major determinants of a person's social status, with the family usually taking its status from the head of

TABLE 9-2.   REASONS FOR WORKING

	Male	*Female*
I enjoy what I do on my job.	29.0%	28.6%
I derive the major part of my identity from my job.	25.8	27.5
Work keeps me from being bored.	17.4	18.2
My work is important and valuable to others.	13.9	10.8
I enjoy the company of my co-workers.	5.3	8.1
I would feel guilty if I did not work.	4.4	3.4
I would continue out of habit.	4.2	3.4

Adapted from Patricia Renwick, Edward Lawler, and the *Psychology Today* staff, "What You Really Want from your Job," *Psychology Today*, May 1978, p. 57.

Responses to the question, "If you would continue to work, what is the one most important reason?"

the household's job. While it would be a mistake to take a prestigious job that is not personally satisfying, high-status jobs and personal fulfillment often go hand in hand. In one survey, about three-fourths of the professionals would not hesitate to choose their same jobs again, compared to fewer than two-thirds of the blue-collar workers (Yankelovich, 1974b).

THE PROCESS OF VOCATIONAL CHOICE

We don't choose a vocation all at once. Eli Ginzberg (1972) says that the process of vocational choice actually begins in childhood and culminates in late adolescence or youth and includes three stages: the fantasy stage, the tentative stage, and the realistic stage. Throughout childhood we remain in the *fantasy stage,* choosing exciting jobs like astronaut and president based mostly on our imagination. By early adolescence we're usually in the *tentative stage,* when we make choices on the basis of our interests and values, which change rapidly with age and growth. It is only with late adolescence and youth that most of us reach the *realistic stage* of vocational choice, when we begin seriously to assess our own abilities and explore viable career choices.

THE MANY NAMES OF WORK

Job, occupation, vocation, career—there are so many words to describe the work we choose to do that it's sometimes confusing. While these terms are often used interchangeably, each term has its own particular emphasis.

When people speak of a *job* or *position,* they usually mean a set of tasks or a type of work to be performed within a particular organization, like a computer programmer at IBM. The term *occupation* is more inclusive and refers to the overall types of activities used to perform work tasks, which are similar from one organization to another. For example, in the occupation of nursing, individuals are trained to perform such activities as taking the patient's temperature whether they are working in a doctor's office or in a hospital. The meaning of the term *vocation* ("to be called") is similar to *occupation* but even broader in scope and denotes an inner purpose in the choice of a life work. The term *career* refers to the overall sequence of jobs and occupations throughout one's life, or a purposeful life pattern of work (Shertzer, 1981).

Ideally, we should choose a vocation and work toward career goals, thereby increasing the possibilities for satisfaction and productiveness in our life work. Yet the rapid changes in supply and demand of workers in our society demand that we keep flexible and be prepared to modify our career goals accordingly. On the other hand, when people become so preoccupied with getting a job and surviving in their day-to-day work, they often fail to discover a sense of their career until it's almost over—usually with less satisfaction, if not regret, about their choices.

By the time we reach high school and certainly college, we are under considerable pressure to make some sort of vocational commitment. Schools require that students choose a curriculum or program of studies as well as specific courses within a chosen field. Parents and friends want to know, "What are you going to do?" But much of the pressure comes from within, from feeling a need to choose a vocation—but without sufficient information, work experience, or guidance. A survey of 32,000 high school students in 33 states showed that 9 out of 10 seniors had spoken with their parents about their career plans, but less than half of them had never discussed their plans with a teacher, counselor, or worker in their field of interest. Over two-thirds of them had never taken any sort of course on career guidance or attended anything like a career day (Noeth et al., 1975).

Stages of Vocational Identity

People often have difficulty choosing a vocation because it involves more than simply selecting some sort of work to do. The choice of a vocation also represents an expression of yourself, or your *vocational identity*. Every step of vocational development is a way of exploring and affirming yourself in the world of work.

People with high self-esteem tend to choose challenging vocations. (Ken Karp)

The choice of a vocation is a public declaration of the way you see yourself. Those who feel good about themselves may readily choose challenging vocations that require hard work, risk, and growth. But individuals who are plagued by self-doubt, feelings of unworthiness, and fear of failure may choose less challenging vocations that are beneath their abilities, or they may have trouble choosing at all.

Although adolescence is a critical time in the achievement of a vocational identity, the process lasts throughout life and includes five developmental tasks or stages (Super et al., 1963).

> *Crystallization:* getting ideas about one's life work as a basis for educational planning (mid- to late teens)
>
> *Specification:* seeking the necessary training for one's vocational choice, whether in college or an apprenticeship (late teens through early twenties)
>
> *Implementation:* looking for suitable opportunities or jobs in which to use one's training (early to mid-twenties)
>
> *Stabilization:* settling down to an appropriate career choice, including further training and specialization in one's chosen field (mid-twenties to mid-thirties)
>
> *Consolidation:* acquiring expertise, experience, and status in one's chosen career (from mid-thirties on)

Super (1974) has proposed the concept of *vocational maturity* as a way of determining how well individuals are progressing toward their vocational identity. Vocational maturity reflects the ability to plan and explore vocational possibilities, to seek out relevant information about oneself and viable career options, and to make realistic vocational commitments. One longitudinal study using Super's theory found that more than three-fourths of the men had stabilized their vocational identity by 25 years of age. A similar study including both women and men, however, found that only one-half to two-thirds of the individuals had stabilized their vocational identities by the age of 25. The most probable explanation offered was that between ages 18 and 25 many of the young women had quit work to pursue marriage and family goals. Interestingly, individuals who changed their vocational choices during and after high school were found to possess greater vocational maturity than those who did not change (Gribbons & Lohnes, 1968, 1969).

It is important to point out that the ages at which people attain these respective developmental levels vary considerably. An older veteran or homemaker, for example, might well begin the cycle of tasks anew, hopefully with greater experience, maturity, and sense of direction. Furthermore, with the increasing frequency of job and career changes characteristic of today's society, many people go through two or three cycles of Super's stages in reshaping their vocational identities to match their personal growth and goals in life.

Sex Differences

Although sex is a diminishing factor in vocational choice, it is still present because of social and psychological influences, especially sex-role differences. Traditionally, the career choices of both sexes have been highly sex-typed, with males not only considering a wider range of vocations, but also being more likely to choose the high-status occupations than females (Hoult & Smith, 1978). A typical study of high school seniors showed that boys generally preferred high-status careers offering opportunities for independence and leadership, while girls preferred lower-status occupations in the social service fields (Singer, 1974). The influence of sex-role stereotypes may be modified to some extent by family influences. That is, individuals growing up with opposite-sex siblings, mothers who work outside the home and fathers who encourage both sexes toward a career, and who have a positive attitude toward both parents demonstrate greater flexibility and maturity in their choice of a career (Miller, 1978). Nevertheless, the cumulative effect of sex-role differences can be seen in the uneven distribution of men and women in the various professions. For example, men still account for 95 percent of dentists, 87 percent of physicians, and 87 percent of lawyers, while women account for 96 percent of nurses, 84 percent of elementary school teachers, and 81 percent of librarians (U.S. Bureau of the Census, 1981).

Fortunately, this situation is steadily changing. More than 9 out of 10 women work outside the home at some point in their lives, with more than half of them employed at any given time (U.S. Bureau of the Census, 1981). More women are working before marriage, delaying marriage longer, and combining careers with marriage and family responsibilities. Also, the number of women attending college and graduate or professional schools has been increasing faster than the number of men. Furthermore, the number of women entering traditionally male-dominated fields such as law, medicine, business, and engineering more than doubled between the mid-sixties and mid-seventies (American Council on Education, 1975). Also, more men are working in traditionally female-dominated fields as, for example, elementary school teachers, nurses, and telephone operators.

Not surprisingly, a college education tends to increase career aspirations among women. One longitudinal study showed that career orientation among women increased steadily from the freshmen to the senior year and beyond college. Upon entering college, 18 percent of the women were career minded and 33 percent were definitely noncareerists. By graduation, the overall changes in orientation resulted in a fairly even percentage of careerists (40 percent) and noncareerists (46 percent). Seven years later, the same women showed an even larger percentage of career minded graduates, with 48 percent careerists, 30 percent mainly oriented to family goals and working only occasionally, and 22 percent keeping partial work commitments but without career goals (Angrist, 1972).

Career aspirations are higher among college-educated women. (Ken Karp)

What About Going to College?

Until recently, the advantages of going to college have been largely taken for granted. College is supposed to make you better informed and provide access to the higher status, better paying jobs. More than three-fourths of the population still believes that a college education is fairly to very important in life (Dearman & Plisko, 1979). Yet more young people are thinking twice before attending college. One reason for this is the increasingly high cost of a college education. Another reason is the difficulty many college graduates are having getting jobs, especially jobs appropriate to college-level training. Still another reason has to do with the decreased economic payoff of a college education. Although college graduates continue to have higher lifetime earnings than do high school graduates, the gap is narrowing. Whereas 25- to 34-year-old college graduates earned 40 percent more than high school graduates did in 1970, they earned only 24 percent more in 1977 (U.S. Bureau of the Census, 1980).

All of this has affected young people's decisions about whether to go to college, what kind of college, and their reasons for attending. Today more young people are delaying their entry into college, whether out of a desire to gain more experience before making educational and vocational commitments or a need to earn money. Almost half the college-bound youth now wait one or more years before enrolling in college. A larger proportion of students are attending public colleges than in the past, with enrollment at two-year community colleges almost doubling in the decade ending in 1977 (Dearman & Plisko, 1979). There has also been a rise in career orientation among students throughout the seventies and eighties. While many students at two- and four-year colleges choose to pursue a liberal arts or science major, there is a greater emphasis on keeping flexible, with more students carrying dual majors, such as business and computer science or education and psychology. There is also less hesitation in changing their major, with the realization that a compatible career is more important than the convenience of pursuing their original plans. Then too, there is a greater tendency to drop out of college, with almost 70 percent of the students in two-year community colleges dropping out at one time or another, although many re-enroll at a later date (Golladay & Noell, 1978). While older students may feel apprehensive about returning to school, most of them soon discover that their greater maturity and sense of direction make their college experience even more meaningful and satisfying.

It is not unusual for people to choose a vocation after college for any number of reasons. In the *Psychology Today* survey, almost 40 percent of the respondents reported that they had gotten into their occupation by chance without much deliberation. Another 16 percent said they had settled for their present occupation because they couldn't get a job in their preferred field. Only 23 percent of the respondents were working within their occupation of choice (Renwick & Lawler, 1978). Another survey found that two-thirds of the men and half of the women had decided on their occupation after leaving college. When asked whether their education had given them the skills needed for their current jobs, 38 percent replied that it has been "very useful" while another 50 percent said that it had been "somewhat useful." Only 12 percent felt that college had not been useful at all. When asked which courses they would recommend for job preparation in any field, they favored courses on how to communicate and get along with people as well as handling figures and general business practices (*The New York Times*, Nov. 7, 1976).

CHOOSING A COMPATIBLE OCCUPATION

Many people work at jobs they dislike or can't cope with, resulting in considerable personal maladjustment and millions of dollars wasted in inefficiency. As a result, it is increasingly important to choose an occupation that is compatible with your interests and abilities. But this is something that you and I must do mostly for ourselves.

Personal Characteristics

A good beginning point is to take stock of your own interests and abilities. You are a unique combination of personal traits, interests, skills, and values. The better you get to know yourself, the wiser decisions you can make.

What interests you most—people, data, or things? What subjects do you like best in school? Which extracurricular activities do you prefer? How about part-time jobs? Try to find out what it is about these things that makes them interesting to you. Is it the activity itself? Or is it the people you do it with?

How about your abilities? What sorts of things do you do best? The least best? No matter how many or few abilities you possess, it is important to realize that each of us is qualified for many different occupations, not just for one. For just as most athletic games involve only a limited number of muscles or skills, so most jobs require only a few specific skills or characteristics. The secret lies in finding those types of jobs that require the particular strengths that you possess.

To some extent both your interests and abilities will change with experience and time. Yet research has shown that broad categories of interests, such as those in the fields of medicine, engineering, or business, remain remarkably stable from young adulthood on (Campbell, 1971). If you like something in your teens and early twenties, chances are you will like it in later years as well.

Perhaps you've heard of someone taking a psychological test to help in the choice of a career. Actually, most of these are inventories of your interests rather than a test in the usual sense of the term. Currently, one of the most widely used instruments is the Strong-Campbell Interest Inventory (SCII), which combines many items from the earlier versions of the Strong inventory for males and females with the elimination of the sex-biased items. The results, which are usually shared openly with the individual, show how an individual's interests compare with those of other people in different occupations.

Do such interest inventories really help you make a wise occupational choice? A lot depends on how they are used. If you rely on the results as a substitute for making a personal decision, then the answer would be negative. But if you use the results more as a resource for clarifying your intersts in order to make a decision, then the answer is decidedly more positive. For such instruments have shown great reliability in predicting whether an individual will persist in or drop out of an occupational field. They cannot predict actual success in a given field because of the many subjective factors involved. But it has been found that those who become successful usually demonstrate higher than average interest scores, while those who later drop out usually have lower than average scores (Shertzer, 1981).

Occupational Characteristics

Once you've begun exploring your own interests, abilities, and values, you're ready to look for occupations that are compatible with your personal characteristics. With over 20,000 different occupations to choose from, it's not an easy task. Fortunately, there are resource books to help with this search, such as the widely used *Dictionary of Occupational Titles* (DOT) and *Occupational Outlook Handbook*. Both books are revised regularly by the Government Printing Office. In addition, the various occupations have been organized into basic families, or *clusters* of related occupations. Each of the clusters shown in Figure 9-1 contains hundreds of closely related occupations. For example, the health field includes a vast number of health occupations—physician, nurse, pharmacist, dentist, dental hygienist, to name just a few. It is often helpful to select the two or three occupational clusters you're most interested in, and then begin to explore some of the specific occupations within each cluster.

A helpful device for finding the most compatible occupations for you is John Holland's *Self-directed Search for Vocational Planning,* which can be self-administered. It is based on the fact that people in the same occupational fields often have similar personal traits, interests, and habitual ways of doing things. Holland (1973) describes six of these personality types together with the most favorable occupational environments for them. After checking off a number of activities, interests, and self-estimates of your abilities, you add up the items to find out the three personality types you resemble most. Then, in a separate occupational finder booklet, you match the various personality-type combinations with some

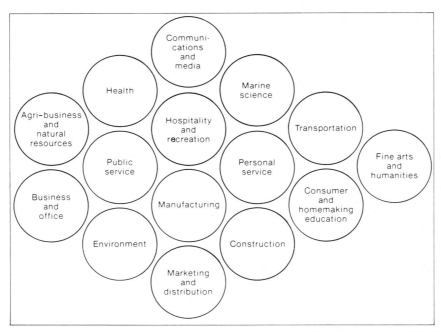

Figure 9-1. Occupational clusters. From *Career Education* (Washington, D.C.: U.S. Government Printing Office, 1971), p. 12.

of the compatible occupations. O'Connell and Sedlacek (1972) have found the *Self-directed Search* highly reliable and quite helpful to those interested in vocational planning.

HOLLAND'S SIX PERSONALITY-OCCUPATIONAL TYPES

The following are descriptions of Holland's six personality-occupational types. These descriptions are, most emphatically, only generalizations. None will fit any one person exactly. In fact, most people's interests combine all six themes or types to some degree. Even if you rank high on a given theme, you will find that some of the statements used to characterize this theme do not apply to you.

The archetypal models of Holland's six types can be described as follows:

REALISTIC: Persons of this type are robust, rugged, practical, physically strong, and often athletic; have good motor coordination and skills but lack verbal and interpersonal skills, and are therefore somewhat uncomfortable in social settings; usually perceive themselves as mechanically inclined; are direct, stable, natural, and persistent; prefer concrete to abstract problems; see themselves as aggressive; have conventional political and economic goals; and rarely perform creatively in the arts or sciences, but do like to build things with tools. Realistic types prefer such occupations as mechanic, engineer, electrician, fish and wildlife specialist, crane operator, and tool designer.

INVESTIGATIVE: This category includes those with a strong scientific orientation; they are usually task-oriented, introspective, and asocial; prefer to think through rather than act out problems; have a great need to understand the physical world; enjoy ambiguous tasks; prefer to work independently; have unconventional values and attitudes; usually perceive themselves as lacking in leadership or persuasive abilities, but are confident of their scholarly and intellectual abilities; describe themselves as analytical, curious, independent, and reserved; and especially dislike repetitive activities. Vocational preferences include astronomer, biologist, chemist, technical writer, zoologist, and psychologist.

ARTISTIC: Persons of the artistic type prefer free unstructured situations with maximum opportunity for self-expression; resemble investigative types in being introspective and asocial but differ in having less ego strength, greater need for individual expression, and greater tendency to impulsive behavior; they are creative, especially in artistic and musical media; avoid problems that are highly structured or require gross physical skills; prefer dealing with problems through self-expression in artistic media; perform well on standard measures of creativity, and value aesthetic qualities; see themselves as expressive, original, intuitive, creative, nonconforming, introspective, and independent. Vocational preferences include artist, author, composer, writer, musician, stage director, and symphony conductor.

SOCIAL: Persons of this type are sociable, responsible, humanistic, and often religious; like to work in groups, and enjoy being central in the group; have good verbal and interpersonal skills; avoid intellectual problem-solving, physical exertion, and highly ordered activities; prefer to solve problems through feelings and interpersonal manipulation of others; enjoy activities that involve informing, training, developing, curing, or enlightening others; perceive themselves as understanding, responsible, idealistic, and helpful.

Vocational preferences include social worker, missionary, high school teacher, marriage counselor, and speech therapist.

ENTERPRISING: Persons of this type have verbal skills suited to selling, dominating, and leading; are strong leaders; have a strong drive to attain organizational goals or economic aims; tend to avoid work situations requiring long periods of intellectual effort; differ from conventional types in having a greater preference for ambiguous social tasks and an even greater concern for power, status, and leadership; see themselves as aggressive, popular, self-confident, cheerful, and sociable; generally have a high energy level; and show an aversion to scientific activities. Vocational preferences include business executive, political campaign manager, real estate sales, stock and bond sales, television producer, and retail merchandising.

CONVENTIONAL: Conventional people prefer well-ordered environments and like systematic verbal and numerical activities; are usually conforming and prefer subordinate roles; are effective at well-structured tasks, but avoid ambiguous situations and problems involving interpersonal relationships or physical skills; describe themselves as conscientious, efficient, obedient, calm, orderly, and practical; identify with power; and value material possessions and status. Vocational preferences include bank examiner, bookkeeper, clerical worker, financial analyst, quality control expert, statistician, and traffic manager.

Pitfalls in Making a Choice

It is important to recognize that choosing an occupation is not a single decision, but involves a series of decisions over a period of many years. In the process, there are certain pitfalls you should especially guard against.

One is the danger of a premature decision. For example, you may become embarrassed answering, "I don't know" to the frequently asked question, "What kind of work do you want to do?" There is a great temptation to answer something like, "I think I want to be an engineer," because of an earlier interest in this field. After learning more of the requirements of this occupation, you may feel less enthusiastic about this choice, but stick with it longer than you should, mostly to save face.

Another pitfall is the accidental choice, such as selecting a major in high school or college with little thought as to the consequences, or remaining in an occupation because of your first job. Selecting an occupation largely because of its external trappings, such as money or prestige, is another common pitfall.

One of the greatest mistakes, according to vocational counselors, is "waiting for things to happen." Instead, you must take the initiative and engage in an active process of looking for compatible occupations. The importance of using relevant educational and occupational literature has already been mentioned. These are usually available in a college library or counseling center. In addition, some colleges are now offering courses and workshops in career guidance, especially designed for those who are undecided. Part-time jobs and work-study programs also offer valuable opportunities to discover which types of jobs you like or dislike.

Another possible pitfall is the failure to realize that your initial choice of an occupation can be modified or changed with experience. In a well-known longitudinal study of men, Daniel Levinson and his colleagues (1978) found that the process of making a firm occupational choice was longer and more difficult than ordinarily portrayed. Men who made strong occupational commitments in their early twenties without sufficient assessment of themselves or exploration of occupational alternatives often regretted it later. On the other hand, those who delayed making a vocational commitment until their thirties usually deprived themselves of the necessary experience to make a wise choice. Levinson concludes, "One of the great paradoxes of human development is that we are required to make crucial choices before we have the knowledge, judgment, and self-understanding to choose wisely. Yet, if we put off these choices until we feel truly ready, the delay may produce other and greater costs" (Levinson, 1978, p. 102). All of this suggests that you need to choose an occupation, but keep that choice open to revision based on subsequent experience and growth.

OCCUPATIONAL ADJUSTMENT

Did you know that you increase your chances of living longer when you are satisfied in your work? According to one long-term study, work satisfaction and personal happiness predicted longevity better than medical examinations or genetic evaluations (Palmore, 1969). On the other hand, dissatisfaction at work may not only shorten your life but also make you more susceptible to the various stress diseases, such as ulcers and hypertension. Among the job-related factors that increase the risk of illness or higher mortality are excessive and continuous change, lack of recognition and support, poor working conditions, and working at a boring, repetitive job.

Satisfaction on the Job

There are many ways to tell how satisfied people are at their work. You can observe their enthusiasm and interest on the job, their productivity, and the quality of their work. Or you can gauge their dissatisfaction by noting their absenteeism or frequency of job changes. But the most direct and frequently used measure is simply to ask people how well they like their work.

Judging by surveys on the subject, a majority of workers are satisfied with their jobs, though the exact percentage varies with the study. A government-financed survey of a cross-section of American workers in the late seventies found that 88 percent of them were either "somewhat" or "very" satisfied with their jobs, a slight decrease from the mid-seventies (*The New York Times,* Dec. 17, 1981). Comparable results can be seen in Yankelovich's poll (1974b) that showed that an average of 80 percent of all workers were either "somewhat" or "very" satisfied with their work. Job satisfaction was highest among professionals and executives and lowest among blue-collar workers, with white-collar workers falling in between.

An even smaller percentage of workers were satisfied with their jobs according to the *Psychology Today* survey cited earlier (Renwick & Lawler, 1978). Only two-thirds of all workers expressed satisfaction with their jobs. About a fifth of the respondents were very satisfied with their jobs, with another fifth definitely dissatisfied with their jobs. Managers, executives, and professionals were more satisfied, less often depressed about their work, and less likely to feel trapped in their jobs than unskilled, semiskilled, and clerical workers. The most dissatisfied workers were the young (under 24), blacks, and those with low incomes. This latter finding is especially relevant since the rising educational level of young workers, coupled with the difficulty of finding suitable jobs, increases worker dissatisfaction. Educated people who are forced to take less challenging, low-paying positions not only express a high degree of job dissatisfaction but also change jobs more frequently (Gooding, 1970).

As you might expect, workers in the *Psychology Today* survey ranked pay and the lack of advancement as major causes of job dissatisfaction. But they were also unhappy with the way their performances were evaluated and the way rewards and praise were distributed. Complaints often centered on the secretive or authoritarian way some organizations go about approving budgets and promotions. Almost half the workers think that getting ahead in an organization depends more on "who you know" than on "how well you've done" (Renwick & Lawler, 1978).

Satisfaction on the job can often be improved by innovations in working conditions. General Motors, for example, has been experimenting with new approaches in several plants plagued by poor morale and low productivity. In these experimental plants, the old assembly-line rules have been replaced by a new approach giving workers a greater voice in decisions affecting their jobs, making their work more challenging and interesting, and treating them with dignity (Yankelovich, 1981).

Among the innovations being tried in other work settings are: a wider use of flexible working hours, a shorter work week, profit-sharing, stock option plans, job sharing, work sharing, and a greater use of part-time employment. Far from producing anarchy, such changes tend to boost employee morale and productivity. More flexible working schedules also increase satisfaction on the job by reducing the conflicts between job demands, family needs, leisure values, and educational needs (Stetson, 1981).

Women and Work

We've already indicated that women have become a more significant part of the labor force, with over half of them employed outside the home at any given time. While people often assume that women work mostly to earn money, this is not always the case, especially when their husbands earn a high income. When women in the *Psychology Today* survey were asked whether they would work even if they could live comfortably without doing so, women were as likely as men to want to continue, which suggests that the psychological significance of work is as important to them as to men (Renwick & Lawler, 1978). A job also takes a woman out of the house, giving her a role with clearer requirements and payoff than housework as well as contact with other people, thus enhancing her sense of competency and self-esteem (Ferree, 1976).

At least one survey has shown that women are generally as satisfied with their jobs as are men. However, women expressed lower levels of satisfaction in certain areas of their work, such as the opportunity to learn new things, freedom on the job, participation in decision making, chances of promotion, and pay (Renwick & Lawler, 1978). Women sometimes complain of discrimination in pay, frequently with good reason. A woman college graduate still earns only about two-thirds the salary of a man with the same education. Women with less education fare even worse (U.S. Bureau of the Census, 1981).

A woman's choice of an occupation goes a long way toward enhancing or limiting her chances of being satisfied on the job. Despite the increased number of women attending college and graduate school, the majority of women still aim for the relatively low-paid, traditionally female occupations where jobs are scarce. Consequently, there are more women trained in kindergarten, elemen-

Women college graduates earn only about two-thirds of the salary of men with the same education. (A.T.&T. Company Photo Center)

tary and secondary school teaching than there are jobs available. At the same time, some experts are projecting that there will be more jobs than qualified candidates in such fields as business, engineering, medicine, and electronic data processing. Yet it is often the highly motivated, exceptional women who seek out such jobs, while the majority of women are still not as informed or willing to explore alternatives to traditionally female jobs (Cerra, 1980).

Another problem area concerns sexual harassment and discrimination on the job. In one survey, women were more apt to complain that their job was not commensurate with their skills and training because of sexual discrimination. Other complaints focused on being denied access to informal sources of communication on the job, being expected to do more work and less prestigious work than other workers with similar jobs, and receiving less pay (Renwick & Lawler, 1978).

Women soon discover that working outside the home does not spare them the housekeeping chores. Since three-fourths of the divorced mothers, compared to only about half of the married mothers, work outside the home, housework can be especially burdensome for unmarried working mothers (U.S. Bureau of the Census, 1980). But married women do not always fare that much better. Reports on both sexes show that women continue to do most of the grocery shopping, cooking, and clearing away after meals. When there are children, women generally take care of them or share responsibilities with their husbands. But the younger the woman, the more likely the household tasks are shared equally, a sign that changes are gradually occurring. When it comes to whose career took priority, however, almost two-thirds of the men claimed their career came first while only one out of ten women adopted this position. Furthermore, the higher a man's income, the more resistant he is to moving for the sake of his wife's job (Renwick & Lawler, 1978). At the same time, the more mutual consideration and cooperation between husbands and wives, the better for all concerned. At least one study has shown that there is a higher degree of happiness in the marriage relationship and home atmosphere when there is moderate rather than high emotional involvement in a career among both partners (Ridley, 1973).

Changes in Supply and Demand

Satisfaction on the job depends partly on whether there is a future in it. This should be taken into consideration when choosing a career. At the same time, all occupations are affected by changes in the supply and demand of workers, though some to a greater extent than others (see Figures 9-2 and 9-3).

The trends toward consolidation in business and farming, along with the rise of technology, all combine to produce significant shifts in employment patterns. This means that farm workers and unskilled laborers will continue to have

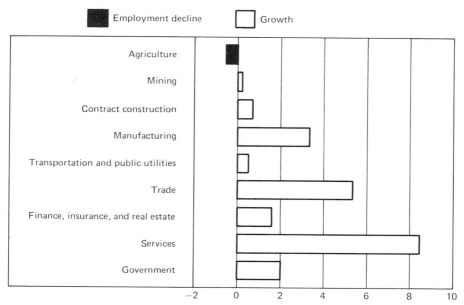

Figure 9-2. Projected changes in employment by industry. From *Occupational Outlook Handbook, 1980-81 Edition* (Washington, D.C.: U.S. Government Printing Office, 1980), p. 19.

trouble finding suitable jobs, while professional and technical workers, managers, sales people, and clerical workers will have much better job opportunities. Since the number of service-producing industries has been increasing at a faster rate than the number of goods-producing industries and is expected to increase further by about 30 percent between 1980 and 1990, employment opportunities should be favorable in such fields as finance, real estate, government, and data processing. Also notice the dramatic increase in the projected job openings for clerical workers, mostly to replace employees who retire, transfer to another occupation, or simply stop working, perhaps to attend college or care for a family.

Job prospects also depend on level of education. Since the median educational level of the work force is now over 12 years, those without a high school education are at a distinct disadvantage. Poorly educated youth with few marketable skills will continue to have the highest unemployment rates, while college graduates will continue to have the lowest. However, the number of college graduates has been increasing faster than appropriate positions for them. Consequently, approximately one out of four college graduates has had to settle for a job pre-

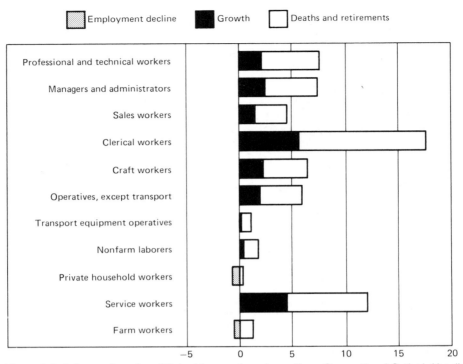

Figure 9-3. Job openings for different types of workers. From *Occupational Outlook Handbook, 1980-81 Edition.* (Washington, D.C.: U.S. Government Printing Office, 1980), p. 22.

viously held by someone with less than four years of college. While college graduates will continue to have a competitive edge over those with less education, their chances will be better in fields that most value a college education, especially professional and managerial positions (*Occupational Outlook Handbook,* 1980-81 Edition).

Changing Jobs

No matter which occupation you choose, chances are that you will change jobs at some time or another. The average person makes about ten major job changes (or changes in employer) during his or her career. Most of these changes occur while people are in their twenties and thirties, when they are actively searching for the most promising job. By the time men and women have reached their

The outlook for jobs is favorable in such fields as data processing. (Western Electric Photographic Services)

forties, they are apt to make only one or two more job changes in their career. Overall, the average number of years a person keeps a job has declined from about four and a half years in 1963 to about three and a half years in 1980. At the same time, over half of all American workers hold jobs that will last five years or more, with job tenure generally rising with age (Crittenden, 1980).

People get restless for a number of reasons. Some discover that changes in the economy have placed their skills in less demand, and they must learn new ones. Others go through a mid-career crisis and are forced to reevaluate their goals. In many instances people realize that they have made poor career choices. One survey found that almost 40 percent of the respondents had happened into their occupation by chance with little deliberation. Another 16 percent admitted they had settled for their present occupation because they couldn't get a job in their preferred field. Only 23 percent of the respondents were working in an occupation of their choice. Almost half the workers felt "locked in" to their jobs, with most of these feeling the time wasn't right for a change. The unskilled and semiskilled workers expressed the strongest feelings about being trapped, with many of them feeling it would be difficult to get a job equal to their present one. Managers and executives, on the other hand, generally felt they had too much at stake to leave their present positions (Renwick & Lawler, 1978).

Generally speaking, changing occupations is more difficult than changing jobs, although both become more difficult with age. In many cases, individuals change to a job in a related field, involving only a minimum of training and readjustment. In other instances where there is deep dissatisfaction, a more drastic change of job or occupation may be needed. The important thing is finding something you really enjoy doing that challenges your abilities, rather than keeping a job mostly because of security or to maintain a reputation. Far too many people are working at jobs beneath their abilities, mostly because they fear unemployment more than boredom. Yet few people fail when they are working at something that they really enjoy and are good at, as long as there is a need for it in society.

LEISURE

Nobody likes to work all the time. Most of us want some time to spend on ourselves and with our families. The term traditionally used for such nonworking time is *leisure,* meaning literally "time free from work or duties." Most of us think that the more leisure time we have the better. But the increase of leisure time now poses a problem for many people.

Increased Leisure Time

At present, many forces are combining to bring us more leisure time. For one thing, the increasing use of computers and other forms of automation are accomplishing more work with fewer workers in less time. At the same time, the entry into the labor market of more young adults, women, and minorities threatens to keep unemployment rates high or modify the distribution of workers. The average worker now has longer paid vacations and holidays, as well as the promise of a longer period of income-supported retirement. While inflation, higher taxes, and the increased costs of education (and just about everything else) threaten to offset these gains, the long-term trend is toward more leisure.

Most people spend about as much time in leisure activities as in work, between 30 and 40 hours a week on the average. Those in the 18-to-25 age bracket and those over 50 years of age spend about twice as many hours in leisure activities as in work. Leisure activities may range from active, outdoor activities such as jogging and bicycling to more passive, indoor pursuits such as watching TV. Although preferred leisure activities vary somewhat by age and sex as well as by what is fashionable, the most popular activities among the general population are in descending order: visiting zoos and parks, picnics, drives, walking or jogging, swimming, sightseeing, attending sports events, playing sports or games, fishing, and nature walks (*Social Indicators III,* 1980).

Another popular form of leisure is the vacation. According to one survey, about half the population takes at least one vacation a year, lasting anywhere from one to three weeks. The most frequently given reasons for taking a vacation, given in order of descending frequency are: relaxation, intellectual enrichment, family togetherness, exotic adventure, self-discovery, and escape. While men generally feel more entitled to a vacation than women, they seem to enjoy them less than women do and are more impatient to return to work. In fact, people tend to carry the same psychological baggage with them wherever they go. Workaholics take their briefcases right along in order to catch up. Physical fitness buffs tend to jog, swim, or play tennis even more than they do at home. All in all, the people who get the most out of their vacations are those who most enjoy their work. And those who don't enjoy their work usually don't have much fun on their vacations. Despite the growing importance of leisure, most people don't seek a leisure-filled life. What they really want is a better balance between work and leisure (Rubenstein, 1980).

Using Leisure Positively

So far we've been discussing leisure ("free") time as if everyone agreed on its meaning. Yet the literature on the subject suggests that leisure is difficult to define. John Kelly (1972) has suggested that leisure can be classified according to two dimensions: the amount of choice the individual has, and the relation of the leisure activity to work. The four types of leisure, including nonleisure, are diagrammed in Table 9-3.

An example of *unconditional leisure* would be the enjoyment of music or meditation. Other examples would be activities undertaken for their own sake, such as swimming, tennis, camping, skiing, or playing a musical instrument. *Coordinated leisure* refers to those activities that are freely chosen but are essentially work-related, such as the person who plays golf with a customer. Examples of

TABLE 9-3. TYPES OF LEISURE

		CHOICE	
		Freely Chosen	*Determined*
WORK	*Nonwork related*	1. Unconditional leisure	3. Complementary leisure
	Work related	2. Coordinated leisure	4. Nonleisure (preparation, recuperation)

Adapted from John R. Kelly, "Work and Leisure: A Simplified Paradigm" *Journal of Leisure Research*, 4 (1972), Figure 3. Reprinted by permission of the publishers. © Copyright National Recreation and Park Association.

complementary leisure would be participation in professional organizations, unions, and civic clubs, as well as community and church organizations. Although these are not directly work related, they are more or less expected of us in our overall role. *Nonleisure time* consists mostly in recuperation and preparation time. An example would be those watching TV because they are too exhausted to do anything else, or the teacher preparing tomorrow's lesson at home.

As you can see, the motivation and use of time rather than the activity itself determines whether something is leisure or work. The truckdriver watching a TV program is doing something different from the TV producer who is checking on the competition. The challenge is learning to view leisure time in a more positive light, not just as recuperation time or as "time on our hands." Those whose work is highly challenging and interesting will continue to experience a close relationship between their work and their leisure. But for the greater number of people whose work is dull, leisure may provide a time for pursuing their own interests and "re-creating" themselves as individuals. Faced with the prospect of increasingly automated and routine work and the desire for more meaningful work, we may come to view leisure as an indispensable means of preserving our wholeness and sanity. It has even been suggested that Freud's classic answer to the question of what normal people should be able to do may be slightly extended to read: They should be able to love, to work, *and to enjoy leisure* (Kimmel, 1974).

SUMMARY

We have seen that attitudes toward work are changing, with fewer people believing that hard work always pays off. Instead, workers are more concerned to find jobs that are interesting and personally satisfying, with friendly co-workers. Although money is still considered important, most people indicate they would continue working even if they didn't need the money. Work also satisfies other motives, such as the need for personal fulfillment, identity, prevention of boredom, serving others, and status and approval.

The choice of a vocation is also an affirmation of vocational identity. Although adolescence is a critical time for such a choice, it has become more acceptable for people of all ages to revise their vocational identities with greater maturity and experience. Women not only are entering the labor force in greater numbers, but are also enjoying a wider range of occupational choices than in the past. While college-bound youth are more apt to think twice before attending college, the majority of college graduates find a college education has been helpful in their careers.

Choosing a compatible occupation involves a process of matching your personal interests, values, and abilities with those of appropriate occupations. Various psychological inventories and theories of vocational choice have proved helpful for this purpose, including Holland's six personality-occupational types. A major pitfall in choosing an occupation is "waiting for things to happen." Therefore, you should engage in an active process of self-assessment and vocational exploration in order to find the most compatible occupation.

Most surveys show that the majority of workers are satisfied with their work, though job satisfaction is usually highest among managers, executives, and professional workers. Most complaints tend to come from women, blacks, and younger workers, and those with low incomes. The constant shifts in the supply and demand for various types of workers also affect occupational adjustment, although college-educated workers continue to have a competitive edge over those with less education. Nevertheless, the average person changes jobs about ten times during his or her lifetime, with most of the changes made during the person's twenties and thirties.

The progressively shorter work week now gives workers more leisure time than they had in the past. While most people spend as much time in leisure activities as at work, they do not always know how to make good use of their leisure. In view of the conflicting prospects of automated work and the worker's desire for meaningful work, a positive use of leisure may provide an indispensable means of preserving the wholeness and sanity of many workers.

QUESTIONS FOR SELF-REFLECTION

1. Do you believe that "hard work always pays off"?
2. What are the three most important things you look for in a job?
3. Which of Don Super's stages of vocational identity are you presently in?
4. To what extent is your preferred occupation sex-typed?
5. In what ways do you expect a college education to benefit your career?
6. Are you actively working to choose a compatible occupation? Or are you mostly "waiting for things to happen"?
7. What kind of supply and demand ratio is predicted for your preferred occupation?
8. Which kinds of jobs have you liked the most, full-time or part-time?
9. How many different jobs have you had so far, including part-time jobs?
10. Which of Kelly's four types of leisure do you engage in most frequently?

EXERCISES

1. Identifying occupational skills—data, people, or things

Perhaps you've heard the old adage that some people work well with people, while others are better at working with things. Although greatly oversimplified, there's some truth to this. More realistically, though, every occupation requires working both with people and things, as well as with information. One of the major differences between occupations, however, is the relative degree to which these three kinds of skills are involved.

Select five or more occupations in which you have some interest. Then, using the classification system listed below, estimate the degree to which each occupation involves the respective skills of working with data (or information), people, or things.

	Occupation	Data	People	Things
1.	_____	_____	_____	_____
2.	_____	_____	_____	_____
3.	_____	_____	_____	_____
4.	_____	_____	_____	_____
5.	_____	_____	_____	_____

The system of classifying the three kinds of skills listed below is the same one used in the *Dictionary of Occupational Titles* (DOT) published by the Government Printing Office. The skills are arranged in a hierarchical order according to the complexity of skills, from the most complex skill (0) to the simpler ones (increasing numbers). The combination of these three numbers corresponds to the last three digits of the DOT coding system. Thus, an occupation with the last three numbers 316 would involve a relatively high level of skills for dealing with data, a high level of skill for dealing with people, but little skill for working with things. Choose the appropriate numbers from the following list to insert under the data/people/things columns on your chart.[1] Check to see how well you estimated by looking up your occupational choices in the DOT.

Data
0. Synthesizing
1. Coordinating
2. Analyzing
3. Compiling
4. Computing
5. Copying
6. Comparing

7. No significant relationship
8. No significant relationship

People
0. Mentoring
1. Negotiating
2. Instructing
3. Supervising
4. Diverting
5. Persuading
6. Speaking, signaling

7. Serving

8. No significant relationship

Things
0. Setting up
1. Precision working
2. Operating, controlling
3. Driving, operating
4. Manipulating
5. Tending
6. Feeding or unloading (machinery)
7. Handling

8. No significant relationship

2. Matching your personality with compatible occupations

Study the list of Holland's six personality-occupational types or themes presented earlier in the chapter. Then select the three types that best characterize your personality in one, two, three order. For example, if you think you are most like the social type personality, and to a lesser extent like the investigative type, and even less like the artistic type, then your top three choices would be SIA.

Now list some occupations that you think would be compatible with your combination of personality types. Suppose you exchange your first and second ranked types; what difference would this make in your list of compatible occupations? Try exchanging all of your rankings systematically to see all the possible combinations of your personality types.

[1]Adapted from Bruce Shertzer, *Career Planning*, 2nd ed. (Boston: Houghton Mifflin Company, 1981), p. 208. Copyright © 1981 by Houghton Mifflin Company. Used by permission.

If you would like to do this type of exercise more systematically, you may be interested in John Holland's *Self-directed Search for Vocational Planning*. Use of Holland's instrument provides you with more specific lists of activities, interests, and abilities, which in turn helps you to determine the personality types most characteristic of you. Then too, his occupational finder booklet provides you with a more comprehensive list of occupations already arranged according to the different possible combinations of the six personality-occupational types. It also indicates the level of education or training required for each occupation.

The *Self-directed Search* should be available at most college counseling centers. Although it is designed to be self-administered (usually in less than an hour), talking over your results with a counselor can be even more rewarding.

3. Matching your interests and skills

Make an exhaustive list of all the accomplishments you have enjoyed doing. This should include anything you feel good about, such as school projects, jobs, hobbies, sports, or community activities. You may include things you have done mostly by yourself or together with others.

Then select a dozen or so of the most enjoyable accomplishments, listing them in order from the most enjoyable down. Be certain to list some of your more recent accomplishments, as well as those from earlier times in your life.

For each accomplishment ask yourself, "What made this so satisfying?" Was it the people involved? Was it because of the "payoff" value, like money or honor? Or was it mostly because of the activity itself? Generally speaking, those activities that are enjoyable in themselves are your best guide to what you will like to do in the world of work.

You may also want to identify the skills involved in your respective accomplishments. Do some skills recur more often than others? You might want to classify the skills according to whether they involve data, people, or things, as described in the first exercise. Are the skills in your list more people oriented, things oriented, or data oriented? What sort of occupations use the skills in your list?

Remember, the things you most enjoy doing and do well provide invaluable clues to the most compatible occupations for you.

4. Vocational requirements

Many people are busily preparing for a career without knowing many of the specific requirements for it or what people actually do in the job. One reason is that young people are expected to select their college major before they have much knowledge or experience in the world of work. Another reason is that people may be attracted to a field because of its prestige, glamor, pay, or rosy future.

In order to provide a more realistic basis for your vocational planning, look up material about your preferred career in some authoritative source, such as the *Occupational Outlook Handbook*. Such books can usually be found in your library, counseling center resource room, or the department of the college responsible for career guidance. Look for specific information about: (1) the educational requirements for your career; (2) what people do in the related jobs; (3) opportunities for advancement in the field; and (4) the outlook for the future, including any trends that may affect this field.

Write up your findings in a page or so. If you still have unanswered questions, you may want to discuss these with a vocational counselor or someone who serves in this capacity in your college. If you have access to someone in your preferred career, you may want to discuss your findings with that person.

5. Job satisfaction

Select a job, full-time or part-time, that you have especially enjoyed and explain why in a page or so. Was it mostly the pay? Or did your satisfaction have more to do with the work setting or people involved? How much did you enjoy the primary work activity itself?

Do you think your rewarding experience was mostly a function of this particular job or time in your life? Or does it also suggest something about the type of career that may be most promising for you?

6. Use of leisure

Take any one-week period of your current life and jot down all the leisure and semileisure activities you engage in. Then classify your leisure activities according to four types of leisure defined by John Kelly in this chapter.

A handy way to do this is to divide an 8½" x 11" sheet of paper into four equal sections. Then label each section as shown in Table 9-3: unconditional leisure, complementary leisure, coordinated leisure, and nonleisure. If possible, estimate the number of hours you spend in each type activity each week.

Which type of leisure do you engage in most frequently? Which leisure activity do you find most enjoyable? Do you find that much of your leisure is work related? How much unconditional leisure do you have? Do you think this type of leisure is a luxury or essential for personal growth?

RECOMMENDED READINGS

Bolles, R. N. *What Color Is Your Parachute?* rev. ed. Berkeley, Ca.: Ten Speed Press, 1981 (paperback). A practical manual for those changing jobs or careers, including an annotated bibliography of helpful books and other resources in the field.

Catalyst Series (paperbacks). An excellent series of books for women in search of a career, including such titles as *Planning for Work* (1973) and *Your Job Campaign* (1975). Available from Catalyst, 14 East 60th Street, New York, N.Y. 10022.

Jackson, T. J. *Guerilla Tactics in the Job Market.* New York: A Bantam Book, 1978 (paperback). A creative and resourceful guide to finding a job by a nationally recognized expert in the field.

Merchandising Your Job Talents. Washington, D.C.: U.S. Government Printing Office, 1980 (paperback). An informative brochure about such practical matters as preparing a resumé, finding out about jobs, and getting ready for the job interview. Available from the Superintendent of Documents, U.S. Government Printing Office, Washington, D.C. 20402.

Occupational Outlook Handbook: 1980–81 Edition. Washington, D.C.: Bureau of Labor, U.S. Government Printing Office, 1980. One of the most frequently used resources for basic information about the major occupations, including a projected outlook for the various fields. (Revised every two years.)

Rohrlich, J. B. *Work and Love.* New York: Crown Publishing Company, 1982 (paperback). Deals with the vital balance between being successful at work and in personal relationships.

Shertzer, B. *Career Planning.* rev. ed. Boston: Houghton Mifflin, 1981 (paperback). An informed overview of career exploration, containing practical exercises at the end of each chapter.

Terkel, S. *Working.* New York: Avon, 1975 (paperback). Candid and colorful first-person accounts of what work means to men and women in a variety of jobs.

Freedom and Decision Making

10

THE IMPORTANCE OF PERSONAL FREEDOM
inner freedom
effects of perceived freedom
loss of freedom and control

FREEDOM AND DECISIONS
available alternatives
freedom and responsibility
group decision making

DECISION MAKING
decision-making strategies
steps in decision making
aids in decision making

DECISIONS AND PERSONAL GROWTH
finding the basic decisions in your life
making new decisions
some practical applications

SUMMARY

There are more choices to make in living today. Many restrictions have been lifted from our personal and social lives. Greater access to publicly supported colleges has provided more opportunities for higher education. Also more types of occupations are available to choose from.

These increased opportunities for personal choice call for greater skill in making decisions. Yet decision making is something most people learn by trial and error, if at all. Worse still, students are under increased pressure to make choices at an earlier age. How often have you been asked what kind of work you want to do? Unduly procrastinating such decisions or making premature ones can reduce your subsequent freedom in an area. Learning how to make good decisions can enhance the freedom and control you have over your life. While decision-making skills may be helpful in simple, everyday choices, they are of critical importance in such life choices as occupation and marriage.

THE IMPORTANCE OF PERSONAL FREEDOM

If someone were to ask you, "Why do you act the way you do?" you would probably reply, "Because I *choose* to!" For this is one of our most prized beliefs—that we are free to choose our own behavior. Today we are more apt to speak of such freedom in terms of *free choice* rather than *free will*. The latter implies a nineteenth-century concept in which a special part of the personality exercises absolute control over the rest through the sheer persistence of effort. Psychologists now regard this as an unrealistic notion. Most of us have discovered this for ourselves whenever we've tried to get rid of some undesirable habit, such as smoking, through sheer willpower without taking into account our overall needs and resistance to change. It is more realistic to speak of free choice as a *relative* freedom exercised by the person as a whole. Accordingly, our freedom is conditioned by all the other determinants of behavior, such as our past behavior, basic needs, personality, and surroundings. At the same time, such freedom enables us to direct our lives one way or the other. As Rollo May defines it, freedom consists in "the capacity to pause in the face of various stimuli, and then to throw one's weight toward this response rather than that one" (1977, p. 7).

Inner Freedom

Considering the advances of science and technology as well as the many constraints placed on our lives by the network of social ties, institutions, and governmental bureaucracies, you may wonder, "In what sense are any of us free?" Carl Rogers reminds us that the freedom which we prize so much is essentially an inner quality, something that exists within us, aside from the degree of outward choices or alternatives we often think of as freedom. It is an inner, subjective freedom through which each of us realizes "I can live my own life, here and now, by my own choices." Rogers adds:

It is the quality of courage which enables a person to step into the uncertainty of the unknown as he chooses himself. It is the discovery of meaning from within oneself, meaning which comes from listening sensitively and openly to the complexities of what one is experienceing. It is the burden of being responsible for the self one chooses to be. It is the recognition of a person that he is an emerging process, not a static end product. The individual who is thus deeply and courageously thinking his own thoughts, becoming his own uniqueness, responsibly choosing himself, may be fortunate in having hundreds of objective outer alternatives from which to choose, or he may be unfortunate in having none. But his freedom exists regardless. So we are first of all speaking of something which exists within the individual, something phenomenological rather than external, but nonetheless prized (1969, p. 269).

This inner freedom complements rather than contradicts our picture of the psychological universe as a sequence of causes and effects. Rogers refers to this as the "paradox of freedom." That is, inwardly we feel free to choose the way we act, while objectively we know that our lives are also shaped by many other forces as well. To deny such freedom, Nietzsche once said, "is foolish" if not "insane." But it is equally foolish, if not naive, to deny the presence of other influences on our behavior. While Rogers admits that he has not resolved the age-old problem of freedom and determinism, he has found a way of living with it. Rightly understood, this inner freedom is a fulfillment by the person of the ordered sequence of his life. "The free man moves out voluntarily, freely, responsibly, to play his significant part in a world whose determined events move through him and through his spontaneous choice and will" (Rogers, 1969, p. 269).

Understandably, such freedom makes us anxious, for it involves envisioning possibilities with consequences we can't fully predict. We can choose in a way that leads to failure as well as to success. Because of this anxiety, people often reject the freedom available to them. It's too much of a burden. They would rather have someone else to blame than accept the anxiety and responsibility that come with freedom.

Yet it is this inner freedom to choose and direct our lives that makes life meaningful and purposeful. Even amid the dehumanizing circumstances of a Nazi concentration camp, Victor Frankl observed that "the sort of person the prisoner became was the result of an inner decision, and not the result of camp influences alone" (1959, p. 66). From his own experience in one of these camps,

---

MORE FREEDOM OF CHOICE TODAY

Judging by a survey of 1,500 people carried out by Yankelovich, Skelly, and White, the majority of Americans feel they have more freedom of choice in how to live their lives than their parents did. Most feel that their parents' lives were hemmed in by all kinds of social, educational, and economic constraints that they themselves have escaped.

The survey showed that 73 percent of Americans feel they have more freedom of choice than their parents did, 17 percent feel they have the same level of choice as their parents, and 8 percent believe they have fewer choices. Only 2 percent were not sure.

Most people felt confident they would be able to carry out their choices and live the way they truly wanted. Typical statements were: "I have more options than my parents did." "I can do what I want to do with my life; my parents couldn't."

People who perceive their parents this way do not necessarily feel they are better people than their parents. But they do believe they have more options in the important areas of education, work, sex, marriage, family, travel, friends, possessions, where to live, and how to live. Would you agree?

Daniel Yankelovich, *New Rules* (New York: Random House, 1981).

Frankl concluded "that everything can be taken from a man but one thing: the last of the human freedoms—to choose one's attitude in any set of circumstances, to choose one's own way" (1959, p. 65).

Effects of Perceived Freedom

Inner freedom is often spoken of as *perceived freedom,* that is, the freedom we perceive ourselves to possess in a given situation. Psychologists such as B.F. Skinner (1972) contend that this subjective freedom is an illusion, since our actions are not caused by an inner self anyway. But many other psychologists observe that all of us act as if our intentions played a significant role in our lives. Even those who espouse a deterministic psychology, as Isidor Chein (1972) has pointed out, are living refutations of it. They live *as if* they were free, while denying such freedom to others. Ivan Steiner (1973) adds that the freedom we attribute to ourselves, however real or illusory, is itself a powerful force with real consequences in our lives. Consequently, researchers are busy tracing the conditions that enhance or diminish our perceived freedom and its effects in our lives.

Perhaps you have noticed how much more you enjoy something when you have chosen to do it. This was demonstrated in an interesting experiment in which volunteers agreed to wear electronic pagers as they went about their activities during an ordinary week. At random intervals throughout each day, the beeper sounded and the respondents were asked to indicate what they were doing, how they felt, and to what extent they would prefer to be doing something else. Half the time they were doing what they wanted to do. About one-fourth of the time they were doing things they felt they had to do. At other times, they checked both options or said they had nothing else to do.

Generally people felt least free when doing things expected of them, such as working, cleaning, and doing household chores. They felt the greatest degree of freedom when engaging in leisure activities, socializing with friends, watching TV, reading, and playing sports and games. On the whole, men felt freer than the women in all but three activities: public leisure, socializing, and eating in a restaurant. At the same time, each sex perceived the same activities differently. For example, women felt less free than men when doing household chores— most likely because such duties are often expected of women. On the other hand, men felt much freer than women when cooking—probably because for most men cooking is a voluntary and occasional activity. The results also showed that the freer people felt in a given activity, the more they enjoyed it. Conversely, when they were doing something compulsory, their attention was divided between performing the task and wishing they were doing something else. The study also showed that to a considerable extent the inner experience of freedom is independent of external conditions; that is, when people felt an activity was freely chosen, regardless of the external conditions, they became more involved with the task and enjoyed it more (Csikszentmihalyi & Graef, 1979).

When you choose to do something, you enjoy it more. (Ken Karp/Sirovich Senior Center)

People are also more likely to change their attitudes when they feel free to do so. The reason is that perceived freedom is a necessary condition for experiencing cognitive dissonance (inner conflict), which in turn may arouse or motivate us to change our attitudes. On the other hand, any external influence that will justify our actions or feelings, such as money, blame, or coercion, tends to reduce the felt dissonance and the possibility of attitude change (Aronson, 1980).

Loss of Freedom and Control

Considering how much the sense of freedom means to us, it is not surprising that people react so negatively when threatened with the loss of freedom. Initially, people assert themselves in an effort to protect that freedom. But when their resistance wears down, they may feel helpless and give up. Let's take a look at both reactions.

When we feel our freedom is being infringed upon, our initial reaction is to redouble our efforts, often with an increased desire to do the opposite of what is called for. Psychologists call this *psychic reactance,* which is essentially a defensive tendency to fight against a threatened loss of freedom or an attempt to regain a freedom we may have lost (Brehm, 1966; Wicklund, 1974). You've probably seen many instances of this in everyday life. Think of the adolescent who is moved to rebellious behavior by harsh, domineering parents. For example, when parents try to end a love affair, the young people involved tend to become even more determined and in love, a reaction that has been called the "Romeo and Juliet effect" (Driscoll et al., 1972). Similarly, when people are being asked for help or a donation, they characteristically react to high pressure appeals by giving less then they would have otherwise given (Fraser & Fujitomi, 1972).

Considering all the restrictions on our personal freedom in everyday life, you may wonder why we don't feel even more psychic reactance. One reason is that we are taught to suppress overt signs of reactance, so that we often respond by learning more subtle ways of asserting our freedom. For example, a student who is compelled to come home unduly early in the evening throughout high school may compensate when away at college by keeping even later hours than he or she would have otherwise kept. Being aware of how people react to restrictions of their freedom may help us to retain a healthy respect for each other's sense of personal freedom at home and at work. When we fail to do so, we shouldn't be surprised at the negative reactions we get. When people experience a severe or prolonged loss of personal freedom or control, their resistance may wear down until they give up. They may become depressed or, in extreme instances, simply die. Martin Seligman (1975) explored the significance of *learned helplessness* for a wide range of human reactions, including depression and unexplained death. He demonstrated experimentally how attitudes of helplessness can be learned. In one study, individuals were subjected to a prolonged loud noise. One group was able to terminate the noise by pressing a button, while the other group could not escape hearing it. Later, when given a shuttlebox that could be manipulated to turn the noise off, the group whose efforts had been futile merely sat and passively accepted the noise. They had *learned* that they were helpless and, even when escape was available, did not take advantage of it.

Seligman has drawn parallels between learned helplessness and *reactive depression,* or extreme sadness occasioned by an external failure or loss. The most prominent symptom of both conditions is a sense of passivity, seen in decreased activity and a general loss of interest in just about everything. While most of us experience disappointment and loss, those most vulnerable to bouts of depression tend to overreact to such experiences because of their attitude of learned helplessness. Case histories of such people have shown that they see themselves as "born losers." Even their dreams are characterized more by frustration, powerlessness, and loss of self-esteem than by a desire for suffering or punishment so often ascribed to depressed people. The fact that more women than men experience such states of depression may be attributed partly to a certain degree of learned helplessness inherent in the female sex role. But as Jessie Bernard (1977) suggests, as women discover that their problem is more oppression than depression, the incidence of depression among women may well decrease.

HELPLESSNESS AND UNEXPLAINED DEATHS

A dramatic example of how the sense of helplessness may contribute to premature death can be seen in a study of unexpected deaths in an old-age home.

Fifty-five women over 65 years of age (their average age was 82) who applied for admission to an old-age home in the Midwest were asked several questions like: "How much choice did you have in moving to this home?" "How many other possibilities were open to you?" and "How much pressure did your relatives apply?"

Seventeen of the women stated that they had had no alternative but to move into the home. After only four weeks in residence, eight of these seventeen women died, with a total of sixteen of them dying after only ten weeks in residence. Only one person of the thirty-eight who voluntarily entered the home died in the same period of time.

All the deaths were called unexpected by the staff, indicating that psychological influences such as a sense of hopelessness and helplessness were definitely involved. Apparently, when the loss of control is severe enough, it leads to the exhaustion stage of stress and to premature death.

N.A. Ferrari, "Institutionalization and Attitude Change in an Aged Population." Unpublished doctoral dissertation, Western Reserve University, 1962. Reprinted in Martin E.P. Seligman, *Helplessness* (San Francisco: W.H. Freeman and Company, 1975), p. 185.

If the sense of helplessness becomes severe enough, it may lead to death. Indeed, this has been offered as an explanation for a variety of enigmatic deaths, including voodoo deaths among natives, higher death rates among inmates in Nazi concentration camps and other institutions, and a variety of premature, unexplained deaths. For example, a frightened woman entered the Baltimore City Hospital pleading for help. She told how she and two other girls had been born of mothers who were assisted by the same midwife in the Okefenokee Swamp on a Friday the thirteenth. The midwife had cursed all three babies, saying that one would die before her sixteenth birthday, another before her twenty-first birthday, and the third before her twenty-third birthday. The first girl had died in an automobile crash when she was fifteen. The second was accidentally shot to death during a fight in a night club on the evening of her twenty-first birthday. Now the third girl was terrified of her own death. Although hospital authorities remained somewhat skeptical, she was admitted for observation. The next morning, two days before her twenty-third birthday, the girl was found dead in her bed of unknown physical causes (Wintrob, 1972).

FREEDOM AND DECISIONS

Given the importance of inner freedom, the relationship between freedom and decision making may be rather obvious. That is, the freer we feel, the better able we are to make autonomous decisions. This is one reason people strive to avoid or escape from all external constraints on their freedom, such as oppressive governments, authoritarian bosses, or possessive mates or friends. Yet many other factors may enhance or diminish our freedom in decision making, such as the alternatives available to us, our willingness to assume responsibility for our decisions, and the influence of others.

Available Alternatives

Common sense tells us that the more alternatives available to us, the freer we feel—which is true up to a point. Yet too many alternatives may make decision making difficult and costly. This is especially true in a competitive, rapidly changing economy when companies proliferate the number of models and styles of their products in an effort to capture a larger share of the market. Too often, though, there is little or no difference between the options, making for pseudo-choices rather than genuine alternatives. Consequently, there comes a time when choice becomes overchoice, thereby diminishing our freedom (Toffler, 1971). Then too, the freedom to decide depends not just on the sheer number of alternatives but also on the ease or difficulty in dealing with them. Studies have shown that when people feel they can evaluate the alternatives quickly and easily, they feel freer with more options. But when it takes a lot of time and trouble to evaluate the options, they feel freer with a smaller number of options (Harvey & Jellison, 1974).

We also tend to feel freer when making decisions involving positive rather than negative outcomes (Harvey, Harris, & Barnes, 1975). For example, it is easier to choose whether to take two one-week vacations or one two-week vacation than it is to choose from which paycheck to have extra income tax withheld. A person's felt freedom also depends on the value differences between alternatives. When there is little or no difference, you may decide just as easily by flipping a coin. But when the differences are great, a wise decision may be more obvious. We enjoy greater subjective freedom when we are choosing among options of approximately equal value. Steiner (1973) found that students in a business school who were given opportunities for investing their money felt the greatest freedom of choice when the net gains among the various choices were approximately equal. All this suggests that the freedom of choice we actually feel depends not just on the number of available alternatives, but also on the types of choices and the real differences between them.

Freedom and Responsibility

The degree of freedom you enjoy in decision making also depends on your willingness to assume responsibility for your decisions. Studies have shown that there is a strong positive relationship between an individual's perceived freedom and his or her felt responsibility for decisions (Harvey, Harris, & Barnes, 1975). For example, students who enroll in college after some deliberation often feel more responsible for their performance than those who simply attend because it's expected of them. We might even generalize by saying that the greater a person's feelings of freedom, the greater the accompanying responsibility in a given situation. But this generalization holds true only up to a certain point. In some instances, a very high degree of freedom also exposes people to increased anxiety, conflict, criticism, and self-recrimination.

A lot depends on how much freedom a person feels comfortable with. Just as an excessive number of difficult alternatives may actually restrict a person's felt freedom, so it is when people are faced with more responsibility (and freedom) than they can handle. They begin to feel anxious and unfree, often attempting to escape from a burdensome responsibility. For example, a wealthy executive ruined his career by forging a relatively small check. When asked why he had done such a stupid thing, he replied, "I really don't know." Later, after attending therapy, he acknowledged that he had felt inadequate for his job and had probably acted out of unconscious feelings of inferiority and guilt, with his self-defeating behavior insuring an escape from a stressful situation.

When we speak of people who are "free," we are usually referring to those who feel accountable for their behavior, who can do what they really want to

AVOIDING FATEFUL DECISIONS

Walter Kaufmann (1973) has coined the word "decidophobia" for the fear of making decisions. People do not necessarily fear all decisions. Indeed, those most plagued by this fear may immerse themselves in making microscopic decisions as a way of avoiding the more significant ones. At one time or another, most of us have used one or more of the following strategies to avoid the serious, fateful decisions that govern our lives.

A common strategy is drifting. Instead of choosing how to live, people simply drift along, either by living according to the status quo or by dropping out, as do those whose lives are guided by no ties, code, tradition, or major purpose.

Another strategy is based on shared decision making, as in committees and marriages. Instead of really deciding, people just talk until something happens. They presume a consensus, often never questioning it. But if things turn out badly, no one feels responsible. Each merely went along.

A frequently used strategy is based on an appeal to some type of authority, such as an expert, a movement, a religion, or an institution. Although individuals may experience a tension between their loyalty and their personal conscience, they find innumerable ways to justify either alternative.

Truly autonomous people rely on none of these strategies. Instead, they accept responsibility for their lives and carefully scrutinize the alternatives available to them. But they also keep their eyes open and have the courage to admit when they are wrong and need to change. The Russian novelist Alexander Solzhenitsyn is an example of the truly autonomous man who resisted all the temptations of the decidophobic, making one fateful decision after another, seemingly against overwhelming odds.

Based on Walter Kaufmann, *Without Guilt and Justice* (New York: Dell Publishing Company, 1975).

do or refrain from doing what they don't want to do. Since freedom in this sense is a function of a well integrated personality, anything that helps us to achieve psychological wholeness affords us greater freedom as well. Freud (1957) held that one of the main goals of therapy is to help the client achieve inner freedom through greater self-awareness and psychic harmony. Many other therapists have discovered that the growth of freedom and responsibility go hand in hand. Carl Rogers (1961) observed that in the early stages of therapy, clients are busy blaming others or circumstances for their predicament, thereby avoiding responsibility for their problems. As therapy proceeds and clients gain greater self-awareness and autonomy, however, they accept more responsibility, though vacillating with anxiety from time to time. As clients continue to grow in therapy, they show an increasing acceptance of responsibility for themselves, their problems, and their growth. Ultimately, the sense of personal freedom is intimately bound up with the acceptance of responsibility for our lives and decisions.

Group Decision Making

Since we spend much of our time exchanging opinions and feelings with others, we often reach a decision through a process of shared decision making. Sometimes this is done informally, as when two or three friends, a married couple, or a family agree on a matter. At other times, the process becomes more formalized, as in a jury or town meeting. In either case, the question becomes: Are group decisions superior to those made by individuals? Actually, it can work either way, depending on the group.

The old saying, "A camel is a horse that was put together by a committee," suggests that group decisions are merely compromises. Irving Janis (1971) has referred to this phenomenon as *groupthink*. That is, the desperate drive for consensus and conformity in groups tends to suppress critical thought, resulting in compromise decisions. Janis hastens to add that for the most part this is a nondeliberate suppression of dissent because of the natural tendency of members to conform to the group norms. Unfortunately, the group members share the illusion of invulnerability, which leads them to take riskier courses of action and fail to heed warnings of danger, which can be disastrous in national policy and military actions. The dynamics of groupthink are such that members

focus on few alternatives, often just two.

spend little time discussing the nonobvious gains and costs of preferred policy.

make little effort to obtain information from outside experts.

ignore facts and opinions contradicting the group consensus.

fail to provide a contingency plan in case of failure.

As a result, group decisions tend to be compromise solutions, which at best make for mediocre performance, but at worst may lead to disastrous consequences.

However, group decisions may also be superior to those of individuals, depending largely on the group process. In a comparison of ad hoc groups and those trained in group effectiveness, Jay Hall (1971) found the latter groups tended to make superior decisions because of better conflict management. In the typical group, conflict is seen as disruptive, with the usual conflict-reducing techniques leading to compromise solutions. In trained groups it is just the opposite. Conflict is seen as a way of generating a wider range of alternatives so that a more creative solution may be found. Consequently, groups trained in conflict management tend to produce solutions that are superior to even the best efforts of individuals.

Some guidelines for achieving creative consensus are:

Present your views, but listen to those of others.

Don't feel that someone has to win and someone has to lose.

Strive for the best possible solution.

A creative use of conflict is the key to good group decisions. (Bethlehem Steel Corporation)

Avoid conflict-reducing techniques such as majority vote.

Realize that differences of opinion are natural and may lead to better solutions.

Hall concludes that group decisions are not inherently inferior. Instead, groups function as their members make them, and properly managed conflict can lead to more creative solutions than those reached by individuals.

DECISION MAKING

From the moment she awoke until she went to sleep at night, Kathy was busy making decisions. When she first awoke she had to decide when to get up and dress. Since it was a dreary day and she felt a bit lazy, she had trouble getting out of bed. Once up, she had to decide what to wear and what to eat for breakfast. Then she had to decide whether to attend her first class or to skip it in order to prepare for a test in her second class. Once in the library, she had to decide what were the most important things to study for the test. After she had begun the test, she had to decide whether to cheat in order to keep up her grade-point average. And so it went throughout the day. Like most of us, Kathy sometimes feels that "life is just one decision after another."

Many of our day-to-day decisions are made with little effort, mostly because of our basic commitments and habits. For example, since Kathy had already enrolled and paid her tuition, she usually attended class and took tests on time. But each day also brings its share of unexpected changes, disappointments, and surprise opportunities, calling for new decisions. In addition, we must also make major decisions, such as whether to change jobs or not. When such decisions arouse anxiety or indecision, we may act impulsively or put off a decision, often making matters worse. Some of these common decision-making strategies will be described in the following pages. We'll also take a look at the essential steps in decision making, along with some suggestions for improving your decision-making skills.

Decision-making Strategies

Most of the time, we're not fully aware of how we reach a decision, unless we're asked to think about it. When high school students were asked about their personal decision making, the results showed that the following types of decision-making strategies were most commonly used:

Impulsive
Taking the first alternative with little thought or examination. (Don't look before you leap.)

Fatalistic
Leaving it up to the environment or fate. (It's all in the cards.)

Compliant
Letting someone else decide. (Anything you say.)

Delaying
Postponing thought and action. (We'll cross that bridge later.)

Agonizing
Becoming overwhelmed analyzing alternatives. (I don't know what to do.)

Planning
Using a rational procedure with a balance between reason and emotion. (Weighing the facts.)

Intuitive
Basing a decision on inner harmony. (It feels right.)

Paralysis
Accepting responsibility but unable to approach a decision. (I can't face up to it.)

The distribution of students who followed each strategy was: planning, 25 percent; impulsive, 18 percent; compliant, 17 percent; delaying, 11 percent; fatalistic, 10 percent; agonizing, 6 percent; intuitive, 6 percent; and paralytic, 6 percent (Dinklage, 1966). Which of these strategies do you use most often? Which is most characteristic of you?

Since all important decisions involve some risk or uncertainty, decision-making strategies can also be classified according to the element of risk involved. At least four types of risk-taking strategies have been identified: the wish, escape, safe, and combination strategies. The *wish strategy* involves choosing the alternative that could lead to the most desirable result regardless of risk. An example would be someone who applies for a position as an astronaut even though the chances of being selected are very small. The *escape strategy* involves choosing the alternative that is most likely to avoid the worst possible results. An example would be the pitcher who, realizing the game is tied and nobody is on base, intentionally walks a batter who leads the league in home runs. The *safe strategy* consists in choosing the alternative that is most likely to bring success. An example would be a part-time student who decides to earn money by taking a job with set hours and salary rather than selling on a commission. The *combination strategy* involves choosing the alternative that combines high probability and high desirability. An example would be a patient who elects to undergo surgery that has a high success rate with highly desirable health benefits (Gelatt, Varenhorst, & Carey, 1972).

It is important to use the strategy that is most compatible for the individual and situation. Because of their training, experience, or interests, some people like to "take a chance" while others prefer to "play it safe." Then too, emotions and personality traits may alter people's estimate of risk. Confident people may underestimate the risk involved, while fearful people may overestimate it. Moreover, a person has to balance the risk against the desired outcome or achievement. That is, people who are fearful of rejection may risk too little, while highly ambitious people may risk too much. On the other hand, those high in achievement motive usually take more moderate risks, thereby increasing their actual chances of success. It is good to keep in mind that the purpose of making a decision is to bring about desired results and avoid undesirable ones. In this sense, what constitutes a "good" or "bad" decision varies with the individual and situation. Yet in order to bring about preferred results consistently, you need to be aware of the essentials of decision making.

WHICH JOB WOULD YOU CHOOSE?

First, make your selection. Then read the rest of the exercise.

A	B	C
A job that pays a low income, but which you are sure of keeping.	A job that pays a good income, but which you have a 50-50 chance of losing.	A job that pays an extremely good income if you do well, but one in which you lose everything if you don't do well.

When 46,000 high school seniors in Minnesota were asked this question, 50 percent of them chose B, with another 25 percent each choosing A or C. But there were important differences within the three groups. Generally boys chose a greater risk than girls; college-bound youth a greater risk than those who went directly to work; and city kids a greater risk than country kids. In fact, boys from the city who went to college chose risk C 44 percent of the time, while girls from the country who went to work after high school chose risk C only 10 percent of the time.

Try to analyze your answer in order to learn more about yourself.

H.B. Gelatt, B. Varenhorst, and R. Carey, *Deciding* (New York: College Entrance Examination Board, 1972), p. 40. Copyright © 1972 by the College Entrance Examination Board, New York. Adapted with permission.

Steps in Decision Making

Books on this subject usually tell us how decisions *ought* to be made. Instead, Irving Janis and Leon Mann (1977) have formulated the following five steps in decision making based on how people have actually made and carried out difficult decisions, ranging from weight loss to national emergencies.

Appraising the challenge. This involves recognizing a challenge for what it is, guarding against both faulty assumptions or oversimplifying a complex problem. Key question: "What are the risks of doing nothing, or not changing?"

Surveying the alternatives. What is most needed here is an attitude of openness and flexibility, with a concern to gather information about all possible alternatives, obvious or not. Key question: "Have I considered all the alternatives?"

Weighing alternatives. All the options are evaluated as to their practicality and consequences, especially the possible gains and costs. Key question: "Which is the best alternative?"

Making a commitment. The cumulative tension of considering alternatives can be resolved only by making a commitment. Yet there is a danger of acting impulsively to "get it over with." Key question: "When do I implement the best alternative and allow others to know my decision?"

Adhering despite negative feedback. Since every decision involves some risk, it is important not to overreact to criticism and disappointment, either by changing your mind prematurely or by justifying your choice and shutting out valuable criticism. Key questions: "Are the risks serious if I don't change? Are they more serious if I do change?"

Successful decision making involves what Janis and Mann call "vigorous information processing." Yet there are situations in which decision makers habitually fail to gather sufficient information, especially the following:

1. When there appears to be a low risk in continuing whatever you are doing, you are unlikely to look for alternatives.
2. When there exist both a high risk to what you're doing and the prospects of a low risk to an obvious alternative, you are likely to choose the latter.
3. If all the obvious alternatives look risky and there appears to be little chance of your coming up with a better one, you are likely to avoid decision making, often denying that a problem exists.
4. If you feel there is a possible alternative that may disappear if you wait to investigate other alternatives, you may panic and choose prematurely.

If you feel that all the obvious alternatives are risky and that there may be a better choice that is not yet obvious, and if there is sufficient time to look, only then will you engage in the necessary information processing. This doesn't necessarily mean that the failure to engage in vigorous information processing always results in poor decisions. Admittedly, collecting information takes time and energy. It disrupts routines and builds tension and conflict, all of which are unpleasant. Consequently, we are more likely to process new information when we expect the benefits to outweigh the costs involved. Yet, Janis and Mann claim that decision makers tend to underestimate the likely benefits of information processing, and often pay too high a price as a result.

Aids in Decision Making

While the process of gathering information, weighing alternatives, and making a commitment is complex enough, it is further complicated by many personal factors, such as our values, attitudes, tolerance for anxiety and conflict, and the like. Consequently, we may improve our decision-making skills by keeping in mind the following principles.

USE SOUNDER JUDGMENT.   Judgment, the raw material of decision making, involves drawing inferences from data. Many decisions are doomed from the start because of poor judgment, often because of the human tendency to simplify complex matters into familiar ideas, especially stereotypes. Richard Nisbett and Lee Ross (1980) suggest replacing simplistic, intuitive strategies with the more empirical orientation that guides scientists, asking ourselves such questions as: What are the facts? How representative are they? What do the alternatives look like? How much is due to situational and chance factors? Sounder judgments may lead to better decisions.

ACKNOWLEDGE CONFLICTS REALISTICALLY.   Every decision involves some degree of conflict, with equal alternatives leading to more intense conflict, especially when choosing between two undesirable results. As you may recall from the chapter on stress, the most common type of conflict is the double approach-avoidance conflict, that is, a conflict between two choices, each of which has positive and negative features. For example, a man who lost his job returned to school to prepare for a better job. When he was offered his old job back, he had to choose between two options, both of which presented advantages and disadvantages. In this case, he decided to reject the job offer and continue his studies.

CLARIFY YOUR VALUES AND OBJECTIVES.   Many conflicts arise from confusion over values rather than over the conflicting alternatives. Since values are neither "good" nor "bad" in themselves, this requires a personal examination. Once you have clarified your values, they can be translated into tangible objectives that guide your decisions. For example, students are sometimes torn between the need to study, work, socialize, or play, often vacillating in their decisions. Yet those who have made a clear choice about what they hope to gain from college will be more likely to resolve their daily decisions effectively.

ACCEPT REASONABLE RESULTS.   Nothing is so devastating to decision making as the wish for an "ideal" solution. People with perfectionistic tendencies are especially susceptible to this. Yet constant striving for perfection guarantees failure. It is usually wiser to accept the most reasonable results under the circumstances. Among the methods of combatting perfectionism suggested by David Burns (1980) are recognizing the advantages and disadvantages of perfectionism and comparing how perfectly you did something with how much you enjoyed it. For example, you may feel that you didn't play tennis very well, but you enjoyed it nevertheless because of the exercise and companionship.

MAKE THE BEST OF FAULTY DECISIONS.   Because of limitations in human judgment, circumstances, and unforeseen events, when it comes to decisions, "You can't win 'em all." But people are apt to waste time berating themselves or trying to justify their poor decisions. Roger Gould (1978) says it may be wiser to realize that more often than not we made the best possible decision at the time, and attempt to learn from our mistakes, whenever possible modifying our decision to achieve a more desirable result. For example, a girl who dropped out of college, married, and had two children regretted giving up her plans to be a writer. Once her children were in school, and encouraged by her husband, she began spending her mornings writing, eventually publishing several novels and winning national recognition.

DECISIONS AND PERSONAL GROWTH

I once asked a colleague who works with alcoholics at what point in the treatment program clients began making significant progress. "It's hard to say," he said, "because so much depends on when a person makes up his mind to change. In fact, we won't even admit people into our program until they have made some sort of commitment to change." A similar realization led Harold Greenwald

(1973) to adopt a new approach in treating clients, namely *direct decision therapy*. Greenwald found the main thing that happens in therapy, regardless of the techniques used, is that the person is helped to make a decision to change and then is supported in carrying out that decision. Decision therapy is aimed at helping clients see their problems as the result of previous decisions, to examine the consequences and alternatives of such decisions, and then to choose a more satisfying alternative. Dr. Greenwald readily admits that this approach has been helpful in his own personal life, including an earlier decision to become a psychologist. He has also found that many people who have never participated in therapy have benefited from applying the principles of decision therapy to their personal lives, especially in terms of personal growth.

Finding the Basic Decisions in Your Life

According to Greenwald, a good beginning point is to find the basic decisions underlying our everyday behavior, especially problem behavior. Although we may be conscious of our behavior being a reaction to people and situations, on closer examination we may find that we have *chosen* to act a certain way. Greenwald speaks of the "decision behind the decision," referring to basic life choices involving our needs and motivation, which we're only dimly aware of if at all. Yet, once such decisions are made, we usually organize our lives around them and our perceptions as well, so that we understand everything that happens to us a certain way. Some practical examples illustrate the point.

Have you ever wondered why people procrastinate or fail to put forth their best efforts on important matters? Often such behavior is the outgrowth of a basic life choice to protect themselves from failure or hurt, though they may not be aware of it. For example, the boy who habitually waits until Friday afternoon to call for a date that evening or the girl who waits until August to apply for college admission have something in common. In both instances, they have a face-saving excuse if they fail—"I was too late." Somewhere in the dim past, each has made a basic decision to play it safe, because of a fear of failure or getting hurt. Only when they change that decision will they put forth their best efforts and enjoy a greater chance of success.

Much negative behavior, such as rebelliousness and defiance, is also the result of a basic life decision though again not in the person's awareness. For example, a young man left home in his mid-teens because of constant fights with his overly strict father. Nevertheless, he was still known to be "touchy" and "hard to get along with," even by his friends. He was always doing the opposite of what people expected of him, often with disappointing results. In opposition to coercive parental authority, at some point in his life this young man had decided "No!" Until that time, he was an appendage of his parents. But from that time on, he felt more in charge of his life. Nor should that surprise us, since the defiance of the young child or adolescent is often the initial step toward autonomy. But as long as this young man remains stuck in this initial but negative stage of independence, his life will be controlled more by what he is against than what he is for.

Other types of behavior, such as undue complaining or suffering, often serve to get the attention people feel they deserve but haven't received. A common example is the married couple's mutual complaints. During a session with the marriage counselor, one husband complained that his wife hadn't shown any signs of being sexually responsive the past week. Then he seemed surprised when his wife said, "Actually, I was kind of horny this week." When the husband said, "Why didn't you let me know?" the wife replied, "If I have to ask you, it's no good." In such instances, the individuals have usually made a decision that they want to be taken care of. Their reasoning is, "If someone really loves me, than he or she will know what I need." One of the most important things about growing up is realizing that no matter how much people may love us, they can't possibly know what we want unless we express our desires. Until such people learn to become more assertive, they will continue to complain or suffer because of their prior choice of wanting to be taken care of.

Making New Decisions

In Greenwald's view, it is only when a *wish* to change leads to a *decision* to change that we really change and grow. For example, many smokers dislike their smoking habit. They say things such as "I'd *like* to stop smoking" and "I *hope* to give it up soon" and "I *plan* to cut down on my smoking." But until they make a basic decision to stop smoking and learn how to implement that decision, nothing happens.

So far we have assumed that people will automatically decide to change for the best. But this is not always the case. In some instances, people may become so overwhelmed with the anxiety and risks of change, that they will decide to remain the way they are, however unsatisfying or painful that may be. Nor can someone be forced into growth, especially by therapists who are militant about people living up to their human potential. As Greenwald (1973) aptly says, "Why the hell does anybody have to live up to his potential unless he wants to?" (p. 295). However well-intentioned such therapists may be, they can make the same mistakes that parents and spouses are prone to make—namely, trying to tell someone else what they ought to decide. Rather, the therapist's task is to help the client first discover what he or she wants to do and then make a personal decision to do it. As most of us have discovered, once you know what you want to do and really decide to do it, you're well on your way.

Some Practical Applications

One of the most common examples of decision making is "decision by default." Putting things off, whether temporarily or indefinitely, is itself a decision. An example that comes to mind is a young man who was having considerable dif-

USING DECISION MAKING FOR PERSONAL GROWTH

Greenwald has outlined the following suggestions for applying the principles of decision therapy to yourself:

1. *State your problem as clearly and completely as you can.* Your problem need not be acute or a crisis, just something you would like to deal with. You may even find it helpful to write things down.

2. *See each problem not as something that just happened to you, but as the consequence of a decision you have made.* Such a problem could be something you decided to do, something you decided to be, or some way you decided to regard other people.

3. *Look for the basic decision behind the decision.* Did you decide to have the problem in order to avoid something? If so, what were you avoiding?

4. *List the advantages and payoffs of the decision.* These may be actual positive gains or may include the avoidance of anxiety. In either case, they are still payoffs.

5. *What was the context in which you made the original decision?* Were you very young? What was the situation then? Was your decision a sound one, given the circumstances?

6. *Ask yourself if the context is different now that you're older.* Maybe the payoffs are not so important or have become more trouble than they are worth.

7. *List the alternatives to each decision you've made.* Examine them in terms of the advantages and disadvantages of each.

8. *Now choose one of the alternatives and decide to put it into practice.* Sharing your decision with friends or colleagues may help you carry it out.

9. *If you have trouble putting the decision into practice, go back to the first suggestion to see if you're still operating under an old decision.* Remember that what you actually do is the best clue to the decision you've made, not what you'd like or wish to do.

10. *Remember that it's not enough to make your decision only once.* You must reaffirm your decision repeatedly. For example, if you decide to lose weight, each time you sit down to eat you must reaffirm your decision.

11. *If you fail occasionally in carrying out your decision, that doesn't mean that you have to give up altogether.* Since most of us are not infallible, we must be able to accept an occasional failure, pick ourselves up, and continue with our decision.

Adapted from Harold Greenwald, *Direct Decision Therapy* (San Diego, Ca.: Edits, 1973).

Only when you make a decision about something do you become involved in it. (Marc P. Anderson)

ficulty completing his doctoral dissertation, partly because of emotional blocks in writing and partly because of conflicts with his advisor. Things became so frustrating that this young man simply turned his efforts elsewhere. He took an administrative post at the university ("while I finish my degree") and spent more time painting ("to take my mind off my problems"). Several years later when I asked him how his degree program was progressing, I wasn't surprised to hear that he had finally "decided" to give it up. Actually, he had made that decision earlier. The failure to make a positive decision is itself a decision with fateful consequences.

Overcoming negative, self-defeating behavior usually involves making a positive decision at a basic level of motivation. An example concerns a 28-year-old librarian who was bothered by depression and a poor relationship with her supervisor. She reported that she was constantly complaining at work, and was especially critical of her boss, often without an apparent reason. During therapy this woman discovered that earlier in her life she had learned to suppress her anger for fear of parental disapproval. She had become a passive, good little girl, but resented those on whom she remained dependent. Gradually, she learned to take more initiative, to show her anger more directly, but as an expression of her feelings rather than as judgmental remarks that might put others on the defensive. As this woman became more assertive, she felt less depressed and enjoyed a more satisfying relationship with those in authority. She also returned to school for a master's degree and later assumed a supervisory position at another library.

Sometimes it is wise to make a decision that counters or reverses an earlier commitment that has led to undesirable consequences. An example is a 45-year-old lawyer who married the daughter of a senior partner in his firm. He admits having married out of "mixed motives." That is, while he had been genuinely attracted to his wife, he had also hoped that his "connections" would enhance his career. Yet he soon discovered that conflicts with his father-in-law complicated his life both at work and at home. Consultation with a specialist about his asthma attacks, which seemed worse during joint vacations at his wife's family summer place, suggested these were brought on by emotional conflicts over his in-laws. Gradually, this man realized that it had not been a good idea to marry the "boss's daughter," and eventually he decided to start his own firm. Although he went through a few lean years, he soon had a flourishing law practice and was much happier in his marriage as well. Failure to make such a courageous decision often results in feeling trapped in one's career, drinking problems, or extramarital affairs.

Sometimes dramatic improvements involve group decision making. In one instance, the quality of work had gotten so bad that a company was considering simply closing an automobile assembly plant. As a final gesture, the manager suggested they inform the workers of the situation and ask for their suggestions. They discovered that the workers themselves were well aware of their poor work, although they justified it because of their poor working conditions. Yet they wanted to improve the situation just as much as the company officials did. A group decision was reached to save the plant, involving concessions from both management and labor. During a six-month probationary period, a new policy was adopted involving workers' suggestions to improve assembly-line production, to improve treatment of workers, and to make the work more meaningful. Each team of workers followed a car through the assembly line and became responsible for the acceptance of the final product. The improvement in productivity and quality of work was so dramatic that the plant not only survived but became a model for the rest of the plants in the parent company.

SUMMARY

We began the chapter by emphasizing the importance of personal freedom, the inner awareness of being able to choose your own course of action. It was pointed out that the greater our perceived freedom, or subjective awareness of being free, in a given situation, the more likely we are to enjoy what we are doing and be open to a change in our attitudes. Yet when our sense of freedom is threatened, we react by asserting it all the harder. When we feel we have little or no freedom, we may give up and succumb to depression or, in extreme instances, suffer premature death.

The intimate association between perceived freedom and decision making was also discussed. It was pointed out that an optimum rather than a maximum number of alternatives increases freedom in making decisions, especially with difficult choices. Moreover, the greater our perceived freedom, the more responsible we feel for our decisions. Although group decision making often produces faulty decisions, mostly because of the pressure of group conformity, training in conflict management may lead to more creative solutions in group decision making.

There are a variety of decision-making strategies, depending on such matters as the degree of rationality, emotions, and risk involved. Janis and Mann have found that in making important decisions people tend to go through a sequence of steps, which include appraising the challenge, surveying alternatives, weighing alternatives, making a commitment, and adhering to a decision despite negative feedback. Some aids to decision making include the use of sound judgment, facing conflicts realistically, clarifying objectives, accepting reasonable results, and making the best of faulty decisions.

Finally, we examined some of the implications of Harold Greenwald's decision therapy for personal growth. Personal problems are to be regarded not as things that merely happened to us, but largely as the consequences of basic decisions we've made. Through examining these decisions and changing them to accord with our basic desires and aims, we may promote personal growth. We also pointed out how people have used the principles of decision therapy to take charge of their lives and change them for the better.

QUESTIONS FOR SELF-REFLECTION

1. Do you feel that people today have more freedom of choice than their parents did? Why?

2. Would you agree with Victor Frankl that we always retain an inner freedom to choose despite outer circumstances?

3. For the most part, do you respect other people's freedom of choice?

4. Do you readily accept responsibility for your decisions and behavior? Or do you engage in a lot of complaining and blaming?

5. What has been your experience in group decision making? Under what circumstances are group decisions likely to be better than those of individuals?

6. How would you characterize your own decision-making skills?

7. When making decisions, are you willing to take risks?

8. What was the best decision you ever made? What was the worst one?

9. Do you learn from faulty decisions? Or are you too busy blaming yourself?

10. Would you agree that personal growth often requires a decision?

EXERCISES

1. Freedom and enjoyment

As you may recall from reading this chapter, we usually derive greater enjoyment from an activity when we have freely chosen to do it. In order to see how this applies to your own experience, select several activities you have enjoyed very much and an equal number you have disliked in the past few weeks. Then compare these activities according to the degree of choice you had in doing them. Do you find that those activities you enjoyed the most were the ones in which you had the most freedom of choice? Conversely, do you find that the activities you disliked were the ones that you were obligated or expected to do?

Since our enjoyment of an activity involves more than the degree of choice involved in doing it, you may discover that this exercise is not as simple as it appears. The degree of choice may be more relevant in some types of activities and situations than in others. Can you think of some activities in which your attitude is most likely to be affected by the freedom of choice involved? Which types of situations are most affected by your having a choice or not? How are your choices affected by sex-role differences?

2. Avoidance of decisions

Do you have a habit of putting off major decisions? If so, look back at Walter Kaufmann's strategies for avoiding decisions and see how these apply to yourself.

When faced with a major decision, do you sometimes drift along, hoping the need for a decision will go away or resolve itself? If you are sharing responsibility for a decision with another person or a group, do you reach a firm decision? Or after talking things over, do you tend to presume a consensus has been reached? Have you ever experienced mis-understanding because of such a mistaken assumption? When making a major decision, do you sometimes rely on the authority of someone else, such as a parent, professor, boss, or physician?

Sometimes sales people are taught how to "close" a presentation, under the assumption that most people need to be helped to make a decision. Have you experienced such pressure when buying things? Do you welcome it, or resent it?

Since sound decision making involves thinking through a problem, looking over the alternatives, and weighing them in terms of their consequences, we are not suggesting that you begin making decisions impulsively. Instead, this exercise is aimed to make you aware of any avoidance tendencies that may undermine effective decision making.

3. Risk taking

Read over the four types of decision-making strategies based on the degree of risk involved: the wish, escape, safe, and combination strategies. How do these strategies relate to your characteristic way of making decisions?

Do you tend to use one of these strategies more than the others? If so, which one? Can you explain the reasons why? Since a "good" decision depends largely on the individual and situation as well as the decision-making strategy involved, can you think of instances in which each of the four strategies is especially appropriate?

When would it be appropriate to use the wish strategy, that is, to choose the most desirable alternative regardless of risk? Or when does it make more sense to utilize the escape strategy to avoid losing? Are there times when it may be preferable to play it safe, that is, to choose the alternative most likely to bring success? How often do you use the combination strategy—choosing an alternative that combines high probability of success with high desirability?

How would you characterize your decision making in regard to taking risks? Do you relish taking risks? Or are you overly cautious? How often do you attempt to regulate the degree of risk involved in order to heighten your chances of success?

4. Which job would you choose?

Review the material in the boxed item on pp. 261–262 and apply it to your own choice of a career or job. Does your career/job choice come closest to option A, B, or C? If it is more like A or C than B, can you explain your reasons for this?

How about your job experience so far? Have you chosen part-time and full-time jobs that are beneath your abilities, or ones that challenge you?

Compare the possible advantages and disadvantages of a career/job similar to each option, A, B, and C. Why is option B preferable in most instances?

5. Steps in decision making

Select some major decision you have already made and analyze it in terms of Janis and Mann's five steps in decision making. Or if you are presently making an important decision, you may want to practice your skills in the suggested steps in decision making. In either case, ask yourself the following questions:

1. Did you realistically evaluate the problem or opportunity requiring a decision? Or did you skip over this stage?
2. Did you gather information about all the possible alternatives? Or did you simply choose from the more obvious ones?
3. To what extent did you compare the alternatives in terms of their respective consequences? Or did you stick with a favorite hunch from the beginning?
4. Did you reach a decision only after considerable deliberation? Or did you make up your mind quickly?
5. Have you persisted in your decision despite the realization of some disappointment or criticism? Or have you changed your mind prematurely or justified your choice to shut out valuable criticism?

While it may not be realistic to expect every decision will be 100 percent correct, use of the appropriate decision-making skills should increase the odds of making the best possible decision under the circumstances.

6. Decision making and personal growth

Apply Harold Greenwald's principles of decision therapy to your own experience. You may select some habit or problem behavior you have already changed or something you would like to change. If you select the latter, you may achieve more by working on a manageable problem, like poor study habits, than on a more severe problem of long-standing.

Would you agree that problem behavior such as procrastination is often a consequence of a decision you have made, whether you are conscious of it or not? Are you convinced that personal growth demands a decision on your part? Remember, it's not enough to make a decision. You must reaffirm it repeatedly.

7. Group decision making

An enjoyable exercise in group decision making is "Lost On The Moon." Participants are to assume they are astronauts who have crash landed on the moon, and must reach the mother ship two hundred miles away. They are asked to rank fifteen items according to how useful each would be to the lunar mission. Items are ranked first by individuals and then again in small groups. The rankings are then compared to NASA's rankings, with individual and group scores tallied. The exercise usually takes about 45 minutes and can be played by any number of participants divided into small groups of three to five members each.

The instructions for this exercise can be found in Jay Hall's article, "Decisions," *Psychology Today,* November 1971, pp. 51–54, 86.

RECOMMENDED READINGS

Cammaert, L. P., and C. C. Larsen. *A Woman's Choice.* Champaign, Ill.: Research Press, 1980 (paperback). A practical handbook to aid women in making the best possible and most realistic decisions about their lives.

Gelatt, H. B., B. Varenhorst, and R. Carey. *Deciding.* New York: College Entrance Examination Board, 1972 (paperback). A workbook on decision-making skills, with three related sections on values, information, and strategy.

Greenwald, H. *Direct Decision Therapy.* San Diego, Ca.: Edits, 1973. A highly readable book on the principles and applications of decision therapy, including numerous examples from the author's clinical practice.

May, R. *Psychology and the Human Dilemma.* New York: W.W. Norton, 1980. A noted existential psychologist explains the meaning of human freedom in relation to the promises and perils of human existence.

Van Over, R. ed. *The Psychology of Freedom.* Greenwich, Conn.: Fawcett, 1974 (paperback). A collection of thought-provoking essays on the psychological aspects of personal freedom by famous authors.

Wheeler, D. D., and I. L. Janis. *A Practical Guide for Making Decisions.* New York: The Free Press, 1980. A practical guide for decision making based on the author's own research studies.

Self-directed Change

Even though you may feel free to change and grow and have made a decision to do so, there is no guarantee that you will. You must also know how to go about it, which brings us to the subject of this chapter.

In the following pages, we will explain how you can achieve greater self-control through altering the sequence of your behaviors and the situational influences involved. Much of the chapter will be devoted to a step-by-step procedure for self-directed change. It includes numerous practical applications as well as three case studies at the end of the chapter. There are also boxed items dealing with such matters as test anxiety, fears, and procrastination.

Because the step-by-step procedure is based on the principles of behavior theory, people sometimes mistakenly assume it is at odds with the concern for personal freedom and growth. Yet, as Michael Mahoney and Carl Thoresen (1974) have pointed out, such a method of self-improvement actually provides us with the "behavioral means for humanistic ends." That is, it is simply another way of implementing the process of personal growth and self-actualization.

ACHIEVING SELF-CONTROL

Whenever someone changes his or her behavior against great odds, such as the person who overcomes a habit of drug abuse, we say that such a person has a lot of willpower. And conversely, when someone eats or drinks too much, we say that this person lacks willpower. But in both cases it is not quite clear what willpower is, much less how we go about acquiring more of it.

Self-control as Learned Behavior

The apparent mystery surrounding the use of willpower disappears when we think of willpower as *self-control*. Psychologists who rely on behavior modification techniques speak of self-control as a learned skill that may be strengthened in accordance with the known principles of learning. B. F. Skinner writes, "When a man controls himself, chooses a course of action, thinks out a solution to a problem, or strives toward an increase in self-knowledge, he is *behaving*" (1953, p. 228). As you'll notice, the term "behavior" here refers not just to overt behavior but to all those internal and external processes and activities that can be observed and measured. Skinner's main point is that the behaviors comprising our ability for self-control can be modified by the same principles as any other behavior.

After what we've said in the last chapter about how behaviorists emphasize the environmental control of behavior, you may be surprised to hear that they also believe in self-control. But they do. Their emphasis, however, is on self-control as a relative, learned skill, as something an individual acquires through interaction with his or her environment. For example, Skinner distinguishes between controlled and controlling behaviors (1972). What he calls *controlled behaviors* are usually the result of biological needs, such as eating, drinking, or sexual intercourse, which are shaped by environmental *reinforcers*—anything that strengthens a given behavior. These are the behaviors we usually want to change in some way. Fortunately, these acts are largely under the power of our *controlling behaviors*, the way we habitually satisfy those needs. Controlling behaviors are primarily learned and thus more susceptible to change. Increasing our self-control, then, consists of increasing our awareness and mastery of these controlling or habitual behaviors.

Awareness of Environmental Influences

One of the earliest examples of this kind of self-control was reported by the Greek poet Homer (Kanfer & Phillips, 1970). In order to protect himself and his crew from the Sirens (whose songs bewitched anyone who heard them), Odysseus commanded his oarsmen to fill their ears with beeswax. He further directed them to tie him to the mast, warning them not to release him under any circumstances, so he could safely hear the song.

Odysseus's success did not lie in the possession of some unusual willpower. Rather, it consisted in his ability to modify some of his controlling behaviors by preparing in advance, which in turn increased his own self-control. This approach stands in contrast to the conventional emphasis on insight and mastery of the internal forces of our behavior. Those who rely on the principles of behavior modification stress that we also need "outsight," or the awareness and mastery of the external influences of behavior. Actually, we need the awareness of both types of influence. But the fact that this approach emphasizes the external influences on behavior may serve as a corrective and complement to the humanistic reliance on insight and internal mastery. Much of our behavior is heavily influenced by situational factors, which is one reason why our willpower fluctuates so from one situation to another. As a result, it has been suggested that the Greek maxim "know thyself" may also be expanded to include "know thy controlling variables" (Mahoney & Thoresen, 1974).

Altering the Cues and Consequences of Behavior

Two types of controlling variables or influences are especially important for behavior, namely, the cues that precipitate behavior and the consequences that follow it. Achieving greater self-control involves altering both types of influence.

Perhaps you have heard of an actor's *cue*, which is a word or sign given as a signal for the actor to do or say something. In a similar way, certain cues in our surroundings or within us may trigger what we say or do. Often we're only dimly aware of these. For example, merely seeing food may make us suddenly feel hungry, or just looking at our watch may tell us it's time to eat. As a result, we often eat when we don't need to.

Often a cue sets off a whole series of behaviors, which psychologists speak of as a *chain of behavior*. A behavior chain is a complex sequence of behaviors that tend to occur together. For example, a man who left work at 5 o'clock found that he drank too much before having dinner at 6:30 P.M., when the other members of his family came home. He found that coming home and sitting down in the living room with time on his hands served as cues to his drinking pattern. So he decided to play tennis two days a week and to take a long walk the other three days. In so doing he also modified his drinking behavior because he altered the cues that set it off.

Many times the consequences of our behavior exert more influence on what we do than the cues that precede it. Psychologists who rely on the principles of *operant learning* refer to the consequences that are contingent on a given behavior as *reinforcement,* as will be explained in greater detail later in the chapter. Reinforcement tends to strengthen a behavior and thereby increase the probability of its occurring again. Such reinforcement does not always have to be positive or even consciously perceived. Even negative attention like criticism often serves to strengthen the very behavior we object to. Many of our habitual behaviors

---

OVERCOMING TEST ANXIETY

While mild to moderate levels of anxiety may improve performance on tests, high levels of anxiety usually impair it. Much depends on the individual, the complexity of the test, and the overall situation. People who are especially prone to test anxiety suffer from low self-esteem and an intense fear of failure. Throughout their preparation and the test itself, text-anxious individuals are preoccupied with negative thoughts such as "I'm no good at this" or "I'll never make it." Such negative self-monitoring then interferes with their performance, leading to a self-fulfilling prophecy.

Studies have shown that test-anxious individuals can be trained to talk to themselves in such a way that they can control their attention and improve their performance. One group of students received cognitive modification training along with some anxiety reducing techniques. They were compared with another group of students who underwent desensitization (to be explained later in this chapter) and with a waiting-list control group. Instead of learning how to get rid of anxiety (as in the desensitization group), students in the cognitive modification group learned how to function better in the face of anxiety. That is, they were taught that some anxiety is inevitable. But rather than view the anxiety as a signal for becoming upset, they were taught to visualize themselves as coping with the anxiety by means of slow, deep breathing and positive instructions for improving their performance.

For example, when faced with a difficult question, they were told to say, "I'll come back to this question after I answer the ones I know," "The more relaxed I remain the better I'll do," and so forth. The results showed that students taught to cope with their anxiety by such positive self-verbalizations improved more than those in the other two groups in terms of their self-confidence, performance in a sample testing situation, and their actual grade-point averages (Meichenbaum, 1974).

Such methods remind us of a simple truth that we tend to overlook because it's so obvious, namely, that we can control our behavior by modifying our private dialogue with ourselves, especially by emphasizing more positive self-instructions.

tend to be followed by some type of reinforcement, such as grades in school or payday at work.

At this point we are ready to describe the actual procedure to be used for self-directed behavior change. As you read the chapter, remember that, although this is a proven method of self-improvement, it is not magic. In order to use this method successfully, you must also want to change. If you should ask, "How much do I have to want to change?" perhaps the best answer I can give you is, "Enough to follow the procedure." The potential benefits are great. You may not only acquire the particular self-improvement you aim for; you may also gain in the kind of self-awareness and self-control that are an integral part of personal freedom itself.

SETTING A GOAL

The first step in achieving better self-control is setting a goal for yourself. Your goal is usually known as your *target behavior*.

Defining Your Target Behavior

It is important to define your target behavior in behavioral terms. In some instances, you may want to decrease or eliminate a problem behavior, such as smoking or eating too much. In other instances, you may want to acquire a more positive behavior, such as exercising more regularly or turning in your class papers on time.

Avoid describing your goal in terms of personality traits like hostility or dependency. Instead, think of specific behaviors associated with these general characteristics. For example, if you want to become more assertive, what kinds of specific behaviors do you associate with this term? Think of concrete situations in your life in which these behaviors would be appropriate. In some instances, you may find it more practical to modify your behavior in only one situation at a time, such as speaking up more frequently in class, and then generalize your assertive behavior to other situations.

It is also preferable to define your target behavior in positive terms: If you want to lose weight, "not being fat" is a negative goal, while "becoming thin" is positive. Focus on what you want to be, not what you are. Furthermore, when you are trying to eliminate an undesired behavior, make your goal an incompatible alternative behavior. For example, if you're cutting down on watching TV, instead of penalizing yourself each time you watch TV (thereby focusing more attention on an undesirable activity), why not make your goal the development of a competing activity like playing the piano, painting, or going out with a friend during the time you normally watch TV?

Selecting an Attainable Goal

Your target behavior must also be attainable. One of the most common mistakes people make in self-improvement programs is to select an overly ambitious or unrealistic goal. A habitual C student who aims to make all As the next semester is probably doomed to failure. A better goal would be to improve by one letter grade in three out of five courses in the first semester. Successfully completing such a modest goal would then help motivate that person to attain the desired goal of making all As in all subjects.

You probably won't be sufficiently motivated to modify your behavior unless it has become bothersome or a problem to you in some way. But if you select some difficult, long-standing problem, like never doing your best in anything you attempt, you may discover that your problem is not only more complex than you realized but that you don't have sufficient objectivity to analyze it correctly, much less to change it. A better strategy would be to select a more limited goal, realizing that the experience of success in achieving your goal will itself provide additional reinforcement for your continuing self-improvement.

It's also important that you be able to measure your progress toward your

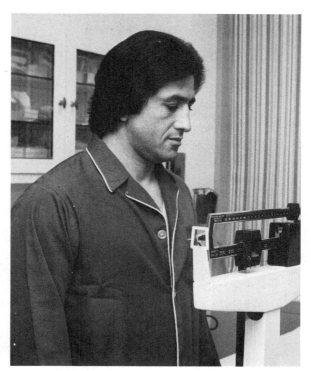

It's important to be able to measure your progress toward a desired goal. (Ken Karp)

target behavior. Otherwise, how will you know how well you are doing? Many overt activities naturally lend themselves to such measurement, like eating, smoking, exercising, working, or sexual behaviors. If you're working on a more general problem such as studying, you may have to define your target behavior in such a way that you can measure it accurately. For example, we all know from experience that just sitting down at your desk and putting your face in a book doesn't necessarily mean that you are studying. You may be staring at the pages and daydreaming. In this case, studying would need to be measured by a more accurate means than amount of time spent in the same room with your books. Such measurements might include the number of pages you've read and understood, your ability to recite the ideas to someone else, writing a short summary of it for yourself, or your next test grade.

RECORDING YOUR BEHAVIOR

Once you've selected a goal, it is essential to observe your present behavior as a basis for measuring your progress later on. This is known as gathering *baseline data* for before and after comparisons.

Methods for Record Keeping

A cardinal rule in recording your own behavior is to use a method that is both practical and portable, for your memory works in a highly selective way. Just think about it. At the end of the day, how well do you remember all the times you took a snack or smoked a cigarette? You can get a more accurate record by carrying around some type of pencil and paper device, which is probably the most common method used. For example, a 3 × 5 card can be inserted inside the cellophane covering of a cigarette package, or in your pocket, or can be attached to one of your books, or even taped on the dashboard of your car for on-the-spot recording. There are also various types of mechanical wrist-counters and bead-counters available for this purpose. Some individuals have also used a knitting-stitch counter that fits over the end of a pencil, which allows you to work while recording your behavior.

How long must you monitor your behavior? The answer to this depends on the individual and the behavior involved. Ordinarily, you should keep records for at least one week, but rarely longer than three to four weeks. If there is a wide variation in the daily frequency of a behavior, such as the number of cigarettes smoked, then take a daily average for later comparisons.

Types of Records

There are three general types of records. Probably the easiest and most widely used type is a frequency count. This consists of counting the number of calories consumed or the number of times you speak up in class. Another type of record

BEN FRANKLIN'S SELF-IMPROVEMENT PLAN

Though Franklin seldom attended church, he was once inspired by a sermon on attaining moral perfection. "I wished to live without committing any fault at any time," he resolved.

He made up a list of thirteen virtues that he wished to achieve: temperance, silence, order, resolution, frugality, industry, sincerity, justice, moderation, cleanliness, tranquility, chastity, and humility.

Franklin found that while he was guarding against one fault, he was frequently overtaken by another. So he decided to concentrate on one virtue a week at a time. Each evening he recorded the violations of the virtues observed that day in his little book, attempting to keep the record entirely clear for the special virtue of the week, such as "temperance."

	Sun.	M.	T.	W.	Th.	F.	S.
Tem.							
Sil.	*	*		*		*	
Ord.	*	*			*	*	*
Res.		*				*	
Fru.		*				*	
Ind.			*				

Franklin completed a course in thirteen weeks, covering four courses a year. To avoid the trouble of making out new pages each week, he later made his daily observations with a pencil on prelined pages which could be easily erased. As he grew older, he completed fewer courses each year until eventually he gave them up altogether because of his busy schedule. "But I always carried my little book with me," Franklin quipped, "more as a reminder."

Surprisingly, Franklin thought that the virtue "order" gave him the most trouble. While he found it was relatively easy to impose order on his days as a printer, it became increasingly difficult in his life as an ambassador. Yet it would be hard to find a more orderly, self-disciplined man than Benjamin Franklin.

Through such conscientious record keeping, Franklin observed, "I was surprised to find myself so much fuller of faults than I had imagined; but I had the satisfaction of seeing them diminish." Later he wrote, "Though I never arrived at the perfection I had been so ambitious of obtaining, I was, by the endeavor, a better and a happier man than I otherwise should have been if I had not attempted it."

How similar is Franklin's method of self-improvement to that described in this chapter? How different?

Benjamin Franklin, *The Autobiography of Benjamin Franklin* (The Spencer Press, N.D.), pp. 97–116.

is a measure of the duration or amount of time invested in the behavior. This is more laborious, but is also more appropriate when the behavior cannot be easily broken down into separate behavioral events. Some examples would be the number of hours spent sleeping, studying, working, or with a particular person. In these instances, a watch may be used to mark the beginning and ending times. A third type of record is counting the products of the behavior, such as a clean room, completed assignments, or money earned.

Graphs are often helpful for recording your initial observations and making comparisons later on. Usually the horizontal axis of a graph measures time, often in days, and the vertical axis measures the behavior, such as frequency, duration, or incidence (see the sample graphs in the case studies at the end of the chapter). It is also recommended that you not attempt to change your behavior until you have discovered your actual behavior patterns through recording them. In fact, many individuals find that the act of observing and recording their behavior itself aids in changing it. This is especially true when a person already has a lot of motivation to change. This is one of the reasons why it is important to select a positive behavior as your goal, since observing a behavior also tends to reinforce it.

ALTERING THE ANTECEDENTS OF BEHAVIOR

As we mentioned earlier, many behaviors occur in close succession or in a sequence known as a chain of behavior. Smoking, for example, tends to occur more frequently when an individual is nervous, bored, drinking, or in casual conversation with others. These conditions are referred to as *precipitating stimuli, cues,* or *antecedents* of behavior, since they tend to trigger a particular act. Changing the sequence or the association of these factors with the behavior in question is one way of modifying the target behavior.

Avoiding and Altering Antecedents

When your goal is to get rid of some undesirable behavior, the best strategy is to reduce the antecedents of it. Thus, individuals who are prone to overeating should avoid fancy restaurants, smokers should avoid passing cigarette machines, and big spenders should avoid expensive stores. One young man fighting a weight problem, for example, was told he could eat to his heart's content. But instead of eating while reading or watching TV, he was to treat food with the dignity it deserved. Even if he ate only a small snack, he was to put it on a plate and sit down and devote himself exclusively to eating. As a result, eating became disassociated from the cues and conditions such as reading or watching TV that precipitated it. Within a week the young man cut out all snacks between meals, telling his therapist, "You've taken all the fun out of it" (Goldiamond, 1965).

Excessive anxiety and lack of preparation set the stage for poor performance. (Ken Karp)

Sometimes just rearranging the various components in a chain of behavior helps. For example Annon (1971) tells of a problem drinker who had consumed up to a pint of vodka before bedtime each night for years. In fact, he couldn't go to sleep without it. By analyzing the usual sequence of events leading up to his drinking, he discovered that he usually came home, turned on the TV, went to the refrigerator, put ice in his glass, poured himself a drink, and then went to the bathroom, took a shower, returning to the kitchen to pour more drinks before going to bed. He then reorganized the sequence of behaviors to reduce his drinking. Immediately upon returning home he took a shower and dressed before going to the refrigerator. Later, he substituted cola for vodka.

Building New Chains of Behavior

When you're trying to establish a desirable behavior, it's best to build in the antecedents and associations that trigger the desired behavior. For example, many students have trouble studying because of the conflicting cues and conditions they associate with studying; a student may go to the student center to do some reading, but may end up socializing instead because of the many convenient opportunities to do so. Or, you may plan to study after watching a ball game on TV, but may find that you're not in the mood for studying later in the evening. In such cases a set of conditions that increase the probability of studying needs to be built up. One way is to set a definite time for studying, such as the early evening hours on weeknights. Reserving a definite place for study also helps. One student found that when he sat down to his desk, he was distracted by the pinup pictures on the wall. He got more studying done by going to the library and using a small study cubicle where there were fewer distractions.

Some individuals have found it helpful to build a strong association betweeen a specific chair and studying by using that chair *only* for studying. All other reading, letter writing, daydreaming, and so forth, is done elsewhere. The same procedure has also been used for eliminating undesirable behavior. Nolan (1968) tells of a smoker whose self-agreement allowed her to smoke only in a certain chair. Once she established this association, she moved the chair to the basement and decreased her smoking even more markedly. A similar approach has also been used for controlling a wide variety of behaviors, including nail biting and hair pulling (Kanfer & Phillips, 1970).

In short, when you want to eliminate an undesirable behavior, reduce the precipitating factors and associations; when you want to establish a desirable behavior, increase them.

OVERCOMING YOUR FEARS

A widely used method for overcoming fears is systematic *desensitization,* developed by Joseph Wolpe (1973). The basic assumption is that a fear response can be inhibited by learning an incompatible response such as relaxation. Although this technique is ordinarily used by therapists with their clients, more people are now using it on a do-it-yourself basis for the milder fears.

There are four steps in desensitizing yourself.

First, write down on a separate 3 × 5 card each situation you associate with a given fear or apprehension. Include at least 10 but no more than 25 items in your stack of cards.

Next, arrange these cards in a hierarchy from the least to the most threatening situations, with small steps of anxiety between each situation. For example, suppose you become anxious when someone criticizes you. You might construct a hierarchy including imagined situations such as the following:

1. A close friend disagrees with your opinion of some minor political figure.

2. A friend mildly kids you for forgetting his or her name in making introductions.

3. Your friend disagrees with your choice of a movie to attend.

Constructing a gradual and realistic hierarchy is one of the hardest parts of this procedure. So take your time writing up the situations and arranging your cards.

The next step is to train yourself in relaxation techniques. First, sit in a comfortable chair or lie on a couch or bed. Then beginning with your forehead and scalp, practice relaxing and letting your muscles go limp. Then move on to the muscles of your jaw, then your neck, and so on, until you have reached your feet and toes. Some people vary this technique by alternately tensing and then relaxing their respective muscles.

Whichever method you choose, take about 15 seconds with each muscle, and anywhere from 15 to 30 minutes for a whole session. You may spend three or four sessions just practicing your relaxation techniques until you are reasonably relaxed.

Now you're ready for the fourth step. Take the top card from the pile and look at it. Then close your eyes and visualize the situation as vividly as you can in your imagination. As soon as you experience *any* anxiety, stop imagining the scene and go back to your relaxation techniques. When you are completely relaxed, then look at the card again. Repeat this until you can look at the card without feeling anxious. Then progress to the next card. Some people use a variation of this technique by listening to a vivid description of their scenes on a tape recorder.

You may want to try a variation of this procedure called behavioral rehearsal. This is especially valuable for dealing with anxiety in interpersonal situations. For example, suppose you have difficulty speaking up to a teacher. Ask a friend of yours to play a teacher who has just given you a low score on a test. Then you can practice being calm and discussing low anxiety-arousing questions with the "teacher"; and then progress to more anxiety-arousing ones. Practice your approach until you feel relatively calm in your behavior.

Still another variation is practicing in real-life situations. Here you gradually approach a feared person or situation while in a relaxed state. For example, a girl who was a senior in college worked on her fear of birds by first approaching birds at a local zoo. When one or two birds were 15 yards away, she would turn and face the birds. Then she would take one step at a time toward the birds. Then when two or more birds were present she would repeat the same procedure. Later, she repeated this procedure beginning 10 yards from the birds, then 5 yards, and so forth. Although she never did come to like birds, she no longer felt nervous around them.

Joseph Wolpe, *The Practice of Behavior Therapy* (New York: Pergamon Press, Inc., 1973). David L. Watson and Roland G. Tharp, *Self-Directed Behavior* (Monterey, Ca.: Brooks/Cole Publishing Company, 1972), p. 176.

ARRANGING EFFECTIVE CONSEQUENCES

Once you've begun to control some of the conditions that trigger your target behavior, you're ready to pay more attention to the consequences of your behavior. In fact, psychologists who rely heavily on the principles of operant learning maintain that much of our behavior is governed more by its consequences than by its antecedents. Increasing self-control, then, consists of arranging the consequences of your behavior so that they strengthen the desired behavior. Technically, this is known as making rewards or reinforcing consequences *contingent* on the target behavior. We don't reward ourselves with the enjoyable or reinforcing activities until we have performed the target behavior we want to strengthen.

A simple example can be seen in the way we go about performing our daily tasks. Most of us have a tendency to do the effortless but pleasant things such as buying toothpaste or notepaper, while putting off the less pleasant tasks such as doing laundry or paying bills. One way to get more things done is to rearrange the sequence of activities so that you do the more enjoyable tasks *only after* doing the less enjoyable ones. In this way, you're using the enjoyable activities as reinforcing consequences for doing the chores.

Types of Reinforcers

A reinforcer, as explained earlier, is anything that strengthens a behavior. It is important, however, to distinguish between the different types of reinforcers.

Positive reinforcement strengthens a given behavior directly. Some activities are inherently more reinforcing than others, such as food, water, love, sleep, or sex. Other things, such as attention, approval, grades, and money, become reinforcing mostly because of their symbolic value or their association with primary reinforcers. It is preferable to use one of these positive reinforcers whenever possible.

Negative reinforcement consists of reducing or eliminating an unpleasant stimulus, like pain, criticism, or anxiety. Whenever we do something that enables us to escape such an unpleasant condition, we engage in escape training. Examples would be taking an aspirin to get rid of a headache or taking a remedial course

Joining a group provides positive reinforcement for changing your behavior. (Ken Karp/Sirovich Senior Center)

or therapy to resolve a problem. Many times, it is desirable to do something to avoid unpleasant consequences before they occur. This is called *avoidance training* or, in plain language, preventive behavior. Much of our self-control, such as studying harder to avoid getting a low grade, is based on this principle.

Aversive reinforcement refers to the use of punishment. Instead of positively reinforcing the correct response or avoiding a negative response, in aversive conditioning, we *punish* the wrong response. There are all kinds of devices and kits to help you apply this type of reinforcement. Ordinarily it is a good policy to deprive yourself of something positive rather than punish yourself with something negative. For example, smokers have penalized themselves for smoking by giving away money to a charitable cause or denying themselves an enjoyable activity like attending the movies. Whenever possible, it is desirable to combine aversive with positive reinforcement, such as denying yourself a privilege for an undesirable act, while rewarding yourself when you perform a desired behavior.

Selecting a Reinforcer

Since few things are equally reinforcing for all people, selecting a reinforcer is a highly personal act. Essentially, an effective reinforcer must meet several criteria. First, it has to be something that is reinforcing for you. Let your own experience be your guide. Jot down on paper some of the reinforcers you're already using. Ask yourself things like: What do I naturally enjoy doing? What are some of my everyday pleasures? What things would I like to buy for myself? Second, how accessible and manipulatable is the reinforcer? It should be something convenient or at hand, since immediacy often takes precedence over abstract value. Don't overlook commonplace things like your favorite food or the use of tokens or points to obtain a more valued long-range goal like buying an article of clothing.

A third requirement is that a reinforcer must be potent or powerful; that is, it should really be an effective consequence to motivate you toward the desired behavior. Frequently, it is good policy to use some of the reinforcers you are already using. A variation of this practice is known as the Premack principle, named after the psychologist who studied it (Premack, 1959). The *Premack principle* states that if behavior B is more likely to occur than behavior A, then we can increase behavior A by making behavior B contingent upon it. Doing your homework (A) before going to a party (B), or earning the money for a car (A) before buying it (B), illustrate this principle.

APPLYING THE INTERVENTION PLAN

At this point you're ready to put your overall plan into action. But, before you begin, experience has shown that you should be especially careful about two things: the agreement with yourself about your goal, and your use of reinforcers.

Making a Self-contract

In order to have a clear agreement with yourself about what you are trying to accomplish, it is best to make a self-contract. Such contracts should be written down and stated in explicit, fair, and generally positive terms. A contract should include

1. A clear description of the target behavior to be attained, including the time limit of your program
2. The actual reinforcers you will use, together with the schedule of applying them
3. A bonus clause for additional positive reinforcement if you exceed the minimal demands of your contract
4. A penalty clause if you do not fulfill your contract within the specified time
5. The means by which you will keep records of your behavior
6. The witness of at least one other person, especially if they are helping you (Kanfer & Goldstein, 1975).

Use of Reinforcers

Ideally, it's best to apply reinforcers immediately after you perform the desired target behavior. Because food or money are usually accessible, many individuals use these as reinforcers. In many instances, however, individuals select a meaningful reinforcer that is not immediately applicable. In this case, there are several ways of bridging the gap between the main reinforcer and the immediate experience.

One way is the use of visual aids. For example, one student with a weight loss program kept a picture of herself at a trim 118 pounds on the table where she ate. Another woman working toward a set of china kept pictures of pieces of china in the place where the undesired behavior took place (Williams & Long, 1979). Variations on this theme are limited only by your imagination.

Another device is the use of tokens. Tokens have two clear advantages: They are easily accessible and can be exchanged for more substantial reinforcement. Students who have used tokens have exchanged them for items like phonograph records, movie tickets, or clothing.

Perhaps the best way of ensuring immediacy of reinforcement is the use of *shaping*. This process is sometimes referred to as the *method of successive approximations* because it entails applying reinforcement to every increment of behavior that approximates the target behavior. For example, suppose you are increasing your study time to three hours an evening for four weeknights. If you wait until the first time you study three consecutive hours at a stretch, you may become discouraged and give up prematurely. Instead, why not reinforce yourself for each thirty minutes of study until you work up to your goal? In this way, shaping

SAMPLE SELF-CONTRACT

December 8, 1982

Goal

Promptness in arriving on time for my classes, part-time job, and all appointments with others.

Self-agreement

I agree to reward myself with a quarter each time I arrive on time for any group meeting or appointment. Whenever I get together with a friend, I'll agree on a specific meeting time as a check on my promptness.

Reinforcers

Quarters, carried in a special purse and not to be spent for anything else under any circumstances. Earned quarters to be put in a jar at home and used for special purchases of new clothes, records, etc.

Bonus Clause (if contract is kept consistently)

Any week I show up on time for all my classes, job, or appointments with others, I will put an extra $2 in the jar. Any two successive weeks of being on time for all meetings and appointments, I'll double the bonus of the previous week.

Penalty Clause (if contract is broken)

If I quit or do not show any consistent improvement over my present habit of being late to meetings after six weeks of my intervention program, then I'll donate all the money earned to the local community chest fund.

Records

I'll record whether I'm on time or late (even as much as a minute) for every meeting or appointment on a 3 × 5 card carried in my wallet; consistent improvement shall be determined by an overall percentage of being on time which is higher than that recorded in my baseline data.

Signed   *Alan Johnson*

Witness   *Jim Stewart*

can enhance your chance of success because it involves taking small steps that can be reinforced immediately.

If your goal is to eliminate an undesirable behavior, it is advisable to aim for an alternative behavior that is incompatible with the undesired behavior. An *incompatible behavior* is one that prevents its opposite from occurring, in the way that smiling prevents frowning or playing tennis prevents sitting in front of the

TV. For example, a student active in campus politics found that he was irritating other members of the student council because of his compulsion to talk. At first he tried not to talk, but found himself impatiently waiting his turn to speak. Then he learned the more positive response of active listening to other students. This not only displaced his incompatible behavior of talking too much, but it also enabled him to learn more and make a better response. Listening also showed other students that he cared about what they thought, which in turn enhanced their evaluation of him (Watson & Tharp, 1972).

When it is not practical to aim for an incompatible alternative behavior, then you may want to use an aversive procedure, as discussed in the section on reinforcers.

ENDING PROCRASTINATION

All of us indulge in procrastination—putting off things that are unpleasant or have to be done.

Sometimes all that's needed is a more efficient use of time. Even a half hour spent on an overwhelming project is better than no time at all. But much of our procrastination is irrational. That is, we postpone things because of inner conflicts and low self-esteem. By doing so we experience hidden payoffs, such as the avoidance of an all-out effort or a true test of our ability. Procrastination may also serve as a means of rebellion against authority. People who are overly self-critical and perfectionistic are especially susceptible to procrastination. Accordingly, procrastinators often need insight and self-mastery to overcome their self-defeating behavior. But most of us may benefit from developing better habits. Here are some suggestions for overcoming procrastination:

Begin now. Take the first appropriate moment to begin some task that must be done. Beginning helps to alleviate anxiety and commits you to the task.

Make a list of things to be done. Assign priorities, then begin completing those tasks you have been putting off. You'll feel good each time you can cross one off your list.

Set aside designated time slots. Arrange specific time periods exclusively for the task at hand, such as studying on Tuesday and Thursday evenings from 7 to 10 P.M.

Use self-reinforcement. Simply getting things done is itself sufficiently satisfying in many instances. But when the task is complex or unpleasant, it may help to give yourself additional rewards at periodic intervals.

Aim for improvement. Concentrate on the achievable goal of improved performance, rather than on the elusive goal of perfection. Use occasional backsliding and failure as opportunities for further learning.

Savor your accomplishments. Take time to appreciate what you've done. Accentuate the positive. Realizing how much you have accomplished may inspire you to get things done more easily in the future.

EVALUATION AND TERMINATION

As in all things, there will be good and bad days in any program of self-improvement. Too often, however, people tend to underestimate their progress because it is not as rapid as they had expected. Most changes in behavior occur gradually and require great patience.

Some Common Problems

When your progress is disappointing, a number of things could be at fault. Probably the most common problems are caused by inadequately defined target behavior, faulty record keeping, or the failure to apply reinforcement properly.

The first problem usually consists of defining the target behavior too generally. For example, equating studying with sitting down at your desk for a given period of time is obviously too general. Studying needs to be defined more precisely in terms of its behavioral results, such as comprehension of what is read or improved performance on tests. Redefining your target behavior more precisely is often the first step in a successful self-improvement program.

Faulty record keeping often results from the failure to obtain adequate baseline data earlier in the program, as well as from not keeping accurate records of your current behavior. Recording your observations in a simple graph sometimes helps make your record keeping more interesting. Some individuals also keep their records in a public place, such as on the dinner table or on their room wall, as a way of gaining social approval or disapproval and of making their progress more evident.

The typical problems in applying reinforcement are twofold. One is not making the reinforcement contingent on the target behavior, which is essentially cheating on yourself. An example might be agreeing to treat yourself to a movie for keeping on a diet for a full week, and then going to the movies even though you fell off your diet for one or two days. A related problem is the failure to apply the reinforcement immediately after the performance of your target behavior. You could enhance the effectiveness of the program in this example by using tokens immediately after each meal, which could then be applied to the price of a movie or some other desired activity.

A Natural Ending

Most people who are successful in their efforts at self-improvement tend to reach a point where they simply quit following their program, as Ben Franklin did. Several months after completing a self-modification program, students were embarrassed about no longer keeping records or using reinforcers (Watson & Tharp, 1972). But then, they were no longer bothered by their problem behaviors either. In other words, such programs tend to come to a gradual, spontaneous end, rather than having a formal termination. Those who had not been as successful in their efforts probably gave up much sooner.

It is a good idea to phase out your program deliberately and gradually. Rather than suddenly dropping your records or reinforcers, you should shift to a less frequent or intermittent schedule of reinforcement. It is also advisable to practice your newly acquired behavior whenever possible. You may want to generalize your behavior to other situations too. For example, if you have successfully learned to speak up more at home or with a close friend, then start doing this in other settings, such as in class or at public meetings.

Success in achieving better self-control is a relative matter. Those who have attained their goals tend to espouse newer, more ambitious ones. Yet, individuals who have not been as successful can learn from their mistakes and can benefit from revised programs of self-improvement. Hopefully, you will find the process of gaining better self-control satisfying, though like Ben Franklin most of us may find that attaining all our goals remains a lifelong quest.

CASE STUDIES

The following case studies illustrate some of the practical applications of the step-by-step procedure explained throughout the chapter. Notice how each person adapts this procedure to his or her own particular problem and situation.

Case Study #1: Speaking up in Class[1]

A student who found it difficult to speak in public undertook a self-directed program with the aim of speaking up in class. Like many people, he was afraid of speaking up because he felt his remarks would appear irrelevant or silly.

He decided on a shaping procedure with the overall goal of speaking up in his large classes. The first step was simply to speak with some other individual in a small class. The next step was to speak to another person about a relevant subject discussed in their class. Then he was to speak out in a small class, with the next step being regular participation. At that point he was to begin speaking up in one of his large classes.

Since he always carried his notebook to class with him, he recorded his behavior by simply checking on a piece of paper each time he spoke out. As you'll

[1]Adapted from *Self-Directed Behavior: Self-Modification for Personal Adjustment*, by D. L. Watson and R. G. Tharp. Copyright © 1972 by Wadsworth Publishing Company, Inc. Reprinted by permission of the publisher, Brooks/Cole Publishing Company, Monterey, California.

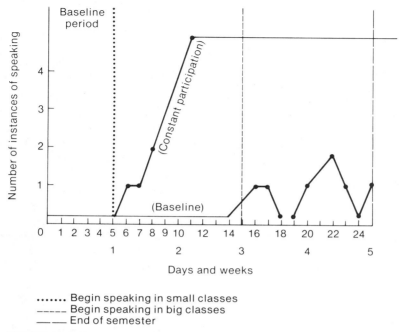

FIGURE 11-1. Frequencies for speaking in class.

.... Begin speaking in small classes
_ _ _ _ Begin speaking in big classes
—— —— End of semester

notice in Figure 11-1, there are only five days in each week since he only counted school days.

This student selected playing in the band as his reinforcer for two reasons. For one thing, he said, "I really enjoy playing my guitar." He also knew if he didn't show up for the practice the "five other guys would wring my neck." Throughout the program, he attended band practice only after he had performed one of the successive steps leading toward his overall goal.

Once he had begun speaking to individuals, he made rapid progress in speaking up in a small group. Within four days of applying the reinforcement, he was participating regularly in a small class (see the slanted line labeled "constant participation" in Figure 11-1).

Most people progress at a slower rate, as shown by this student's behavior in the next stage. As you can see in Figure 11-1, his progress in speaking up in a large class was much more modest. While he didn't speak at all on several days, however, he did make at least one comment for five days, with more than one comment on one day.

What would have been the risks had this student initially attempted to speak up in a large class? Do you see the advantages of his using such a shaping procedure? Disadvantages?

Case Study #2: Smoking Behavior[2]

Sheila, a 37-year-old teacher, had smoked for 20 years and had made several unsuccessful efforts to quit before undertaking a self-directed modification program to stop smoking. She estimated smoking an average of 15 cigarettes a day before beginning her program.

During the initial 27-day period of gathering baseline data, Sheila recorded the number of cigarettes she smoked using two methods. One was to count the number of cigarettes in a package at the beginning and end of a day. The other was to count the number of cigarettes left in an ashtray that had been empty earlier. As Figure 11-2 indicates, Sheila found that she averaged 8.4 cigarettes a day.

Using a mild aversive procedure of giving 25 cents to charity for each cigarette smoked in the next stage of her program, Sheila found that her average dropped to 4 cigarettes a day, with a range of 0 to 8.

In the third stage, Sheila added the additional procedure of not buying cigarettes and thereby having to "bum" them from her friends. During this period she didn't smoke at all for 13 days, averaging less than one cigarette a day for the 16-day period.

During a second baseline check, Sheila reinstated her earlier condition of buying cigarettes, but without paying 25 cents to charity after smoking a cigarette. She then found her average was 6 cigarettes a day for a 3-day period, which was considerably more than when she had not bought cigarettes.

Consequently, in the fifth stage, Sheila again gave up buying cigarettes. She also gave up the practice of contributing 25 cents to charity for each cigarette smoked. Although she smoked 5 cigarettes on one day, she didn't smoke at all for 12 days. She felt considerably more confident that her smoking habit was under control.

Sheila continued the practice of not buying cigarettes, but recorded her behavior only periodically. In the one postcheck recorded, as you can see in Figure 11-2, she smoked only one cigarette in 4 days. One year after formally terminating her program, Sheila reported that she smoked only in stressful situations, such as at the beginning of a school term and during examinations.

Case Study #3: Interpersonal Relationships[3]

Two women found that in the year's time they had worked together, their relationship had deteriorated to the point where "just seeing each other made each of them angry." Every time they talked, both of them inevitably felt angry

[2]Adapted from *Self-Control: Power to the Person*, by M. J. Mahoney and C. E. Thoresen. Copyright © 1974 by Wadsworth Publishing Company, Inc. Reprinted by permission of the publisher, Brooks/Cole Publishing Company, Monterey, California.

[3]Adapted from *Self-Directed Behavior: Self-Modification for Personal Adjustment*, by D. L. Watson and R. G. Tharp. Copyright © 1972 by Wadsworth Publishing Company, Inc. Reprinted by permission of the publisher, Brooks/Cole Publishing Company, Monterey, California.

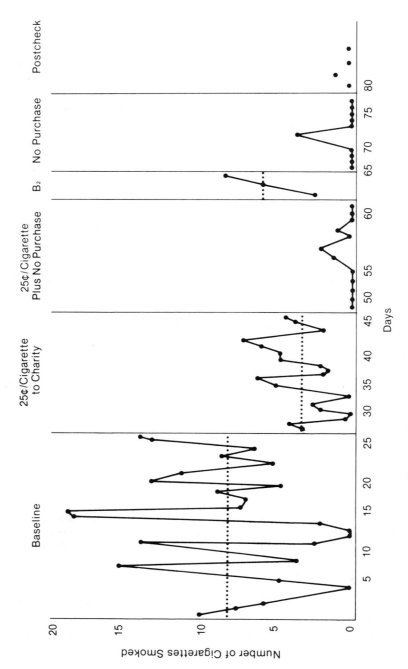

FIGURE 11-2. Altering smoking behavior.

and hurt. However, since they had to work together, the first woman decided to alter their relationship by a two-step procedure.

To begin with, the first woman initiated a "cooling-off period" in which she did not talk with the other woman unless it was absolutely necessary. This strategy was based on her observation that it was the other woman's cutting remarks that precipitated her own angry, defensive behavior. When they did interact, the first woman confined her remarks to their work and tried to be either neutral or mildly pleasant. After a couple of weeks, the first stage proved to be reasonably effective, so that for the next couple of months the women had occasional short and relatively calm interactions.

Since their work would eventually necessitate more substantial interaction, the first woman felt their relationship might deteriorate again unless she initiated the second stage of her program. At this point, she attempted to alter the other woman's behavior through selective reinforcement. She did this in three ways. First, she did not respond to (or reinforce) any anger-producing remarks, such as, "You're not doing that right." Second, she made it a point to respond to (or reinforce) the other woman's pleasant remarks, such as "That seemed to work out very well," with reinforcing remarks like, "Thanks very much. It is kind of you to say that." At the same time, she praised the other woman for her good work and refrained from criticizing her inferior work.

Essentially, what the first woman did was to change her behavior by altering the other woman's responses that precipitated her own undesired behavior. Frequently, problems in interpersonal relationships are a kind of vicious circle in which one person's undesirable behavior precipitates or reinforces that of another. What typically happens in such relationships? Suppose one person ignores the undesirable behavior of another while reinforcing the desired behavior? What might happen if both people followed this procedure?

SUMMARY

In contrast to the conventional view of willpower as a subjective quality, behavioral psychologists speak of self-control as an acquired skill that can be strengthened in accordance with known principles of learning. The step-by-step procedure for increasing self-control may be viewed as the behavioral means for achieving humanistic ends, such as greater personal freedom and self-actualization.

The first step in increasing self-control is to set a goal for ourselves, generally known as our target behavior. It is important that our goal be realistic and attainable, since the experience of success in reaching it will provide additional reinforcement for self-control.

Before attempting to change your behavior, you should take a week or so to record your present behavior as a means of making before and after comparisons of your progress. You may choose to record either a simple frequency count, the duration of time involved, or the outcome of your behavior.

Since many of our complex behaviors occur in close succession to one another or in a chain of behaviors, the next step in achieving self-control is to analyze and control the antecedents and consequences of the target behavior. When our goal is to get rid of undesirable behavior, it's best to reduce the antecedent factors that trigger the behavior; when the goal is to establish a positive behavior, it's more appropriate to increase the precipitating factors.

In order to control the consequences of our behavior, it is best to arrange the sequence of our actions so that reinforcing consequences are made contingent on our target behavior. We may choose to use either positive reinforcement, which strengthens behavior directly; negative reinforcement, which consists of avoiding or escaping something unpleasant; or aversive conditioning, which involves punishing the wrong response.

In order to be clear about what you are trying to accomplish, it is recommended that you write out a self-contract containing an explicit description of your target behavior as well as your use of reinforcers. A key rule is to apply the reinforcer immediately after performing the target behavior. The process of shaping is often advisable because it involves reinforcing many small steps that lead to the desired behavior.

Individuals who succeed in their efforts at self-improvement usually reach a point where they no longer record or reinforce themselves because they have attained their target behaviors. Those who have not been as successful have often encountered one of the common problems, such as defining the target behavior too generally, faulty record keeping, or failing to reinforce properly. They too may learn from their mistakes and eventually benefit from a revised program of self-improvement.

QUESTIONS FOR SELF-REFLECTION

1. Do you find that your willpower is stronger at some times than at others? How do you explain this?
2. Can you identify some external forces, such as situations or other people, that affect your self-control positively or negatively?
3. Which kinds of self-improvement lend themselves to the procedure described in this chapter? Which kinds are not suitable for this procedure?
4. Why does the act of observing our behavior often result in changing it as well? What does this say about our habits?
5. List some cues or associations that tend to precipitate behaviors such as eating, sleeping, studying, sexual intimacy, drinking (alcohol), taking drugs, or leisure activities.
6. Which of your behaviors are strongly influenced by their antecedents?
7. Which behaviors are controlled mostly by their reinforcing consequences?
8. Can you think of some instances where negative reinforcement or aversive conditioning are more appropriate than positive reinforcement? List some of these.

EXERCISES

1. Target behaviors

List some possible target behaviors you would like to achieve; then describe these in concrete, behavioral terms. If you include undesired behaviors you want to get rid of, describe some incompatible alternative behaviors.

2. Record keeping

Observe and record your present behavior in relation to one or two of the target behaviors you have listed. Estimate the occurrence of these behaviors before recording them. How accurate were your estimates? Did the act of recording your behavior actually result in changing it a bit as well?

3. Antecedents and consequences

Write down some of your chains of behavior. Can you identify their major antecedents? Which consequences strengthen these behaviors? Try rearranging or scrambling the sequence of these behaviors, as the habitual vodka drinker did.

4. Reinforcers

List some of the major reinforcers used to motivate people in our society, such as money or approval. Now write down your own personal reinforcers, that is, the influences that especially control your own behavior. How similar or different are your two lists?

5. Systematic desensitization

Select one of your fears that you believe is susceptible to change, and then apply the method of systematic desensitization to your behavior. This procedure was described earlier in the box on Overcoming Your Fears.

6. Self-directed change

The main exercise, of course, is to select some target behavior you would like to achieve or eliminate, as the case may be, and then proceed to modify your behavior according to the six-step procedure described in this chapter.

a. State your target behavior in behavioral terms.

b. Keep a record of your present behavior for a week or so.

c. Avoid or alter the factors that precipitate your undesired behavior, or establish such factors to help you acquire desired behaviors.

d. Arrange the sequences of your behavior so that reinforcing consequences are made contingent on your target behavior.

e. Apply your intervention plan for a specified period.

f. Evaluate your progress.

Remember that success in achieving a modest goal strengthens your self-control more than frustration in pursuit of an idealized goal.

RECOMMENDED READINGS

Benson, H., M.D. *The Relaxation Response.* New York: Avon, 1976 (paperback). A synthesis of age-old wisdom and scientific data regarding the relaxation response evoked by meditational techniques, along with a simple, proven method for learning to relax.

Ellis, A., and W. Knaus. *Overcoming Procrastination.* New York: National American Library, 1979 (paperback). A rational-emotive approach to resolving the common problem of procrastination.

Mahoney, M. J. *Self-Change.* New York: Norton, 1981. Practical strategies for solving personal problems, with an emphasis on the cognitive and behavioral approach.

Rosen, G. *Don't Be Afraid.* Englewood Cliffs, N.J.: Prentice-Hall, 1976 (paperback). A program for overcoming your fears and phobias.

Wenrich, W. W., H. H. Dawley, and D. A. General. *Self-directed Systematic Desensitization.* Kalamazoo, Mich.: Behaviordelia, 1976 (paperback). An attractive and readable book providing step-by-step instructions for individuals to cope successfully with their fears, with sample hierarchies for dealing with specific fears, such as test anxiety, airplane travel, or fear of sexual intercourse, included in the appendix.

Williams, R. L., and J. D. Long. *Toward a Self-managed Life Style,* 2nd ed. Boston: Houghton Mifflin, 1978 (paperback). A concise but readable account of self-directed behavior change, with most of the book devoted to applications of this procedure, including sports, study, and interpersonal behavior.

Zastrow, C. and H. Dae. *The Personal Problem-Solver.* Englewood Cliffs, N.J.: Prentice-Hall, 1977 (paperback). Contains suggested strategies for coping with various emotional, sexual, health, and interpersonal problems as well as selected crisis situations. Based on a survey of desired information among students and the general population.

Psychotherapy

Few of us escape having problems at home or at work at one time or another. Most of the time we manage to cope with such difficulties on our own. Often we feel better simply with the help of friends. Or the situation may change by itself. But when these are not sufficient, we may need psychotherapy.

Some people are reluctant to enter therapy because of the stigma associated with it. In the popular mind, psychotherapy is for people who are "sick" or "crazy." Yet it is usually just the opposite, as you'll see in this chapter. The people most likely to seek out a therapist are often the least seriously disturbed. Sometimes they seek relief from distressing symptoms, such as a crippling anxiety or a marriage problem that has become intolerable. But in other instances, people see therapy as a means of overcoming some of their personal limitations or personal growth.

Let's begin by taking a look at psychotherapy as a whole, including the typical clients and goals of therapy. We will also describe some of the major types of therapy, such as insight, behavioral, and group therapy. Then the question of what makes therapy work will be examined, as well as some of the ethical problems posed in therapy and how to choose a therapist.

AN OVERVIEW OF PSYCHOTHERAPY

Psychotherapy means literally "healing of the soul." Yet, in an age oriented to science and secular values, therapy is usually defined somewhat differently. Essentially, it is a help-giving process in which a trained, socially sanctioned healer performs certain activities that will facilitate a change in the client's attitudes and behavior (Frank, 1973b). Since psychotherapists rely primarily on verbal and psychological methods, psychotherapy has been referred to as the "talking cure." But in practice, other therapeutic measures such as tranquilizing or antidepressant drugs are sometimes used to supplement the talking cure, especially when the therapist has a medical orientation.

Many times people are helped by counseling, a process that overlaps considerably with psychotherapy. For practical purposes, we can say that *counseling* is a process dealing with the so-called normal person who has mild symptoms and rather specific problems, while *psychotherapy* refers to work with those who have more serious problems and usually takes place in a clinical or medical setting. But such a distinction does not hold consistently true in practice. As a result, C. H. Patterson has concluded that "there are no essential differences between counseling and psychotherapy" in terms of the therapist-client relationship, the methods or goals of therapy, or even in the types of clients seen (1973, p. xii). Consequently, most of the things said about psychotherapy throughout this chapter apply equally well to counseling.

Who Seeks Therapy or Counseling?

An obvious answer to this question would be "those who need it." But this is not always the case. While estimates of those who need help or could benefit from it range anywhere from one out of ten people to one our of four, the proportion of people seeking therapy is considerably smaller. It has been estimated that only about 6 million Americans receive some form of psychotherapy each year. About 2.4 million people are seen in outpatient psychiatric clinics, with 1.5 million in community health centers, and another 1.5 million in therapists' offices. Several hundred thousand people are also treated in mental hospitals (Gross, 1978).

Sometimes people are simply not aware of the resources available to them. Or they may feel that therapy is excessively expensive. Perhaps an even greater factor is a person's attitude toward getting help. A willingness to talk about personal problems generally reflects a favorable attitude toward therapy more than the severity of the symptoms does.

Fortunately, recent surveys have shown that people in the 1980s have a greater willingness to admit their need for personal help and to seek it than people in earlier eras. Americans are generally more inclined to admit the anxieties, problems, and inadequacies in their personal lives and to talk over their problems with close friends or professional helpers. In part, this improved attitude toward psychotherapy reflects a greater desire for personal well-being, as well as an increased orientation toward psychology to explain experience (Veroff, Kulka, & Douvan, 1981).

Kenneth Howard and David Orlinsky (1972) have identified three types of clients most likely to enter psychotherapy. The most visible client is the affluent, college-educated person who exhibits what Schofield (1964) has called the *YAVIS syndrome;* that is, he or she is *y*oung, *a*ttractive, *v*erbal, *i*ntelligent, and relatively *s*uccessful. These people are not seriously impaired psychologically. Most of them have rather common "neurotic" complaints and regard therapy as a means of growth.

In contrast, a second type of client comes from a lower- or working-class background and has less than a high school education. These people tend to be more seriously disturbed, with a greater percentage of the disabling psychotic disorders, especially schizophrenia. They are also less skilled in talking about their problems, have a less receptive attitude toward psychotherapy, but are driven to seek help because of the severity of their problems.

A third type of client tends to seek help from religious rather than secular sources. These people are usually over 30 years old, from a conservative Protestant background, and are seldom college-educated. When faced with a personal crisis, they tend to turn to their minister rather than to a psychiatrist or psychologist for guidance.

Women tend to make up a disproportionately greater number of all three types of clients. They suffer from more psychosomatic complaints, enter psychotherapy, and are admitted to both general and psychiatric hospitals in greater numbers than men (Gove & Tudor, 1973). Explanations for this range from the stressful effects of being a woman in a male-oriented society to the greater willingness of women to admit weakness and seek help in our society.

Psychiatrist Jerome Frank (1973a) has suggested that people also seek out therapy because they have become demoralized. These individuals have become bewildered and disheartened by their problems. They are conscious of having failed to meet the expectations of themselves and others. They feel their lives are boxed in, but they feel powerless to do anything about it. As a result, they may feel they are going crazy. Sometimes their loss of morale results from a situation that is transitory and may be easily resolved, such as the loss of a job.

At other times, it may be severe enough to require hospitalization, as in the case of an older person who is depressed. But, in both instances, Frank believes that psychotherapists must treat the underlying condition of demoralization as well as the symptoms that drive people to seek help. The therapist must rekindle the clients' hope and belief that they can regain their morale and mastery over their lives.

Major Goals of Therapy

Frank's notion of why people seek therapy brings up the matter of the purpose of psychotherapy. Once a person has begun therapy, what can he or she expect to gain from it? What is the major goal of therapy? The answers to such questions vary among different therapists. But according to Norman Sundberg, Leona Tyler, and Julian Taplin (1973), there are seven major goals that are common to most kinds of therapy.

1. *To strengthen the client's motivation.* This may be achieved through accepting and encouraging clients in their efforts to change and often occurs in self-help groups, such as Alcoholics Anonymous, as well as in professional therapy.
2. *To facilitate the expression of feelings.* Clients are encouraged to express or reenact feelings that are especially intense or painful to them in safe settings, as in psychoanalysis, primal therapy, or client-centered therapy.
3. *To release the potential for growth.* Assuming that everyone has a basic tendency toward growth, therapists remove the obstacles and allow people to get in touch with their potential for growth, as expressed in Everett Shostrom's actualization therapy.
4. *To modify the client's thinking.* Believing that many problems are caused by misconceptions about ourselves and others, therapists such as Albert Ellis help clients to replace irrational beliefs with more rational thinking.
5. *To develop insight or self-understanding.* Therapists help clients to see themselves more accurately, which in turn may reduce their anxiety and symptoms, and facilitate healthier behavior.
6. *To modify behavior.* Since insight does not necessarily lead to different behavior, some therapists prefer to focus on the process of modifying behavior directly, as in the various forms of behavior therapy.
7. *To improve the client's interpersonal relationships.* While some therapists accomplish this through helping their clients uncover early family relationships that may be influencing their present behavior, other therapists emphasize the client's present pattern of relationships with family, friends, and co-workers, as in transactional analysis.

Each of the major kinds of therapy described in this chapter emphasizes some of these goals more than others. But, in actual practice, many therapists tend

A warm, supportive relationship is an important part of most psychotherapies. (Gail Atwater)

to be eclectic; that is, they combine these goals in varied ways and rely on techniques from a number of different approaches.

Psychotherapy and Personal Growth

There is a growing realization that therapy is not just for the treatment of illness. It is also for the actualization of growth and health. In part this reflects a shift away from the medical model of mental health, with its emphasis on pathology and sickness, toward a growth model, as described in the opening chapter of this book. Part of the reason may also be that, as a lifestyle of affluence, leisure, and freedom from constraints spreads to more of the population, people become less concerned with their basic needs and more concerned with self-actualization. As a result, many individuals now seek therapy more for the purpose of growth than for the relief of symptoms (London, 1974).

Therapists influenced by the growth model tend to view problems not so much as symptoms of a mental illness but as inhibitions of the normal growth process. They recognize that all of us have problems in growing up. But it is important not to misinterpret these as signs of illness, especially at the critical stages of growth such as adolescence. For example, the overly rebellious teenager often gets that way because of undue dependency in relation to overprotective parents. The wise therapist will seek to readjust the balance between freedom and limits to encourage growth toward independence with less attendant rebelliousness. Or many times problem behavior occurs when a life situation actually inhibits growth, as in the case of a person who drinks too much because of a dissatisfying job or marriage. In these situations, the therapist's job is not only to help individuals to eliminate their self-defeating behaviors, but also to help them get in touch with their potential for growth. While many times this entails helping clients acquire needed skills and problem-solving strategies, the focus is on helping them regain responsibility and mastery over their own lives.

The degree to which therapists are influenced by the growth model depends partly on their background and training. Many therapists are trained in a particular theory and method of therapy that continues to characterize much of their work despite the eclectic tendency typical of most therapists. We'll describe some of the better known schools of therapy in each of the major types—insight, behavior, and group therapy—in the next three sections of this chapter respectively. But it would be good to remember that individual therapists tend to modify their orientation with experience and growth.

INSIGHT THERAPIES

The term *insight* (meaning literally to "see into" or understand) is associated with those therapies that facilitate change or growth through increasing the client's inner awareness or self-understanding. For many years the most prestigious type of insight therapy was psychoanalysis, developed by Sigmund Freud. But since the 1950s, clients have had many more insight therapies to choose from, including those based more directly on a growth model, such as Carl Rogers's client-centered therapy.

Psychoanalysis

Sigmund Freud's (1965) approach to therapy was an integral part of his theory of personality and development. In his view, the driving forces of personality came from the *id,* the unconscious reservoir of psychic energy derived from biological instincts. These instincts are primarily sexual and aggressive in nature. Early in the child's life, part of the id is modified through parental control to help inhibit these unruly forces of the unconscious. This part is known as the *superego* or, roughly speaking, conscience. Another part of the personality that develops more gradually out of the id through the effects of life-long socialization is the *ego,* the center of self-consciousness and rational control. The ego serves as the manager of personality, enabling us to integrate the conflicting demands of id, superego, and society.

According to Freud, psychological disturbances are due to anxiety that we feel about hidden conflicts between the different parts of our unconscious personality. If not expressed directly, these unconscious impulses and conflicts seek indirect release in all kinds of symptoms and neurotic activities. The therapist's purpose is to help the individual gain insight into or conscious awareness of these unconscious desires or conflicts, thereby gaining emotional release and eventual mastery of them.

The psychoanalyst may use a variety of techniques to accomplish this end. One of the earliest of these was *free association*. The client is asked to lie down on a couch, relax, and talk about anything that comes to awareness. Sometimes the client is encouraged to talk about his or her dreams. Though these recollections might appear irrelevant, the well-trained analyst may see relationships and meanings that eventually shed light on the client's problems.

When an individual hesitates or is reluctant to talk about some painful experience, this is seen as a sign of the client's resistance. The therapist may simply wait or may use another approach to the area of resistance, so that eventually this can be overcome. By analyzing an individual's resistances, the therapist helps the client to see how he or she handles anxiety-provoking material. The overall process of free association, dream association, and the interpretation and overcoming of the resistance is called "working through."

Freud also discovered that his clients would often treat him in the same way as they had treated the significant figures earlier in their life, especially their parents. This is called *transference*. At the appropriate time, the therapist interprets these feelings and actions to the client, thereby helping the client to achieve additional self-insight.

Psychoanalysis tends to be a prolonged procedure, usually involving one or more 50-minute sessions each week for several years. As such, it is more appropriate for normal people with relatively mild disorders who can afford to pay for such a procedure. The goal of psychoanalysis is to strengthen the client's ego, thereby facilitating greater self-understanding and self-mastery. Freud held that psychoanalysis does not do away with the common unhappiness of life, but it does help the individual to become his or her best self or the kind of person each would have been under the most favorable conditions.

Client-centered Therapy

One of the major alternatives to psychoanalysis is client-centered therapy, developed by psychologist Carl Rogers.

Rogers formulated his view of therapy out of his own experience as a therapist. Early in his career he was counseling a mother whose son was having problems. But no matter what strategy he tried, he got nowhere. Finally, he admitted his failure. As the mother walked toward the door, she turned and asked Rogers if he ever saw adult clients. When he replied, "Yes," the woman returned to her seat and began pouring out her own problems. She spoke of her own sense of confusion and failure and her despair about her marriage, all of which was more pertinent to her son's problems than the sterile case history approach they had followed before. After many more interviews, the woman felt better about her marriage, and her son's problem behavior dropped away as well. Rogers felt the improvement had come because he had followed her lead, because he had listened and understood rather than imposed his diagnostic understanding on her. This was the first of many experiences that gradually led Rogers to the view that therapeutic progress comes mostly from respecting and responding to the client's own frame of reference (Rogers, 1973).

Accordingly, Rogers's use of the term *client* rather than *patient* suggests a more democratic relationship in therapy than in Freudian analysis. The client-centered therapist does not probe or interpret what an individual says. Instead, the therapist provides an atmosphere conducive to the client's self-exploration. The therapist facilitates this through an accepting attitude toward the client, which Rogers calls *unconditional positive regard,* and through expressing an empathetic understanding of the client's experience in terms of his or her own frame of reference. The assumption is that in such a warm and nonjudgmental relationship individuals may relax their defenses and begin to experience feelings and self-perceptions that have been denied or distorted. Gradually, as clients come to trust in their own experience and resources and perceive themselves more positively, they tend to actualize their potentialities more fully themselves (Rogers, 1961).

Rational-emotive Therapy

Developed by psychologist Albert Ellis, this approach was originally called rational psychotherapy to emphasize the role of reason in changing problem behavior. According to Ellis, emotional problems are caused primarily by faulty assumptions and irrational thinking. Although much of an individual's illogical thinking stems from earlier experiences with parents and surroundings, it is unwittingly perpetuated by the individual's own self-verbalizations. As a result, individuals become blinded by their own faulty thinking and overreact to potential problem situations, thereby making them worse.

The therapist attempts to help the client identify and change these faulty thought patterns that lead to self-defeating behavior. The assumption is that, as individuals learn to see themselves and their relationships in a more rational, problem-solving manner, they will adopt more appropriate and satisfying behaviors. (See the boxed material on p. 308.)

A Variety of Approaches

Although the proliferation of different therapeutic techniques and theories continues, many of the newer approaches can be seen as attempts to add or emphasize an element missing in existing therapies. For example, in *existential therapy,* practiced by Rollo May, and *direct decision therapy,* advocated by Harold

SOME IRRATIONAL IDEAS COMMONLY HELD

Ellis has identified a dozen irrational ideas or assumptions that are widespread in our society and when believed tend to lead to self-defeating behavior. These are:

1. The idea that you must—yes, *must*—have sincere love and approval almost all the time from all the people you find significant.

2. The idea that you must prove yourself thoroughly competent, adequate, and achieving, or that you must at least have real competence or talent at something important.

3. The idea that people who harm you or commit misdeeds rate as generally bad, wicked, or villainous individuals and that you should severely blame, damn, and punish them for their sins.

4. The idea that life proves awful, terrible, horrible, or catastrophic when things do not go the way you would like them to go.

5. The idea that emotional misery comes from external pressures, and that you have little ability to control your feelings or rid yourself of depression and hostility.

6. The idea that if something seems dangerous or fearsome, you must become terribly occupied with and upset about it.

7. The idea that you will find it easier to avoid facing many of life's difficulties and self-responsibilities than to undertake more rewarding forms of self-discipline.

8. The idea that your past remains all-important, and that because something once strongly influenced your life, it has to keep determining your feelings and behavior today.

9. The idea that people and things should turn out better than they do, and that you have to view it as awful and horrible if you do not quickly find good solutions to life's hassles.

10. The idea that you can achieve happiness by inertia and inaction or by passively and uncommittedly "enjoying yourself."

11. The idea that you must have a high degree of order or certainty to feel comfortable, or that you need some supernatural power on which to rely.

12. The idea that you can give yourself a global rating as a human being, and that your general worth and self-acceptance depend upon the goodness of your performances and the degree that people approve of you.

Albert Ellis and Robert A. Harper, *A New Guide to Rational Living* (Englewood Cliffs, N.J.: Prentice-Hall, Inc.; and Hollywood: Wilshire Books, 1975), pp. 83–85. Reprinted by permission of the publishers and the author.

Greenwald, the emphasis is on the need for clients to choose solutions and take responsibility for their own problems and lives. *Gestalt therapy,* founded by Fritz Perls, also puts great value on individual responsibility, but there is also more use of here-and-now behavior in the therapy session to help the client to unify feelings and actions. *Reality therapy,* developed by William Glasser, also emphasizes the need for clients to take responsibility for their own problems and differs from rational-emotive therapy mainly in focusing on rational behavior rather than on rational thinking. One of the newer types, *actualization therapy,* espoused by Everett Shostrom, actually combines elements from client-centered, gestalt, rational-emotive, and existential therapies, but the emphasis is on self-actualization rather than adjustment as the purpose of therapy. Actually, an increasing number of therapists would probably characterize themselves as eclectic in the sense that they use a combination of techniques as appropriate for their individual clients.

BEHAVIOR THERAPIES

It is commonly thought that behavior therapists treat their clients' behavior directly, rather than searching for deeper, underlying causes. Yet behaviorists themselves maintain that if "underlying" is taken to mean "not immediately obvious" rather than "unconscious," then they too look for underlying causes in the sense of the most significant causes of behavior (Davison & Neale, 1974). However, they tend to see these causes more in terms of the influences directly associated with behavior than in terms of deeper, intra-psychic forces.

The rapid increase in activity and publication by behaviorists during the 1960s brought forth an impressive array of different therapeutic approaches. But most of these approaches are based on the learning principles of either classical conditioning (Pavlov and Watson) or operant conditioning (Skinner) and differ mostly in terms of their techniques.

Desensitization

Developed by Joseph Wolpe in the 1950s, this approach is based on the assumption that a fear response can be inhibited by learning an incompatible response such as relaxation and calmness.

Wolpe (1973) tells of a 24-year-old art student who came for treatment because of her fear of taking examinations, which had resulted in repeated failures. Wolpe began by making up a hierarchy of imagined situations that made her anxious, culminating with the day of the examination. Then he taught her how to relax her body muscles and gradually associate such a relaxed state with each of the feared situations. After seventeen sessions, the art student felt free from anxiety at the highest level of the hierarchy. Four months later she took and successfully passed her examinations without any disruptive anxiety.

In addition to confronting the client with imagined scenes of the situation, as in systematic desensitization, therapists may also use variations of this technique. In behavior rehearsal, for example, the client role-plays the feared situation, while in the real-life method, the individual gradually approaches the feared situation directly.

Assertiveness Training

Even in our individualistic, competitive society, there are many people who are not sufficiently assertive in the sense of being able to express themselves effectively or to say "no" to demands made on them. Often these people are afraid of being rejected or punished if they act assertively. Such individuals may find that assertiveness training counteracts the fears and anxieties associated with a particular situation. By noticing that assertive behavior does not necessarily lead to negative reactions by others, individuals gradually acquire more confidence in their ability to act appropriately in a given situation.

In one version of this approach, the client is first told to reenact an inappropriate behavior in which he or she is being stepped on, such as acting timidly as a checker in a supermarket. Then the therapist role-plays the other person, whether an authoritarian manager or irate customer. After pointing out the flaws in the client's behavior, the roles are reversed, and the therapist models a more assertive response. Then the roles are switched again to allow the client to imitate the assertive response. The process is repeated until the client feels able to transfer the newly acquired behavior to a real-life situation (Alberti & Emmons, 1970). Some therapists, however, have found that individuals don't

---

SAYING NO MAY BE POSITIVE

Kathy, an unmarried woman in her early 30s, had an enviable position as secretary to one of the top executives in her company, but she felt depressed and intimidated in her job. She said that her boss and co-workers were always imposing on her, so that she worked harder than the other secretaries did but without extra pay. As a result, she felt resentful, depressed, and complained a lot both at work and at home.

After consulting a therapist, Kathy learned that part of the problem was her own passivity and compliance. She realized that she had been oversocialized to the point where she always did what was asked of her, mostly to gain others' approval. Gradually, with the encouragement of her therapist, Kathy learned to act more assertively and to express her needs and rights more forthrightly. When other secretaries wanted to unload their extra jobs, she began saying "no" more frequently, explaining that she had enough work of her own to do. Kathy also told her boss she resented being asked to cover for his colleague's secretaries without her permission. Because he had not been aware of her feelings, he said, "I'm glad you spoke up." Then they agreed that she wouldn't be expected to do extra work unless she was consulted ahead of time and paid extra for it.

Kathy's newly acquired assertiveness gave her a much-needed sense of control over her life. She reported feeling less resentful and depressed about her job, and wasted less time in needless complaining. Furthermore, Kathy discovered that once others know you are an assertive person, they are less likely to impose on you.

usually generalize their newly acquired assertive behavior until they have practiced it in other areas of their lives as well (Morris, 1975).

Modeling

Another technique for modifying problem behavior, developed by Albert Bandura (1970), consists of allowing individuals to observe and imitate appropriate models. In the first stage, a client learns by watching another person perform the desired behavior, including the consequences or reinforcement experienced by the model. Then, in a second stage, the client may be externally reinforced for doing the behavior, in addition to the intrinsic reward of performing the behavior itself.

Bandura and his associates applied this technique to four groups of people with a fear of snakes. Each group was treated differently. Individuals in the first group watched a film showing children and adults fearlessly handling a king snake. This was called *symbolic modeling*. Those in the second group saw a live model handling a king snake and then were told to imitate the model's actions. They did this through graduated steps, such as first letting the snake coil around their arms, and finally allowing the snake to crawl over their bodies. This second procedure was called *live modeling with participation.* A third group of people were taught to relax while they imagined handling snakes (desensitization), and a fourth group received no training at all. While all individuals performed better than those in the fourth group, individuals in the participant modeling group improved the most of all. Eleven out of the twelve people in this group overcame their fear of snakes (Bandura, 1970).

Modeling techniques have been used for people of all ages and types of problems, including phobias, alcoholism, delinquency, schizophrenia, as well as for the training of professional personnel.

Contingency Management Methods

Contingency management is a flexible treatment strategy including various techniques of operant learning, such as positive reinforcement, shaping, and modeling, which can be used in modifying adaptive behaviors in many settings.

In one case, a 37-year-old housewife had become depressed over the recent death of her mother. Whenever she complained, cried, or withdrew, other family members responded with sympathy, which thereby reinforced her feelings of helplessness. In an effort to help this woman recover an adequate level of functioning, family members were instructed to reinforce her positive behaviors such as cleaning or cooking with encouragement, while gradually ignoring the depressed behavior. Within a week, there was a notable increase in this woman's adaptive behavior, with a decrease in her depression (Liberman & Raskin, 1971).

This method has been especially useful for individuals with severe problems.

For example, Ayllon and Azrin (1965) used it to teach chronic schizophrenics how to perform certain self-care behaviors and work assignments on and off the ward. Others have used this approach to help patients adjust to leaving the hospital and returning to the larger community. One study showed only a 12 percent readmission rate to the hospital as compared to the usual 65–80 percent for patient populations (Atthowe & McDonough, 1969). As a result, Atthowe (1973) holds that most treatment and rehabilitative programs should use some form of contingency management.

There are a number of other forms of behavior therapy, but two techniques deserve special mention. *Implosion therapy* is a technique in which the therapist attempts to reverse the conditional avoidance of feared situations by flooding the client with anxiety-arousing stimuli under safe conditions. In one application of this technique, seven out of ten people who were afraid of snakes were able to pick up a snake after only a single 45-minute session (Hogan & Kirchner, 1968). *Aversion therapy* is used with behaviors that are immediately pleasurable but may have negative effects in the long run, such as smoking, drinking, drug addiction, gambling, and some forms of sexual behavior. Aversion therapy consists of replacing the pleasurable associations with a negative one (when using classical conditioning techniques) or punishing the undesired behavior directly (when using operant techniques). Because some people consider the consequences used to be too harsh—giving alcoholics liquor that has a drug in it that will make them throw up, for example—aversion therapy is a controversial technique. However, it may have value in suppressing undesirable behavior when other methods have not been effective.

GROUP THERAPIES

Although groups have been used for healing purposes since recorded time, they have literally mushroomed in their number and variety since the 1940s and constitute one of the most promising approaches to therapy.

Groups offer several advantages over individual therapies. The most obvious one is that a therapist can see many individuals at the same time, though many groups have co-leaders. Perhaps even more important is that groups present a microcosm of the larger society, thus facilitating the transfer of learning from therapy to outside life. Groups also offer opportunities for individuals to interact with others of similar problems, thus releasing the powers of empathy, mutual support, and control among their members.

Virtually every theory or technique employed in individual therapy has been or can be applied to groups as well, so that we find psychoanalytic groups, client-centered groups, and behavioral groups along with countless others. The brief overview of groups in the following pages, however, is based on more important

WHO ARE THE THERAPISTS?

Unlike law or medicine where there is a single path to professional practice, there are at least a half dozen routes to becoming a psychotherapist. Since few states regulate the practice of psychotherapy as such, the question of who may legitimately conduct psychotherapy is governed by state law or professional boards within the respective professions.

Psychiatrists are medical doctors who specialize in the treatment of mental illness. They usually spend three to four years training in a clinical setting following their medical degree and can treat the serious mental disturbances requiring drugs and hospitalization.

Psychoanalysts are generally psychiatrists who have received several years of additional training in personality theory and the therapeutic methods of one of the founding analysts, such as Freud, Jung, Adler, or Sullivan.

Psychologists are individuals who receive clinical training in the methods of psychological assessment and treatment as part of a program in clinical, counseling, or school psychology. They may have a Ph.D., Ed.D., or Psy.D. degree.

Psychiatric social workers receive supervised clinical training as part of their master's degree program in the field of social work, and some earn a doctorate as well. They tend to be community oriented and usually work as part of a clinical team, though sometimes in private practice.

Counselors are people who receive training in personality theory and counseling skills, usually at the master's degree level. Their counseling emphasis tends to reflect their respective professional affiliations, depending on whether they are doing marriage counseling, guidance counseling, pastoral counseling (clergy), or some other type of counseling.

Paraprofessionals (*para* meaning "akin to") are people with 4- or 2-year degrees (or sometimes no degrees at all) who work in the mental health field. Sometimes as many as half the staff members of a community mental health center work at the paraprofessional level, assisting in the helping process in a variety of ways.

distinctions between groups, such as those composed of preexisting groups like families and those consisting of strangers, or the difference between traditional groups and those primarily designed for growth.

Marriage Counseling and Therapy

What brings couples to therapy is often some specific problem, such as infidelity, finances, or trouble with in-laws. Often they come because one partner has threatened to leave, while the other wants to stay in the relationship.

Although couples coming for help often blame their partners for their problems, professionals in this field tend to focus more on their interaction or the

Although couples tend to blame their partners for their problems, marriage counselors focus more on their interaction or the marriage relationship itself. (Ken Karp)

marriage relationship itself. The therapist may begin with the specific problems presented by a couple, but attention is also given to how such problems are related to their marital interaction. If one partner has committed infidelity, instead of joining in the blame for that partner, the therapist may ask what brought it about. Perhaps one partner sought to fill a void in an empty marriage or indulged in a hostile attempt to get back at the other partner. Either way, the therapist helps each partner become more aware of their give-and-take relationship, how they compete with and hurt each other, and so forth. The therapist also helps them clarify the decision as to whether they want to separate or work at their marriage. If it becomes evident that the partners are willing to work at their marriage, the therapist helps them express better communication and supportive concern for each other.

Professionals sometimes complain that couples don't seek help until it is too late. As a result, some professionals have begun leading marriage enrichment groups focused more on growth. Once a marriage is in trouble, the actual benefit a couple may derive from marriage counseling or therapy depends on many factors, especially their receptiveness to help and their motivation to make their marriage more meaningful and satisfying.

Family Therapy

Sometimes an individual who has benefited from therapy will regress while at home unless the family itself is treated. So in family therapy the entire family becomes the client, with the focus on the interaction among the family members. Each family is seen as a distinct entity that builds up its own patterns of interactions, including role expectations, modes of communication, and overt and covert family rules. Whatever problems they are experiencing are understood in relation to their primary interactions with each other.

Often one person plays the role of the family scapegoat. The therapist views such a role as determined by the group. For example, if Bill, an adolescent, is a problem in school and has become quarrelsome and obstinate at home, the therapist may increase the family's awareness by raising pertinent questions such as, "How long has Bill acted this way?" or "What has happened to make him that way?" The therapist may observe that Bill takes a seat somewhat away from the rest of the family members and ask them, "I notice nobody asked Bill to sit with the rest of you. Why is that?" In other words, the therapist examines the needs and pressures within the family as a whole that encourage Bill to act the way he does (Lecker, 1976).

As in marriage therapy, the family therapist attempts to clarify expectations, open up clearer lines of communication among family members, and help them to achieve more mutually satisfying interactions in which they each can more fully be themselves. Because of the complexity of family interactions, family therapy has a here-and-now quality that sometimes necessitates the use of co-therapists and videotapes to avoid undue subjectivity on the part of the therapist. Yet most family therapists would agree that family problems are best solved in the same setting in which they occur, that is in the family group itself. Furthermore, many other problems such as drug abuse and anorexia nervosa (an eating disorder) are often an expression of the individual's attempted solution to family dysfunction, and are best treated in family therapy.

Therapy and Growth Groups

There was a time when the term *group therapy* referred to professionally led groups that consisted of individuals labeled as patients who had some type of psychological illness and were treated according to their individual needs. People with more severe problems might be treated supportively to strengthen weak defenses, while those with less disabling symptoms would be treated in a manner facilitating deep-seated personality changes.

The rapid rise of numerous sensitivity and encounter groups in the 1960s, however, has made the current scene of healing groups more confusing. Ostensibly, the human potential groups are based on an educational or growth model rather than a treatment model. Yet many leaders of such groups come from the traditional professions of psychiatry and psychology. Also, many of the techniques used by therapy and growth groups overlap. Jerome Frank sees a major difference between the participants of the respective groups, with "those of the therapy groups having more to unlearn and, being more anxious, are less able to respond more positively to new experiences" (1973b, p. 268). But he hastens to add that there is considerable overlap between the types of people who participate in both groups. As a result, many observers find the differences between therapy and growth groups blurred.

In an effort to relate these new groups to traditional group therapy, Lieberman (1975) has visualized the various healing groups along a continuum according to the appropriate clients and the major functions of the groups. At one end are the socially sanctioned, professionally led groups that adhere more closely to the traditional notion of group therapy. At the opposite end of the continuum are a variety of self-help groups that are led by nonprofessionals and have restricted membership, such as Alcoholics or Gamblers Anonymous. In between, but more toward the group therapy end of the spectrum, are the newer types of encounter groups. Although their activities are aimed at those who want to grow and change, there is considerable overlap between the leaders, methods, types of participants, and goals of the two types of groups. Consequently, the newer groups are sometimes referred to as the *new group therapies* because the difference between the two types of groups is relative.

A key issue in conducting any therapeutic group concerns the selection of participants or clients. In the traditional groups, clients are selected according to their individual needs and symptoms as assessed by a professionally trained therapist. In the new groups, however, there is little or no screening of participants. One reason is the assumption that everyone who desires to grow has the same basic needs because all modern people are alienated and cut off from their feelings to some extent. As a result, individuals with serious psychological problems are sometimes admitted to these new groups. This is unfortunate because previous psychological disturbance is one of the most accurate predictors of negative group experience (Hartley et al., 1976). Other studies have shown that a negative experience or dropping out is also associated with a number of other personal characteristics, such as unrealistically high expectations of the group, low esteem, being overly sensitive to others, fear of attack or rejection, and the fear of intimacy and self-disclosure (Lieberman, 1973). Consequently, professionals now urge that participants be better screened and better prepared for the group experience.

A second issue concerns the qualifications of the leaders of group therapy. Traditional therapy groups must be led by individuals certified by their respective professions or licensed by the state, both of which ensure a minimum level of training. The lack of corresponding laws for leaders of growth groups, however, means that anyone can lead such a group. While groups are often led by professionals certified by their profession or those from nationally recognized programs of group training, it is possible to move from participant to leader status with no more than workshop-type training in some such groups. A major difficulty in this area, however, is that there is no consistent proof that professionally trained leaders are superior with groups. For the group process itself has an inherent potential for facilitating change so that positive gains among the participants may not be a simple function of the leader to the same degree as in individual therapy (Lieberman, 1975).

Whatever you may think of the new groups, their presence has certainly affected the approach to group healing. For one thing, traditional therapy groups have incorporated some of the innovative features of the newer groups, such as use of nonverbal and marathon techniques. Another impact of the new groups concerns the relative importance of the group experience in healing. In traditional therapy, the group experience tends to supplement individual therapy, but in many of the newer therapies the group supplants or displaces individual therapy entirely. A third influence of the human potential groups concerns the shift in goals of therapy, from the treatment of symptoms and illness to facilitating growth and psychological health.

Another change toward an increased consumer orientation on the part of the

RADIO'S NEW PSYCH JOCKEY

This is the label given to the new breed of psychologists who dispense psychological advice on call-in radio shows. While many professionals believe it is dangerous to give advice to unknown and undiagnosed people, psych jockeys defend their programs by saying that they routinely refer people with serious problems and provide support and hope to others (Foltz, 1980). After a lengthy debate, the American Psychological Association has taken the position that its members may provide "advice" but may not "diagnose" or perform "psychotherapy" on the air. But so far, this appears to be a fine but hardly enforceable line (Rice, 1981).

Most of the psych jockeys are young, attractive women with earned doctorates, many of them having had experience in private practice. Apparently, listeners of both sexes feel more comfortable revealing their problems to a woman. One of the best-known psych jockeys is Dr. Toni Grant, who conducts a call-in radio show from 1 to 4 PM on weekdays in Los Angeles, now reaching over 100,000 people. The calls are screened, partly to keep out cranks and psychotics. Yet many of the calls are about dramatic problems, such as rape, wife-beating, and incest. But there are also less dramatic ones, such as the woman concerned about her teenage son dating an older woman (*Time,* May 26, 1980).

A key to the program's success is the psychological involvement between the psychologist and listener. The callers seem to want personal support and encouragement. A 50-year-old man who sucked his thumb was reassured that there were worse ways of relieving his anxiety. But an even greater benefit may be experienced by the silent majority of listeners, who vicariously receive information and advice without jeopardizing their privacy (Rubinstein, 1981).

participants may be more mixed. While the therapist makes a professional judgment as to when therapy has been successful in traditional group therapy, in the newer groups it is the participants' enthusiastic response that is paramount. Yet, as Lieberman (1975) warns us, "change and enthusiasm" are not necessarily the same thing, which brings us to the question of how we evaluate the effectiveness of therapy.

DOES PSYCHOTHERAPY REALLY WORK?

For many years, hardly anyone asked this question. Therapists and clients alike held to a kind of blind faith that psychotherapy works. Then Hans Eysenck shocked the professional community by reviewing the existing literature on therapy, and concluded that about as many patients improve with the passage of time without treatment as those who undergo therapy. Like practically all findings in the field of therapy, Eysenck's claims were hotly contested by other professionals and counterchallenged by later studies of his own (Eysenck, 1952, 1966).

Although there are no definitive answers on this issue, more recent studies have confirmed that psychotherapy does work (Bergin & Suinn, 1975). Individuals in therapy generally improve more than those in control groups or on waiting lists (Sloane et al., 1975). Even the fact that some people suffer negative effects from therapy is evidence that people may be influenced by therapy. At this point, then, the issue regarding the effectiveness of therapy revolves around more specific questions such as "What makes therapy work?" "Why do some people benefit from it more than others?" and "Why are some therapists more effective than others?"

Insight Therapies

It now appears that the type of person who enters psychotherapy may affect the outcome more than the type of therapy itself. Surveying many studies in the field, Luborsky (1971) concluded that, while all individuals benefit from therapy, those who are intelligent, educated, upwardly mobile, motivated, and not seriously disturbed show greater gains than those having less of these characteristics. Also, individuals who seek therapy under situational stress, such as the loss of a job or the failure of a marriage, tend to perform better in therapy than those whose difficulties arise in the absence of external pressure (Frank, 1973).

How much you expect to benefit from therapy also powerfully affects the outcome. For example, outpatients in the United States and England have shown a positive association between their estimates of how well they expected to feel after 6 months of therapy and their reported relief at the later date (Friedman, 1963). As a result, there have been some attempts to enhance the effectiveness of therapy through preparing the client for it. After individuals participated in a preparatory interview in one such study, they showed more appropriate behavior in therapy as well as a better outcome than those who had not received this training (Sloane et al., 1970).

The therapist's personal qualities also affect the outcome of psychotherapy. A composite image of the "good therapist" is one who is a "keenly attentive, interested, benign, and concerned listener—a friend who is warm and natural, is not averse to giving direct advice, who speaks one's language, makes sense, and rarely arouses intense anger" (Strupp et al., 1969, p. 117).

Jerome Frank (1973b) stresses that the effectiveness of therapy depends in part on the therapist's belief in the power of his or her therapy. Others point to the importance of the therapist's motivation for doing therapy. For example, one analysis of 12 successful therapists showed that they experienced personal growth and fulfillment themselves in the process of helping their clients to grow (Burton, 1972).

The willingness of the therapist to disclose himself or herself also tends to heighten the client's self-disclosure. However, if the therapist overdoes it, clients may feel that the focus of therapy has shifted from their own problems to those of the therapist (Derlega & Chaikin, 1975).

It may be obvious by now that many of these desirable personal qualities cannot be readily procured merely by having completed a certain period of training. A lot depends on the kind of personality and attitudes one brings to therapy. Frank has remarked that "anyone with a modicum of human warmth, common sense, some sensitivity to human problems, and a desire to help can benefit many candidates for psychotherapy" (1973b, p. 167). Some support for this notion comes from an interesting study in which students seeking therapy were treated either by a highly experienced therapist or by college professors from a variety of fields chosen for their ability to relate to people. The results showed that the students seen by the professors showed about as much improvement as those seen by professional therapists (Strupp & Hadley, 1979). Yet Frank himself would be the first to admit that the weight of evidence shows that experienced therapists, regardless of their orientation or training, get better results than novices.

The actual relationship between therapist and client also vitally affects what happens in therapy. For example, one study showed that, while therapists who provided warm, active, and personal relationships did better with hospitalized schizophrenics, those who offered a less active and objective relationship did better with outpatient neurotics. However, both types of therapists did equally well with patients hospitalized with other disorders (McNair, 1967). Therapist-client compatibility is also affected by such things as the similarity of values and interpersonal needs for affection and control (Pande & Gart, 1968). Many therapists recognize this and select their clients carefully. For example, some therapists will not attempt to treat alcoholics, while others avoid hysterics, and still others believe they do best with depressed patients or schizophrenics. Perhaps all of this implies that success in therapy depends on the willingness of both therapist and client to become emotionally involved in the therapeutic relationship.

Behavior Therapies

Behavior therapies have shown an impressive record of success for many types of problems, though Wolpe's much-cited claim of a 90-percent cure rate has been criticized because he omitted all clients who had dropped out of therapy before the fifteenth session (1960). A more realistic picture can be gained from a study of 50 therapists and 1,000 clients, which revealed success rates from 60 percent up to the 90 percent claimed by Wolpe (Paul, 1969). Behavior therapy has been found to be especially effective in treating phobias, with desensitization and implosive techniques being generally superior to insight therapies for this problem (Boulgouris et al., 1971). At the same time, a comparison of patients with relatively mild disorders receiving behavior therapy and psychoanalytic therapy respectively showed that neither therapy was superior overall (Sloane et al., 1975).

One of the difficulties in evaluating the effectiveness of behavior therapy is that the diversification among behavior therapists is no less extensive than that between behavioral and nonbehavioral practitioners (Loew et al., 1975). Also, many behavior therapists have moved beyond their behaviorist heritage and have become more inclusive in their techniques. This is especially true in their tendency to include their clients' "private events" and "covert processes"—thoughts and feelings—in the treatment process. As behavior therapists increasingly deal with cognitive factors, they must also deal with the corresponding ambiguity of human experience, which lessens the distance between their approach and the insight therapies (Lazarus, 1977). Perhaps it is a compliment to behavior therapists that because they are so concerned with helping their clients, they have been accused of mixing in many aspects of insight therapies as well (Weitzman, 1967).

Group Therapies

Some of the most reliable findings on the effect of groups come from a study by Lieberman, Yalom, and Miles (1973). They studied 210 Stanford students who volunteered and were later randomly assigned to one of the 18 different types of encounter groups. Several related measures were used to assess their reactions before the group, immediately following the group experience, and six months later.

Immediately after the group experience, the students' responses were 57 percent positive, 29 percent neutral, and 14 percent negative. Six months later, the positive reactions had decreased somewhat, along with a corresponding increase in neutral and negative responses. Almost 8 percent of the participants were classified as casualties, defined as those who seemed more psychologically distressed or employed more maladaptive behavior at the time of the six-month follow-up. However, there were wide variations between groups, with some groups reporting no dropouts, while others had more than half their members quitting.

One of the most important factors affecting the participants' reactions was the leadership style of the group leaders. Six styles were identified—the energizer, provider, social engineer, laissez-faire, impersonal, and manager. The providers, who ranked high on caring and giving feedback but low on imposing structure on the group, turned out to be the most effective leaders overall. They produced the most positive changes with the least negative ones. The energizers, who were the most charismatic and likely to impose their beliefs on others, produced many positive changes, but also had a high rate of negative and casualty reactions. The least effective leaders were the laissez-faire, impersonal, and man-

The most effective group leaders rank high on caring and giving feedback but low on imposing structure on the group. (Ken Karp)

ager types. The first two types did not invest themselves sufficiently in the leadership role, while the managers were seen as "top sergeants" who controlled too much.

Most participants reported increased satisfaction with themselves and maintained their initial enthusiasm about their group experience throughout the six-month follow-up period. But more individuals in the provider-led groups actually experienced gains in the positive evaluation of their experience. The enthusiasm individuals felt for their leaders changed somewhat over time. Enthusiasm for the energizer leaders dropped, and feelings for the provider leaders remained fairly stable across the six-month period.

An important implication of this study is the need to distinguish between the participants' enthusiasm and their actual personality or behavior change. Using several related measures to assess change, the researchers found that about one-third of the participants showed positive change, a little more than a third showed no change, while the remainder had negative experiences. The discrepancy between this modest level of change and the high degree of enthusiasm among participants suggests that subjective enthusiasm is not necessarily the same thing as lasting change. This is supported by other studies showing that the therapist's ratings of client success tends to be considerably lower than the client's own ratings, suggesting that client satisfaction can supplement but should not displace professional evaluation of the outcome of therapy (*APA Monitor,* 1977).

Comparative Effectiveness

It is natural for practitioners of each type of therapy to point to their successes, especially with clients who had not benefited from other methods. Yet, as we look at the entire spectrum of psychotherapy, the more obvious it becomes that the respective claims of the different therapies tend to cancel each other out. For example, after reviewing many studies of the effects of psychotherapy mainly with nonpsychotic clients, Luborsky (1971, 1972) has drawn several significant conclusions. First, no one school of psychotherapy has been proven consistently superior to any other. Second, clients in individual and group therapy have shown similar gains. Third, there have been no significant differences in the benefits to clients in insight therapy compared to those in behavior therapies. The only exception is the treatment of certain phobias, which seem better suited for behavioral techniques. And finally, comparison of time-limited with unlimited individual therapy has shown similar gains for each.

Such findings confirm what many therapists and clients have long suspected, namely, that the different therapies have more in common than their respective theoretical orientations imply. What makes therapy effective or not depends more on common factors, such as the type of people who enter therapy, their expectations, the personal qualities and experience of the therapist, the therapist-client relationship, and so forth. Thus, each therapist should be willing to use techniques of empirically proven worth regardless of their field of origin (Lazarus, 1977). The implication is that eclecticism among therapists will continue to increase with time.

ETHICAL CONSIDERATIONS

A process like psychotherapy that is capable of producing profound changes in people's lives inevitably poses certain ethical considerations.

One important issue has to do with personal freedom and the extent to which individuals can decide for themselves whether, when, and how they will change. Probably no group has been more criticized on this issue than behavior therapists. They have been accused of manipulating people, treating clients like Pavlovian dogs, and subjecting them to inhumane shock treatments. As a result, many behaviorists are now paying more attention to the relationship aspects of therapy, realizing "that without a favorable helper-client relationship, client change will rarely occur" (Goldstein, 1975, p. 49). However, Bandura (1972) reminds us that all forms of therapy affect behavior change through deliberate and unwitting controlling influences. So the critical issue is not so much whether therapists exert controlling influences or not, as much as how knowingly and voluntarily the clients submit to such influences. Many behaviorists themselves now question the effectiveness of techniques imposed on a reluctant client, who may in turn resist such treatment all the more. Respect for personal freedom has also become an important issue in treating clients with a diminished mental capacity in institutional settings, such as a mental hospital or prison. In these instances, it is recommended that the goals of therapy be approved by an independent review committee to safeguard an individual's civil rights (Wilson & Davison, 1975).

Another issue concerns the therapist's bias toward his or her clients. Criticism in this area has taken several forms. One is the accusation that therapists tend to impose their middle-class values on all their clients regardless of the client's own values. Some people wonder if a white therapist can carry out unbiased therapy with a black client. More recently, attention has been focused on sex bias in therapy. For example, in one study therapists were asked to describe the characteristics of a healthy person. The results showed that most of the socially desirable characteristics were those traditionally assigned by society to males. Even more striking, female therapists gave the same responses as men, showing that this bias toward males is deeply ingrained in all our social values (Broverman et al., 1970). Since most psychotherapists are men but the majority of their clients are women, the male sex bias is an issue that has serious implications for psychotherapy.

Still another issue has to do with the place of values in psychotherapy. The earlier naive notion that psychotherapy, unlike religious forms of healing, is neutral is being dispelled by empirical findings showing otherwise. According to one study, the longer therapy continues, the more similar the values of clients and therapists become (Welkowitz, 1967). Even though there is a mutual influence of values between therapist and client, clients appear to change more toward the values of their therapists (Pande & Gart, 1968). Compatibility of values is an important ingredient in the success of psychotherapy (Frank, 1973b). But it is important that the therapist be aware of the role that values and value judgments have in psychotherapy and show due respect for the client's own value system in the process.

The question of values suggests still another issue, the goal of psychotherapy. The traditional notion that therapy should improve the client's adjustment to society continues to have some merit because everyone needs a minimal degree of social adequacy to cope with the demands of everyday life. Yet this approach unwittingly makes the therapist an agent of social conformity at a time when we are becoming more aware that our views of normality as well as psychological illness and health are themselves largely determined by cultural values.

Accordingly, changing social values have led the therapists and clients alike to put less emphasis on being well-adjusted and more on attaining one's own potential or self-actualization. There is a fresh appreciation that each of us has talents and strengths that, if sufficiently cultivated, will help us function better than will blind conformity to other's demands. As a result, therapists are becoming more concerned with helping their clients attain their optimal functioning, however like or different from the majority they may become. The emphasis is on strengthening such competencies as autonomy, self-control, freer expression of needs and desires, and the acquisition of various problem-solving skills—all of which make for self-directed growth or self-actualization.

SUMMARY

Psychotherapy has been defined as a help-giving process in which a trained, socially sanctioned therapist performs certain activities to facilitate changes in the attitudes and behavior of those seeking help.

A major factor in the willingness of clients to participate actively in therapy has to do with their favorable attitudes toward therapy. Although there are many different ideas regarding the purpose of therapy, seven major goals are implicit in most kinds of therapy, ranging from strengthening the client's motivation to modifying their behavior or interpersonal relationships. A goal of increasing importance is personal growth, with many individuals now seeking therapy for the purpose of personal growth as well as for the relief of symptoms.

Most psychotherapies can be classified into one of three main types: insight therapies, behavior therapies, or group therapies.

Insight therapies are based on the assumption that verbal discussion of a client's problems can bring insights into the possible causes and solutions. While psychoanalysis was the most widely admired form of psychotherapy for many years, there are a variety of other insight therapies today, including client-centered therapy and rational-emotive therapy.

Behavior therapists tend to focus their efforts on the client's behavior itself. Although there are more than a dozen different behavior therapies, most of them are based on the principles of classical and operant learning and differ mostly in terms of their techniques. Behavior therapies include desensitization, assertiveness training, modeling, contingency management methods, implosion therapy, and aversion therapy.

The different group therapies can be seen along a continuum, with approaches using a medical model with the aim of treatment of illness at one end, followed closely by those approaches using more of a growth model, to a variety of self-help groups led by non-professionals at the other end of the spectrum. Because of the considerable overlap between leaders, methods, type of participants, and goals of the former two types of groups, the difference between the old and new group therapies is a relative one.

Although the nature of the therapeutic process makes it difficult to evaluate its effectiveness, the weight of evidence indicates that psychotherapy does work for most people. However, its effectiveness depends on a number of factors, such as the type of clients who enter therapy, their attitudes toward therapy, the personal qualities and experience of the therapists, as well as the client-therapist relationship. There is no consistent evidence that any one type of therapy, whether insight, behavioral, or group, is consistently superior to any other. Actually, it appears that the different types of therapy have more in common than their respective differences imply.

A process like psychotherapy that is capable of producing profound changes in people's lives inevitably poses certain ethical considerations. One key issue has to do with the extent to which individuals can decide for themselves whether, when, and how they will change. Other ethical issues have to do with the bias of the therapist toward clients of a different class, race, sex, or set of values, as well as the appropriate goal of therapy.

QUESTIONS FOR SELF-REFLECTION

1. In what ways do you and I act as psychotherapists for each other?
2. Under what conditions would you suggest that a friend or a member of your family seek professional psychotherapy? Yourself?
3. If you were being psychoanalyzed, which areas of your life would you be most reluctant to discuss?
4. What are some personal qualities you would look for in selecting a psychotherapist for yourself?
5. Do you believe people can really change in therapy?
6. What sort of persons or problems are best suited for Rogers's client-centered therapy?
7. Which behavioral techniques do you think would be most helpful if you suffered from excessive test anxiety?
8. What kind of impression do you have of growth groups, based on your own experience or conversations with those who have participated in such groups?
9. Under what conditions do you think it would be ethical to use behavior modification techniques on mental hospital patients or prisoners?
10. What are some of the implications of the trend to seek psychotherapy more for self-actualization than for the relief of symptoms?

EXERCISES

1. A first-person account of therapy

If you have ever taken part in any type of counseling or psychotherapy, it may be helpful to reflect on your experience. A wide variety of experiences qualify here, ranging from vocational counseling with a guidance counselor to personal counseling or therapy with a psychologist or psychiatrist. Write up your experience in a page or so, telling how you have benefited from the therapy. Do you have any criticism or misgivings about your experience? Would you recommend it to others?

If you now feel the need for professional help for an academic, vocational, or personal problem, you might consult someone in your college counseling center, local community mental health center, or a professional person in private practice, and write up your experience as indicated above.

2. A therapist's point of view

Ask your instructor to invite a therapist or counselor to speak to your class. This could be a psychiatrist, psychologist, marriage counselor, family therapist, or social worker. Other possibilities include people who work with alcohol or drug abusers, unwed mothers, runaways, or school dropouts.

At some point, you might ask what kind of therapy this person does, specific techniques used, typical problems encountered, and ways in which clients benefit from therapy.

3. Class demonstration

You may prefer to have your instructor invite someone who will present a specific therapeutic approach or technique that lends itself to a class demonstration. Some possibilities are assertiveness training, desensitization, biofeedback, hypnosis, and psychodrama. It is especially valuable to provide opportunities for class participation without making individuals feel threatened or obliged to take part.

4. Choosing a type of therapy

You are a therapist who can draw on any of the therapeutic methods described in the chapter. Now, suppose each of the clients described below comes to you for help. Which type of therapy would you use for each of them? What are the reasons for your choices?

a. Joan feels pretty adequate as a student when doing papers and discussing topics in class. But she says she freezes up for a test, especially final exams. Although she does high B-level work in her papers and projects, her poor grades on tests bring her overall course grades down to low Bs and sometimes Cs.

b. Brad has difficulty making up his mind. Sometimes he makes decisions too hastily just to get rid of the anxiety over decision making. At other times when he acquires a lot of information and weighs alternatives, he is so afraid of making a mistake that he procrastinates for weeks, disrupting his sleep and concentration during other activities. As a result, he has changed his college major three times, but still has no idea what he really wants to do.

c. Although Nancy leads a relatively normal life, attending classes at college and occasionally going out socially with friends of both sexes, she says she also spends a lot of time doing nothing. "I just don't feel like doing anything," she says, complaining of feelings of listlessness, unworthiness, and just not caring what she does. Yet her family doctor has assured her there is no medical problem involved.

d. Jeff is overweight by about 85 pounds. Part of the problem, he says, is his "oral fixation," which makes it difficult for him to resist food any time or place. His physician says there is no medical basis for his obesity. Jeff himself says he really wants to lose weight, but can't seem to stick to any of the diets prescribed for him. He also loathes exercise.

5. The group experience

The counseling centers in many colleges offer various types of growth groups at little or no cost to the student. If your college offers such groups, select the one you are most interested in and enroll in it. Assertiveness training has been a popular choice for many students, as has career guidance and female or male awareness groups. How much is your group experience like or unlike your expectations of it?

6. Self-help groups

Interview someone who attends a self-help group such as Alcoholics Anonymous to speak to your class. How alike or different are such groups from professionally led therapy groups? Growth groups? What are the strengths and weaknesses of self-help groups?

7. Some films to see

If your instructor includes films in the course, try to see a film on psychotherapy. There is a four-reel series by the title of "Gloria" that features three one-hour sessions of the same client with Carl Rogers doing client-centered therapy, Fritz Perls doing Gestalt therapy, and Albert Ellis doing rational-emotive therapy. There is also a one-reel color film by the title of "Actualization Therapy," which includes excerpts from "Gloria" along with commentaries by Everett Shostrom on combining the elements from these three therapies into an actualization therapy. One of the best films of an encounter group is "Journey into Self," featuring excerpts from a weekend encounter group led by Carl Rogers.

RECOMMENDED READINGS

Binder, V., A. Binder, and B. Rimland, eds. *Modern Therapies.* Englewood Cliffs, N.J.: Prentice-Hall, 1976 (paperback). An overview of the different major types of therapy based on articles by their founders and leading practitioners.

Ellis, A., and R.A. Harper. *A New Guide to Rational Living.* Englewood Cliffs, N.J.: Prentice-Hall, 1975 (paperback). An application of rational-emotive therapy to everyday life.

Frank, J. *Persuasion and Healing.* New York: Schocken Books, 1974 (paperback). A comparative study of psychotherapy by one of America's leading practitioners, summarizing research findings and critical topics in a clear, nontechnical way.

Kovel, J. *A Complete Guide to Therapy.* New York: Pantheon Books, 1977 (paperback). A therapist's view of what motivates people for therapy, along with clear descriptions and candid evaluations of the different therapeutic approaches.

Rogers, C. *Carl Rogers on Encounter Groups.* New York: Harper & Row, 1973 (paperback). The dean of the encounter group movement describes the typical group process as well as discussing selected topics such as group leaders, the effects of encounter groups, and research findings.

Shephard, M. *The Do-It-Yourself Psychotherapy Book.* New York: Permanent Press, 1980 (paperback). A self-improvement book using many of the insights and principles of psychotherapy.

Verny, T. *A Practical Guide to Encounter Groups and Group Therapy.* New York: McGraw-Hill, 1975. A psychiatrist's highly readable account of what happens in the various therapy groups, with illustrative dialogues between participants, guidelines for group members, and resource material on the different types of groups.

Growth and Adult Life Stages

13

It is common to stereotype those older than ourselves as "old" and simply continuing a static existence. A 20-year-old may regard a 40-year-old person as "past her prime." That same 40-year-old, however, may see herself as a youthful person who continues to change and grow, though she may in turn regard a 55-year-old friend as definitely "over the hill." And so it goes. As soon as you reach an age you previously regarded as "old," that is no longer so, because you do not want to think of yourself as old. Only those older than you are old. You begin to see through the stereotyped notions of age and development. You realize you are still a vital person, perhaps a bit mellower, but still interested in taking on new challenges and acquiring new insights about life. In short, you discover that you never stop growing.

We will begin this chapter by taking a look at the nature of adult development and how people continue to grow with age. Then we will examine some of the characteristic changes that occur throughout three broad stages—early, middle, and late adulthood.

ADULT GROWTH

Paul Baltes (1979) distinguishes between two influences in adult development: age-graded and non-age-graded influences. *Age-graded influences* are events that commonly occur at a given stage of life, such as puberty and graduation from high school. *Non-age-graded influences,* on the other hand, are experiences and events that are unique to the individual's development. For example, one person may drop out of college at 21 because of financial difficulties, delay marriage until 35 because of responsibilities at home, and change careers at 45 because of stagnation at work. Such a person will have a different development and outlook from someone who graduates from college at 22, marries at 24, and remains in the same career throughout middle age.

Since life experiences that are unique to the individual, or non-age-graded influences, have a greater influence on development after adolescence, there are no clear-cut stages of adult development. In fact, some social scientists have found little evidence for uniform age-graded stages in adulthood (Lacy & Hendricks, 1980). Yet the self-perceptions and life situations of a 35-year-old tend to differ from those of a 55-year-old much the same as these would differ from those of a 75-year-old. Furthermore, people in the same age bracket often experience "predictable life crises" (Sheehy, 1977) that occur in sequence, such as the mid-life transition, the empty nest, and retirement. Consequently, different investigators have proposed different adult life stages, though there is no consensus favoring one theory over another. Rather, each viewpoint emphasizes a different aspect of development which, combined with others, may enrich our understanding of adult life stages as a whole. We will draw on various studies and viewpoints in our discussion of adult development, and organize the material around three broad stages: early, middle, and late adulthood respectively, realizing that age boundaries are somewhat blurred.

Stability and Change

A key issue is whether people really change once they have reached adulthood. Can adults really grow? Or do they remain essentially the same? Longitudinal studies provide some evidence for both views, though some aspects of personality tend to change more than others.

Paul Costa and Robert McCrae (1980) kept track of people's scores on personality tests on two or three occasions at intervals of six, ten, or twelve years and found a high degree of stability in some personal traits. They found that the most stable trait was extroversion-introversion, which measures how gregarious and assertive a person is. They found almost as much stability in specific traits such as anxiety, impulsiveness, hostility, and depression. A person's level of activity also seems to remain quite stable throughout adult life; that is, those who are active in their youth also tend to be the most active and energetic throughout middle and late adulthood (Haan & Day, 1974).

Some personal traits are more likely than others to change with life experience.

Because of the maturing effect of life experiences, people are especially apt to increase in their self-esteem and the control and mastery they have over their lives (Brim, 1980). Furthermore, there is a tendency for people to change toward health and adaptation. For example, some studies have shown that adolescents who were characterized as passive, brittle, and negativistic changed the most in their transition to adulthood, while the more cooperative and productive adolescents changed the least (Block, 1981). Similarly, women are especially apt to exhibit marked changes in personal growth throughout adulthood.

While Maas and Kuypers (1975) found that early adulthood styles set the tone for old age styles for most people, this was not the case for many people. These people were more often women than men, especially women who in their thirties had the lowest levels of energy and were the most dissatisfied, depressed, and unambitious. Yet when their dissatisfaction reached a crisis level as a result of a divorce or the death of a child, these women changed markedly for the better. They began working outside the home, developed friendships and hobbies, and exhibited a more gregarious lifestyle in their later sixties.

Authorities differ somewhat in regard to which is the more dominant theme in adult development—stability or change. Costa and McCrae claim that many of the changes in adult personality are the result of "mellowing," but that an individual's personality remains essentially the same. For example, a warm, outgoing person may become more reserved with age but remain an extrovert in relation to his or her peers. Other researchers such as Orville Brim believe that people tend to change in many important aspects of their personality such as self-esteem, *unless* they become stuck because of some tragic life experience or adverse circumstances.

A Sequence of Psychosocial Changes

Actually, much of adult growth is occasioned by psychosocial changes that occur in an orderly sequence. In studying 524 men and women of all ages for evidence of such stages. Roger Gould (1978) found there was a developmental sequence of adult life that was somewhat predictable with age. For example, he found 16- and 17-year-olds predominantly concerned about escaping from parental dominance and 18- to 22-year-olds actively substituting friends for family. Individuals in their mid-twenties were busy establishing themselves in the adult world, but they characteristically became more self-reflective as they moved into their thirties. The mood of self-assessment usually became more intense for those 35 or older, with middle age being an uncomfortable and unstable time for most people. By the time most people reached 50, however, they had become more accepting of themselves and others, as well as more tolerant of the complexities of life.

Perhaps the best-known theory of psychosocial stages is that of Erik Erikson (1968). In Erikson's view, personal growth consists of eight stages or critical turning points extending from infancy to old age. Each stage consists of a positive achievement along with a related threat especially appropriate for that age, such as the achievement of a personal identity at adolescence accompanied by the danger of identity confusion. Optimal personal growth consists of a successful resolution of each stage, with the resulting personality composed of the acquired strengths and weaknesses. Biological changes that tend to occur at given ages set the stage for the first four life tasks, which are achieving a sense of trust, autonomy, initiative, and industry. The four stages of adolescent and adult growth—the achievement of identity, intimacy, generativity, and integrity—are defined more by psychosocial changes, which results in less precise age spans for adult growth. Consequently, the sequence in which these life tasks are mastered is more important than the particular age at which they occur. For example, Gruen (1964) found that older people were not necessarily any further along in the sequence of stages than younger people, but he did find that those who had established a strong sense of identity at adolescence were more likely to be successful in achieving interpersonal intimacy during young adulthood. Personal growth, in other words, is cumulative, with each stage building on the strengths and weaknesses of earlier stages.

Since many of the proposed adult life stages are based on research involving only male subjects, some authorities question whether such stages apply equally well to women. For instance, Rosalind Barnett and Grace Baruch (1978) have pointed out that Levinson's (1978) view of adult development reflects men's preoccupation with careers. But their own research has shown that women's experience in early and middle adulthood depends more on specific decisions about work, marriage, and child rearing than careers. Consequently, different psychosocial changes tend to shape women's development than men's, as will be pointed out in our discussion of adult growth. In fact, one study found that social class, and to a lesser extent sex and race, were better predictors of adult development than age, challenging the assumptions about the existence of uniform age-related stages (Lacy & Hendricks, 1980).

Individual Differences

Because of the greater importance of non-age-graded influences throughout adulthood, people tend to become more diverse with age. For example, two 40-year-olds are likely to be more different from each other in regard to their personalities and values than two 20-year-olds.

The sequential nature of growth, however, results in individual lifestyles or characteristic ways of thinking and problem-solving that remain relatively consistent throughout adult life. Bernice Neugarten (1977) has found that personality becomes more predictable with age, and that an individual's success in adjusting to adult crises remains relatively consistent throughout that person's life. People who have been relatively successful in their earlier stages of growth also seem to cope well with critical stages of adult life such as marriage, parenthood, and retirement. On the other hand, those who tend to fall apart at these critical times are often the individuals who have been vulnerable and less successful in the earlier stages of their life. We can even predict to some extent how older people will react to stressful events according to their previous lifestyles (Lowenthal, 1972).

Of course, we should be cautious in predicting an individual's reaction to the changes of adult life because we can't fully predict growth. People inevitably change with age, but they don't necessarily grow. They *may* grow. A great deal depends on a person's openness to change and new experience. Some individuals tend to fear change and to shut out new influences, thereby unduly accentuating the contraction or disengagement tendencies associated with aging. They seek stability at the expense of growth. Perhaps an even greater number of people tend to regulate the input of new experiences to maintain a balance between change and stability, resulting in only moderate growth with age. Other adults tend to be more growth oriented. Each experience that contradicts their existing orientation leads them to reach out for new information and skills, resulting in greater adaptive abilities and richer satisfactions with increasing age. One study of more than 2,500 people who lived to 75 years or older showed that they tended to be flexible and quick to change, suggesting that personal growth may actually enhance one's chance of survival (*The Philadelphia Inquirer*, Nov. 25, 1976).

EARLY ADULTHOOD

More authorities now recognize what parents and young people themselves have long suspected, namely that adolescence doesn't end in adulthood. Instead, adolescents tend to grow into yet another transitional stage which is neither adolescence nor adulthood. Kenneth Keniston (1970) has proposed calling this the *youth* stage of life. He sees it more as a time for transformation than completion, a further period of preparation for living in a complex and technological society. Quentin and Emmy Schenk (1978) characterize young people at this stage as NQAs—"not quite adolescents, not quite adults." A common problem among NQAs and their parents alike is the sense of ambivalence over the prolonged dependence on the family throughout this period, usually occasioned by the lengthy educational requirements for young people. Daniel Levinson and his colleagues (1978), drawing on their longitudinal studies of young men, found that early adulthood lasted well into the thirties and included several substages: the early adult transition (late teens and early twenties); entering the adult world (mid-twenties); the age 30 transition (late twenties and early thirties); and a settling down phase in the early thirties prior to the midlife transition. All these views suggest that the transition to adulthood is more lengthy and complex than ordinarily understood.

Leaving Home

A major task at this stage of life is separation from our family of origin. The external aspects include moving out of the family home, becoming less dependent financially on our parents, and entering new roles and responsibilities. The internal aspects include increasing differentiation of ourself from parents and reduced emotional dependence on them. Leaving home also includes separation from adolescence, from adolescent activities, roles, and groups. It is the psychosocial transition, however, that is most essential for entering adulthood. That is, some youth may run away from an unhappy home at an early age, but take a long time before growing up emotionally. Others, mostly because of a lengthy education, may remain home well into their twenties, choosing to achieve self-sufficiency in other ways. In both cases, it is the "symbolic" leaving home that is so crucial to attaining emotional autonomy. Levinson (1978) points out that, since the separation from home is never complete, it is more accurate to speak of the changes in the degree and kind of attachment with parents that take place during this period.

Up to age 18, many young people feel and often exclaim, "I've got to get away from my parents." But they lack the financial resources to set out on their own and often have a stronger desire to remain at home at least until graduation from high school. After that, young people are more inclined to act on their convictions and begin pulling up stakes in earnest. Graduation from high school provides the occasion for their departure, with college, military service, jobs, and short-term trips serving as the accepted vehicles for getting away from home. In his book *Leaving Home,* Jay Haley (1980) points out that maladjustments at this stage often reflect problems in separating both from home and from the dynamics of the family itself. Separation troubles can take many forms, including drug addiction, delinquent behavior, emotional disturbances, failure at school or work, paralyzing apathy, or suicide. In many instances young people have difficulty leaving home because of their parents' unwillingness to "let go." Such parents may complain of a young person's problems at school or with drugs, while deriving an unconscious satisfaction from knowing they are still needed as parents. Young people themselves also experience conflicts over leaving home. On the one hand, they may feel impatient and resentful toward their parents for their attempts to control them, but they may also feel anxious about their ability to make it on their own.

Going away to college often tips the balance of forces toward independence, and in the process improves the relationship between young people and their parents. This can be seen in a study by Kenneth and Anna Sullivan (1980) which included 242 male students from 12 high schools in Pennsylvania, New Jersey, New York, and Massachusetts. They compared two groups of students: those who attended residential colleges and those who remained at home and commuted to school. Questionnaires completed by students and their parents at the

Going to college is frequently the occasion for leaving home. (Marc P. Anderson)

high school and college stage included questions about the affection and communication between parents and students as well as the latter's independence. The level of the young man's independence was measured first by whether his family encouraged him to make his own decisions or criticized him and tried to dictate such things as hair style, and second by the degree to which he made decisions without their help. The results showed marked differences between the groups. Those who had gone away to college reported that they not only enjoyed better communication with their parents, but also that they and their parents had more affection for each other than did students living at home.

A similar study involving both sexes showed that women tended to have more extreme feelings of anxiety and anger toward their parents than men did, as well as a greater tendency to idealize what college would be like. But as the students adjusted to college, they felt an increased attachment to their parents. One implication of this finding was that anxiety and anger toward parents are a normal part of the emotional disengagement from the family upon leaving for college. Only when they persisted long after the transition to college did such feelings seem to indicate a deeper problem (Kurash, 1980).

Taking Hold in the Adult World

How well young people take hold in the adult world depends partly on their ability to manage time, money, and adult work roles. Many young people have already had considerable experience through part-time and summer employment. During, the college years, half the full-time students and almost all the part-time students have held part-time jobs (Dearman & Plisko, 1979). Work experience helps young people learn how to handle competing demands on their time and how to get along with all kinds of people. While young people do not always like their jobs, they usually enjoy the independence that comes from earning their own money, which is an important means of moving toward adulthood (Cole, 1980).

Assuming responsibility for a full-time job is a major step toward economic independence. Yet the degree of independence depends largely on the educational requirements, type of job, and pay. School dropouts must usually take the lower-level jobs, such as manual labor and farm work. High school graduates generally fare much better in terms of job tenure, pay, and satisfaction. College graduates enjoy even greater advantages in many of the same areas and also have the lowest rates of unemployment (U.S. Bureau of the Census, 1981). Yet many young people who have been brought up with the belief that a college education is the key to personal fulfillment and career advancement are experiencing frustration in their careers because of the difficulties associated with inflation, recession, and tight job markets.

Young women may experience added difficulties in achieving independence. Traditionally, the majority of women have sought economic security primarily through marriage and family. Today, however, more women are working before marriage, marrying later, having fewer children, and combining career or work with marriage and child rearing. Furthermore, a larger proportion of women are attending college, which in turn heightens career aspirations among women (Angrist, 1972). Yet many women experience conflict over the priorities of having a family or pursuing a career. As Gail Sheehy (1977) has pointed out, many women find it difficult to balance the claims of marriage and career until they are in their thirties. The added fact that women 25 years and over are paid on the average only two-thirds as much as men this age for the same work makes it difficult for women to achieve economic independence during this period of their lives (U.S. Bureau of the Census, 1981).

Early adulthood is an unstable time in the lives of many young people, partly because of all the critical choices to be made, such as college, career, and marriage. Almost half the college-bound youth delay their enrollment in college because of uncertainty over their goals or lack of finances. Then too, more students interrupt their college education at some time or another. Approximately half the students in four-year colleges and more than two-thirds of those in two-year colleges interrupt their education, though many of them return to school at a later date (Golladay & Noell, 1978). Moreover, the typical young

THE MENTOR RELATIONSHIP

Some people become highly successful early in their careers because they are fortunate enough to have a mentor who takes a special interest in them. A mentor is a person of greater experience and seniority who acts as your informal sponsor or advisor, usually in a work setting. By believing in you and encouraging you, a mentor may facilitate your career development.

In their study of adult development, Daniel Levinson and his colleagues (1978) found that the presence or absence of such a figure in the early adult years was a significant factor in a man's career development. At the same time, they observed that the mentor relationship lasted only two or three years on the average, ten years at the most. Furthermore, highly successful men usually outgrew the mentor relationship by the time they entered middle age.

Up until recently, women had less mentoring in many fields, probably because a career was not deemed as important for them as for men. Also, as Gail Sheehy (1977) points out, women were more likely to have a male mentor, with the added danger that the mentor relationship might be transformed into a romantic or sexual one. In recent years, however, the women's movement has helped to bring about both a more extensive support system for women in the workaday world and freedom from sexual exploitation in "moving up the ladder" of their chosen occupation.

Have you ever had a mentor relationship at school or work? Did you find it helpful to your career? Would you agree that it is natural to outgrow a mentor relationship?

worker holds a number of brief jobs for the first few years after leaving school before settling into a position that will last several years. Furthermore, people are changing jobs more often now than in the past, so that the average worker in his or her mid-twenties has had five different employers (Crittenden, 1980). A major reason for such frequent job changes is the desire to find an optimal fit between themselves and their jobs, with interesting, satisfying work commonly being regarded as more important than pay for many people.

Establishing Intimate Relationships

Erikson (1974) has long held that the establishment of intimate relationships outside the family becomes all important in the early adult years. There is abundant evidence for this. Just look around at the young people of this age you know, and you will probably discover that they are actively substituting friends for family. At this stage, both college and noncollege youth agree that the two most important things in life are having a good marriage and family life *and* strong friendships (Astin, 1977). Yet, in shifting their emotional involvement from family to friends, there is also greater risk in experiencing loneliness, so that Erikson holds the attendant danger accompanying the pursuit of intimacy is isolation.

In Erikson's view, a firm sense of identity is necessary for the establishment of healthy intimacy. Whether in friendship, love, marriage, or at work, intimate relationships involve a fusing of personal identities while each partner retains a sense of self. Those with only a weak or unclear identity may be so fearful of losing themselves that they can only enter into superficial, unstable, or dependent relationships. Those who are more certain of themselves are freer to enter into the give and take of close relationships. Studies of college students have shown that men and women with a firm sense of identity enjoy deeper and more committed relationships than those who have not developed a clear identity (Kacerguis & Adams, 1980).

Yet this does not prove that such matters as a clear vocational identity necessarily precede intimacy. As you may recall from our discussion in an earlier chapter, Erickson's prediction of a successful resolution of the identity crisis preceding success in intimacy applies mostly to men. Women follow a more varied pattern. While some women who follow the male pattern may indeed concentrate on a career before focusing on their intimacy needs, others who follow the stereotyped feminine pattern tend to be more concerned about interpersonal crises in romance, sex, or sex role before clarifying their vocational identity. Still other women who follow more of an androgynous pattern may experience crises in both realms simultaneously. All of this suggests that there is a great variety in the ways women go about establishing their identity and relating vocational identity and intimacy (Hodgson & Fischer, 1979).

Traditionally, true intimacy has been associated with the marriage relationship, in which the couple's commitment is backed up by all sorts of legal sanctions. But in recent years, there is a growing conviction that intimacy is also a function of the quality of interpersonal relationships, such as mutual sharing and fulfillment, and may occur just as readily among friends and lovers as marriage partners. Consequently, more unmarried couples are having sexual intercourse and living together, sometimes deciding to marry at a later date and sometimes not to marry at all. Nevertheless, the vast majority of people marry, mostly while both partners are in their twenties. While the median age of *all* marriages has been rising steadily in recent years, this is largely because of the increasing number of divorces and remarriages among young couples. As we mentioned in an earlier chapter, the median age of *first* marriages has remained stable for many years, at about 21 years of age for women and 23 for men (U.S. Bureau of the Census, 1981).

Starting a Family

Early adulthood is also the time for starting a family. Today, however, couples are giving more thought to whether they want children, and, if so, when to have them. One result is more voluntary childlessness. Yet few couples resolve this issue directly. Usually, couples decide to postpone having children until they eventually make the postponement permanent. Those who decide to have children tend to wait longer before doing so than did couples during the 1950s. Today many couples do not have their first child until they are in their late twenties or early thirties. The advantages and disadvantages of each pattern were shown in a series of interviews with couples in three different generations who had their children early (in their twenties) or late (in their late twenties or early thirties). Couples who had their children early pointed to the advantages of growing up with their children and getting free of their children at a relatively early age. A major disadvantage was missing the freedom to do things on their own early in the marriage. Couples who waited to have their children cited the advantages of having a chance to strengthen their marriage, advance their careers, and generally grow up before having children. A common disadvantage was the conflict over balancing the claims of career and child rearing (Daniels & Weingarten, 1981).

Having children may affect a couple's marriage in several ways. On the positive side, many couples report that having children makes them feel more responsible and adult. They also report increased satisfaction in sharing affection and learning experiences with their children, all of which enhance their sense of purpose

Some couples prefer having time to strengthen their marriage and advance their careers before having children. (Ken Karp)

in life (Hoffman & Manis, 1979). But, on the negative side, taking care of small children is also an added stress on the marriage, leaving less time for the parents to be alone with each other. This also comes at a time in the marriage relationship when romance is giving way to the realities of married life, with many couples characteristically expressing decreased marital satisfaction and loneliness at this stage of life (Gould, 1978).

Maintaining a satisfying relationship in one's personal or family life as well as one's career is also a challenge at this period. Although men and women often have different priorities regarding the relative importance of career or marriage, they face the common problem of balancing their emotional involvement in both realms. Gail Sheehy (1977) says that the *integrator* pattern is the ideal for both men and women. But it is also the most difficult to achieve. For men, it consists of balancing career ambitions with a genuine commitment to family. Men at this stage often feel torn between spending long hours to get ahead at their jobs and not having the time for their wives and families. Women have an even more difficult time, largely because the twenties is both an ideal time for having children as well as pursuing graduate school and a successful career. As a result, many women feel they must choose between a career and marriage. Gail Sheehy observes that those who successfully combine career and marriage tend to do so in their thirties since "before then, the *personal* integration necessary as a ballast simply hasn't had a chance to develop."[1]

Doubts and Reappraisals at Age 30

As individuals move into their thirties, their mood becomes more self-reflective. Pipe dreams, so invigorating in the twenties, have begun to be replaced by experience in the adult world. Life now looks more complex and inconsistent than it did earlier. The gap between aspirations and achievements leads to more inner doubts and questioning, and individuals at this age typically feel that something is missing. "More often it begins as a slow drum roll, a vague but persistent sense of *wanting to be something more*" (Sheehy, 1977, p. 198).

Part of the reappraisal comes from the sense that time is running out. Roger Gould (1978) found that up to the mid-thirties, both men and women felt there was still plenty of time to do the things they wanted to do. But at that point, there was a sharp increase in the opposite feeling, that it was getting too late to make any major changes in their careers. As a result, individuals in their late twenties and early thirties tend to make job changes while there is still time to do so.

The mood of self-questioning spreads to intimate relationships as well, reflecting much of the strain on marriage and family in this period. Gould found that individuals in their late twenties and early thirties expressed a sharp rise in

---

[1]Gail Sheehy, *Passages: Predictable Crises of Adult Life* (New York: E. P. Dutton, 1976), p. 340. Copyright © 1974, 1976 by Gail Sheehy. Reprinted by permission of the publisher. E. P. Dutton, Inc.

agreement with the statement "I wish my mate would accept me for what I am," with a gradual decreasing agreement with "For me marriage has been a good thing" (1975). As a result, there is a good deal of restlessness and change at this period, leading couples to question their marriages, with some ending in divorce.

All in all, the over-30 period is a time of active psychological change in preparation for the more stressful forties.

MIDDLE ADULTHOOD

While the average individual thinks of a middle-aged person as someone in their forties or fifties, this period actually begins in the mid-thirties, literally the midpoint of the average lifespan.

Physical and Intellectual Changes

The most obvious signs of middle age are certain physical changes in appearance. People tend to gain weight around the waist, especially after 40. Men's hairlines may begin to recede around the temples, with a greying of hair for both sexes. All these changes reflect a gradual slowing down in the overall physical system. There is less physical energy and stamina. People get tired more easily and take more time to bounce back from fatigue or stress.

There is actually some improvement in general health in the sense that middle-aged adults get fewer colds, allergies, or minor illnesses, and they experience fewer accidents. But they become more susceptible to the chronic and serious illnesses, such as diabetes, heart attacks, strokes, and cancer (Troll, 1975). As a result, there is increasing concern over health and more attention paid to keeping fit.

Slower mental reactions are among the most obvious intellectual changes, resulting largely from a slowing down of the central nervous system. As a result, middle-aged people don't usually perform as well on tests or on problems that require quick thinking. At the same time, they may continue to function well, if not better, in tasks depending on vocabulary, memory, or problem solving.

Much depends on the individual. For example, Verhage (1965) found that those who test well to begin with tend to maintain their level of intellectual performance longer than those who have tested poorly. There is also some evidence that people who are dissatisfied with their lives and try harder may gain more in IQ points between the ages of 18 and 40 than the average person (Honzik & Macfarlane, 1970). Others have shown that individuals born more recently tend to experience less decline of general intelligence with age, perhaps because our modern way of life demands more use of our minds (Schaie & Strother, 1968).

As a result, middle-aged people may compensate for their slower mental reactions with more seasoned judgment as well as a tendency to work with more deliberation and efficiency in solving problems. Not surprisingly, when people of all ages were asked who they turned to most often for advice, the most favored age span by all was 35 to 55 years of age (Gibson, 1977).

The Midlife Transition

Sooner or later, men and women must make the transition from early to middle adulthood, commonly known as the midlife transition. Essentially, this is a time of personal reevaluation that comes from the realization that life is half over. Although people at this age may hide some of the more obvious changes of age or compensate by trying harder, it is more difficult for them to ignore other fundamental changes that come at this age. For one thing, their parents retire, become ill, and die during these years. More of their friends and acquaintances are also lost through death, with death from all causes rising sharply at this time of life. Children grow up and leave home, and middle-aged parents feel more aware of the mistakes they have made raising their children than in earlier years (Gould, 1978). As a result, the early part of middle adulthood becomes an uncomfortable and unstable time for many people, intensifying the mood of restlessness and self-questioning of the early thirties. While some individuals may experience considerable emotional turmoil or a *midlife crisis* during this period of their lives, many others make the shift relatively smoothly, more as a *midlife transition.*

In Erikson's view (1968), the main life task at this stage is achieving *generativity,* which involves looking beyond one's immediate family and extending life in more meaningful ways into the larger community. The realization that life is half over prompts people this age to ask themselves what they would like to do with the rest of their lives. Such self-questioning may lead to changes in their careers, marriages, or personal relationships. It often leads them to take up new interests or become active in community or national affairs as a way of making their world a better place in which to live. In Carl Jung's view (1957), middle age is a time for actualizing potentials for growth that have remained unconscious during the active young adult years. It's a time for becoming aware of the "opposite," unrealized side of one's personality. For example, at this time of life, a hard-driving businessman may take more of an interest in helping others, or a mother may go back to school as a way of developing her skills as a research scientist. In either view, middle age is a time for shifting gears and developing new interests and values. Not doing so may result in undue self-absorption or stagnation.

Career Changes

How the midlife transition affects a person's career depends on many factors, such as sex and earlier successes or failures. Since men are usually deeply involved in their career, they tend to feel much of the effect of the midlife crisis in their work. If they have not fully achieved their ambitions, this becomes a time for now-or-never decisions. Men often redouble their efforts to achieve their career goals at this age, which increases their stress and susceptibility to heart attacks. Or, if they sense they will never make it in their present jobs, they may switch positions or even careers. Even those who have been successful run the risk of going stale unless they continue to grow. Sometimes the needed challenge comes from new responsibilities with advancement. Or it may come from a job that is challenging and rewarding in different ways than before, especially one that puts people before profits.

John DeLorean chose the latter path. He had had a highly successful career at General Motors, having been appointed head of a division at the age of 32. Yet, by his late forties he had grown tired of the same thing. "Sure," he said, "I could have coasted for seventeen more years at $750,000 a year without trying too hard, but coasting is not my style." Instead, he left General Motors and took a job more directly involved in helping people. "I must be working twice as hard as I did before," he said. "but no amount of money or success remotely approaches the feeling you get inside from doing a good thing for somebody" (Sheehy, 1977, p. 402).[2]

Women react to their midlife crisis somewhat differently from men, depending largely on whether their involvement is focused on their family or on a career. The most common pattern is seen among women who married in their twenties. Their children are in school, and their husbands are working longer hours. Having spent much of her married life caring for her husband and children, the typical woman feels the need to fulfill herself in other ways, using abilities not developed in her role as a homemaker. She begins to reexamine her life. Such self-questioning often leads to erratic changes, with the mid-thirties being the characteristic age for extramarital affairs, the runaway wives, women returning to school, or taking a job outside the home.

Women who have spent their lives in a career outside the home experience the midlife crisis differently. These women often sense a need to bring out their nurturant, maternal sides. Single-mother adoptions reach a peak among women between the ages of 35 and 39. Others feel a need to have their own child before it is too late. This is what Irma Kurtz did. As an unmarried free-lance jounalist who had reached the top of her profession, she felt the need for something more in her life. She decided to have a baby at 37 years of age. Despite the broken sleep and hectic schedule that come with having a child, she felt thoroughly gratified saying it was "an end to vanity" and "my own egocentric childhood" (Sheehy, 1977, p. 383). It also brought new perceptions of herself and others that helped her to be a deeper, more fulfilled person.

---

[2]Gail Sheehy, *Passages: Predictable Crises of Adult Life* (New York: E. P. Dutton, 1976). Copyright © 1974, 1976 by Gail Sheehy. Reprinted by permission of the publisher, E. P. Dutton, Inc.

THE EMPTY NEST

There is a popular notion that when the last child leaves home, the parents become tearful and sad; women especially become depressed and lack a sense of purpose. Yet there is little basis to this view. A comparison of working and nonworking mothers whose children had just left home or were in the process of doing so showed that almost all of them responded to the departure of their children with a decided sense of relief. While most women experienced temporary feelings of anxiety, disappointment, and sadness, these feelings were quickly superseded by an equally powerful need to turn attention to their own lives. Many women regarded this period as the exciting beginning of a new phase of their lives (Rubin, 1979). According to other studies, a majority of men and women look forward to the empty nest stage (Lowenthal & Chiriboga, 1972). After having children in the home for 25 years or so, parents welcome the prospect of a more private life and an opportunity for pursuing personal fulfillment not possible in earlier periods.

Sexual Changes

The bilogical and psychological changes accompanying the loss of reproductive powers contribute significantly to the midlife crisis in both sexes. The adolescent changes in sexuality that lead to distinctively male and female sex roles have reached a peak by about 40 years of age. From this point on, the loss of biological reproductivity with its associated changes tends to blur former sex-role distinctions. While this poses new anxieties for both men and women, it also presents new opportunities for personal growth.

The most significant change in women is the rather abrupt stop of the menstrual cycle (menopause), with the loss of a woman's child-bearing capacities. These related changes tend to occur in women sometime between 45 and 55 years of age. The physical effects vary from a certain degree of atrophy in the uterus, vagina, and breasts to a variety of other symptoms such as hot flashes, dizzy spells, headaches, and other psychosomatic complaints. About half the women between 45 and 55 years of age in one survey found menopause mostly a negative experience, with adverse effects on their appearance and on their physical, emotional, and sexual lives. The other half experienced little or none of these effects. When asked to check the worst effect of middle age, only 4 percent of these women checked the menopause. However, about half of them said "losing your husband," suggesting that the psychological effects of menopause outweigh the physical ones (Neugarten, 1968).

Some positive changes also occur during this period. For example, the lessened fear of pregnancy can lead to increased sexual responsiveness for many women of this age. How well a woman adjusts to the changes of menopause depends on the particular woman. According to three-fourths of the women in Neugarten's survey, the women who have trouble at this stage are either "expecting trouble" or "have nothing to do with their time." As a matter of fact, research on menopause suggests that other events of middle adulthood, such as changes in the marital relationship, freedom from child-care responsibilities, and return to work outside the home are usually more important to women than menopause itself (Notman, 1979).

Although men are not subject to a menopause, they do go through a male *climacteric,* defined technically as the loss of reproductive powers. There is a gradual reduction in fertile sperm, a diminution of testosterone resulting in less aggressive behavior, and reduced sexual vigor along with increasing impotency in some men. However, men tend to reach their climacteric 5 or 10 years later than women, and do so in a more gradual way, with fewer physiological consequences (Troll, 1975). The most significant effects are psychological. Men tend to feel they are losing their masculinity and react in a variety of ways. Some men feel depressed at the prospect of waning sexual vigor. They may become critical of their wives, wishing they had a younger, more sexually attractive partner. Sometimes men compensate by extra efforts at keeping fit and looking younger. Perhaps the most common reaction is a last attempt to recapture adolescent sexual fantasies by having an extramarital affair or marrying a younger wife, thus attempting to deny the aging process.

Men and women who take these changes in stride often find their lives even more satisfying than before. For one thing, the changes and anxieties of this period may make each individual more aware of their need for a spouse and the security of marriage. Nothing helps a man or woman through the turmoil of this stage as much as an understanding and supportive partner. Actually, there is a rise in marital happiness among many couples at this period, with individuals in their late forties and fifties reporting levels of marital happiness surpassing couples in their twenties (Gould, 1978). The fact that men and women tend to become more like each other also brings each a new sense of freedom in sex and marriage. As Carl Jung put it,

> *The other sex has lost its magic power over us, for we have come to know its essential traits in the depths of our own psyche. We shall not easily "fall in love," for we can no longer lose ourselves in someone else, but we shall be capable of a deeper love, a conscious devotion to the other"* (Jacobi, 1973, pp. 282–283).

As a result, there is an overall "settling down" in the lives of individuals as they move into their fifties and the final stage of life looms closer.

LATE ADULTHOOD

Now that the average life expectancy is increasing, the elderly are becoming a larger proportion of American society. While those over 65 represented only 4 percent of our population in 1900, they now make up over 10 percent of all

Americans. By the year 2000, the elderly will comprise about 12 percent of the population.

The "greying of America" will affect every aspect of society—business, education, government spending, housing, leisure, and medicine. Attitudes toward older people will also change. As individuals, most of us tend to hold stereotyped ideas about people older than ourselves. Once we reach the same age, however, we get more understanding and insight into people that age. Much the same is occurring on a larger scale as society grows older. Gradually, we are getting a better understanding of aging and are adopting a more humane attitude toward older people. After all, one day each one of us will be an older person.

Interestingly, our attitudes toward aging are influenced by our experiences with older people while we are growing up. If the only elderly people we know are very old and sickly, we may acquire a negative image of aging. On the other hand, if we are fortunate enough to know some elderly people who are active and vigorous, we may get a more positive image of aging. For example, interviews with older adults averaging 79 years old have shown that those who had lived with a relatively youthful grandparent when they were very young are themselves more alert, more active, and less dependent than older people who learned about aging in the usual fashion that emphasizes the debilitating effects of aging (Langer, 1981).

Physical and Intellectual Changes

As individuals get older, there is a progressive slowing down of all bodily processes. As a result, older people eat less, exercise less, and have less zest for life. They also sleep less restfully, though they spend more time in bed compensating for their lack of sleep. Their senses become less efficient, and difficulties in hearing and vision (especially in the dark) are common problems at this age. Older people also have more trouble maintaining their sense of balance. Deaths from falls occur twice as frequently as those from other accidents. Chronic diseases and deaths from all causes increase with age, with the greatest percentage of deaths resulting from heart and circulatory disorders (Kalish, 1975).

Fortunately, with improved understanding of aging and the importance of health care and supportive environments for the elderly, we are discovering that older people can remain in reasonably good health and function better at the same age than their parents and grandparents did. We're also learning that many of the negative changes associated with aging are due to stress and disease rather than to the aging process itself. Senility, which is associated with symptoms such as impaired attention, memory loss, and disorientation in time or place, is actually a disease caused by damage to the brain's cells and affects only a small number of very old people.

Intellectual functions are also affected by the aging process, though rarely to the extent justifying the stereotype of the absent-minded old person. *Fluid intelligence,* which refers to those mental abilities most affected by aging of the nervous system, such as the speed of mental reactions and visualizing an old problem in new ways, does decline somewhat in middle age and more sharply in late adulthood. As a result, older people exhibit slower mental reactions and are often less adept in processing new information. But *crystallized intelligence*, which refers to those abilities most affected by learning, such as verbal skills and vocabulary usage, remains the same and in many instances continues to improve with age (Botwinick, 1978). Consequently, even though young people may beat their grandmother in a ping-pong match because of their greater speed, she will probably win playing Scrabble or doing cross-word puzzles.

It is also thought that individuals can maintain their creativity well into late adulthood, depending on their type of work. Studies of total productivity (not just outstanding work) of creative people have shown that artists hit their peak in their forties, scientists maintain their creativity well into their sixties, while those in the humanities (for example, historians and philosophers) have shown a steady increase in creativity through their seventies (Dennis, 1966). For example, Benjamin Franklin invented the bifocal lens at age 78, and Will and Ariel Durant continued working on their story of philosophy series well into their eighties. Furthermore, it just may be that the decreased creativity ordinarily seen among older people is due more to their restricted environments than to aging (Stevens-Long, 1979).

Personal and Social Adjustment

In order to discover how people change with age, Bernice Neugarten (1977) interviewed 700 men and women over a seven-year period. These were people between the ages of 40 and 90 years of age who lived in homes and apartments (not institutions) in the Kansas City area. She found that as these people grew older, they exhibited both continuity and change in their personalities.

Their basic personality traits remained remarkably stable, with an accentuation of these traits increasing with age. For example, an overly dependent adult would probably become even more helpless as an old person. People's adaptive skills also remained stable, with those who were well-adjusted in earlier years continuing to cope more successfully with their surroundings than those who had been poorly adjusted.

There were also some important changes in personality with age. For one thing, men and women saw their respective sex roles reversed. Males were perceived as more submissive and females as more authoritative. A second change was a marked tendency toward a more interior orientation. Older people saw their environments as more complex and dangerous and tended to focus more on their inner feelings and interests. Another related change was a shift in coping style, from active to passive mastery, with individuals conforming rather than attempting to change their environments to meet their needs.

Another area of change has to do with the presence of family and friends. Although the majority of older people in the United States have living children,

Grandparents can assist their grown children with child care. (Action)

only about one in eight of them lives with a grown child. The major reason is the mutual desire for independence and privacy among older people and their children. At the same time, one study found that about half the older people lived within ten minutes of a grown child and visited frequently (Shanas, 1979). Elderly parents can assist their grown children with child care, while the latter can help their parents with finances and emotional support in times of illness.

Because most married women will outlive their husbands, there are more widows than widowers among the elderly. More than half the women in the United States are widowed by their early sixties; 80 percent are widowed by their early seventies. Among those over 65, widows outnumber widowers four to one (Hendricks & Hendricks, 1977). Yet women tend to adjust to the loss of their spouse more readily than men. Although widowers are usually better off financially than widows, they tend to have more difficulty coping with routine household tasks, feel lonelier, and are less happy than widows (Barrett, 1978). Interestingly, people who have remained single throughout their lives often feel more satisfied in late adulthood than do widows or widowers the same age, possibly because they have chosen a single lifestyle and become better adjusted to it (Gubrium, 1974).

With the reduction of social contacts in late adulthood, friendship becomes even more important for the elderly. Older people especially value the emotional

ARE WE BECOMING AN AGE-IRRELEVANT SOCIETY?

It just may be. People are no longer surprised to see a 24-year-old mayor or a 28-year-old university president. Professional football players no longer retire automatically when they turn 30. Actresses no longer quit acting when they reach 40. Nor do actors stop working in front of the cameras when their hair turns grey. While people may still blink when a 55-year-old man marries a 26-year-old woman or a 40-year-old woman marries a 25-year-old man, they are no longer shocked or outraged.

Bernice Neugarten says that the whole internal clock that tells us when we're ready to marry or to reitre is no longer as powerful or compelling as it used to be. Instead, age has become a poorer and poorer predictor of the way we live. Greater affluence and higher educational levels are helping us to move toward an age-irrelevant society. Another reason is that men and women are finding that getting older isn't all losses. There are gains as well. Parents with grown children are enjoying middle age as a time for taking on new challenges and personal growth. Older people are finding that they are much younger and more vigorous than their parents were at the same age and are able to do more things. All in all, an age-irrelevant society allows people of all ages to engage in a wider variety of lifestyles without fear of being told "act your age."

B.L. Neugarten and E. Hall, "Acting One's Age: New Rules for Old," *Psychology Today,* April 1980, pp. 66–80.

and personal aspects of friendship, with the quality of the relationship being more important than the frequency of interaction. Several studies have shown that friends play an even more important role than relatives in preventing loneliness among the elderly (Perlman, Gerson, & Spinner, 1978). Because older people enjoy having friends the same age, they may prefer living in a retirement home or a community for the elderly.

Retirement

This is a major milestone in a person's life. Although retirement has been traditionally regarded as more stressful for men because of the abrupt change in their major activity, work, there is some evidence that women take a longer time adjusting to retirement (Atchley, 1976).

Most people adjust reasonably well to retirement and find it a satisfactory experience (Ward, 1979). Yet the retirement experience varies considerably from one person to another, depending on a number of factors. How retirement is perceived by the individual is of major importance. Attitude toward retirement is one of the most important predictors of later adjustment and satisfaction during retirement. Furthermore, the more voluntary the retirement, the better the adjustment (Kimmel, Price, & Walker, 1978). On the other hand, forced early retirement ranks ninth among forty major stress-producing events in life

(Shapiro, 1977). Having good health is also very important during this period, with continued good health an important predictor of life satisfaction in the retirement years (Kimmel et al., 1978).

An adequate income is very important for retirement. Yet it is the "perceived adequacy" of the income that is more crucial. That is, even though retired people usually have a reduced income, they usually have fewer major expenses such as college tuition, so that their income may be sufficient for their lifestyle. Nevertheless, those from upper-level occupations generally have the best retirement experience because they have ample income and good health (Bengston, Kasschau, & Ragan, 1977). Retired people also need to learn how to deal with increased leisure. Since many people have simply watched TV in their spare time, they may have difficulty learning how to use leisure time more adequately. Again, those with higher incomes who have been accustomed to leisure-oriented activities throughout their lives often make an easier transition to retirement (Cottrell & Atchley, 1969).

While some people may choose to retire in a warmer part of the country, such as in the sunbelt states, the vast majority of people tend to grow old in place. Most remain in the same house. The majority of those who move remain in the same community. (Neugarten & Hall, 1980). Only a small percentage of the retired people, about 5 percent, move into some type of institution. Women are especially likely to be institutionalized because they live longer than men. Also, those who have never married and lack family may be forced to be institutionalized (Palmore, 1976). It is important to point out, however, that there is a wide variety of institutions for the elderly, ranging from luxurious hotels and expensive nursing homes to state-supported mental hospitals. At the same time, there is a tendency for institutionalized older people to become more dependent on others, thereby hastening their deterioration. Consequently, there is a move to provide better services for the elderly at the local level, whether in the form of day care centers or retirement communities, enabling older people to remain in their own homes and take care of themselves as much as possible.

Successful Aging

Some older people seem to have nothing else to do but to sit in a rocking chair and talk about the "good old days." Others remain at their jobs past the usual retirement age, take up new activities, and relish keeping up with their friends. Which ones would you say are doing the most "successful" job of aging?

According to the *disengagement theory* (Cumming & Henry, 1961). successful aging consists of gradually disengaging from society with advancing age. Some investigators have found that psychological disengagement usually precedes social withdrawal by about ten years, with the latter more likely to occur during a person's sixties or seventies (Neugarten, Moore, & Lowe 1965). A related notion is the theory of *differential disengagement,* which holds that disengagement occurs at different rates and degrees according to the roles a person plays. For example, retirement would not necessarily become a crises for someone who has already begun making the appropriate transition from an active worker's role to a more passive retiree's role (Streib & Schneider, 1971).

Those favoring the *activity theory* of aging, on the other hand, say that the more active a person remains, the more satisfied and better adjusted that he or she is likely to be, regardless of age. According to this view, people want to remain active as they get older, but disengage mostly because society provides so few outlets for their energies. Proponents of this view have found that the more active older people are, the higher their morale and life satisfaction (Maddox, 1970).

Bernice Neugarten (1977) emphasizes the importance of individual differences in regard to the question of successful aging. She has found that an individual's success and style of coping with life crises remains relatively consistent throughout that person's life. Consequently, each person tends to select a style of aging that best suits his or her personality, needs, and interests. Thus, an energetic, hard-working person will continue to tackle new projects with age, while a more contemplative person will probably do more reading. Yet Neugarten found that some older people tend to benefit from activity more than others. For example, while those with a well-integrated personality generally adjusted better to old age regardless of how active they were, the less well-integrated exhibited better adjustment with higher levels of activity.

Keeping active may enhance older people's morale. (Ken Karp/Sirovich Senior Center)

Another approach to successful aging is defined more in terms of inner satisfactions than in external adjustment. According to Erikson (1968), the developmental task of older people is to establish a sense of integrity—a sense that one's life as a whole has been meaningful and satisfying. Those who have experienced a great deal of frustration and suffering may have more misgivings than satisfactions, experiencing despair and depression. Actually, people ordinarily experience both ego integrity and despair, but the healthier the person, the more self-acceptance and satisfaction will prevail.

Robert Butler (1963) speaks of the increased importance of the *life review* at this age. The life review is seen as a naturally occurring process prompted by the realization that life is approaching an end. While such a process potentially leads to wisdom and serenity in the aged, it may also evoke some negative aspects, such as regret, anger, guilt, depression, or obsessional rumination about past events. The process consists of reminiscence, thinking about one's self, reconsideration of past events and their meanings, along with mirror gazing. For example, a passing glance in the mirror may remind old people of the obvious— that they are getting older. Some older people may prefer to review their lives privately, while others may enjoy doing it more externally, such as by making a family tree or telling their children and grandchildren about the significant aspects of their family history. Such reminiscing serves to provide them with a final perspective of their lives, while leaving a record of the past to their family and friends. At least one study found that old people who reminisced frequently were found to be better adjusted than people the same age who didn't (Boylin, Gordon, & Nehrke, 1976).

SUMMARY

Now that the average person can expect to live almost a generation longer than people did at the beginning of the century, the adult years are increasingly viewed as a time for continued change and personal growth. Because adult growth depends more on psycho-social changes and experiences that are unique to the individual, we have discussed adult development in relation to three broad stages: early, middle, and late adulthood.

Early adulthood is usually a time for leaving home, with college, jobs, military service, and short trips being the accepted means of departure. This is a time when many critical decisions are made, especially in relation to marriage, preparing for a career, and economic independence. Young people this age are busy actively substituting friends for family, and they put a high value on intimate relationships, especially friendship and marriage. It is also a time for starting a family, though couples are waiting longer before having children, and more couples are deciding to remain childless. We also mentioned that the late twenties and early thirties are often a time of self-doubt and reappraisal, setting the stage for the midlife transition.

Somewhere between the mid-thirties and early forties marks the beginning of middle adulthood, a time of more intensive reevaluation of one's life and active growth. A major task at this age is to reach out and establish new meaning in life, especially in relation to things set aside in the course of taking hold in society, often leading to changes in career and intimate relationships. While the loss of reproductive powers poses new tensions between the sexes at this age, successful adaptation to these changes makes possible new levels of cooperation between men and women during the latter part of middle adulthood.

An increasingly larger proportion of our population now enters late adulthood and functions better at the same age than their parents did. Although many women are widowed by their sixties, the increased importance of friends helps make this a satisfying time of their lives. Most people adjust reasonably well to retirement, especially those who enjoy an adequate income and continued good health. While some older people remain more active than others, each person tends to adapt the style of aging that best suits his or her personality, needs, and interests.

QUESTIONS FOR SELF-REFLECTION

1. In what ways has your personality changed with age?
2. At what stage of adulthood are you now: early, middle, or late adulthood?
3. When did you leave home? Under what conditions?
4. Have you found close friends you enjoy being with? Are most of them your age or all different ages?
5. Have you experienced the midlife transition yet?
6. Do you find that many women become more self-confident and assertive in middle age? How would you explain this?
7. Have you personally known someone who switched careers in midlife? How has it worked out?
8. What kind of elderly person do you think you will become?
9. When would you like to retire? Why?
10. What do you think it means to age "successfully"?

EXERCISES

1. Age and growth

To what extent have you grown as a person with age? To find out, you might engage in a bit of self-reflection using the following questions as your guide.

Which aspects of your personality have changed the most? Which have changed the least? Be certain to include inner qualities such as self-confidence and judgment as well as outer behavior. What has been the occasion for your growth? Has it been stimulated by people or events in your surroundings? Or has it come mostly from dissatisfaction and stirrings within yourself? Try to distinguish between the usual physical changes and mellowing that come with age and the more deliberate changes in personality that have resulted from your unique experience in a crisis, continuing education, or psychotherapy.

Has your growth made you more distant from your old friends? If you are married, has your growth brought a strain to the marriage? Or has the personal relationship between you and your spouse (or friends) become even more satisfying with your growth?

Would you agree that people become more different from each other with age?

2. Mentors

Make a list of all the people who have influenced your career development, mostly from your high school years and up. Then analyze your list in terms of the following questions: Would you call any of these people a mentor in the sense described in this chapter? Are they people of the same sex as yourself? Opposite sex? Both? What effect have they had on you? Has their influence been mostly helpful, or not?

3. Leaving home

This is an exercise in self-reflection on the developmental task of separating from your family of origin.

Have you left home yet? If so, in what sense? Are you living in another house or apartment? Or are you away most of the year at college? If you are still living at home most of the year, have you considered moving out?

How have your living arrangements affected the relationship with your parents? If you are living away from home, do you find that you get along with them better? If you are living at home, do you find the relationship with your parents strained at times? Or has it become unbearable?

Regardless of where you live, to what extent have you achieved emotional autonomy or psychosocial emancipation from home? Do you have a steady job or source of money separate from your parents? Can you come and go as you please? Do you feel free to select your own friends? How important is your parents approval for the major decisions in your life?

How has the achievement of emotional autonomy affected the relationship with your parents? Would you say that the more autonomous and mature you become, the better you get along with your parents?

4. Satisfaction and stress in early adulthood

It is often said that early adulthood is a time of great emotional intensity, making it one of the most exciting times of your life and also one of the most stressful. For many people, the late twenties and early thirties are every bit as stressful as middle age. Take a minute to reflect on your experience of early adulthood, especially with an eye toward the balance of satisfactions and stresses at this time of life.

At this stage, two major areas of adjustment are career development and intimate relationships. Typical sources of stress are indecision over your career or college major, slow or disappointing career development, difficulty finding the right job, and financial dependence on parents. By the same token, positive accomplishments in these areas are a source of satisfaction. Another major area of adjustment has to do with the realm of intimate relationships, including the relation to your parents, finding close friends, marriage, and family life. How satisfying or stressful has life been in these areas?

All things considered, how do you see the balance of satisfaction and stresses in early adulthood? Has your own experience been more satisfying than stressful? Or has it been the other way around?

Another way to do this exercise is to select the most fulfilling experience you have had at this stage of life and tell why it has been so satisfying. Then take the most stressful experience you have had, and explain why it has been so stressful. How is life satisfaction and stress related at this stage of life?

5. The midlife transition

If you are going through or have completed the midlife transition, write up your experience as a means of self-reflection on this stage of life. Compare your experience with the descriptions and findings of the midlife transition given in the book. How has your experience been like and unlike that portrayed in this chapter? In what ways has your experience been unique? Would you say that you experienced more of a midlife crisis or a transition? Explain your answer.

What has been the most stressful thing for you? What has been the most gratifying part of your experience? Do you feel that women have to make a greater adjustment at this age than men? Or do you feel that the midlife transition is equally stressful for both sexes?

If you have not reached this stage, you might interview your parents or some other middle-aged people to get their reactions.

6. Retirement

Have you thought about your own retirement plans? At what age do you want to retire? Where? Are you or your employer now setting aside part of your income for retirement? Based on the projected retirement pension and possible social security benefits plus any other funds you may have, what kind of retirement lifestyle do you envision?

Interview a retired person to get a better understanding of what retirement is like. Under what conditions did the person retire? Was it voluntary or forced? Was it an early retirement? How long has the person been retired? What has been the biggest adjustment? How has the person's retirement experience been affected by such things as health, income, and the spouse's health or death? Did this person choose to retire in the same community or in a special retirement community? Any regrets about this?

Do you avoid thinking about your retirement? Or are you looking forward to it?

7. Successful aging

Interview one or more persons who have reached late adulthood, orienting your questions to the three views of successful aging discussed in this chapter. It may be helpful to review the disengagement theory, the activity theory, and the life satisfaction theory of successful aging.

What evidence is there that this person has disengaged from society? Has this been mostly social? Or does the person show less interest and emotional involvement in others as well? Was the process of disengagement voluntary or not?

How active has the person remained in his or her job or career? In keeping up with friends? In community organizations such as the church? In regard to Bernice Neugarten's emphasis on the increased importance of individual differences in aging, how much of this person's orientation reflects his or her lifestyle? How like or unlike is this person from others the same age?

What about the person's inner satisfaction? Does this person have a positive outlook on life? Or did you hear a lot of complaining? What effect has the life-review process had on this person? Has it made the person more satisfied and serene? Or has it evoked guilt and regret?

All things considered, how successfully is this person aging?

8. Facts and myths about aging

Select several subjects in each of the four broad age groups, including adolescents, young adults, middle-aged people, and older people. Then ask them the following true or false questions on aging. Since all the questions are false, the number of correct responses can be figured out quickly. What is the overall average score? Are there any differences between age groups? Between sexes? Do you think people are well informed on aging or not?

1. Most older people live in a nursing home or some other institution.
2. Individuals naturally recognize when they are getting older.
3. People tend to become more alike as they get older.
4. Most older people have given up sexual activity or desires.
5. Older people usually prefer to live alone.
6. People become more fearful of death as they get older.
7. Most people become senile after 85 years of age.
8. Individuals tend to become more fault-finding with age.
9. Most older people are absent-minded or deficient in memory.
10. Older people act like children in the sense that they become more dependent on others.

RECOMMENDED READINGS

Comfort, A. *A Good Age.* New York: Simon & Schuster, 1978 (paperback) Rejecting many of the myths of aging, a famous gerontologist provides factual knowledge as well as advice for those who wish to lead an active and meaningful life well into late adulthood.

Kalish, R. A. *Late Adulthood.* Monterey, Ca.: Brooks/Cole, 1975 (paperback). A well-informed but succinct account of the physical, personal, and social development of older persons, written by an expert in the field.

Levinson, D. J. *The Seasons of a Man's Life.* New York: Ballantine, 1979 (paperback). A Yale psychologist explains adult development in terms of the major psychological influences, such as the young man's "dream," "loved one," and "mentor," based on a study of 40 men between the ages of 18 and 47.

Rubin, L. B. *Women of a Certain Age.* New York: Harper & Row, 1979. A look at how women are meeting the challenges of the middle years in a way that dispels many of the myths associated with this period.

Schenck, Q. F. and E. L. Schenk. *Pulling Up Roots.* Englewood Cliffs, N.J.: Prentice-Hall, 1978 (paperback). A practical guide for parents and youth facing the transitional stage between adolescence and adulthood.

Sheehy, G. *Passages: Predictable Crises of Adult Life.* New York: Bantam Books, 1977 (paperback). A highly readable account of the adult life stages from adolescence through middle age, with an emphasis on the inner changes of adult development. Rich with personal illustrations from the life stories of over 100 men and women interviewed by the author.

Troll, L. E. *Early and Middle Adulthood.* Monterey, Ca.: Brooks/Cole, 1975 (paperback). A concise overview of adult development through middle age, with the material arranged according to topical chapters on the physical, intellectual, personal, family, and vocational aspects of adult development.

Death and Bereavement

14

In his book The Hour Of Our Death, *Philippe Ariés (1981) notes that we live in the era of "invisible death." People act as if it doesn't occur. Death is a subject that is evaded, ignored, and denied. It is as though death were another problem or disease to be conquered. It happens only to the unfortunate, and becomes an embarrassment to the family of the deceased. Bereavement has become a private affair, with little or no display of grief. The old black hearse has become a grey limousine blending in with the rest of traffic. Society no longer pauses at the sight of the funeral procession. Everything goes on as if nobody had died.*

But deep within, we all know better. The fact is, death is inevitable. While the average life expectancy has been prolonged, sooner or later we all die. Yet death need not be regarded as a morbid subject. Instead, death should be seen as an integral part of life, which in turn gives meaning to human existence. Death sets a limit on life, reminding us to make the most of the time we have. Coming to terms with the possibility of our own death long before it is imminent is one of the most important adjustments we can make. Grieving over the loss of the dead may deepen our relationships with the living.

We will begin this chapter by taking a look at the social and religious attitudes toward death. Then we will examine the experience of dying, bereavement, and the problem of unresolved grief. Finally, we will put the whole issue of life and death in perspective by discussing such matters as the right to die, dying a natural death, funerals, and the relation of death to personal growth.

ATTITUDES TOWARD DEATH

In many ways, our attitudes toward death reflect our attitudes toward life. In earlier eras when life was short and hard, death was regarded as a familiar fact of life. It was not that death was passively accepted as a crude fact of nature, but it was "tamed" or domesticated through beliefs and rituals so that people could deal with it openly (Ariès, 1981). Today, in our youthful, progress-oriented society, the average person expects to live a longer and more affluent life, and the subject of death is avoided like a dreaded disease. In some ways, death is to our generation what sex was to the Victorians—although it occurs regularly, we deny its existence. The most characteristic attitude toward death is the denial of death.

The Denial of Death

The denial of death takes many forms. One is the putting off of death until old age. In societies with higher death rates, people die more frequently at all ages, and death is considered separate from old age. But the low death rate in our society makes it possible for more people to survive into old age, so death becomes associated with old age. Consequently, much of the abhorrence of old age is a denial of death itself (Kalish, 1976). A related form of the denial of death can be seen in the search for longevity or the reversal of aging and death. The frantic search for pleasure, material possessions, fame, or self-fulfillment so often seen in middle-aged people is motivated largely by anxiety over death. Probably the most blatant denial of death can be seen in the unrealistic belief that "It won't happen to me"—a common delusion.

The denial of death can also be seen in the way people are protected or isolated from the event of death itself. How many times have you seen someone die? Most people have never witnessed death directly, only on TV. Our first exposure to death usually comes with the loss of our grandparents, other relatives, friends or acquaintances, or a family pet (Shneidman, 1971). Most people are well into their twenties before a parent dies and into their thirties by the time the surviving parent dies (Eisenstadt, 1978). When people have a heart attack or become gravely ill, they are usually taken to a hospital. When death occurs, it is usually in relative isolation from loved ones. Moreover, as soon as a patient dies, the body is whisked away to the hospital morgue or to an undertaker's establishment. When people ask what happened, the response among medical personnel and family alike is often euphemistic—he "expired" or she "passed away." Death is an individual and isolated affair. Here, as in so many other areas of our lives, we have turned the business of death and dying over to specialists, with the resulting embarrassment that occurs from unfamiliarity.

Burial practices also express the denial of death. Prevalent practices favor embalming and dressing up the deceased so that he or she looks as "real" as possible. At funerals, people tend to act stiff and formal and give flowers, mostly because they don't know how to act in the event of death. Like zombies, they move passively through the funeral rites.

Fortunately, the taboo against death is weakening, partly because of more openness toward many aspects of life that were traditionally repressed, such as homosexuality and divorce. Consequently, there is greater social recognition of death as a natural part of life. There are books and college classes on the subject. At least two journals are devoted to a better understanding of death. And professionals and laity alike are working to ensure that people die with dignity, as in the hospice movement.

Religious Attitudes

Practically all religions provide beliefs and practices to help their adherents cope with death. Yet there is little consensus on how religion affects people's attitudes toward death because of the variety of factors present. One of the most important factors is the individual's emotional involvement in religion. For example, in a study of terminally ill patients, one of the best predictors of emotional adjustment was religious orientation. But it was the quality of religious orientation, rather than mere religious affiliation that most helped patients. Intrinsically, religious people who integrated their religious beliefs into their lifestyles generally made the best adjustment to a limited life expectancy (Carey, 1975).

However, the *Psychology Today* questionnaire on death showed that even nominal religious affiliation affected people's attitudes toward death. For instance, 55 percent of all the Roman Catholics, 42 percent of all the Protestants, and 18 percent of all the Jews surveyed believed or tended to believe in some type of afterlife. Interestingly, in every group there were more people who *wished* there were an afterlife than believed in one. The more religious, the more likely people were to wish for an afterlife (Shneidman, 1971). Generally, the belief in an afterlife has a beneficial effect on people's attitudes toward death, with a high proportion of people who believe in an afterlife reporting less fear of death, compared to those who do not hold to such beliefs (Dempsey, 1975). At the same time, Kalish (1976) found both strongly convinced atheists and deeply religious people had less fear of death than people with nominal religious beliefs, suggesting that it is the certainty of one's attitudes toward death rather than assent to religious belief that helps a person face death with serenity.

While most religions condemn suicide or the taking of one's life, people who belong to an organized religion are no less likely to attempt suicide than those with no affiliation, at least in the survey cited above. In fact, those with Protestant ties or no religious affiliation committed a slightly greater proportion of suicide attempts than would be expected by chance, while those with Jewish ties committed slightly less. Apparently, when it comes to moments of heightened emotion and despair, a formal belief in the sinfulness of suicide is not a sufficient deterrent to the act (Schneidman, 1971).

Awareness of Death

When asked, "How often do you think about your own death?" over half the people in one survey said "occasionally," slightly fewer than one fourth of them said "frequently" or "very frequently," and an equal number said they rarely thought about their own death. When asked how they felt about their own death, over half of the people said it made them feel more resolved in relation to life or pleasure in being alive. Only one-third of them said thoughts of their own death made them fearful or depressed. Interestingly, those in their late twenties were the most fearful group of all (Shneidman, 1971).

As they get older, people become more aware of death but less fearful of it. For one thing, older people have already lived a reasonable lifespan and see less of a usable future for themselves. Then too, aging and chronic disease as well as the increasing frequency of death among their friends are constant reminders of death as a personal reality. The strong association between a positive attitude toward death and a belief in some kind of afterlife among the aging also suggests that such a belief provides an important mechanism for dealing with the anxieties of aging and death (Dempsey, 1975).

In many instances, people lack a realistic awareness of the possibility of their own death. In one survey, students were given actuarial tables on life expectancies and asked to estimate how long they expected to live. Students generally estimated they would live 10 to 20 years longer than their projected ages. When asked to explain why, the most typical remarks were, "It won't happen to me," "I'm not like other people," "I'm unique" (Snyder, 1980).

Actually, there is considerable misunderstanding about the actual risk of death among many people. According to one study, people greatly overestimate the frequency of deaths from sensational causes such as accidents and homicides, and underestimate the frequency of deaths from nonspectacular causes that claim one victim at a time, such as diabetes and strokes. Such misjudgment has to do partly with the tendency to judge an event as likely or frequent if instances are easy to imagine or recall, which is further compounded by the biases of the mass media. For example, even though newspapers carry about three times as many articles about homicide as death from diseases, the latter take about one hundred times as many lives as homicide. People also tend to underestimate the risk of death when dealing with familiar hazards under their control, such as motor vehicles, smoking, and X-rays. They are also unrealistically optimistic about their chances of surviving a crisis such as a heart attack. In short, there is a marked discrepancy between our awareness of the risk of death and the actual risk of death from a given cause or event (Slovic, Fischhoff, & Lichtenstein, 1980).

DEATH AND DYING

Now that people are most likely to die in a hospital, often sedated and isolated from all but their immediate family and hospital personnel, the experience of death has become something of a mystery. Many people have never been in the presence of a dying person, and have little awareness of what it is like. Those who have sat with a loved one or friend who is dying often have little awareness of the dying person's internal state, much less how to communicate with that person. For people who are heavily sedated, perhaps the final moments of dying are meaningless, if they are aware at all. But some remain alert right up to the

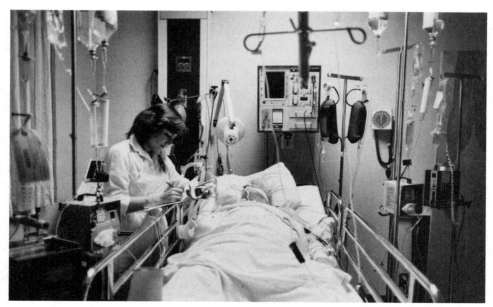

Most people die in the hospital, often isolated from all but their immediate family and hospital personnel. (Ken Karp)

end, and have expressed their thoughts and feelings about dying, giving us a more accurate understanding of it.

Near-death Experiences

For many years, when a person's heart stopped beating or lungs stopped breathing, that person was considered dead. But progress in medical technology has changed all that. Now a person can survive a temporary cardiac arrest or respiratory failure with the aid of life-saving machines, raising questions as to when death actually occurs. Consequently, the definition of death now includes failure of the brain as well as of the heart and lungs. Death can be determined by the following criteria: when there has been no movement or breathing for at least one hour, no reflexes, no brain-wave activity for at least 24 hours, and no change in these conditions for 24 hours.

The use of life-saving technology has also made possible a new kind of experience among those brought back from the verge of death—the near-death experience. Psychiatrist Raymond Moody (1977) found that various accounts of such experiences show striking similarities. Initially, individuals experience a detachment from their bodies and being pulled through a dark tunnel. Then, they find themselves in another kind of "spiritual body," in which physical objects present no barrier and movement from one place to another is almost instantaneous. While in this state they may experience a reunion with long-lost friends and loved ones. One of the most incredible elements is the appearance of a brilliant light, perceived as a warm, loving "being of light," which fosters a kind of life-review, but in a nonjudgmental way. Finally, people report being drawn back through the dark tunnel and experiencing a rapid reentry into their bodies. For most people, the near-death experience brings a profound change in attitudes. They not only become less fearful of death, but they are more concerned with learning and loving and valuing the life they have.

Cardiologist Michael Sabom (1981), using a random sample of patients who had suffered near-fatal medical crises, found that 40 percent of them had vivid memories of their brush with death. He too was struck with the uniformity of the patients' accounts. But Sabom found no religious similarities among people who reported such experiences. Atheists and church-goers were equally likely to report them. Nor were there any similarities in regard to education, race, or occupation among people reporting such experiences. Curiously, though, women with near-death experiences were more likely to recall seeing their loved ones.

People have made a variety of claims about such experiences, including that they are mystical or peak experiences or glimpses of the afterlife. Some researchers believe these experiences are little more than hallucinations brought on either by the patient's physical condition or intense emotions aroused by the nearness of death. While Sabom personally believes in life after death, he readily admits his work does not prove it. He does, however, believe that such experiences suggest dying brings about a splitting apart of the nonphysical part of our being from our bodies, but feels that we still have much to learn about this.

The Experience of Dying

There is also a new interest in learning more about the experience of dying. One of the best-known pioneers in this field is Elisabeth Kübler-Ross. Since 1964, she and her colleagues have interviewed more than 500 terminally ill people at the University of Chicago hospital. She also started a course on The Dynamics of Death and Dying. Dr. Kübler-Ross (1975) has found that even when patients were not told of the seriousness of their illness, they usually sensed that fact as well as the approximate time of their death. Hence, there is a growing realization that when a person indicates a willingness to know the truth about his or her impending death, it may be wiser to share the relevant knowledge than to protect the patient with a conspiracy of concealment. How this knowledge is shared becomes more important than the particular facts communicated. Furthermore, dying people have benefited from the opportunity to face death openly, with the opportunity to talk about it removing much of the fear of death, the sense of isolation, and the mystery of dying.

Dr. Kübler-Ross noted that individuals tend to go through several stages in dying, even though there is considerable overlap between these stages. The first stage consists of a *denial* of death, with people characteristically feeling "No, not me." Such denial protects one against the deep emotions associated with death and provides time to cope with the disturbing facts. Later, individuals tend to show small signs that they are now willing to talk about it. But at this stage a friend or a professional should talk about it only for a few minutes at a time, allowing the dying person time to make the needed adjustment. In the second stage, denial eventually gives way to the emotions of *anger* and *resentment*. "Why me?" people ask. The sight of others enjoying their health evokes the emotions of envy, jealousy, and anger. They often take their feelings out on those closest to them, but mostly because of what these people represent—life and health. Consequently, it is important for those nearby not to take these remarks personally, but rather to help the dying person express his or her feelings.

The third stage characteristically consists of attempts to *bargain* for time. Individuals at this stage often say, "I know I'm dying *but.....*" And then they indulge in a bit of magic, thinking, "If I cooperate with the doctor or my family, maybe God will let me live till my daughter graduates or my son gets married." When individuals tend to drop the "but" and admit "Yes, I'm dying," they enter the fourth stage of *depression*. In a sense this is a natural response to the threat of losing one's life, and it's very important to allow a person to grieve and express his or her feelings of sadness. One of the worst things a friend can do is deny these feelings and say "Cheer up." This is why it is so important for family and friends as well as professionals to learn to accept their own feelings about death in order that they can help dying people accept their own impending death without dwelling on it unduly.

The final stage is the *acceptance* of death, though not all dying persons reach this stage. By this time, most people who are dying have pretty much disengaged themselves from others and ask for fewer visitors. But they don't want to die alone, which is why most people prefer to die at home, though they are more likely to die in a hospital. In fact, much of the pain of dying comes from the mental anguish, especially the fear of being separated from loved ones.

Unfortunately, the popularization of Elisabeth Kübler-Ross's views has resulted in a stereotyped view of the experience of dying as a fixed, inevitable process, which it is not. Elisabeth Kübler-Ross was the first to point out that many people do not follow these stages. For some, anger remains the dominant mood throughout, while others are depressed until the end. Furthermore, Robert Kastenbaum (1981) points out that Kübler-Ross's theory does not account for the nature of the various diseases and types of deaths, age and sex differences, personality and cognitive styles, and cultural backgrounds. Accordingly, he has found that individual differences are more prominent in the experience of dying than are any stages.

Dying the Way You Live

You may recall from the chapter on adult life stages that each person's uniqueness becomes accentuated in old age. As a result, there is a tendency for people to die the same way they have lived. For a hostile, belligerent person who has lashed out at others throughout life, the dominant mood in the face of death may be anger and blame. Such a person may blame herself, her spouse, the doctor, or even God. On the other hand, for a passive, long-suffering person who has derived a lot of attention from being sick, the dominant mood in the face of death may be despair and depression, with a drawn-out illness requiring months of special care in a nursing home.

One of the most common reactions to death is seen among those with a strong will to live. Even when they are suffering from a physical illness, such people tend to live without the use of machines longer than predicted by medical diagnosis. Yet, when such people are themselves convinced that their time has come, they face death with equal deliberation. An example would by the 86-year-old widow, who despite her good health felt her time was near, consulted her lawyer, sold her house, and within a week was dead. Another common reaction is seen among those who have always coped with stress by denying it. Such a person tends to give only a passing acknowledgment to his or her impending death without altering the daily routine. For them, death comes as an annoying interruption in a life they live as long as possible.

Psychiatrist Edwin Shneidman (1973) tells of his investigations among elderly people suffering from terminal illnesses, who with unexpected energy have ended their lives in a manner similar to the way in which they have lived. Such patients have succeeded in taking out their tubes and needles, climbing over the bed rails, opening heavy windows, and throwing themselves to the ground below. When their past lives were examined, these people had one thing in common—they had never been fired; they had always quit first.

The author recalls a rugged self-made man who for years had enjoyed his wealth by over-indulging himself in food, alcohol, and sex. When informed by his physician that he must eat less and stop smoking, drinking, and running around, this man chose to continue his indulgent way of life. Within four years he was dead at the age of 48. In his own words, he had "died with his boots on."

BEREAVEMENT

To lose someone very close to us through death is to lose a part of ourselves. It is a very emotional and painful experience, labeled variously as grief, mourning, or bereavement ("to be deprived").

Societies often provide social customs to facilitate the expression and resolution of bereavement. In former times widows dressed in black and widowers wore black armbands. This served partly to excuse any oddities of behavior due to bereavement; even more important, such dress afforded the bereaved an occasion to talk about their loss and to receive the sympathy they needed. In recent times, many of the social sanctions for bereavement have been given up. Funerals are abbreviated and more formal; wakes and visitations have been replaced by memorial services; the bereaved are expected to resume their usual dress and behavior at home and at work as soon as possible. In short, it is assumed that people will manage the emotional burden of grief in a highly rational and controlled way. Yet this is precisely why so many people are having trouble handling death and bereavement. Grief has become too private, with excessive suppression of emotion.

The Process of Bereavement

Bereavement can be experienced at varying levels of intensity, depending on the seriousness of the loss. For most of us, the first experience of bereavement is usually occasioned by a less dramatic loss, such as the death of a grandparent, uncle, or aunt, rather than a member of our immediate family. While we may feel such loss acutely at the moment, we usually get over it rather quickly. Those who lose a parent, especially at an early age, or a brother, sister, or spouse, however, tend to experience a more intense grief because of the close emotional ties involved.

The process of bereavement parallels the experience of dying, with many of the same emotions and mechanisms involved. For instance, our initial reaction to someone's death is usually denial, especially when it is sudden. We say things such as, "I can't believe she is dead. I just talked with her on the telephone a couple of hours ago." Anger is another emotion commonly seen in bereavement. People sometimes project their anger onto other people, such as a family member or doctor. Or when there is guilt involved, we may blame ourselves. Some guilt may refer to specific things done or undone—"If only I had not asked him to drive home that night." But in other instances, we may feel guilt just because we have survived and the other person has not.

Professionals are well aware that grief can assume many disguises, including physical symptoms. According to one survey of people during the first month they were widowed, the most common symptoms included crying, depressed feelings, difficulties in concentration and sleeping, lack of appetite, and weight loss. Over half of these people relied on sleeping pills and tranquilizers at some point during the initial month of bereavement (Clayton, Halikes, & Maurice, 1971). One authority on bereavement observed that consultation for physical symptoms tends to rise about 50 percent following a death in the family (Parkes, 1972).

There are also age differences in the experience of bereavement. Young children who are incapable of understanding the full significance of death tend to rely on primitive and immature responses, such as denial through fantasy. Older children may use coping mechanisms, such as projection, passive-aggressiveness, and acting-out behavior, especially delinquency. While adolescents and young adults may rely on some of the same mechanisms, they also use the so-called "neurotic" responses, such as intellectualization and displacement, as well

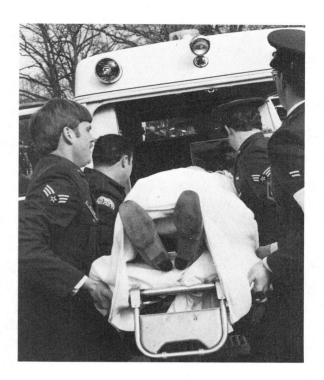

Sudden, unexpected death makes bereavement all the harder. (Marc P. Anderson)

as the more "mature" responses, such as the suppression of emotion. Although middle-aged and elderly people are more likely to rely on mature coping mechanisms, such as altruism and sublimation, older people are also more apt to have physical illnesses or symptoms in the course of bereavement (Pattison, 1978). Husbands and wives also tend to react to the loss of their spouses somewhat differently. Glick (1974) found that women tend to feel abandoned or deserted, while men are more likely to feel dismembered ("deprived of their arms"). These different reactions are probably related to what marriage has meant to each partner. Wives tend to look at their husbands as breadwinners and protectors, while husbands regard their wives as someone who sustains their capacity for work. As a result, wives often get over their grief by going to work, while husbands tend to become all the more disorganized in their work.

Unresolved Grief

Ordinarily, people get over their bereavement within six months to a year, depending on the individuals, the occasion of death, and their prevailing attitudes. When grief remains unduly suppressed or unacknowledged, however, people may suffer from more serious and lasting consequences. The longer the resolution of grief is postponed, the more severe the symptoms.

Unresolved grief may be expressed in a variety of forms, from unexplained physical complaints to psychological symptoms. In some instances, the psychological reactions are obviously related to the loss. For example, some people can't bring themselves to return to the house, hospital, or room where a patient has died because of unresolved grief. In other cases, unresolved grief may be more disguised. One woman complained that when her father died, she had not really experienced any grief. She recalls that she never cried, nor experienced the usual grief reactions. Much of the reason for this was found to be that she was left out of the family bereavement process. No one in the family had talked to her about her father's death. She had not been allowed to accompany them when they attended the funeral or burial afterwards. Years later, this woman discovered that much of her resentment toward her mother and her apprehensiveness over her husband's traveling were related to unresolved grief over her father's death. As she expressed the pent-up tears and anger over her father's death, she gradually worked out her grief, which resulted in more satisfying relationships with her mother and husband.

People suffering from the broken-heart syndrome also have a higher rate of physical illness, including cancer, and higher mortality rates from natural causes, most likely from reduced resistance to illness because of stress. In one study, it was found that women who suffered a recent loss and had reacted to it with feelings of hopelessness and depression were much more likely to contract cancer of the cervix than women without such symptoms of grief (Schmale, 1972). Another study showed that suicide rates were five times as high among people who had recently lost a parent or spouse than among a comparable group in the general population (Bunch, 1972).

Men are more likely to die within a few years after the death of their spouse than men of the same age who remain married. But women's mortality rates are almost unaffected by a husband's death. While there is little difference in the death rates between persons who have lost a spouse in the past year and married people the same age, in the ensuing years widowed men suffer a much greater mortality rate than their married counterparts; those between the ages of 55 and 65 die at a 60 percent higher rate than married men the same age. One explanation is that the quality of life changes more drastically for men than women, possibly because of their greater reliance on wives for their emotional and daily needs. Women also seem to have a better support system for coping with their grief. Yet when widowers remarry, they have an even lower mortality rate than their married counterparts who have never lost a spouse (Helsing, Szklo, & Comstock, 1981).

Good Grief

So far, we've seen that it is better to go through the full experience of bereavement, however painful it may be, than to get over it too quickly. But there are also more positive aspects of grief. That is, grief may be a learning experience that helps us grow. It is sometimes said that we don't fully appreciate something until we have lost it, which is especially applicable to human relationships. While people are still with us, we often have ambivalent feelings toward them. One moment we love them, another we don't. In retrospect, however, grief helps us appreciate loved ones and friends more fully despite their shortcomings. Grief also helps us value our relationships with those still living. In short, good grief means that we have learned and grown in our bereavement.

Edgar Jackson (1973) has suggested several ways to make the experience of bereavement more effective: talking it out, feeling it out, and acting it out. Even though it may be very difficult to talk about the death of a loved one for the first several weeks, this is the time when talking it out can be most helpful. The main thing to remember is that the focus is on the feelings of the bereaved. Some things may sound trivial or hollow, such as "at least he is out of his misery," but whatever it takes, a friend should attempt to listen and help the bereaved person to talk out his or her feelings as much as possible.

Encouraging the bereaved to express their feelings may also be cathartic. People tend to feel less embarrassment when they can do this in the company of a few close friends, especially those who consider themselves "private" people. Men usually have more difficulty expressing feelings of bereavement, largely because society considers a show of emotions by men a sign of weakness. It is also important to realize that each person's characteristic way of expressing his or her emotions differs somewhat from one person to another. For some, moistened eyes and a warm handclasp are about as close as they ever come to expressing grief. Others may cry openly and unashamedly. Still others seem to be inclined toward more dramatic, and at times hysterical, expressions of grief, such as screaming and tearing their hair and clothes.

Another way of resolving grief is to act it out in appropriate ways. Sometimes just sheer physical activity helps to alleviate the tension and sadness of bereavement, at least temporarily. Funeral rituals may afford an outlet for grief. Also, taking care of the affairs of the deceased may be therapeutic as well as helpful. As the executor of my father's estate, I found myself faced with a great deal of correspondence and many legal transactions. Initially I regarded it as a burden, but I soon realized it was one of the few tangible things I could do for my father. It became a way of showing my respect for him and helping me express my own grief.

LIFE AND DEATH IN PERSPECTIVE

Now that the average life expectancy is about seventy years, more people are apt to suffer from chronic diseases such as cancer, heart disease, and kidney failure. As a result, death comes more slowly and usually occurs in the hospital. Yet hospitals tend to be large and impersonal institutions, geared more to the treatment of acute illnesses and the prolonging of life. Consequently, the change in the context of death presents us with new ethical issues, such as the life-saving machines and the right to die in a dignified way. Examining such issues may help us put life and death in better perspective.

The Right to Die

If machines are being used to prolong life needlessly, perhaps the answer is to pull the plug. At least, this is the view of those who advocate passive *euthanasia* (easy, painless death). This notion is increasingly popular among ministers, doctors, and others who disapprove of needlessly extending a meaningless existence, but who do not approve of actively hastening a patient's death with drugs. A poll of medical doctors found that 80 percent of them practised passive euthanasia, with 87 percent approving of it in principle. Yet only 15 percent of them approve of actively putting a patient to death with drugs (Hendin, 1973). The public, however, is even more willing for doctors to practice active euthanasia, with slightly more than half (53 percent) of the adults in a Gallup poll agreeing that a doctor should be allowed to end a patient's life by painless means if the patient and family request it. The proportion favoring active euthanasia is even higher among those under 30 and the college educated (Gallup, 1978). Perhaps it is no accident that doctors are given such a significant role in these matters, since almost all euthanasia occurs in hospitals, a good part of it in intensive care and geriatric units.

Ironically, the public seems less in favor of voluntary euthanasia for one's self as a means of obtaining relief from an incurable disease. According to the same Gallup poll cited above, less than half (40 percent) of adults felt it was morally right for someone with an incurable disease to end his or her own life (Gallup, 1978). The clearest cases for voluntary euthanasia involve those who are mentally competent and refuse further treatment. For example, a 33-year-old man who had lived on an artificial kidney machine for three years refused further treatment. For him, being inactive and having no chance to do anything was not a meaningful existence. Understandably, the doctor insisted on a waiver relieving him from the responsibility for the action. But no one challenged the patient's decision, and morphine was used to deaden the pain of his final days.

A greater problem lies with those who are not in a position to make such a decision, such as someone who is unconscious and being kept alive by a machine. Who speaks for them? In one instance, when the mother of a 22-year-old girl refused permission for a spleen operation and blood transfusion on religious grounds, the hospital applied to the courts to become the girl's guardian and carried out the operation successfully, enabling the girl to survive. Had the girl been in a position to make the decision herself, the courts might have ruled against the hospital (Dempsey, 1975).

There are also dangers in voluntary euthanasia. Many people have a self-destructive drive that may be easily aggravated by their claim to the right to die. In some instances, this right could be used in a hostile way to punish survivors.

DO YOU BELIEVE PEOPLE CONTRIBUTE TO THEIR OWN DEATHS?

Or do you share the more fatalistic notion that people tend to die when their time comes? Almost all of the respondents in a *Psychology Today* questionnaire (Shneidman, 1971) believed that psychological factors can influence death. Although half these people felt most deaths are caused by events over which we have no control, 43 percent felt most deaths include some conscious or unconscious participation of the person who dies.

One coroner's office in California classifies the intentionality in death as high, medium, low, and absent. Not counting suicides, records kept over a two-year period disclosed that one-fourth of all deaths showed some degree of intention, whether the person was aware of it or not. Among accidental deaths, 44 percent showed some degree of intentionality. For homicides, which are often considered accidental, the figure was 54 percent (Dempsey, 1975).

People often hasten their own death through self-destructive habits. A survey of physicians in England found that nearly 40 percent of the 250 people under 50 who died in hospitals had contributed to their own deaths by overeating, drinking, smoking, or ignoring their doctors' orders. Practically all those who died of cancer of the throat and lungs were addicted to cigarettes. Many of those who died of heart attacks were grossly overweight or smoked. Several of the heart attack victims had had symptoms long before consulting their doctors. And two of the diabetics did not follow the prescribed treatment (*The Philadelphia Inquirer,* October 24, 1978).

After his mother's premature death from a heart attack at the age of 42, Elvis Presley once told others he probably wouldn't make it past 30. Later, Presley died of a heart attack at 42 years of age, precisely two days later in the same month his mother had died. But the conditions surrounding Elvis's death suggest his chronic drug abuse also hastened his own death.

Do such experiences make us hesitant to estimate how long we expect to live, for fear that expecting it may make it so?

In any event, even when people are dying, they not only sense the fact, whether told or not, but often can estimate the approximate time of their deaths even more accurately than others (Kastenbaum, 1981).

Then too, there is more enthusiasm for euthanasia among the young and healthy than the elderly, making for severe legal problems if there is any ambiguity in the documents. There are also problems with the "Living Will"—a document specifying what one wants done when there is no reasonable chance of a recovery from a physical or mental disability. Such documents are made out when there is little emotional concern with one's own death. What if a person has a change of mind when the contract becomes operative? In some cases the patient may feel obligated to keep the decision out of subtle social coercion from doctors and relatives. The right to die has become a duty. Partly because of these dangers, an elderly doctor appearing before a senate committee on the subject argued that we also need right-to-live legislation to protect patients against the abuse of the right-to-die laws (Dempsey, 1975).

A Natural Death

One of the dangers of the right-to-die movement is that it may unwittingly program people to die quickly. It is often said that death is more of a problem for the survivors than for those who die. For this reason, sudden death from a heart attack or an automobile accident is more appreciated than death from a drawn-out illness. On the surface, at least, the dying are supposed to have been spared the suffering of a terminal illness. But they have also saved the rest of us the burden of taking care of an invalid or having to watch someone die slowly. Hastening death also helps us to avoid our social responsibilities, such as caring for the lingering convalescent and the aged. Ironically, the revolt against needless prolongation of life may incline us toward an equally "unnatural" hastening of death. Yet a quick, induced death does not answer the key questions: How old is old? How ill is ill? At what point should a person on the heart-lung machine be allowed to die? When does a life cease to have meaning? (Dempsey, 1975)

What is needed is a more supportive environment and humane attitudes that will encourage people to die in character. According to Simone de Beauvoir (1973), people rarely see their own death as natural. Each of us regards our own death as an accident. Even when we know and consent to it, our own death is seen as an unjustifiable violation. Perhaps the nearest we come to a natural death is helping people to die at their own pace and style. For example, if a young person has been an active, outdoor type and doesn't have the will to adjust to an invalid state, perhaps that person should be allowed to die a dignified death. Others who may suffer from equally disabling handicaps but who prefer making the adjustment to their diminished capacities should be encouraged and supported in their efforts to go on living.

The hospice movement for the terminally ill represents a giant step toward the kind of humane and supportive community needed for a dignified death. In the Middle Ages the hospice was a shelter for travelers who had nowhere else to go. Today the hospice is a place to take care of those approaching the end of their lives. As we mentioned earlier, much of the suffering of the terminally ill consists of the treatments, the impersonal atmosphere, and the sense of isolation experienced in hospitals. In contrast, the hospice is a community that helps people to *live*, not merely exist, while they are dying.

One of the pioneer communities for the dying is St. Christopher's Hospice in London. It is situated in a suburb, surrounded by spacious grounds with flower gardens. Visiting hours run all day until eight o'clock in the evening, and there are no restrictions on children. Even family pets are permitted when appropriately accompanied. There are no nursing stations, so that nurses spend more time visiting with patients. Some ward patients have brought their own furniture to make themselves feel more at home. Drugs are given on demand.

But even more common is a special cocktail containing alcohol and cocaine that is administered at four-hour intervals. Throughout the community, care for the dying consists not just in the management of physical pain, but also in coping with psychological pain, social concerns, and the spiritual pain of the dying person.

In short, the hospice consists of a humane community for the dying, including ongoing support for family members as well as staff members and volunteers. Begun in England, the hospice movement is rapidly expanding elsewhere, with more than three dozen programs in America and Canada (Dempsey, 1975; Woodson, 1978).

Funerals

Like birth, coming of age, and marriage, death is a rite of passage to be recognized by both family and community. In most societies parting with the dead is recognized by some kind of funeral, the rituals and ceremonies connected with burial or cremation of the dead. Such rituals have enabled people to main-

Funerals are for the benefit of survivors, as well as for remembering the dead. (Irene Springer)

tain order and defend themselves against the untamed forces of nature (Ariès, 1981).

In earlier eras, when belief in an afterlife was a more dominant influence in human affairs, funerals were held primarily for the benefit of the dead. Death was seen as a passage to heaven or eternal life. Hence, some ancients not only buried the corpse, but included personal items of the deceased to be used on the journey. In today's secularized society, however, the emphasis tends to be humanistic and materialistic. While it is the dead who are remembered at funerals, the ceremony is more for the benefit of the survivors. Funerals have become the occasion for according the dead the recognition and honor they may not have achieved in life. Families get caught in a status game, selecting expensive bronze caskets, ornate headstones, and choice burial sites to maintain their position in society. Consequently, funerals have become increasingly lavish and expensive. While the funeral industry has been criticized for exploiting people in their bereavement, their spokesmen point out that bereaved family members themselves are partly to blame because they choose on the basis of their emotions rather than through reason. Thus, whether out of respect for the dead, guilt, or vanity, many of the expensive funeral practices continue.

Criticism of the funeral industry has spurred a movement toward simpler, less expensive funerals. Many funeral directors now provide a wider range of funeral options and are more sensitive to the needs of the bereaved family. Some widows have reported that they found the funeral director more helpful than the family physician or clergyman, partly because funeral directors are there to deal with much of the immediate effect of grief (Silverman, 1974). But clergy are also receiving training to deal with the bereaved, and suggest that, whenever it is appropriate, funerals should be held in churches, thereby exercising more control over such matters as open caskets and floral displays.

Some groups, such as the Unitarians, prefer cremation rather than embalming. While cremation (burning of the body into ashes) is widely practiced in such countries as England and Japan, only a small percentage of Americans prefer this practice so far. People who are accustomed to traditional funerals with caskets and viewings often feel "something is missing" at a memorial service, especially when there is no urn of ashes present. The percentage of people preferring cremation is higher among educated, professional groups, and is growing in the general population.

Another movement toward simpler funerals can be seen in the nonprofit funeral and memorial societies springing up all around the country. Members have access to expert guidance and can specify what they want done with their bodies and what kind of funeral they want. All of this helps people to end their lives in a way that reflects their lifestyle and values, while sparing their relatives the worry of how best to carry out their wishes. For example, Charles Lindbergh requested that he be buried without embalming or eulogies within eight hours of his death in a tiny church cemetery in Hawaii. The only mourners present were his wife and one son. It was a fitting end for a man who cherished privacy (Dempsey, 1975).

Death and Growth

It may seem strange relating death to growth. Ordinarily, death is seen as the end of growth and existence. Yet, in the larger scheme of things, death is an integral part of life that gives meaning to human existence. It sets a limit on our lives, reminding us to spend our days on the things that matter most. Those who are fortunate enough to have some warning of their end often find it a time of personal growth. Similarly, grieving over the loss of a loved one may help us relate more deeply to those who remain.

Whether you are young or old, if you can begin to see death as an inevitable companion of life, it may help you live your life fully rather than passively. Not

Death is a natural part of life that puts life in perspective. (Marc P. Anderson)

that you should rush out and begin doing all those things people fantasize about. Instead, the awareness that you have only so much time to live may help you make the most of your life—the disappointments and pains as well as the joys. As one recent widower told me, "I've begun to take time to smell the roses." Usually, it is those who have not lived their lives fully who are the most reluctant to die. Haunted by broken relationships and unfulfilled dreams, they grow ever more anxious and fearful in the face of death.

Far from being morbid, thinking about your own death may give you a new perspective on life. For instance, if you were dying from a terminal illness, what things would you like people to say to you? Are you prepared to cope with all the practical and legal matters connected with death? If you were told you have only a limited time to live, how would you spend it? How do you want your body disposed of when you die? Whatever things make your life most meaningful, plan to do them before it's too late. As Elisabeth Kübler-Ross reminds us, the greatest lesson we may learn from the dying is simply "LIVE, so you do not have to look back and say, 'God, how I wasted my life'" (1975, p. xix).

SUMMARY

We began the chapter by noting that the prevalent attitude of denying death in our youthful, progress-oriented society has begun to weaken, and there are now more open discussions, books, and courses on death. Although people become more aware of death with age, older people are not necessarily more fearful of it. The fact that both deeply religious people and strongly convinced atheists have less fear of death than people with nominal beliefs suggests that it is the certainty of one's beliefs about death rather than the influence of religion itself that helps a person face death with serenity.

Despite the preference for a sudden death or a quiet dignified death at home, the majority of people die in hospitals, often after extended treatment. Interviews with dying patients have taught us about the experience of dying. Observers have pointed out the importance of individual differences, reminding us that people tend to die the way they have lived.

Bereavement, or the experiences of loss, tends to parallel the experience of dying and involves many of the same emotions. Since people are expected to handle the emotional burden of bereavement in a private, rational manner that encourages the suppression of emotion, they may suffer from unresolved grief. Yet grief may be a valuable learning experience, helping us to deepen our lives and relationships with others.

Medical advances pose thorny issues that may help to put life and death in better perspective. Consequently, the practice of needlessly prolonging life has brought about a concern for a natural, dignified death, including right-to-die legislation and the hospice movement. There is also a movement toward simpler funerals that benefit the bereaved while remembering the dead. Although people may avoid the subject of death for understandable reasons, the realization that death is an integral, natural part of life may help us put our lives in order, and make the most of our time and talents.

QUESTIONS FOR SELF-REFLECTION

1. When learning of a friend's death, do you ever feel, "It won't happen to me?"
2. What do you believe happens to us after death?
3. Are you afraid of dying?
4. Have you had a near-death experience?
5. How do you think you will probably die?
6. Can you recall your first experience of grief? Whose death was it?
7. Have you ever experienced "good grief"?
8. Do you have any self-destructive habits that might hasten your death?
9. If you were suffering from a terminal illness, how would you prefer to spend your last few weeks?
10. What kind of funeral would you like?

EXERCISES

1. Subjective life expectancy[1]

Simply knowing a person's age does not tell you how that person feels about his or her future. To discover this, try the following exercise in subjective life expectancy. You may want your friends or other individuals to try it as well.

[1]Robert J. Kastenbaum, *Death, Society, and Human Experience,* 2nd ed. (St. Louis: The C. V. Mosby Co., 1981).

1. I *expect* to live to age (circle your answer)
   25 30 35 40 45 50 55 60 65 70 75 80 85 90 95 100

2. I *want* to live to age (circle your answer)
   25 30 35 40 45 50 55 60 65 70 75 80 85 90 95 100

Are there discrepancies between the expressed desire and expectation? If so, what are the possible reasons? Are there differences in desires with increasing age?

Usual findings have shown that those past middle-age expect and wish to live to a later age than younger subjects do. Did you find this to be true? When people expect to live less than the average life expectancy for their age, do they have a good reason? Did you find some people afraid to specify an age for fear this will somehow make death occur at a given age?

2. Do you deny your death?

In order to assess your attitudes in this area, answer *yes* or *no* to the following questions:

Do you avoid the idea that you will eventually die?

Are you afraid to joke about your death?

Have you put off making a will?

Are you afraid of dying?

Does reading about death make you depressed?

Do you dread visiting someone who is dying?

Look back over your *yes* answers and explain the reasons for your response. Since denial is a normal mechanism for coping with stress, it is understandable that each of us denies our own death to some extent. Yet undue reliance on the denial of death may result in too little precaution about the hazards of living as well as the postponement of things you really want to do, often until it's too late.

3. Your attitude toward death

Do a self-analysis of your attitudes toward death. First, write down your actual experiences with death, such as the loss of a friend or loved one, the ages at which this occurred, and so forth. Then describe some of your feelings and attitudes toward death. Include your own responses to the subjective life expectancy exercise as well.[2]

4. Death as an altered state of consciousness

Some people have observed a similarity between dying and the marginal state of awareness experienced just before sleep. Try to catch yourself in this state some night and make a mental note of your reactions. Was it a peaceful state? Did you find yourself naturally giving into it? How did you feel after the loss of control or power?[2]

[2]From Carol R. Hoffman, Montgomery County Community College, Blue Bell, Pa., 1981. Used by permission.

You might want to read Raymond Moody's book *Life after Life,* which contains personal accounts of those who have had deathlike experiences and survived. What other states of awareness like dying have you had? Fainting? Anesthesia before surgery? Hypnosis? Blurred awareness from alcohol or drugs?

5. Reflections on the experience of bereavement

Try to recall a personal experience of loss of someone close to you, whether a friend, colleague, or relative. Then describe your experience of bereavement in a page or so, using the following questions as a guide.

To what extent did your experience resemble the process of bereavement described in the chapter? Were you more susceptible to various bodily complaints, such as lack of appetitie, difficulties in concentration and sleeping, and reliance on sleeping pills or tranquilizers?

Did you experience most of the reactions described by Elisabeth Kübler-Ross? Was it difficult to acknowledge the person's death? Did you experience anger, either toward others or yourself? Did you feel any guilt? What were you the most guilty about? Were you sad or depressed? To what extent was your experience of bereavement distinctive? That is, did it reflect your own personality and relationship with the deceased?

How has your experience of grief affected you? Has it made you more cautious or bitter toward life? Or has it left you more resolved to make the most of life and to reach out to others in a more meaningful way? Has your experience become a "good grief"?

6. Disposing of your body

If you had a choice, how would you want your body disposed of? Do you want to be embalmed and buried? Or would you rather be cremated? If so, what do you want done with your ashes? While some people ask that their ashes be scattered over water or a favorite spot on land, many people prefer that their ashes be left in a mausoleum or buried in a cemetery. People sometimes write down such preferences and leave them with their families or a memorial society.

Have you thought about donating organs from your body? If so, which ones? Are you interested in leaving your body for use by medical science?

7. Write your own obituary

This isn't as strange as it may seem. Major newspapers usually have a file of obituaries written while celebrities and national figures are still alive, and then they update these accounts at the time of death.

Try writing your own obituary in two or three paragraphs. In addition to giving the standard information, such as your name, age, and position at work, point out some of your major accomplishments in life. Which community activities would you mention? Who are your survivors?

In addition, list your funeral and burial plans. What day and time do you prefer to be buried? Where is your service being held? Do you have any preferences regarding financial contributions to charities in lieu of flowers? Where do you want to be buried or your ashes deposited?

RECOMMENDED READINGS

Ariès, P. *The Hour of Our Death.* New York: Alfred A. Knopf, 1981. An interpretative account of the meaning and customs associated with death in different historical eras.

Kübler-Ross, E. *Death: The Final Stage of Growth.* Englewood Cliffs, N.J.: Prentice-Hall, 1975 (paperback). A collection of essays and case studies showing how awareness of death may serve as a means of personal growth.

Kübler-Ross, E. and M. Warshaw. *To Live Until We Say Good-bye.* Englewood Cliffs, N.J.: Prentice-Hall, 1978 (paperback). A pictorial account of leavetaking, especially appropriate for patients choosing to die at home.

Kushner, H. *When Bad Things Happen To Good People.* New York: Shocken, 1981. A philosophical and religious explanation of the occurrence of misfortune and untimely death.

Lynch, J. J. *Broken Heart.* New York: Basic Books, 1979 (paperback). A physician discusses the medical consequences of grief and loneliness.

Ramsay, R. W., and R. Noorbergen. *Living With Loss.* New York: William Morrow, 1980. A guide for coping with bereavement based on a dramatic new breakthrough in grief therapy.

Sabom, M. B. *Recollections of Death.* New York: Harper & Row, 1981. A physician's interpretation of the near-death experience, including the author's own studies.

References

ALBERTI, R. E., and M. L. EMMONS. *Your Perfect Right*. San Luis Obispo, Cal.: Authors, 1970.

ALTMAN, I., and D. TAYLOR. *Social Penetration*. New York: Holt, Rinehart & Winston, 1973.

AMERICAN COUNCIL ON EDUCATION, "National Survey of 1975 College Freshmen," in R. E. Grinder (ed.), *Adolescence* (2nd ed.). New York: John Wiley, 1978.

ANGRIST, S. S. "Variations in Women's Adult Aspirations during College," *Journal of Marriage and the Family*, 34 (1972), 465–468.

ANNON, J. "The Extension of Learning Principles to the Analysis and Treatment of Sexual Problems." Unpublished doctoral dissertation, University of Hawaii, 1971.

ARAFAT, I., and B. YORBURG. "On Living Together without Marriage," in *Annual Editions: Readings in Marriage and Family 76/77*. Guilford, Conn.: The Dushkin Publishing Group, Inc., 1976.

ARIÈS, P. *The Hour of Our Death*. New York: Knopf, 1981.

ARNOLD, M. B. (ed.). *Feelings and Emotions*. New York: Academic Press, 1970.

ARONSON, E. *The Social Animal* (3rd ed.). San Francisco: W. H. Freeman & Company Publishers, 1980.

ASTIN, A. W. *Four Critical Years*. San Francisco: Jossey-Bass, 1977.

ATCHLEY, R. C. "Selected Social and Psychological Differences between Men and Women in Later Life," *Journal of Gerontology*, 31 (1976), 2, 204–211.

ATHANASIOU, R., P. SHAVER, and C. TAVRIS. "Sex," *Psychology Today* (July 1970), pp. 37–52.

ATKINSON, J. W., and N. T. FEATHER. *A Theory of Achievement Motivation*. New York: John Wiley, 1966.

ATTHOWE, J. M. "Behavior Innovation and Persistence," *American Psychologist*, Vol. 28 (1973).

ATTHOWE, J. M., and J. M. McDONOUGH. *Operations Re-entry*. (Film of Veterans Administration Hospital, Palo Alto, Cal.). Washington, DC: United States Department of Health, Education and Welfare, Social and Rehabilitation Services, 1969.

AYLLON, T., and N. H. AZRIN. "The Measurement and Reinforcement of Behavior of Psychotics," *Journal of The Experimental Analysis of Behavior,* 8 (1965).

BACH, G. R., and P. WYDEN. *The Intimate Enemy.* New York: Morrow, 1969.

BACHMAN, J. G., and L. D. JOHNSTON. "The Freshmen, 1979," *Psychology Today* (September 1979).

BALTES, P. B. "Life-span Developmental Psychology," in P. B. Baltes and C. G. Brim (eds.), *Life-span Development and Behavior,* Vol. 2. New York: Academic Press, 1979.

BANDURA, A. in A. C. Bergin and H. H. Strupp (eds.), *Changing Frontiers in the Science of Psychotherapy.* Chicago: Aldine Publishing Co., 1972.

BANDURA, A. "Modeling Therapy," in W. S. Sahakian (ed.), *Psychopathology Today: Experimentation, Theory and Research.* Itasca, Ill.: F. E. Peacock Press, 1970.

BANE, M. J. "Marital Disruption and the Lives of Children," in G. Levinger and O. C. Moles (eds.), *Divorce and Separation.* New York: Basic Books, 1979.

BARDWICK, J. "The Dynamics of Successful People," in *New Research on Women.* Ann Arbor: University of Michigan Press, 1974.

BARDWICK, J. *Psychology of Women: A Study of Biocultural Conflicts.* New York: Harper & Row, Pub., 1971.

BARNETT, R. C., and G. K. BARUCH. "Women in the Middle Years: A Critique of Research and Theory," *Psychology of Women Quarterly,* 3 (1978), 187–197.

BARRETT, C. J. "Effectiveness of Widows' Groups in Facilitating Change," *Journal of Consulting and Clinical Psychology,* 46 (1978), 20–31.

BEAUVOIR (DE), S. *A Very Easy Death.* New York: Warner Paperback Library, 1973.

BEIER, E. G. "Nonverbal Communication: How We Send Emotional Messages," *Psychology Today* (October 1974), pp. 53–56.

BELL, A., and M. WEINBERG. *Homosexualties.* New York: Simon & Schuster, 1978.

BELL, R. R. *Marriage and Family Interaction.* Homewood, Ill.: The Dorsey Press, 1975.

BEM, S. "Sex-role Adaptability: One Consequence of Psychological Androgyny," *Journal of Personality and Social Psychology,* 31 (1975), 4, 634–643.

BEM, S. "The Measurement of Psychological Androgyny," *Journal of Consulting and Clinical Psychology,* 42 (1974), 2, 155–162.

BEM, S. L., and E. LENNEY. "Sex Typing and the Avoidance of Cross-sex Behavior," *Journal of Personality and Social Psychology,* 33 (1976), 48–54.

BENGSTON, V. L., P. L. KASSCHAU, and P. K. RAGAN. "The Impact of Social Structure on Aging Individuals," in J. E. Birren and K. W. Schaie (eds.), *Handbook of The Psychology of Aging.* New York: Van Nostrand Reinhold, 1977.

BERGIN, A. E., and R. M. SUINN. "Individual Psychotherapy and Behavior Therapy," in M. R. Rosenzweig and L. W. Porter (eds.), *Annual Review of Psychology,* Vol. 26. Palo Alto, Cal.: Annual Reviews, 1975.

BERMANN, E., and D. MILLER. "The Matching of Mates," in R. Jessor and S. Feshback (eds.), *Cognition, Personality and Clinical Psychology.* San Francisco: Jossey-Bass, 1967.

BERNARD, J. Quoted in "Psychology for the Taking," *Psychology* (April 1977).

BERNARD, J. *The Future of Marriage.* New York: World Publishing Company, 1972.

BERNARD, J. *Remarriage: A Study of Marriage.* New York: Russell and Russell, 1971.

BERNARD, J. "The Eudaemonists," in S. Z. Klausner (ed.), *Why Man Takes Chances: Studies in Stress Seeking.* Garden City: Doubleday, 1968.

BERNE, E. *Games People Play.* New York: Grove Press, 1964.

BERSCHEID, E., E. WALSTER, and G. BOHRNSTEDT. "The Happy American Body: A Survey Report," *Psychology Today* (November 1973).

BERSCHEID, E., K. DION, E. WALSTER, and G. W. WALSTER. "Physical Attractiveness and Dating Choice: A Test of the Matching Hypothesis," *Journal of Experimental Social Psychology,* 7 (1971), 173–189.

BLAKE, W. "A Poison Tree," in *The Oxford Dictionary of Quotations* (2nd ed.). London: Oxford University Press, 1955.

BLOCK, J. "Some Enduring and Consequential Structures of Personality," in A. I. Rabin et al. (eds.), *Further Explorations in Personality.* New York: John Wiley, 1981.

BOHANNAN, P. "The Six Stations of Divorce," in R. E. Albrecht and W. Bock, *Encounter: Love Marriage and Family.* Boston: Holbrook Press, 1975.

BOLLES, R. C. *Theory of Motivation.* New York: Harper, 1967.

BOTWINICK, J. *Aging and Behavior* (2nd ed.). New York: Springer, 1978.

BOULGOURIS, J. C., I. M. MARKS, and P. MARSET. "Superiority of Flooding (Implosion) to Desensitization for Reducing Pathological Fear," *Behavior Research Therapy,* 9 (1971), 7.

BOWLBY, J. *Attachment and Loss: Separation,* Vol. 2. New York: Basic Books, 1973.

BOYLIN, W., S. K. GORDON, and M. F. NEHRKE. "Reminiscing and Ego Integrity in Institutionalized Elderly Males," *The Gerontologist,* 16 (1976), 118–124.

BRADFORD, D. L., and S. KLEVANSKY. "Nonutopian Communities—the Middle-class Commune," in K. C. W. Kammeyer (ed.), *Confronting the Issues.* Boston: Allyn & Bacon, Inc., 1975.

BREHM, J. W. *A Theory of Psychological Reactance.* New York: Academic Press, Inc., 1966.

BRIM, O. G., and J. KAGAN (eds.). *Constancy and Change in Human Development.* Cambridge, Mass.: Harvard University Press, 1980.

BROVERMAN, I. K., D. M. BROVERMAN, F. E. CLARKSON, P. S. ROSENKRANTZ, and S. S. R. VOGEL. "Sex-role Sterotypes and Clinical Judgments of Mental Health," *Journal of Consulting and Clinical Psychology,* 34 (1970), 1, 1–7.

BROVERMAN, L., S. VOGEL, D. BROVERMAN, F. CLARKSON, and P. ROSENKRANTZ. "Sex-role Stereotypes: A Current Appraisal," *Journal of Social Issues,* 28 (1972), 2, 59–78.

BUNCH, J. "Recent Bereavement in Relation to Suicide," *Journal of Psychosomatic Research,* 16 (1972), 361–366.

BURTON, A. *Twelve Therapists.* San Francisco: Jossey-Bass, 1972.

BURNS, D. *Feeling Good.* New York: Morrow, 1980.

BUTLER, R. N. "The Life Review: An Interpretation of Reminiscence in the Aged," *Psychiatry,* 26 (1963), 65–76.

BYRNE, D. "Interpersonal Attraction and Attitude Similiarity," *Journal of Abnormal and Social Psychology,* 62 (1961), 713–15.

CAMPBELL, D. P. *Handbook for the Strong Vocational Interest Blank.* Stanford, Cal.: Stanford University Press, 1971.

CAREY, R. G. "Living until Death: A Program of Service and Research for the Terminally Ill," in E. Kübler-Ross, *Death: The Final Stage of Growth.* Englewood Cliffs, N.J.: A Spectrum Book/Prentice-Hall, 1975.

CARLSON, E. R. "The Affective Tone of Psychology," *Journal of General Psychology,* 75 (1966), 65–78.

CARTWRIGHT, R. D. "Happy Endings for our Dreams," *Psychology Today* (December 1978), pp. 66–76.

CERRA, F. "Study Finds College Women Still Aim for Traditional Jobs," *The New York Times,* May 11, 1980, p. 46.

CHEIN, I. *The Science of Behavior and the Image of Man.* New York: Basic Books, Inc., 1972.

CLAYTON, P. J., J. A. HALIKES, and W. L. MAURICE. "The Bereavement of the Widowed," *Diseases of the Nervous System,* 32 (1971), 9, 597–604.

COLE, S. "Send Our Children to Work?" *Psychology Today* (July 1980), pp. 44–68.

COLEMAN, J. C., and C. L. HAMMEN. *Contemporary Psychology and Effective Behavior.* Glenview, Ill.: Scott, Foresman, 1974.

COLEMAN, J. C., and W. E. BROEN. *Abnormal Psychology and Modern Life.* Glenview, Ill.: Scott, Foresman, 1972.

COLLINS, J. K. "Adolescent Dating Intimacy: Norms and Peer Expectations," *Journal of Youth and Adolescence,* 3 (1974), 317–328.

CONSTANTINE, L., and J. CONSTANTINE. "Where Is Marriage Going?" *The Futurist,* 46 (April 1970).

COOMBS, R. H., and W. KENKEL. "Sex Differences in Dating Aspirations and Satisfaction with Computer-selected Partners," *Journal of Marriage and the Family,* 28 (1966), 62–66.

COOPERSMITH, S. *Antecedents of Self-Esteem.* San Francisco: W. H. Freeman and Company Publishers, 1967.

COSTA, P. T., and R. R. McCRAE. "Still Stable after All These Years: Personality as a Key to Some Issues in Adulthood and Old Age," in P. B. Baltes and O. G. Brim (eds.), *Lifespan Development and Behavior,* Vol. 3. New York: Academic Press, 1980.

COTTRELL, F., and R. C. ATCHLEY. *Women in Retirement: A Preliminary Report.* Oxford, Ohio: Scripps Foundation, 1969.

CRITTENDEN, A. "One Life, 10 Jobs," *The New York Times,* November 23, 1980.

CROOKS, R., and K. BAUR. *Our Sexuality.* Menlo Park, Cal.: The Benjamin/Cummings Publishing Company, Inc., 1980.

CSIKSZENTMIHALYI, M., and R. GRAEF. "Feeling Free," *Psychology Today* (December 1979).

CUBER, J. F., and P. B. HARROFF. *Sex and the Significant Americans.* Baltimore: Penguin, 1965.

CUMMING, E., and W. H. HENRY. *Growing Old.* New York: Basic Books, 1961.

DANIELS, P., and K. WEINGARTEN. *Sooner or Later.* New York: W. W. Norton & Co., Inc., 1981.

DARWIN, C. *The Expression of Emotions in Man and Animals.* New York: Philosophical Library, 1872.

DAVISON, C., and J. M. NEALE. *Abnormal Psychology: An Experimental Clinical Approach.* New York: John Wiley, 1974.

DAVITZ, J. R. "A Dictionary and Grammar of Emotions," in M. B. Arnold (ed.), *Feelings and Emotion.* New York: Academic Press, 1970.

DEARMAN, N. B., and V. M. PLISKO (eds.). *The Condition of Education: 1979 Edition.* Washington, DC: U. S. Government Printing Office, 1979.

DEMENT, W. C. *Some Must Watch While Some Must Sleep.* San Francisco: W. H. Freeman & Company Publishers, 1974.

DEMPSEY, D. *The Way We Die.* New York: Macmillan, 1975.

DENNIS, W. "Creative Productivity between the Ages of 20 and 80 Years," *Journal of Gerontology,* 21 (1966), 1–8.

DENTLER, R. A. and P. PINEO. "Sexual Adjustment, Marital Adjustment and Personal Growth of Husbands: A Panel Analysis," *Marriage and Family Living* (February 1960), 45–58.

DERLEGA, V. J., and A. L. CHAIKIN. *Sharing Intimacy.* Englewood Cliffs, N.J.: Prentice-Hall, 1975.

DIEPOLD, J., JR., and R. D. YOUNG. "Empirical Studies of Adolescent Sexual Behavior: A Critical Review," *Adolescence,* 14 (1979), 45–64.

DINKLAGE, L. B. *Adolescent Choice and Decision-Making.* Cambridge, Mass.: Harvard University Press, 1966.

DION, K., E. BERSCHEID, and E. WALSTER. "What Is Beautiful Is Good," *Journal of Personality and Social Psychology,* 24 (1972), 285–290.

DRISCOLL, R., K. E. DAVIS, and M. E. LIPITZ. "Parental Interference and Romantic Love: The Romeo and Juliet Effect," *Journal of Personality and Social Psychology*, 24 (1972), 1–10.

DUTTON, D. G., and A. P. ARON. "Some Evidence for Heightened Sexual Attraction under Conditions of High Anxiety," *Journal of Personality and Social Psychology*, 30 (1974), 510–517.

EDWARDS, M., and E. HOOVER. "A Positive Vision of the Single Life," in A. Arkoff (ed.), *Psychology and Personal Growth* (2nd ed.). Boston: Allyn & Bacon, 1980.

EIBL-EIBESFELDT, I. *Ethology*. New York: Holt, Rinehart & Winston, 1970.

EISENSTADT, J. M. "Parental Loss and Genius," *American Psychologist* (March 1978), pp. 211–223.

EKMAN, P., and W. V. FRIESEN. "Constants across Cultures in the Face and Emotions," *Journal of Personality and Social Psychology*, 17 (1971), 124–129.

EKMAN, P., E. R. SORENSON, and W. V. FRIESEN. "Pancultural Elements in Facial Displays of Emotion," *Science*, 164 (1969), 86–88.

ELLIS, A., and R. A. HARPER. *A New Guide to Rational Living*. Englewood Cliffs, N.J.: Prentice-Hall, 1975.

EPSTEIN, S. "The Self-concept Revisited: Or a Theory of a Theory," *American Psychologist* (May 1973).

EPSTEIN, S., and W. D. FENZ. "Steepness of Approach and Avoidance Gradients in Humans as a Function of Experience: Theory and Experiment," *Journal of Experimental Psychology*, 70 (1965), 1–12.

ERIKSON, E. H. *Dimensions of a New Identity*. New York: W. W. Norton & Co., Inc., 1974.

ERIKSON, E. H. *Identity: Youth and Crisis*. New York: W. W. Norton & Co., Inc., 1968.

EYSENCK, H. J. "Introverts, Extroverts, and Sex," *Psychology Today* (January 1971), pp. 49–51, 82.

EYSENCK, H. J. "The Effects of Psychotherapy: An Evaluation," *Journal of Consulting Psychology*, 16 (1952), 319–24.

EYSENCK, H. J. *The Effects of Psychotherapy*. International Science Press, 1966.

FELT, J. W. "How to Be Yourself," *America*, May 25, 1968.

FERRARI, N. A. "Institutionalization and Attitude Change in an Aged Population." Unpublished doctoral dissertation, Western Reserve University, 1962. Reprinted in E. P. Seligman, *Helplessness*. San Francisco, Cal.: W. H. Freeman & Company Publishers, 1975.

FERREE, M. M. "The Confused American Housewife," *Psychology Today* (September 1976).

FESTINGER, L. *A Theory of Cognitive Dissonance*. Stanford, Cal.: Stanford University Press, 1957.

FISHER, S. *Body Consciousness*. Englewood Cliffs, N.J.: Prentice-Hall, 1973.

FISHER, S. *The Female Orgasm*. New York: Basic Books, 1973.

FLEMING, J. D. "What Mother Knows Best: If One Baby's Nice, What's Wrong with Two?" *Psychology Today* (May 1975).

FOLTZ, D. "Psychologists in the Media," *APA Monitor* (May 1980).

FOX, C. A., et al. "Studies on the Relationship between Plasma Testosterone Levels and Human Sexual Activity," *Journal of Endocrinology*, 52 (1972), 51–58.

FRANK, J. D. "The Demoralized Mind," *Psychology Today* (April 1973a).

FRANK, J. D. *Persuasion and Healing*. Baltimore, Md.: Johns Hopkins University Press, 1973b.

FRANKL, V. E. *From Death-Camp to Existentialism*. Boston: Beacon Press, 1959.

FRANKLIN, B. *The Autobiography of Benjamin Franklin*. Spencer Press, n.d.

FRASER, S., and I. FUJITOMI. "Perceived Prior Compliance, Psychological Reactance, and Altruistic Contributions," *Proceedings of the*

80th Annual Convention of the American Psychological Association (1972), 247–248.

FREUD, S. *New Introductory Lectures on Psychoanalysis*, J. Strachey (trans.). New York: W.W. Norton & Co., Inc., 1965.

FREUD, S. *The Ego and the Id*, Joan Riviere (trans.). London: The Hogarth Press, Ltd., 1957.

FREUD, S. *Collected Papers*, J. Strachey (ed.). New York: Basic Books, 1959.

FRIEDMAN, H. J. "Patient Expectancy and Symptom Reduction," *Archives of General Psychiatry*, 8 (1963), 61–67.

FRIEDMAN, M., and R. F. ROSENMAN. *Type A Behavior and Your Heart*. New York: Knopf, 1974.

FROMM, E. *The Art of Loving*. New York: Harper & Brothers Publishers, 1956.

GALLUP, G. *Public Opinion 1972-1977*, Vol. I. Wilmington: Scholarly Resources, Inc., 1978.

GARTRELL, N., and D. MOSBACHER. Unpublished study; reported by C. T. Cory in "Newsline," *Psychology Today* (November 1979), p. 29.

GEBHARD, P. H. "Factors in Marital Orgasm," *Journal of Social Issues*, 22 (1966), 2, 88–95.

GELATT, H. B., V. VARENHORST, and R. CAREY. *Deciding*. New York: College Entrance Examination Board, 1972.

GERGEN, K. F. "Multiple Identity: The Healthy, Happy Human Being Wears Many Masks," *Psychology Today* (May 1972), pp. 31–35, 64–65.

GERGEN, K. F. *The Concept of Self*. New York: Holt, Rinehart & Winston, 1971.

GIBSON, J. E. "The Best Years of Your Life," *Family Weekly*, April 17, 1977.

GILMORE, J. V. "Parental Influences on Academic Achievement," *Normline*, 2 (1969), 2, 1–4.

GINZBERG, E. "Toward a Theory of Occupational Choice: A Restatement," *Vocational Guidance Quarterly*, 20 (1972), 169–176.

GLICK, I. O., R. S. WEISS, and G. M. PARKES. *The First Year of Bereavement*. New York: John Wiley, 1974.

GLICK, P. C. "Children of Divorced Parents in Demographic Perspective," *Journal of Social Issues*, 35 (1979), 4, 170–182.

GODENNE, G. D. "Sex and Today's Youth," *Adolescence*, 9 (1974), 67–72.

GOLDIAMOND, I. "Self-control Procedures in Personal Behavior Problems," *Psychological Reports*, 17 (1965), 851–868.

GOLDSTEIN, A. P. "Relationship-enhancement Methods," in F. H. Kanfer and A. P. Goldstein (eds.), *Helping People Change*. New York: Pergamon Press, 1975.

GOLDSTEIN, B. *Human Sexuality*. New York: McGraw-Hill, 1976.

GOLEMAN, D. "Staying Up: The Rebellion against Sleep's Gentle Tyranny," *Psychology Today* (March 1982), pp. 24–35.

GOLLADAY, M. A., and J. NOELL (eds.). *The Condition of Education: 1978 Edition*. Washington, DC: U. S. Government Printing Office, 1978.

GOODING, J. "The Fraying White Collar," *Fortune* (December 1970), pp. 78–81, 108.

GOODMAN, M. "Expressed Self-acceptance and Interpersonal Needs: A Basis for Mate Selection," in J. Heiss (ed.), *Family Roles and Interaction*. Chicago: Rand McNally College Publishing Company, 1976.

GORDON, S. "But Where Is Sex Education?" *APA Monitor* (November 1977), p. 13.

GORDON, T. *Parent Effectiveness Training*. New York: Peter H. Wyden, Inc., 1970.

GOTTMAN, J. M., and A. L. PORTERFIELD. "Communication Competence in the Non-verbal Behavior of Married Couples," *Journal of Marriage and the Family*, 43 (1981), 4, 817–824.

GOULD, R. *Transformations*. New York: Simon & Schuster, 1978.

GOVE, W. R., and J. F. TUDOR. "Adult Sex Roles and Mental Illness," *American Journal of Sociology*, 78 (1973).

GRAHAM, B. "Loneliness: How It Can Be Cured," *Reader's Digest* (October 1969), 135–138.

GRAYBILL, D. "Relationship of Maternal Child-rearing Behaviors to Children's Self-esteem," *Journal of Psychology,* 100 (1978), 1, 45–47.

GREELEY, A. M. "The State of the Nation's Happiness," *Psychology Today* (January 1981).

GREENWALD, H. "Decision Therapy," *Personal Growth* (January 1974).

GREENWALD, H. *Direct Decision Therapy.* San Diego, Cal.: Edits Publishers, 1973.

GRIBBONS, W. D., and P. R. LOHNES. *Career Development from Age 13 to Age 25.* Washington, DC: U. S. Department of Health, Education and Welfare, 1969.

GRIBBONS, W. D., and P. R. LOHNES. *Emerging Careers.* New York: Teachers College, Columbia University, 1968.

GROSS, M. L. *The Psychological Society.* New York: Random House, 1978.

GRUEN, W. "A Study of Erikson's Theory of Ego Development," in B. L. Neugarten and associates (eds.), *Personality in Middle and Late Life.* New York: Atherton Press, 1964.

GUARDO, C., and J. BOHAN. Personal communication between authors, 1973; found in Judith E. Gallatin, *Adolescence and Individuality.* New York: Harper & Row, Pub., 1975.

GUBRIUM, J. F. "Marital Desolation and the Evaluation of Everyday Life in Old Age," *Journal of Marriage and the Family,* 36 (1974), 107–113.

GUNDERSON, M. P., and J. L. McCARY. "Sexual Guilt and Religion," *Family Coordinator,* 28 (1979), 353–357.

GURIN, G., J. VEROFF, and S. FELD. *Americans View Their Mental Health.* New York: Basic Books, 1960.

HAAN, N., and D. DAY. "A Longitudinal Study of Change and Sameness in Personality Development: Adolescence to Later Adulthood," *International Journal of Aging and Human Development,* 5 (1974), 11–39.

HAAS, L. "Domestic Role Sharing in Sweden," *Journal of Marriage and the Family,* 43 (1981), 4, 957–967.

HACKETT, T. P., and N. H. CASSEM. "Psychological Reactions to Life-threatening Illness—Acute Myocardial Infarction," in H. S. Abram (ed.), *Psychological Aspects of Stress.* Springfield, Ill.: Charles C Thomas, 1970.

HALEY, J. *Leaving Home.* New York: McGraw-Hill, 1980.

HALL, J. "Decisions, Decisions, Decisions," *Psychology Today* (November 1971).

HARITON, E. B. "The Sexual Fantasies of Women," *Psychology Today* (March 1973), pp. 39–44.

HARRIS, T. A. *I'm Ok—You're OK.* New York, Harper & Row, Pub., 1967.

HARTLEY, D., H. B. ROBACK, and S. L. ABRAMOWITZ. "Deterioration Effects in Encounter Groups," *American Psychologist,* Vol. 31 (March 1976).

HARTMANN, E. L. *The Functions of Sleep.* New Haven, Conn.: Yale University Press, 1973.

HARVEY, J. H., B. HARRIS, and R. D. BARNES. "Actor-observer Differences in the Perceptions of Responsibility and Freedom," *Journal of Personality and Social Psychology,* 32 (1975), 22–28.

HARVEY, J. H., and J. M. JELLISON. "Determinants of the Perception of Choice: Number of Options and Perceived Time in Making a Selection," *Memory and Cognition,* 2 (1974), 539–544.

HEIMAN, J. R. "Women's Sexual Arousal," *Psychology Today* (April 1975), pp. 91–94.

HELSING, K. J., M. SZKLO, and G. W. COMSTOCK. "Factors Associated with Mortality after Widowhood," *American Journal of Public Health,* 71 (August 1981), 802–809.

HENDIN, D. *Death as a Fact of Life.* New York: W. W. Norton & Co., Inc., 1973.

HENDRICKS, J. H., and C. D. HENDRICKS. *Aging in Mass Society.* Cambridge, Mass.: Winthrop, 1977.

HERMANS, H. J. M., J. J. F. LAAK, and C. J. M. PIET. "Achievement Motivation and Fear of Failure in Family and School," *Developmental Psychology,* 6 (1972), 520–528.

HERON, W. "Cognitive and Physiological Effects of Perceptual Isolation," in P. Solomon et al. (eds.), *Sensory Deprivation*. Cambridge, Mass.: Harvard University Press, 1961.

HILLIX, W. A., H. HARARI, and D. A. MOHR. "Secrets," *Psychology Today* (September 1979), pp. 71–76.

HITE, S. *The Hite Report*. New York: Macmillan, 1976.

HODGSON, J. W., and J. L. FISCHER. "Sex Differences in Identity and Intimacy Development in College Youth," *Journal of Youth and Adolescence*, 8 (1979), 37–50.

HOFFMAN, L. W. "Changes in Family Roles, Socialization and Sex Differences," *American Psychologist*, 32 (1977), 8, 644–657.

HOFFMAN, L. W. "Fear of Success in 1965 and 1974: A Follow-up Study," *Journal of Consulting and Clinical Psychology*, 45 (1977), 310–321.

HOFFMAN, L. W., and J. D. MANIS. "The Value of Children in the United States: A New Approach to the Study of Fertility," *Journal of Marriage and the Family*, 41 (1979), 583–596.

HOGAN, R. A., and J. H. KIRCHNER. "Implosive, Eclectic, Verbal and Bibliotherapy in the Treatment of Fears of Snakes," *Behavior Research and Therapy*, 6 (1968).

HOGAN, R., and D. SCHROEDER. "Seven Biases in Psychology," *Psychology Today* (July 1981), pp. 8–14.

HOLLAND, J. L. *Making Vocational Choices*. Englewood Cliffs, N.J.: Prentice-Hall, 1973.

HOLMES, T. H., and M. MASUDA. "Psychosomatic Syndrome," *Psychology Today* (April 1972).

HOLMES, T. H., and R. H. RAHE. "The Social Readjustment Rating Scale," *Journal of Psychosomatic Research*, 11 (1967), 213–218.

HONZIK, M. P., and J. W. MACFARLANE. "Personality Development and Intellectual Functioning from 21 Months to 40 Years." Paper presented at the American Psychological Association Symposium on Maintenance of Intellectual Functioning with Advancing Years, Miami Beach, Florida, 1970. Reprinted in L. E. Troll, *Early and Middle Adulthood*. Monterey, Cal.: Brooks/Cole, 1975.

HORNER, M. S. "Toward an Understanding of Achievement-related Conflicts in Women," *Journal of Social Issues*, 28 (1972), 157–175.

HORROCKS, J. E. *The Psychology of Adolescence* (4th ed.). Boston: Houghton Mifflin Company, 1976.

HOULT, P. P., and M. C. SMITH. "Age and Sex Differences in the Number and Variety of Vocational Choices, Preferences and Aspirations," *Journal of Occupational Psychology*, 51 (1978), 2, 119–125.

HOWARD, K. I., and D. E. ORLINSKY. "Psychotherapeutic Processes," in P. Mussen and M. Rosenzweig (eds.), *Annual Review of Psychology: XXIII*. Palo Alto, Cal.: Annual Reviews, 1972.

HOWARD, S. M., and J. F. KUBIS. "Ego Identity and Some Aspects of Personal Adjustment," *Journal of Psychology*, 58 (1964), 459–466.

HUNT, B., and M. HUNT. *Prime Time*. New York: Stein & Day, 1975.

HUNT, M. "The Limits of Intimacy," in A. Arkoff (ed.), *Psychology and Personal Growth* (2nd ed.). Boston: Allyn & Bacon, 1980.

HUNT, M. *Sexual Behavior in the 1970s*. Chicago: Playboy Press, 1974.

HYDE, J. S., and B. G. ROSENBERG. *Half the Human Experience*. Lexington, Mass.: Heath, 1976.

IZARD, C. E. *Human Emotions*. New York: Plenum, 1977.

IZARD, C. E., and S. CAPLAN. "Sex Differences in Emotional Responses to Erotic Literature," *Journal of Counseling and Clinical Psychology*, 42 (1974), 468.

JACKSON, E. "On the Wise Management of Grief." Paper for a Foundation of Thanatology conference, New York, November 2–3, 1973. Reprinted in D. Dempsey, *The Way We Die*. New York: Macmillan, 1975.

JACOBI, J. *The Psychology of C. G. Jung.* New Haven: Yale University Press, 1973.

JACOBS, L., E. BERSCHEID, and E. WALSTER. "Self-Esteem and Attraction," *Journal of Personality and Social Psychology,* 17 (1971), 84–91.

JAMES, W. *Talks to Teachers on Psychology and to Students on Some of Life's Ideals,* pp. 33–36. New York: Henry Holt & Company, 1899. Unaltered republication, New York: Dover, 1962.

JANIS, I. L. *Stress and Frustration.* New York: Harcourt Brace Jovanovich, Inc., 1971.

JANIS, I. L. "Groupthink," *Psychology Today* (November 1971), pp. 43–46.

JANIS, I. L., and L. MANN. *Decision Making.* New York: Free Press, 1977.

JESSOR, S. L., and R. JESSOR. "Transition from Virginity to Non-virginity among Youth: A Social-psychological Study Over Time," *Developmental Psychology,* 11 (1975), 473–484.

JEWELL, L. N. "Differential Responding to Anxiety: Are There 'Facilitators' and 'Debilitators'?" *Studies in Higher Education,* 95 (1968), 28–45.

JONGEWARD, D., and M. JAMES. *Winning With People.* Reading, Mass.: Addison-Wesley, 1973.

JOURARD, S. M. "Growing Experience and the Experience of Growth," in A. Arkoff (ed.), *Psychology and Personal Growth,* pp. 307–315. Boston: Allyn & Bacon, Inc., 1975.

JOURARD, S. M. *The Transparent Self.* New York: Van Nostrand Reinhold, 1971.

JOURARD, S. M., and T. LANDSMAN. *Healthy Personality* (4th ed.). New York: Macmillan, 1980.

JOUVET, M. "The Sleeping Brain," *Science Journal,* 3 (1967), 5, 105–111.

JUNG, C. G. Taped interview in R. I. Evans, *The Making of Psychology.* New York: Knopf, 1976.

JUNG, C. G. *The Undiscovered Self.* New York: Mentor Books, 1957.

KAATS, G. R., and K. E. DAVIS. "The Dynamics of Sexual Behavior of College Students," *Journal of Marriage and Family,* 32 (1970), 390–399.

KACERGUIS, M. A., and G. R. ADAMS. "Erikson Stage and Resolution: The Relationships between Identity and Intimacy," *Journal of Youth and Adolescence,* 9 (1980), 117–126.

KALISH, R. A. "Death and Dying in a Social Context," in R. Binstock and E. Shanas (eds.), *Handbook of Aging and Social Sciences.* New York: Van Nostrand Reinhold, 1976.

KALISH, R. A. *Late Adulthood: Perspectives on Human Development.* Monterey, Cal.: Brooks/Cole, 1975.

KALISH, R. A., and D. K. REYNOLDS. *Death and Ethnicity.* Los Angeles: University of Southern California Press, 1976.

KANFER, F. H., and J. S. PHILLIPS. *Learning Foundations of Behavior Therapy.* New York: John Wiley, 1970.

KANIN, E. J., and S. R. PARCELL. "Sexual Aggression: A Second Look at the Offended Female," *Archives of Sexual Behavior* (1977), 67–76.

KANTER, R. M. *Commitment and Community.* Cambridge, Mass.: Harvard University Press, 1972.

KASTENBAUM, R. J. *Death, Society and Human Experience* (2nd ed.). St. Louis: C. V. Mosby Company, 1981.

KATZ, J., et al. *No Time for Youth: Growth and Constraint in College.* San Francisco: Jossey-Bass, 1968.

KAUFMANN, W. "Do You Crave a Life without Choice?" *Psychology Today* (April 1973).

KELLER, S. "The Female Role: Constants and Change," in V. Franks and V. Burtle (eds.), *Women in Therapy.* New York: Brunner/Mazel, 1974.

KELLY, J. R. "Work and Leisure: A Simplified Paradigm," *Journal of Leisure Research,* 4 (1972), 50–62.

KENISTON, K. "Youth: A 'New' Stage of Life," *The American Scholar*, 39 (1970), 4, 631–654.

KEPHART, W. M. *The Family, Society, and the Individual* (4th ed.). Boston: Houghton Mifflin Company, 1977.

KIMBLE, C., and R. HELMREICH. "Self-esteem and the Need for Social Approval," *Psychonomic Science*, 26 (1972), 339–342.

KIMMEL, D. C. *Adulthood and Aging*. New York: John Wiley, 1974.

KIMMEL, D. C., K. F. PRICE, and J. W. WALKER. "Retirement Choice and Retirement Satisfaction," *Journal of Gerontology*, 33 (1978), 4, 575–585.

KING, K., et al. "The Continuing Premarital Sexual Revolution among College Females," *Journal of Marriage and The Family*, 39 (1977), 455–459.

KINKADE, K. "Commune: A Walden-Two Experiment," *Psychology Today* (January 1973), pp. 35–42, 90–93; (February 1973), pp. 71–82.

KINSEY, A. C., W. B. POMEROY, and C. E. MARTIN. *Sexual Behavior in the Human Male*. Philadelphia: Saunders, 1948.

KINSEY, A. C., W. B. POMEROY, C. E. MARTIN, and P. GEBHARD. *Sexual Behavior in the Human Female*. Philadelphia: Saunders, 1953.

KRAUT, R. E., and R. E. JOHNSON. "Social and Emotional Messages of Smiling: An Ethological Approach," *Journal of Personality and Social Psychology*, 39 (1979), 9, 1539–1553.

KÜBLER-ROSS, E. *Death*. Englewood Cliffs, N.J.: Prentice-Hall, 1975.

KULIK, J. A., and J. HARACKIEWICZ. "Opposite-sex Interpersonal Attraction as a Function of the Sex Roles of the Perceiver and the Perceived," *Sex Roles*, 5 (1979), 4, 443–452.

KUNZ, P. R., and J. SUMMERS. "A Time to Die: A Study of Birthdays and Time of Death," *Omega: Journal of Death and Dying*, 1980.

KURASH, C. Reported in D. Goleman, "Leaving Home: Is There a Right Time to Go?" *Psychology Today* (August 1980), pp. 56, 59.

LACY, W. B., and J. HENDRICKS. "Developmental Models of Adult Life: Myth or Reality," *International Journal of Aging and Human Development*, 11 (1980), 2, 89–110.

LALLJEE, M., and M. COOK. "Uncertainty in First Encounters," *Journal of Personality and Social Psychology*, 26 (1973), 1, 137–141.

LANDIS, J. T. "Social Correlates of Divorce or Nondivorce among the Unhappy Married," in R. E. Albrecht and W. Bock (eds.), *Encounter: Love Marriage and Family*. Boston: Holbrook Press, 1975.

LANGER, E. J. "Automated Lives," *Psychology Today* (April 1982), pp. 60–71.

LAO, R., W. UPCHURCH, B. CORWIN, and W. GROSSNICKLE. "Biased Attitudes toward Females as Indicated by Ratings of Intelligence and Likability," *Psychological Reports*, 37 (1975), 1315–1320.

LAWS, J. L., and P. SCHWARTZ. *Sexual Scripts*. Hinsdale, Ill.: Dryden Press, 1977.

LAZARUS, A. A. "Has Behavior Therapy Outlived its Usefulness?" *American Psychologist*, 32 (1977), 550–554.

LAZARUS, R. S. "Little Hassles Can Be Hazardous to Health," *Psychology Today* (July 1981), pp. 58–62.

LECKER, S. *Family Therapies*, in B. Wolman (ed.), *The Therapist's Handbook*. New York: Van Nostrand Reinhold, 1976.

LEDERER, W. J., and D. D. JACKSON. *The Mirages of Marriage*. New York: W. W. Norton & Co., Inc., 1968.

LEE, J. A. "The Styles of Loving," *Psychology Today* (October 1974).

LERNER, R. M., and S. A. KARABENICK. "Physical Attractiveness, Body Attitudes and Self-concept in Late Adolescents," *Journal of Youth and Adolescence*, 3 (1974), 307–316.

LERNER, R. M., J. B. ORLOS, and J. R. KNAPP. "Physical Attractiveness, Physical Effectiveness, and Self-concept in Late Adolescence," *Adolescence*, 11 (1976), 313–326.

LEVIN, R. J. "The Redbook Report on Premarital and Extramarital Sex," *Redbook Magazine,* October 1975, pp. 38–44, 190–192.

LEVIN, R. J., and A. LEVIN. "Sexual Pleasure: The Surprising Preferences of 100,000 Women," *Redbook Magazine,* September 1975, pp. 51–58.

LEVINGER, G. "Sources of Marital Dissatisfaction among Applicants for Divorce," *American Journal of Orthopsychiatry,* 36 (1966), 803–807.

LEVINSON, D. J. et al. *The Seasons of a Man's Life.* New York: Knopf, 1978.

LIBERMAN, R. P., and E. E. RASKIN. "Depression: A Behavioral Formulation," *Archives of General Psychiatry* (June 1971).

LIEBERMAN, M. A. "Group Methods," in F. H. Kanfer and A. P. Goldstein (eds.), *Helping People Change.* New York: Pergamon Press, 1975.

LIEBERMAN, M. A., I. D. YALOM, and M. B. MILES. *Encounter Groups: First Facts.* New York: Basic Books, 1973.

LINDAUER, M. S. "Pleasant and Unpleasant Emotions in Literature: A Comparison with the Affective Tone of Psychology," *Journal of Psychology,* 70 (1968), 55–67.

LOEW, C. A., H. GRAYSON, and G. H. LOEW (eds.). *Three Psychotherapies.* New York: Brunner/Mazel, 1975.

LONDON, P. *Beginning Psychology.* Homewood, Ill.: Dorsey Press, 1978.

LONDON, P. "From the Long Couch for the Sick to the Push Button for the Bored," *Psychology Today* (June 1974).

LOWENTHAL, M. F. "Some Potentialities of a Life-cycle Approach to the Study of Retirement," in F. M. Carp (ed.), *Retirement.* New York: Behavioral Publications, 1972.

LOWENTHAL, M. F., and D. CHIRIBOGA. "Transition to the Empty Nest," *Archives of General Psychiatry,* 26 (1972).

LOWRY, R. (ed.). *Dominance, Self-esteem, Self-actualization: Germinal Papers of A. H. Maslow.* Monterey, Cal.: Brooks/Cole, 1973.

LUBORSKY, L. "Comparative Studies of Psychotherapy—Is It True that Everybody Has Won and All Must Have Prizes?" Paper presented at Third Annual Meeting of the Society for Psychotherapeutic Research, Nashville, June 6, 1972.

LUBORSKY, L., et al. "Factors Influencing the Outcome of Psychotherapy: A Review of Quantitative Research," *Psychological Bulletin,* 75 (1971), 145–182.

LUCE, G. G. *Current Research on Sleep and Dreams.* Public Health Service Publications No. 1389. Bethesda, Md.: National Institute of Health, 1965.

LYNCH, J. J. *Broken Heart.* New York: Basic Books, 1979.

MAAS, H. S., and J. A. KUYPERS. *From Thirty to Seventy—A Forty-year Longitudinal Study of Adult Life Styles and Personality.* San Francisco: Jossey-Bass, 1975.

McCLELLAND, D. C. *Motivational Trends in Society.* New York: General Learning Press, 1971.

McCLELLAND, D. C. "Towards a Theory of Motive Acquisition," *American Psychologist,* 20 (1965), 321–333.

McCLELLAND, D. C., and R. I. WATSON. "Power Motivation and Risk-taking Behavior," *Journal of Personality,* 41 (1973), 121–139.

MACE, D. R. "Contemporary Issues in Marriage," in R. E. Albrecht and W. E. Bock (eds.), *Encounter: Love Marriage and Family.* Boston: Holbrook Press, 1975.

McKAIN, W. *Retirement Marriage.* Storrs Agricultural Experiment Station Monograph 3, University of Connecticut, 1969.

MACKLIN, E. D. "Cohabitation in College: Going Very Steady," *Psychology Today* (November 1974), pp. 53–59.

McNAIR, D. M., D. M. CALLAHAN, and M. M. LORR. "Therapist 'Type' and Patient Response to Psychotherapy," *Journal of Consulting Psychology,* 26 (1967), 425–429.

MADDI, S. R. *Personality Theories: A Comparative Analysis.* Homewood, Ill.: Dorsey Press, 1972.

MADDOX, G. L. "Themes and Issues in Sociological Theories of Human Aging," *Human Development,* 13 (1970), 17–27.

MADDOX, G. L. "Persistence of Life Styles among the Elderly: A Longitudinal Study of Patterns of Social Activity in Relation to Life Satisfaction," *Proceedings of the 7th International Congress of Gerontology,* Vienna, 6 (1966), 309–311.

MAHONEY, M. J., and C. E. THORESEN. *Self-Control: Power to the Person.* Monterey, Cal.: Brooks/Cole, 1974.

MANN, J., J. SIDMAN, and S. STARR. "Effects of Erotic Films on Sexual Behavior of Married Couples," *Technical Report of the Commission on Obscenity and Pornography,* Vol. 8. Washington, DC: U. S. Government Printing Office, 1971.

MANZ, W., and H. LUECK. "Influence of Wearing Glasses on Personality Ratings," *Perceptual and Motor Skills,* 27 (1968), 204.

MARCIA, J. E. "Development and Validation of Ego Identity Status," *Journal of Personality and Social Psychology,* 3 (1966), 551–558.

MARTINDALE, D. "Sweaty Palms in the Control Tower," *Psychology Today* (February 1977).

MASLOW, A. H. "Health as Transcendence of Environment," in T. J. Cottle, and P. Whitten (eds.), *Readings in Personality and Adjustment.* San Francisco: Canfield Press, 1978.

MASLOW, A. H. *The Farther Reaches of Human Nature.* New York: Viking, 1971.

MASLOW, A. H. *Motivation and Personality* (2nd ed.). New York: Harper & Row, Pub., 1970.

MASLOW, A. H. *Toward a Psychology of Being* (2nd ed.). New York: Van Nostrand Reinhold, 1968.

MASLOW, A. H. "A Theory of Metamotivation," *Journal of Humanistic Psychology,* 7 (1967), 2.

MASTERS, W. H., and V. F. JOHNSON. *The Pleasure Bond.* Boston: Little, Brown, 1974.

MASTERS, W. H., and V. F. JOHNSON. *Human Sexual Inadequacy.* Boston: Little, Brown, 1970.

MASTERS, W. H., and V. F. JOHNSON. *The Human Sexual Response.* Boston: Little, Brown, 1966.

MAY, R. "Freedom Determinism and the Future," *Psychology* (April 1977).

MEAD, M. "Marriage in Two Steps," in H. Otto (ed.), *The Family in Search of a Future.* New York: Appleton-Century-Crofts, 1971.

MEICHENBAUM, D. "Cognitive Factors in Behavior Modification: Modifying What People Say to Themselves." Paper presented at the Fifth Annual Meeting of the Association for the Advancement of Behavior Therapy, Washington, DC, 1971. Reprinted in M. J. Mahoney and C. E. Thoresen (eds.), *Self-Control: Power to the Person.* Monterey, Cal.: Brooks/Cole, 1974.

MENNINGER, K., M.D. *The Vital Balance.* New York: Viking, 1963.

METTEE, D. R. "Changes in Liking as a Function of the Magnitude and Effect of Sequential Evaluations," *Journal of Experimental Social Psychology,* 7 (1971), 157–172.

METTEE, D. R. "The True Discerner as a Potent Source of Positive Affect," *The Journal of Experimental Social Psychology,* 7 (1971), 292–303.

MILLER, M. F. "Childhood Experience Antecedents of Career Maturity Attitudes," *Vocational Guidance Quarterly,* 27 (1978), 2, 137–143.

MILLER, P. Y., and W. SIMON. "The Development of Sexuality in Adolescence," in J. Adelson (ed.), *Handbook of Adolescent Psychology.* New York: John Wiley, 1980.

MONTEIRO, L. A. Reported in "College Women and Self-esteem," *The New York Times,* December 10, 1978, p. 85.

MOODY, R. A., JR. *Reflections on Life After Life.* Atlanta: Mockingbird, 1977.

MOORE, J. "Loneliness: Personality, Self-discrepancy, and Demographic Variables." Unpublished doctoral dissertation, York University, Toronto, Canada, April, 1972.

MORGAN, J. "Survey Research Center Findings," in *Work in America.* Cambridge, Mass.: MIT Press, 1972.

MORRIS, R. J. "Fear Reduction Methods," in F. H. Kanfer and A. P. Goldstein (eds.), *Helping People to Change.* New York: Pergamon Press, 1975.

MORSE, S., J. GRUZEN, and H. REIS. "The 'Eye of the Beholder': A Neglected Variable in the Study of Physical Attractiveness." Unpublished manuscript, New York University, 1973. Reprinted in K. Gergen (ed.), *Social Psychology.* Del Mar, Cal.: CRM Books, 1974.

MURSTEIN, B. I. "Physical Attractiveness and Marital Choice," *Journal of Personality and Social Psychology,* 22 (1972), 8–12.

MURSTEIN, B. I. *Theories of Attraction and Love.* New York: Springer Publishing Company, 1971.

MYRICK, F. L. "Attitudinal Differences between Heterosexually and Homosexually Oriented Males and between Covert and Overt Male Homosexuals," *Journal of Abnormal Psychology,* 83 (1974), 81–86.

NAVRAN, L. "Communication and Adjustment in Marriage," *Family Process,* 6 (1967), 2, 173–184.

NEUGARTEN, B. L. "Personality and Aging," in J. E. Birren and K. W. Schaie (eds.), *Handbook of The Psychology of Aging.* New York: Van Nostrand Reinhold, 1977.

NEUGARTEN, B. L. "Adult Personality: Toward a Psychology of the Life Cycle," in B. L. Neugarten (ed.), *Middle Age and Aging.* Chicago: University of Chicago Press, 1968.

NEUGARTEN, B. L., and E. HALL. "Acting One's Age: New Rules for Old," *Psychology Today* (April 1980), pp. 66–80.

NEUGARTEN, B. L., J. W. MOORE, and J. C. LOWE. "Age Norms, Age Constraints, and Adult Socialization," *American Journal of Sociology,* 70 (1965), 6, 710–717.

NEWMAN, G., and C. R. NICHOLS. "Sexual Activities and Attitudes in Older Persons," *Journal of the American Medical Association,* 173 (1960), 33–35.

NEWMAN, H. F. "Vibratory Sensitivity of the Penis," *Fertility and Sterility,* 21 (1970), 11, 791–793.

NEWTON, M. "Trebly Sensuous Woman," *Psychology Today* (July 1971).

NISBETT, R., and L. ROSS. *Human Inference.* Englewood Cliffs, N.J.: Prentice-Hall, 1980.

NOETH, R. J., J. D. ROTH, and D. J. PREDIGER. "Student Career Development: Where Do We Stand?" *Vocational Guidance Quarterly,* 23 (1975), 210–218.

NOLAN, J. D. "Self-control Procedures in the Modification of Smoking Behavior," *Journal of Consulting and Clinical Psychology,* 32 (1968), 92–93.

NOTMAN, M. "Midlife Concerns of Women: Implications of the Menopause," *American Journal of Psychiatry,* 136 (1979), 1270–1274.

NOWLIS, V. "Mood, Behavior and Experience," in M. B. Arnold, (ed.), *Feelings and Emotions.* New York: Academic Press, 1970.

O'CONNELL, T. J., and W. E. SEDLACEK. *The Reliability of Holland's Self-directed Search for Educational and Vocational Planning.* College Park, Md.: University of Maryland, 1972.

O'NEILL, N., and G. O'NEILL. "Open Marriage: A Synergic Model," in *Annual Editions: Readings in Marriage and Family 76/77.* Guilford, Conn.: The Dushkin Publishing Group, Inc., 1976.

ORLOFSKY, J. L., J. E. MARCIA, and I. M. LESSER. "Ego Identity Status and the Intimacy versus Isolation Crisis of Young Adulthood," *Journal of Personality and Social Psychology,* 27 (February 1973), 2, 211–219.

OTTO, H. A. "New Light on Human Potential," in *Families of the Future,* Iowa State University Home Economics Department. Ames, Iowa: Iowa State University Press, 1972.

PALMORE, E. "Total Chance of Institutionalization among the Aged," *The Gerontologist,* 16 (1976), 504–507.

PALMORE, E. "Predicting Longevity: A Follow-up Controlling for Age," *The Gerontologist,* 9 (1969), 247–250.

PAM, A. "A Field Study of Psychological Factors in College Courtships." Unpublished doctoral dissertation, State University of New York at Buffalo, 1970.

PANDE, S. K., and J. J. GART. "A Method to Quantify Reciprocal Influence between Therapist and Patient in Psychotherapy," in J. Schlien, H. F. Hunt, J. D. Matarazzo, and C. Savage (eds.), *Research in Psychotherapy,* pp. 395–415. Washington, DC: American Psychological Association, 1968.

PARKES, C. M. *Bereavement.* London: Tavistock, 1972.

PARLEE, M. B., and the editors of *Psychology Today.* "The Friendship Bond," *Psychology Today* (October 1979).

PATTERSON, C. H. *Theories of Counseling and Psychotherapy.* New York: Harper & Row, Pub., 1973.

PATTISON, E. M. "The Living-Dying Process," in C. A. Garfield (ed.), *Psychosocial Care of the Dying Patient.* New York: McGraw-Hill, 1978.

PAUL, G. L. "Outcome of Systematic Desensitization. II. Controlled Investigations of Individual Treatment Technique Variations and Current Status," in C. M. Franks (ed.), *Behavior Therapy: Appraisal and Status.* New York: McGraw-Hill, 1969.

PEELE, S., and A. BRODSKY. "Love Can Be an Addiction," *Psychology Today* (August 1974).

PELLEGRINI, R. J. "Impressions of the Male Personality as a Function of Beardedness," *Psychology,* 10 (1973), 29–33.

PENNEBAKER, J. W., M. A. DYER, R. S. CAULKINS, D. L. LITOWITZ, P. L. ACKREMAN, D. B. ANDERSON, and K. M. MCGRAW. "Don't the Girls Get Prettier at Closing Time: A Country and Western Application to Psychology," *Personality and Social Psychology Bulletin,* 5 (1979), 1, 122–125.

PEPLAU, L. A., Z. RUBIN, and C. T. HILL. "Sexual Intimacy in Dating Relationships," *Journal of Social Issues,* 33 (1977), 86–109.

PEPLAU, L. A., Z. RUBIN, and C. T. HILL. "The Sexual Balance of Power," *Psychology Today* (November 1976), pp. 142–147, 151.

PERLMAN, D., A. C. GERSON, and B. SPINNER. "Loneliness among Senior Citizens: An Empirical Report," *Essence,* 2 (1978), 239–248.

PHILLIPS, D. P., and K. A. FELDMAN. "A Dip in Deaths before Ceremonial Occasions: Some New Relationships between Social Integration and Mortality," *American Sociological Review,* 38 (1973), 678–696.

PIETROPINTO, A., and J. SIMENAUER. *Beyond the Male Myth.* New York: Quadrangle, 1977.

PLECK, J. H. "Prisoners of Manliness," *Psychology Today* (September 1981), pp. 69–83.

PLECK, J. H. "The Male Sex Role: Definitions, Problems and Sources of Change," *Journal of Social Issues,* 32 (1976), 3, 155–164.

PLUTCHIK, R. *Emotion.* Homewood, Ill.: Learning Systems Company, 1975.

POGREBIN, L. C. *Growing Up Free.* New York: McGraw-Hill, 1980.

POPE, H., and C. W. MUELLER. "The Intergenerational Transmission of Marital Instability," in G. Levinger and O. C. Moles (eds.), *Divorce and Separation.* New York: Basic Books, 1979.

PREMACK, D. "Toward Empirical Behavioral Laws: Positive Reinforcement," *Psychological Review,* 66 (1959), 219–233.

RABOCH, J. "Men's Most Common Sex Problems," *Sexology* (November 1969), 60–63.

RAINWATER, L. *Family Design: Marital Sexuality, Family Size, and Contraception.* Chicago: Aldine, 1965.

RAUSH, H. L., et al. *Communciaton, Conflict, and Marriage.* San Francisco: Jossey-Bass, 1974.

RENWICK, P. A., E. E. LAWLER, and the *Psychology Today* staff. "What You Really Want from Your Job," *Psychology Today* (May 1978).

RHEINGOLD, H., and K. COOK. "The Content of Boys' and Girls' Rooms as an Index of Parents' Behavior," *Child Development,* 46 (1975), 2, 459–463.

RHYNE, D. "Bases of Marital Satisfaction among Men and Women," *Journal of Marriage and the Family,* 43 (1981), 4, 941–955.

RICE, B. "Call-in Therapy: Reach Out and Shrink Someone," *Psychology Today* (December 1981).

RIDLEY, C. A. "Exploring the Impact of Work Satisfaction and Involvement on Marital Interaction when Both Partners are Employed," *Journal of Marriage and the Family,* 35 (1973), 2, 229–237.

RISMAN, B., C. T. HILL, Z. RUBIN, and L. A. PEPLAU. "Living Together in College: Implications for Courtship," *Journal of Marriage and the Family,* 43 (1981), 1, 77–83.

ROBERTS, A. E., and W. L. ROBERTS. "Factors of Lifestyles of Couples Married over 50 Years." Paper presented at the annual meeting of the National Council on Family Relations, Salt Lake City, August 1975.

ROBERTS. E. J., K. KLINE, and J. GAGNON. *Family Life and Sexual Learning.* Cambridge, Mass.: Population Education, 1978.

ROGERS, C. R. "My Philosophy of Inter-personal Relationships and How It Grew," *Journal of Humanistic Psychology,* 13 (1973), 2.

ROGERS, C. R. *Freedom to Learn.* Columbus, Ohio: Chas. E. Merrill, 1969.

ROGERS, C. R. *On Becoming A Person.* Boston: Houghton Mifflin Company, 1961.

ROGERS, C. R. *Client-centered Therapy.* Boston: Houghton Mifflin Company, 1951.

ROGERS, C. R., and B. STEVENS, et al. *Person to Person.* Lafayette, Cal.: Real People Press, 1971.

ROGERS. D. *Adolescents and Youth* (4th ed.). Englewood Cliffs, N.J.: Prentice-Hall, 1981.

ROLLINS, B. C. and H. FELDMAN. "Marital Satisfaction over the Family Cycle," *Journal of Marriage and the Family* (February 1970), 20–28.

ROSENBERG, M. *Society and the Adolescent Self-image.* Princeton, N.J.: Princeton University Press, 1965.

ROSENTHAL, R., D. ARCHER, M. R. DiMATTEO, J. H. KOIVUMAKI, and P. L. ROGERS. "Body Talk and Tone of Voice: The Language Without Words," *Psychology Today* (September 1974), pp. 64–68.

RUBIN, L. B. *Women of a Certain Age.* New York: Harper & Row, Pub., 1979.

RUBIN, T. I. *The Angry Book.* New York: Macmillan, 1969.

RUBIN, Z. *Liking and Loving.* New York: Holt, Rinehart & Winston, 1973.

RUBINSTEIN, C. "Survey Report: How Americans View Vacations," *Psychology Today* (May 1980).

RUBINSTEIN, C. "Who Calls In? It's Not the Lonely Crowd," *Psychology Today* (December 1981).

RUBINSTEIN, C., P. SHAVER, and L. A. PEPLAU. "Loneliness," in N. Jackson (ed.), *Personal Growth and Behavior 82/83.* Guilford, Conn.: The Dushkin Publishing Group, Inc., 1982.

SABOM, M. *Recollections of Death.* New York: Harper & Row, Pub., 1981.

SAEGERT, S., W. SWAMP, and R. B. ZAJONC. "Exposure, Context and Interpersonal Attraction," *Journal of Personality and Social Psychology,* 25 (1973), 234–242.

SANDERS, J. S., and W. L. ROBINSON. "Talking and Not Talking about Sex: Male and Female Vocabularies," *Journal of Communication,* 29 (1979), 2, 22–30.

SATIR, V. *Conjoint Family Therapy.* Palo Alto, Cal.: Science and Behavior Books, 1967.

SCHACHTER, S. *Emotion, Obesity and Crime.* New York: Academic Press, 1971.

SCHACHTER, S. *The Psychology of Affiliation: Experimental Studies of the Sources of Gregari-*

ousness. Stanford, Cal.: Stanford University Press, 1959.

SCHACHTER, S., and J. SINGER. "Cognitive Social and Physiological Determinants of Emotional State," *Psychological Review*, 69 (1962), 379–399.

SCHAFFER, K. F. *Sex-role Issues in Mental Health*. Reading, Mass.: Addison-Wesley, 1980.

SCHAIE, K. W., and C. R. STROTHER. "The Effects of Time and Cohort Differences on the Interpretation of Age Changes in Cognitive Behavior," *Multivariate Behavioral Research*, 3 (1968), 259–294. In L. E. Troll, *Early and Middle Adulthood*. Monterey, Cal.: Brooks/Cole, 1975.

SCHENK, Q. F., and E. L. SCHENK. *Pulling Up Roots*. Englewood Cliffs, N.J.: Prentice-Hall, 1978.

SCHMALE, A. H. Noted in C. M. Parkes, *Bereavement*, pp. 18, 198. London: Tavistock, 1972.

SCHOFIELD, W. *Psychotherapy: The Purchase of Friendship*. Englewood Cliffs, N.J.: Prentice-Hall, 1964.

SCOTT, J. P. *Early Experience and the Organization of Behavior*. Belmont, Cal.: Brooks/Cole, 1968.

SEARS, D. O., and R. E. WHITNEY. *Political Persuasion*. Morristown, N.J.: General Learning Press, 1973.

SEEMAN, M. "The Urban Alienations: Some Dubious Theses from Marx to Marcuse," *Journal of Personality and Social Psychology*, 19 (1971), 135–143.

SELIGMAN, M. E. P. *Helplessness*. San Francisco: W. H. Freeman & Company Publishers, 1975.

SELYE, H., M.D. *Stress without Distress*. Philadelphia: Lippincott, 1974.

SERMAT, V. Personal communication to P. N. Middlebrook. 1972. Reprinted in P. N. Middlebrook, *Social Psychology and Modern Life*, p. 249. New York: Knopf, 1974.

SERMAT, V., and M. SMYTH. "Content Analysis of Verbal Communication in the Development of a Relationship: Conditions Influencing Self-disclosure," *Journal of Personality and Social Psychology*, 26 (1973), 332–346.

SHANAS, E. "Social Myth as Hypothesis: The Case of Family Relations of Old People," *The Gerontologist*, 19 (1979), 3–9.

SHAPIRO, H. D. "Do Not Go Gently . . ." *New York Times Magazine*, Feb. 6, 1977, 36–40.

SHAVER, P., and J. FREEDMAN. "Your Pursuit of Happiness," *Psychology Today* (August 1976), pp. 26–32.

SHEEHY, G. *Passages*. New York: Bantam, 1977.

SHERTZER, B. *Career Planning* (2nd ed.). Boston: Houghton Mifflin Company, 1981.

SHNEIDMAN, E. S. *Deaths of Man*. New York: Quadrangle, 1973.

SHNEIDMAN, E. S. "You and Death," *Psychology Today* (June 1971), pp. 43–45, 74–80.

SHOPE, D. "Why Virgins Make Happier Marriages," in K. C. W. Kammeyer (ed.), *Confronting the Issues*. Boston: Allyn & Bacon, 1975.

SHOSTROM, E. L. "Group Therapy: Let the Buyer Beware," *Psychology Today* (May 1969).

SILVERMAN, P. "Another Look at the Role of the Funeral Director." Paper for a Foundation of Thanatology conference, March 29–30, 1974. Reprinted in D. Dempsey, *The Way We Die*. New York: Macmillan, 1975.

SINGER, J. L. "Navigating the Stream of Conscousness: Research in Daydreaming and Related Inner Experience," *American Psychologist*, 30 (1975), 7, 727–738.

SINGER, J. N. "Sex Difference-similarities in Job Preference Factors," *Journal of Vocational Behavior*, 5 (1974), 357–365.

SKINNER, B. F. *About Behaviorism*. New York: Knopf, 1974.

SKINNER, B. F. *Beyond Freedom and Dignity*. New York: Bantam/Vintage, 1972.

SKINNER, B. F. *Science and Human Behavior*. New York: Macmillan, 1953.

SKINNER, B. F. *Walden Two.* New York: Macmillan, 1948.

SLOANE, R. B., A. H. CRISTOL, M. C. PEPERNIK, and F. R. STAPLES. "Role Preparation and Expectation of Improvement in Psychotherapy, *Journal of Nervous Mental Disorders,* 150 (1970), 18–26.

SLOANE, R. B., F. R. STAPLES, A. H. CRISTOL, N. J. YORKSTON, and K. WHIPPLE. *Psychotherapy versus Behavior Therapy.* Cambridge, Mass.: Harvard University Press, 1975.

SLOVIC, P., B. FISCHHOFF, and S. LICHTENSTEIN. "Risky Assumptions," *Psychology Today* (June 1980), pp. 44–48.

SMITH, G., and J. DEBENHAM. "Computer Automated Marriage Analysis," *American Journal of Family Therapy* 7 (1979) 1, 16–31.

SMITH, K. "The Homophobic Scale," in G. Weinberg, *Society and the Healthy Homosexual.* New York: Anchor, 1973.

SNYDER, C. R. "The Uniqueness Mystique," *Psychology Today* (March 1980), pp. 86–90.

SORENSEN, R. C. *Adolescent Sexuality in Contemporary America.* New York: World Publishing Company, 1973.

SPANIER, G. B. "Romanticism and Marital Adjustment," *Journal of Marriage and the Family* (August 1972), pp. 486–487.

SPENCE, J. T. "Achievement and Achievement Motives." Paper presented at meeting of the American Psychological Association, New York, 1979. Reprinted in Z. Rubin and E. B. McNeil, *The Psychology of Being Human* (3rd ed.). New York: Harper & Row, Pub., 1981.

SPENCE, J., and R. HELMREICH. *Masculinity and Femininity.* Austin: University of Texas Press, 1978.

STEINER, I. D. "The Illusion of Freedom is No Mirage," *Psychology Today* (August 1973), pp. 51–55.

STETSON, D. "Work Innovations Improving Morale," *The New York Times,* September 20, 1981.

STEVENS-LONG, J. *Adult Life.* Palo Alto, Cal.: Mayfield, 1979.

STOTLAND E., and R. E. DUNN. "Empathy, Self-esteem and Birth Order," *Journal of Abnormal and Social Psychology,* 66 (1970), 532–540.

STOUFFER, S., E. SUCHMAN, L. De VINNEY, S. A. STAR, and R. WILLIAMS. *The American Soldier: Vol. I., Adjustment During Army Life.* Princeton, N.J.: Princeton University Press, 1949.

STRAUS, M. A. "Leveling, Civility, and Violence in the Family," in K. C. W. Kammeyer (ed.), *Confronting the Issues.* Boston: Allyn & Bacon, 1975.

STREIB, G. F., and C. SCHNEIDER. *Retirement in American Society.* Ithaca: Cornell University Press, 1971.

STRUPP, H. H., R. E. FOX, and K. LESSLER. *Patients View their Psychotherapy.* Baltimore: The Johns Hopkins University Press, 1969.

STRUPP, H. H., and S. W. HADLEY. "Specific versus Nonspecific Factors in Psychotherapy: A Controlled Study of Outcome," *Archives of General Psychiatry,* 36 (1979), 1125–1136.

SULLIVAN, K., and A. SULLIVAN. "Adolescent-parent Separation," *Developmental Psychology,* 16 (1980), 2, 93–99.

SUNDBERG, N. D., L. E. TYLER, and J. R. TAPLIN. *Clinical Psychology: Expanding Horizons* (2nd ed.). Englewood Cliffs, N.J.: Prentice-Hall, 1973.

SUPER, D. E. *Measuring Vocational Maturity for Counseling and Evaluation.* Washington, DC: National Vocational Guidance Association, 1974.

SUPER, D. E. *The Psychology of Careers.* New York: Harper & Row, Pub., 1967.

SWENSEN, C. H., R. W. ESKEW, and K. A. KOHLHEPP. "Stage of Family Cycle, Ego Development, and the Marriage Relationship," *Journal of Marriage and the Family,* 43 (1981), 4, 841–853.

TAVRIS, C. "You Are What You Do," in N. Jackson (ed.), *Personal Growth and Behavior 82/*

83. Guilford, Conn.: The Dushkin Publishing Company Inc., 1982.

TAVRIS, C. "Men and Women Report their Views on Masculinity," *Psychology Today* (January 1977), pp. 35–42, 82.

TAVRIS, C., and T. E. JAYARATNE. "How Happy Is Your Marriage? What 75,000 Wives say about their Most Intimate Relationship," *Redbook Magazine*, June 1976, pp. 90–92, 132.

TERKEL, S. *Working*. New York: Pantheon, 1972.

THIBAUT, J. W., and H. H. KELLEY. *The Social Psychology of Groups*. New York: John Wiley, 1959.

THOMPSON, D. F., and L. MELTZER. "Communication of Emotional Intent by Facial Expression," *Journal of Abnormal and Social Psychology*, 68 (1964), 129–135.

TILLICH, P. *The Courage To Be*. New Haven: Yale University Press, 1952.

TOFFLER, A. *Future Shock*. New York: Bantam, 1971.

TOUHEY, J. C. "Comparison of Two Dimensions of Attitude Similarity on Heterosexual Attraction," *Journal of Personality and Social Psychology*, 23 (1972), 8–10.

TRESSMER, D. "Fear of Success: Popular but Unproved," *Psychology Today* (March 1974), pp. 82–85.

TROLL, L. E. *Early and Middle Adulthood*. Monterey, Cal.: Brooks/Cole, 1975.

UDRY, J. RICHARD. *The Social Context of Marriage* (3rd ed.). Philadelphia: Lippincott, 1974.

U. S. BUREAU OF THE CENSUS. *Social Indicators III*. Washington, DC: U.S. Government Printing Office, 1980.

U. S. BUREAU OF THE CENSUS. *Statistical Abstract of the United States 1981* (102nd ed.). Washington, DC: U. S. Government Printing Office, 1981.

U. S. BUREAU OF THE CENSUS. *Statistical Abstract of the United States 1980* (101st ed.). Washington, DC: U. S. Government Printing Office, 1980.

U. S. BUREAU OF LABOR, BUREAU OF LABOR STATISTICS. *Occupational Outlook Handbook: 1980–1981*. Washington, DC: U. S. Government Printing Office, 1980.

VEEVERS, J. E. "Voluntary Childless Wives: An Exploratory Study," *Sociology and Social Research*, 57 (1973), 356–366.

VERHAGE, R. "Intelligence and Age in a Dutch Sample," *Human Development*, 8 (1965), 238–245.

VEROFF, J., E. DOUVAN, and R. A. KULKA. *The Inner American*. New York: Basic Books, 1981.

VEROFF, J., R. A. KULKA, and E. DOUVAN. *Mental Health in America*. New York: Basic Books, 1981.

WALLERSTEIN, J. S., and J. B. KELLY. *Surviving the Break-up*. New York: Basic Books, 1980.

WALSTER, E., V. ARONSON, D. ABRAHAMS, and L. ROTTMANN. "Importance of Physical Attractiveness in Dating Behavior," *Journal of Personality and Social Psychology*, 4 (1966), 508–516.

WALSTER, E., E. BERSCHEID, and G. W. WALSTER. "New Directions in Equity Research," *Journal of Personality and Social Psychology*, 25 (1973), 151–76.

WANG, J. "Breaking Out of the Pain Trap," *Psychology Today* (July 1977).

WARD, R. A. *The Aging Experience*. Philadelphia: Lippincott, 1979.

WATERMAN, A. S., P. S. GEARY, and C. K. WATERMAN. "A Longitudinal Study of Changes in Ego Identity Status from the Freshman to the Senior Year at College," *Developmental Psychology*, 10 (1974), 387–392.

WATERMAN, A. S., and C. K. WATERMAN. "A Longitudinal Study of Changes in Ego Identity Status during the Freshman Year in College," *Developmental Psychology*, 5 (1971), 167–173.

WATSON, D. L., and R. G. THARP. *Self-Directed Behavior: Self-Modification for Personal Adjustment*. Monterey, Cal.: Brooks/Cole, 1972.

WEBB, W. B. *Sleep: The Gentle Tyrant.* Englewood Cliffs, N.J.: Prentice-Hall, 1976.

WEIDIGER, P. *Menstruation and Menopause.* New York: Knopf, 1976.

WEISS, J. M. "Psychological Factors in Stress and Disease," *Scientific American,* 226 (1972), 106.

WEITZMAN, B. "Behavior Therapy and Psychotherapy," *Psychological Review,* 74 (1967), 300–317.

WELKOWITZ, J., J. COHEN, and D. ORMEYER. "Value System Similarity: Investigation of Patient-therapist Dyads," *Journal of Consulting Psychology,* 31 (1967), 48–55.

WESTOFF, L. A. "Two-time Winners," *The New York Times Magazine,* August 10, 1975, pp. 10–15.

WHITE, G. L. "Jealousy and Partner's Perceived Motives for Attraction to a Rival," *Social Psychology Quarterly,* 44 (1981), 1, 24–30.

WICKLUND, R. A. *Freedom and Reactance.* Potomac, Md.: Lawrence Erlbaum Associates, Publishers, 1974.

WILLIAMS, R. L., and J. D. LONG. *Toward a Self-managed Life Style,* 2nd ed. Boston: Houghton Mifflin, 1979.

WILSON, G. T., and G. C. DAVISON, "A Road to Self-control," *Psychology Today* (October 1975), pp. 54–60.

WINCH, R. F. *The Modern Family* (3rd ed.). New York: Holt, Rinehart & Winston, 1971.

WINER, J. A., et al. "Sexual Problems in Users of a Student Mental Health Clinic," *Journal of Youth and Adolescence,* 6 (1977), 117–126.

WINTROB, R. M. "Hexes, Roots, Snake Eggs? MD versus Occult," *Medical Opinion,* 1 (1972), 7, 54–56.

WOLPE, J. *The Practice of Behavior Therapy.* New York: Pergamon Press, 1973.

WOODSON, R. "Hospice Care in Terminal Illness," in C. Garfield (ed.), *Psychosocial Care of the Dying Patient.* New York: McGraw-Hill, 1978.

WYLIE, R. C. *The Self-Concept* (rev. ed.). Lincoln: University of Nebraska Press, 1974.

YANKELOVICH, D. *New Rules.* New York: Random House, 1981.

YANKELOVICH, D. "The Meaning of Work," in J. M. Rosow (ed.), *The Worker and The Job.* Englewood Cliffs, N.J.: Prentice-Hall, 1974a.

YANKELOVICH, D. *The New Morality.* New York: McGraw-Hill, 1974b.

YANKELOVICH, SKELLY, and WHITE, INC. *Raising Children in a Changing Society.* Minneapolis, Minn.: General Mills, Inc., 1977.

YOGEV, S. "Do Professional Women Have Egalitarian Marital Relationships?" *Journal of Marriage and the Family,* 43 (1981), 4, 865–871.

ZELNIK, M., and J. F. KANTNER. "Sexual Activity, Contraceptive Use, and Pregnancy among Metropolitan-area Teenagers: 1971-1979," *Family Planning Perspectives,* 12 (1980), 5, 230–237.

ZELNIK, M., and J. F. KANTNER. "Sexual and Contraceptive Experiences of Young Unmarried Women in the United States: 1976 and 1971," *Family Planning Perspectives,* 9 (1977), 55–71.

ZIMBARDO, P. G., and R. FORMICA. "Emotional Comparison and Self-esteem as Determinants of Affiliation," *Journal of Personality,* 31 (1963), 141–162.

ZIMBARDO, P. G., P. A. PILKONIS, and R. M. NORWOOD. *The Silent Prison of Shyness.* Glenview, Ill.: Scott, Foresman, 1974.

ZIMBARDO, P. G., and F. L. RUCH. *Psychology and Life* (10th ed.). Glenview, Ill.: Scott, Foresman, 1980.

ZUCKERMAN, M. *Sensation Seeking.* New York: Halstead Press, 1979.

ZURCHER, L. A., JR. *The Mutable Self.* Beverly Hills, Cal.: Sage Publications, Inc., 1977.

Glossary

acting out: The unconscious mechanism by which we relieve anxiety or unpleasant tensions through expressing them in overt behavior.

actualization therapy: An approach that stresses self-actualization as the goal of psychotherapy.

adjustment: The process of changing ourselves and our circumstances to achieve a satisfactory relationship with others and our surroundings.

adulthood: The period of life from physical maturity on, consisting of a sequence of psychosocial changes throughout early, middle and late adulthood.

aging: A decline in the biological processes that come with advancing years, usually accompanied by appropriate psychosocial changes, increasing risk of illness and death.

androgyny: The combination of masculine and feminine traits and behaviors facilitating optimal adjustment and growth in both sexes, in contrast to stereotyped sex roles.

anger: The feeling of extreme displeasure, usually brought about by frustration of our needs and desires.

antecedents of behavior: Anything which immediately precedes a given behavior and which may contribute to it.

anxiety: A vague, unpleasant feeling warning us of impending threat or danger.

assertiveness training: A therapeutic strategy aimed at helping individuals express their personal rights more effectively through developing assertive skills.

avoidance training: Learning those behaviors which enable us to avoid unpleasant consequences, such as studying to avoid failing a test.

baseline data: Observations of habitual behavior that provide a basis of comparison in regard to learning new behavior.

behavior therapies: Those therapies aimed at helping the client change specific behaviors through action-oriented techniques.

bereavement: The process of adjusting to the experience of loss, especially the death of one's friends or loved ones.

body image: That part of the self-concept based on the individual's perception of his or her own body.

career: One's purposeful life pattern of work, as seen in the sequence of jobs held throughout one's life.

client-centered therapy: A form of psychotherapy developed by Rogers, which facilitates change through acceptance and empathetic understanding of the client's own experience and frame of reference.

climacteric: The loss of reproductive ability, occurring along with the menopause in women but over a longer period of time in men with a gradual reduction of fertile sperm.

coefficient correlation: A statistic showing the degree to which two sets of scores are related to each other.

cognitive theory of emotion: The view that our mental set and surroundings vitally affect the way we interpret our inner sensations and thus the emotions we feel.

cohabitation: Unmarried persons living together, sharing bed and board.

commune: Three or more persons who wish to live together and share a given style of life, with or without legal marriage.

compatibility: A congenial relationship between two or more persons based on their shared interests and satisfaction of needs.

compensation: The unconscious mechanism by which we cover up a sense of inferiority by exaggerated feelings of adequacy.

complementary need theory of mate selection: The view that individuals tend to select partners with traits or behaviors that are complementary to their own.

conflict: The felt pressure to respond simultaneously to two or more incompatible forces.

contingency management methods: A general term for a flexible treatment strategy using the various techniques of operant learning, such as positive reinforcement and shaping.

coping devices for minor stress: A variety of largely spontaneous responses which reduce one's felt tensions during stressful times, such as eating, drinking, crying, or vigorous physical exercise.

counseling: A help-giving process that facilitates changes in the client's attitudes and behaviors, similar to therapy. *(See psychotherapy.)*

death: The cessation of biological life, as measured by the absence of breathing, heartbeat, and electrical activity of the brain.

decision making: The process of gathering information about relevant alternatives and making an appropriate choice.

decision-making strategies: The variety of ways individuals go about making decisions, such as the impulsive, compliant, and intuitive strategies.

defense mechanisms: Unconscious, automatic mechanisms which protect us from the awareness of anxiety, thereby enabling us to maintain a sense of self-worth and adequacy in the face of threat.

denial: The unconscious mechanism by which we protect ourselves from unpleasant aspects of reality by refusing to perceive them.

denial of death: The characteristic attitude toward death in our society in which the subject of death is evaded, ignored, and denied.

desensitization: A method of controlling anxiety through learning to associate an incompatible response, such as relaxation, with the fear-provoking stimulus.

differential disengagement: The idea that the disengagement that accompanies aging occurs at different rates and degrees according to the roles a person plays.

direct decision therapy: The view that therapy is best aimed at helping clients see their problems in terms of previous decisions and choosing a more satisfying alternative.

disengagement theory: The idea that aging is normally accompanied by a decreasing involvement or engagement between individuals and society.

displacement: The unconscious mechanism by which we redirect unconscious impulses to less dangerous objects.

distress: Stress that affects us in an unpleasant or harmful way, such as excessive competition.

divorce: The legal dissolution of marriage, usually accompanied by psychological, social, and financial adjustments.

drive-reduction model of motivation: The view that we act mostly to reduce the tension of unmet needs.

ego: According to Freud, the rational, managerial part of personality that integrates the conflicting demands of the id, superego, and society.

emotion: A complex state of awareness involving inner sensations and outer expressions which has the power to motivate us to act.

emotional mood: A generalized emotional state such as elation or apathy that persists over a period of time, whether hours or days.

empathy: Experiencing another's attitudes or feelings through imaginative awareness, "as if" you were in that person's place.

empty nest: A popular phrase for the stage of adult development in which one's grown children have left home.

erogenous zones: Any part of the skin which when stroked brings pleasure and sexual arousal.

eustress: Sress that affects us in a stimulating or beneficial way, such as moderate aspirations for achievement.

euthanasia: A merciful, painless death as a way of ending a person's suffering, especially someone who is terminally ill.

existential therapy: An approach that emphasizes the client's capacity for growth and transcendence through affirmation of his or her personal values and free choice.

fantasy: The process of relieving unfulfilled desires through imaginary action, such as daydreaming. When this becomes excessive or a substitute for reality, fantasy tends to serve as a defense mechanism.

fantasy stage: According to Ginzberg, the stage in which vocational choices are based on imagination, mostly in childhood.

fight or flight response: A way of classifying emotional arousal in terms of whether it turns us against or away from something.

foreplay: Sexual stimulation for the purpose of increasing readiness for intercourse, including erotic caressing and handling of the genitals.

free association: A technique used in psychoanalysis in which the client is asked to say whatever comes to mind.

frustration: The blocking of our needs or desires or the absence of suitable goal objects to satisfy them.

general adaptation syndrome: Selye's view that humans tend to adapt to stress in three progressive stages: an initial alarm reaction, followed by a resistance stage, and finally exhaustion.

gestalt therapy: An approach that utilizes the here and now behavior to facilitate the client's integration of self.

good grief: The positive benefits that may result from grief as a learning experience.

grief: The intense emotional suffering associated by loss or misfortune, especially the death of a loved one. *(See bereavement.)*

group decision making: The process of reaching a joint decision which involves the drive for consensus and conformity in addition to the usual process of decision making.

group marriage: The situation of three or more people who consider themselves married to each other, as distinguished from individuals merely living together in cooperative households.

group therapies: Those forms of therapy in which a leader meets with a group of clients, including preexisting groups such as families and those consisting of strangers.

groupthink: The tendency for groups to reach compromise decisions because of the conformity and suppression of critical thought in groups.

growth model of motivation: Maslow's view that humans act out of survival and growth motives, with both kinds of motivation necessary for human fulfillment.

guilt: The emotion that follows the violation of our conscience or moral principles, involving self-reproach and apprehension over the fear of punishment.

helplessness: The subjective sense of being powerless in a given situation, especially as this is affected by one's past experience.

homeostasis: The tendency of organisms to maintain a steady state or level of physiological functioning.

homosexual behavior: Erotic stimulation and sexual activity with persons of the same sex.

hospice: A humane and supportive environment providing for a dignified death, such as a special home for terminally ill patients.

id: According to Freud, the unconscious reservoir of psychic energy derived from biological instincts.

ideal self: The self I would like to be, including my aspirations, moral ideals, and values.

identification: The unconscious act of attributing characteristics to ourselves which we perceive in others whom we admire. When characteristics so acquired serve to cover up one's own feelings of self-devaluation, identification may function as a defense mechanism.

implosion therapy: A technique that uses anxiety-provoking material in a way that eventually lessens the client's fear of a particular situation.

impression formation: The process of forming initial judgments about other people on the basis of such things as their appearance, dress, age, sex, and speech.

incompatible alternative behavior: Behavior that prevents its opposite from occurring, such as smiling prevents frowning.

inner freedom: The subjective sense of being free to determine one's own life over and above the outward choices available to us. *(See also perceived freedom.)*

insight therapies: Those types of therapy that facilitate change or growth through increasing the client's inner awareness or self-understanding.

insulation: The unconscious mechanism by which we protect ourselves from hurt by emotional withdrawal from others.

interpersonal attraction: Feelings of attraction toward others based on such things as physical proximity, similarity of social background and personality, mutual liking, and physical appearance.

intimacy: Interpersonal closeness between two or more persons, such as friends or lovers, which may or may not include physical, sexual intimacy.

learned helplessness: The subjective realization that your actions have little or no effect on the environment, frequently leading to passivity and depression.

leisure: Time free from work or duty that may be spent in recreative activities.

love: A complex emotional state accompanying our needs for attachment as well as the satisfaction of these needs. The term love is also used more generally, as in interpersonal intimacy.

marriage relationship: The personal relationship or companionship aspects of marriage, as distinguished from marriage as a legal role relationship.

masturbation: The act of manipulating the genitals or sex organs to produce pleasure, usually without the help of another person.

menopause: The cessation of menstrual cycles in a woman's life.

midlife transition: The period of reevaluation and adjustment at about 35 to 40 years of age accompanying the realization that life is half over.

modeling: A technique for modifying problem behavior in which a client observes and imitates an appropriate model performing the desired behavior.

motivation: The tendency toward goal-seeking behavior which results from inner conditions such as physiological or psychological needs.

motive: A specific goal-directed activity, such as the hunger motive to satisfy the need for food.

mutual accommodation: The willingness of two or more persons to empathize with each other and modify their own behavior when necessary for cooperation.

near-death experience: The distinctive state of recall associated with being brought back to life from the verge of death.

need: A state of tension or deprivation which arouses us to seek appropriate gratification.

nonverbal expression of emotion: Communicating emotions through various facial expressions and body language, with or without words.

occupation: The responsibilities and activities needed to perform given work tasks, as in the occupation of nursing.

open marriage: A concept of marriage that encourages the maximum personal freedom and growth of the partners without undermining their essential commitment to marriage.

operant learning: A type of learning that results from the application or withdrawal of rewards.

oral-genital sex: The stimulation of the penis or vulva by the lips or tongue of another person.

organismic model of personality: The notion that the human organism behaves as a unified whole of mind and body and is best understood as such.

orgasm: An extremely pleasurable peak of sexual activity, involving the release of tensions from sexual excitement, usually accompanied in the male by ejaculation.

paradox of freedom: The realization that we are inwardly free to choose the way we act, despite the fact that our lives are also shaped by other forces.

perceived freedom: The subjective sense of freedom one feels in a given situation.

personal growth: Change or development in a desired direction, including the fulfillment of one's inborn potential.

petting: The erotic caressing and fondling of another person, which may or may not culminate in orgasm.

phenomenology of growth: An account of the growth process as subjectively experienced by individuals themselves.

physiological motives: Motives stemming from bodily needs, such as hunger, thirst, and sleep.

precipitating stimuli: Anything that triggers or sets off a given sequence of behavior.

Premack principle: The principle by which a behavior that occurs with great frequency can be used to reinforce or strengthen a behavior that occurs with less frequency.

pressure: Inner or outer demands which constitute a form of stress, such as the pressure to succeed.

problem-solving approaches to stress: Attempts to modify stress directly, either through increasing our tolerance for stress or modifying the source of stress through assertiveness, withdrawal, or compromise.

projection: The unconscious mechanism by which we attribute our unacceptable desires or impulses to others.

psychic reactance: The defensive response of asserting our personal freedom all the more in the face of external threats and restrictions against it.

psychoanalysis: A form of psychotherapy developed by Freud, aimed at helping the client gain insight and mastery over unconscious conflicts.

psychological motives: Motives that are primarily learned and associated with our psychological well-being rather than with our physical survival, such as the striving for achievement.

psychotherapy: A helping process in which a trained therapist performs certain activities that will facilitate a change in the client's attitudes and behavior.

rational-emotive therapy: A form of psychotherapy developed by Ellis, in which the client is encouraged to replace irrational ideas with a more rational, problem-solving approach to life.

rationalization: The unconscious mechanism by which we attempt to justify our unacceptable behavior through "good" reasons.

reaction-formation: The unconscious attempt to control unacceptable desires by adopting conscious feelings and behaviors opposite to the repressed ones.

reactive depression: A state of depression that has presumably come about because of changes in the environment, sometimes known as exogenous depression.

realistic stage: According to Ginzberg, the stage in which vocational choices are based on a realistic assessment of our abilities and career options.

reality therapy: An approach that focuses on the client's ability to live responsibly in accordance with his or her own values.

reinforcers: Anything that strengthens a given behavior, such as attention.

repression: The automatic, unconscious denial of a feeling to awareness, which if consciously admitted would be threatening.

retirement: Withdrawal from regular occupational activity and status, usually because of the changes in age or health.

role: The expected behavior associated with a given position or status in society.

romantic love: Physical attraction and strong emotional attachment to a person of the opposite sex, with a marked tendency to idealize one's partner.

self-actualization: The process of fulfilling our inborn potential, involving an unconscious actualizing tendency as well as our self-conscious effort at growth.

self-concept: Generally defined as the overall pattern of self-perceptions as viewed by the individual himself or herself. *(See subjective self.)*

self-control: As used in this book, the individual's awareness and control of the various stimuli that influence personal behavior.

self-directed behavior modification: A step-by-step procedure for modifying a given behavior

through increasing awareness and control of the antecedents and consequences of the behavior.

self-disclosure: The voluntary disclosure of our deeper thoughts or feelings to others.

self-esteem: The sense of personal worth we associate with our self-concept.

self-identity: The sense of coherence between our past and present, private and public selves, as well as our sense of personal uniqueness.

sex drive: The desire or need for sexual activity, conditioned by biological forces and learning.

sex role: The complex of attitudes, expectations, and behaviors associated with maleness and femaleness, based in part on biological gender but heavily influenced by learning.

sexual arousal: The momentary level of sexual excitement resulting from a variety of sensual stimulation, such as sight, smell, and touching, including the genitals.

sexual intercourse: The penetration of the female vagina by the male penis, characteristically accompanied by pelvic thrusting and orgasm for one or both partners.

shaping: Applying reinforcement to every increment of behavior that approximates one's goal or target behavior.

singles: A general term designating various types of unmarried individuals, including young adults who have not yet married, older persons who probably will not marry, and the formerly married who are now divorced or widowed.

social exchange model: The view that human relationships are regulated by a fair exchange between the parties, or the mutual satisfaction of needs.

social selves: All those self-perceptions derived from our social roles and interactions with others.

stages of dying: According to Elizabeth Kübler-Ross, the view that individuals suffering from a terminal illness go through a series of stages in dying, such as denial, anger, bargaining, depression, and acceptance.

stereotyped sex roles: Widely held generalizations about the characteristics of males and females that exaggerate the differences between the sexes.

stress: Any adjustive demand, external or internal, that requires an adaptive response from us.

stress tolerance: The degree and duration of stress we can tolerate without becoming irrational and disorganized.

subjective self: The self I see myself to be.

superego: According to Freud, the part of personality that imposes constraints on the impulses of the id and ego.

suppression: The conscious and deliberate control of our emotions.

tentative stage: According to Ginzberg, the stage in which vocational choices are based on the adolescent's changing interests and values.

transference: In psychoanalysis, the tendency of clients to relate to their therapists the same way they did to other important authorities in their formative years, especially their parents.

transactional analysis model: The view that human relationships consist of transactions between different ego states (child, parent, adult) of the individuals involved, with the meaning of the transaction depending on the type of transaction.

trial marriage: Refers to proposals for a more flexible form of marriage, easier to enter and dissolve than conventional legal marriage.

unconditional positive regard: In client-centered therapy, this refers to the therapist's attitude of respect and acceptance toward the client.

undoing: The unconscious mechanism by which we attempt to do things to cover up unacceptable impulses or misbehavior, such as the excessive washing of hands to get rid of guilt.

unresolved grief: A psychological state in which your emotional reaction to loss remains suppressed and is often manifested in unexplained physical or psychological symptoms.

verbal expression of emotion: Communicating your emotions through appropriate words or sounds.

virgin: A person of either sex who has not experienced sexual intercourse.

vocational choice: The process of selecting an occupation as one's life work.

vocational identity: The sense of personal identification with a given vocation or type of work.

vocational maturity: According to Super, the degree to which individuals progress toward their vocational identity, which reflects the ability to plan, explore, and make realistic vocational commitments.

work: Physical or mental activity that produces something useful, usually as a means of earning a livelihood.

work ethic: Valuing hard work and success as an expression of self-worth and responsibility.

yavis syndrome: An acronym designating the types of clients most likely to benefit from psychotherapy; namely, those who are young, attractive, verbal, intelligent, and successful.

Name Index

Adams, G. R., 339
Alberti, R. E., 310
Altman, I., 133, 145
Angrist, S. S., 226, 337
Annon, J., 283
Arafat, I., 211
Ariès, P., 359–60, 375–76
Arnold, M. B., 80, 82
Aron, A. P., 99
Aronson, E., 138, 252
Astin, A. W., 338
Atchley, R. C., 350, 351
Athanasiou, R., 177
Atkinson, J. W., 36
Atthowe, J. M., 312
Ayllon, T., 312
Azrin, N. H., 312

Bach, G. R., 201, 202
Bachman, J. G., 132, 189, 220
Baltes, P. B., 331
Bandura, A., 311
Bane, M. J., 209
Bardwick, J., 15, 164, 171

Barnes, R. D., 256
Barnett, R. C., 333
Barrett, C. J., 349
Baruch, G. K., 333
Baur, K., 171, 175, 177, 182
Beier, E. G., 91
Bell, A., 178
Bell, R. R., 191, 200
Bem, S. L., 162
Bengston, V. L., 351
Bergin, A. E., 319
Bermann, E., 148
Bernard, J., 198, 209, 212, 254
Berne, E., 134, 136
Berscheid, E., 115, 116, 133, 139
Blake, W., 95
Block, J., 332
Bohan, J., 121
Bohannan, P., 208
Bohrnstedt, G., 115
Bolles, R. C., 25
Botwinick, J., 348
Boulgouris, J. C., 320
Bowlby, J., 34
Boylin, W., 353
Bradford, D. L., 211

Subject Index